SAN FRANCISCO'S F-LINE

The story of how America's most exciting and successful new transportation experience was built!

By Peter Ehrlich

Bulletin 150 of the Central Electric Railfans' Association

ISSN 0069-1623

©2019 by Peter Ehrlich

CERA DIRECTORS 2017

Irwin William Davis
John D. Nicholson
Lenard Marcus
Joseph Reuter

William Reynolds
Andrew Sunderland
Jeffrey L. Wien

All rights reserved. No part of this book may be commercially reproduced or utilized in any form except for brief quotations nor by any means electronic or mechanical including photo-copying and recording, nor by any informational storage / retrieval system, without permission in writing from the publisher

San Francisco's F-Line was designed by Peter Ehrlich
Production was coordinated by John D. Nicholson

CERA Bulletins are technical, references prepared as historic projects by members of the Central Electric Railfans' Association working without salary due to their interest in the subject. This bulletin is consistent with the stated purpose of the corporation: To foster the study of the history, equipment, and operation of electric railways.

Library of Congress Cataloging-in-Publication Data
Names: Ehrlich, Peter, 1946- author. | Central Electric Railfans' Association, issuing body.
Title: San Francisco's F-Line / Peter Ehrlich.
Description: Chicago, Illinois : Central Electric Railfans' Association 2019. | Series: Bulletin ... of the Central Electric Railfans' Association, ISSN 0069-1623 ; 150 | Includes bibliographical references and index. | Summary: "The reader is taken on a joyously meandering ride over a thirty year span, telling how San Francisco's F-line came about, through the efforts of a multitude of San Franciscans including visionaries, planners and engineers, politicians and community activists, transit operators and everyday transit riders. The idea of vintage streetcar operations was born in the 1970s, and then becomes tangible with the "Trolley Festivals" in the 1980s. It took another 20 years for the "F-Line" to become a permanent part of San Francisco's transit scene, and that saga is told as well"
-- Provided by publisher.

Identifiers: LCCN 2019021617 | ISBN 9780915348510 (hardcover)
Subjects: LCSH: San Francisco Municipal Railway--History. | Street-railroads--California--San Francisco--History. | Cable cars (Streetcars)--California--San Francisco--History. | Local transit--California--San Francisco--History.
Classification: LCC HE4491.S43 E47 2019 | DDC 388.4/60979461--dc23
LC record available at https://lccn.loc.gov/2019021617

Central Electric Railfans' Association
PO Box 503
Chicago, IL 60690
U.S.A.

About The Author

Peter Ehrlich, born in 1946, currently resides in Brewster, New York. He lived in San Francisco for 44 years, from 1966 to 2010. Mr. Ehrlich was employed by the
San Francisco Municipal Railway as a streetcar operator from 1979 to 2005,
the last ten years as an F-Line operator. He broke in on Muni's vintage fleet in 1982, and was assigned to the 1987 Trolley Festival.
Throughout his employment, he studied San Francisco's transit history closely,
and followed the events that led to the creation of today's F-Line with a keen eye.

Mr. Ehrlich also began developing his photographic skills during his time in
San Francisco. His main film farmers were a series of Minolta X-700s, a Nikon F3, and later a Nikon F100 and others. He graduated to digital photography in 2002 with a Nikon D100. He now uses a D700. His photographs have appeared in the
Market Street Railway's "Museums In Motion" calendars, and extensively on Yahoo's Flickr site, *www.flickr.com/milantram/* and the *www.nycsubway.org* site.
He has his own photography website, *www.pdephotography.net* ,
and also sells on *www.ebay.com*.

Mr. Ehrlich is also an accomplished musician. Before joining Muni in 1979, he ran his own music business teaching recorder and selling Renaissance woodwinds
and music for recorders.

+ + + + + + + + + +

Fourth Printing, November 2018
In this fourth printing, I've added and updated some information throughout the book, added 20 pages, and made editorial corrections where needed. San Francisco's

San Francisco's F-Line

By Peter Ehrlich

San Francisco's F-Line
Table Of Contents

Foreword by Peter Straus — ix
Preface — x
Acknowledgments — xii
Introduction — 1
The Ballad Of An F-Line Trip by Bruce Battles — 3
Chapter 1 - Before The F-Line — 6
    Horse Cars And Cable Cars - The Making Of A Streetcar City - The Great Earthquake And Fire; Muni Opens - The People's Road - The "Roar Of The Four" - Market Street Railway Succeeds URR; The "White Front Cars" - The Ferry Building Loop - Consolidation! - Retrenchment Continues - BART and Muni Metro - Ordering Replacement Streetcars
        The PCC Car: An American Success Story — 24
        Muni And The PCC–1939-1982 — 28

Chapter 2 - Planning for New Historic Streetcar Lines — 34
    Market Street Without Trolleys? - The Market Street Beautification Act - The *San Francisco Tomorrow* Plan - Early Talk of an Embarcadero Line, and the Cauthen Report to Dianne Feinstein - The I-280 Transfer Fund - Urgency To Get Historic Streetcars Running On Market - Working with the Wharf Merchants

Chapter 3 - The Trolley Festivals — 46
    Cable Cars Shut Down, Too - Gathering A Truly International Fleet - 1983–First And Foremost! - 1984–Serving the Democratic National Convention - 1985–Seven Days A Week - 1986–All Cars on One Route - 1987–All Good Things Must End
        The 1987 Embarcadero Demonstration — 64
        Four Who Made It Happen — 66

Chapter 4 - Rebuilding The Tracks — 68
    The Facelift Begins - Phase Two; MSR Regroups - Phase Three-Rails Return To Upper Market - PCCs Arrive; Rewiring Geneva Yard -
Phase Four-Bureaucratic Frustration Replaced by speedy Construction

Chapter 5 - The F-Line Opens! — 82
    A Glorious Sight! - Settling Down - More Exotic Cars - Service Expansion, Of sorts - Torpedoes and Vintage Cars - Politics, The Castro and The City - Citizens Keep Cars Clean - More Frequent Weekday Service Finally Added - Valencia Grade and First Street - Streetcar Named Desire Arrives - Last Run to Transbay Terminal
        Market Street Railway: Promoting Museums In Motion — 98

Chapter 6 - Bound for Fisherman's Wharf   **100**
  At Last! Trolleys To The Wharf! - Building The Line In Phases - First Streetcars Reach The Wharf; Setting A Date - A New Fleet For Wharf Service - Riders Quickly Overwhelm The Trolleys - 2001: First Major Improvement - The Need For More Trolleys - Choke Points: What To Do About Them? - Everyday Vintage Car Service A Reality
    Milan's Icons: The Peter Witt Trams [sidebar]   **114**

Chapter 7 - Expansion In The Works   **118**
  Muni Metro Runs First E-Line - Preparing for E-Line Vintage Operation - Missing: Cars and Cash - To Loop, Or Not To Loop? That Is The Question - The Torpedo Project - On to Fort Mason - Finally! The E-Line Begins Regular Service! – G for Golden Gate Park - Union Iron Works Loop - Into The Presidio? - Why Are There No Vintage Cars On the N-Line? - Gimme Shelter! - Extension into Fort Mason Stalled Again - Proposed 7th Street Loop - Heritage Weekends!

Chapter 8 - The Colorful F-Line Fleet   **142**
  Selecting A Fleet - PCCs Represent Many Cities - Contract Option for 3 Torpedoes - Milan Peter Witts Add International Color - Vintage San Francisco Treasures - Gems From Afar - The New Jersey PCCs Arrive - The Last Four Torpedoes Go To Rebuild - Stockpiling PCCs For The Future - 1006 and 1040: Two Notable PCCs - A Muni "Eleven" Represents St. Louis - For Trolley Festival Use Only - Three That Didn't Make It - The Brookville Philly PCC Rehab Contract - A New Brookville Contract Wrinkle - Rebuilding the Milan and Vintage Cars

Chapter 9 - Behind The Scenes   **188**
  The men and women who operate, maintain and guide the F-Line

The Operators - On The Street - Signups And Runs - Operations and Support Staff - Trolley Maintenance - Other Staff at Muni

    Jack Smith: A Gentleman Motorman [sidebar]   195

Chapter 10 - So, What's A Ride On The F-Line Like?   196
A Ride To The Wharf (inbound) - A Ride To Castro Street (outbound)

Chapter 11 - More Tours Of Discovery   226
The Muni Metro Subway - The L-Taraval Line - K-Ingleside and M-Ocean View Lines - The N-Judah Line - The J-Church Line - MMX and The T-Line - The Central Subway —The Cable Cars - Muni's Trolley Coach System - Golden Gate Bridge; Twin Peaks by Muni Bus - BART - Light Rail and Vintage Cars in San Jose - Western Railway Museum - SMART - Sacramento - Los Angeles - San Diego

Chapter 12 - Vintage Cars (and modern ones) in other U. S. Cities   250
New Orleans - Detroit - Seattle - Dallas - Memphis - Portland - Kenosha - Tampa - Tacoma - Little Rock - Charlotte - Tucson - Atlanta - Salt Lake City - Washington - Kansas City - Cincinnati - Detroit (again) - St. Louis - Oklahoma City - El Paso - Milwaukee - Tempe - Other Possibilities - Fort Collins - Fort Smith - Lowell - Yakima - Los Angeles (San Pedro) - Philadelphia and Boston - Self-Propelled Streetcars In The U. S. - Trolley Museums across the U. S. - SUMMARY

    New Orleans and Portland-Two Cities Where Streetcars Work Well [sidebar]   252
    Nostalgia Rides The Subway, Too [sidebar]   280
    Modern Streetcars [sidebar]   284

Chapter 13 - Muni's 100th Anniversary, and Photo Addendum   286
Car 1 Reinaugural - The Promise Of Good Things To Come - Photos added in August 2014

Bibliography, Discography and Internet   296
Glossary   298
Index   307
Picture Index   316
List of Points Of Interest   320
Addendum - 2013, etc.   324

Foreword

"IT TAKES A VILLAGE to raise a child." Welcome to the F-Line!

Some projects are derived from a single person's efforts or are achieved through a single champion's vision and drive to bring them to fruition. Not so Muni's F-Line. In celebration of the Municipal Railway's centenary year, author Peter Ehrlich takes you on a joyously meandering ride over a thirty year span to tell you how San Francisco's F-Line came about, through the efforts of a multitude of San Franciscans including visionaries, planners and engineers, politicians and community activists, transit operators and everyday transit riders.

Come aboard for the journey! This story is told by someone who was along for the ride, well, *almost* from the beginning, and from the vantage point of a transit user and then transit operator, and finally as a streetcar operator on the F-Line itself. Peter is also well known nationally as a transit photographer, and has been able to illustrate much of the story with his own photographs.

Peter's tale begins with background on the development of transit in San Francisco, one of the nation's most transit-oriented cities, then as now. He continues as the idea of vintage streetcar operations was born in the 1970s, and then becomes tangible with the "Trolley Festivals" in the 1980s. It took another 20 years for the "F-Line" to become a permanent part of San Francisco's transit scene, and that saga is told as well.

Looking around, Peter also goes on to describe first a ride on today's F-Market and Wharves streetcar line, and then other transit attractions in the City, the Bay Area, and the State of California. Lastly, Peter takes you on a tour of other vintage streetcar operations throughout the U.S., many of which can trace their origins to the success of the F-Line here in the City by the Bay.

Climb on board!

--Peter Straus
San Francisco, January 2012

Peter Straus started as a streetcar operator at Muni in 1973, and was Director of Planning for Muni from 1980 to 2009.

Preface

WHEN I RETIRED FROM THE San Francisco Municipal Railway as a transit operator in 2005, San Francisco's F-Line had established itself as a necessary and colorful part of the city's transit scene. I had been employed as a streetcar operator and bus driver for 26 years, and considered myself lucky in that, as a rookie, I broke in on the PCC streetcars right away. These had ruled San Francisco electric street railways since 1957, and, in turn, were about to be replaced. Of course, I had to drive buses, but that was because I got "bumped" out of the rail division–at that time, it was called Geneva Division–in September 1979. By 1985, as my seniority improved, I was able to sign permanently at Muni's Green Light Rail Division, from which all of Muni's streetcars, both modern and vintage, are based. And I got trained on the historic two-man cars, the Boeing and Breda Muni Metro LRVs, and the F-Line cars as they entered service.

I'm one of those "dyed-in-the-wool" railfans who grew up riding the New York subways, and I endured the sometimes painful transition from the wonderful and noisy original subway stock to the new cars that erased historical memories without necessarily improving the subway experience. Moving to San Francisco in 1966, I quickly became a Muni enthusiast. It happened immediately–the second day I was in the Bay Area, to be exact–when I stepped off a bus at the Transbay Terminal, went downstairs, and lo and behold, there was a gaggle of green and cream trolley cars waiting to whisk me away up Market Street. The sheer variety of transit modes Muni operated was truly amazing–streetcars, cable cars, electric trolley buses, and buses *not* built by General Motors! I got involved politically and made friends with many operators, learning much about Muni, even learning to operate a PCC or two on the sly. On my first day of Muni employment–March 21, 1979–Curtis Green, the Muni General Manager, a man whose acquaintance I had made years before and a manager for whom I had a great deal of respect, came to visit the new class, looked over in my direction, and said, "Ah, I see, we have an old friend with us today." Immediately, I felt right at home.

I learned how to run vintage cars in 1982. Between 1985 and 1995, I worked Muni Metro, with occasional assignments to vintage cars, and watched as the F-Line got built, hoping for the day that I could leave the problem-plagued subway behind. That happened on September 1, 1995, and I jumped for joy. I was careful, though, to maintain my qualifications on Muni Metro and on buses, and would work these on run trades or even on entire signups to keep my skills sharp.

By 2001, I could sign on a vintage car run full-time, and I operated the historic streetcars until retirement. In a way, these were closest to the charm and the music I remembered from my childhood days riding the 3rd Avenue El and the subways in New York City–a dream come true.

As my career progressed, I also developed my photography skills. I maintain that it's important to document the changes in public transit because of its role in developing our cities and maintaining their livability, and one of the ways of doing that is through photography. But capturing the creation of a rail transit line, or the "Roar Of The Four" on Market Street in the 1930s, or the transformation of the terminal at 17th and Castro into a pedestrian-friendly "piazza," on film, is a permanent historical record and one that future generations will enjoy.

The F-Line and the cable cars are probably the most photographed transit vehicles in the world, and each photograph captures some of that living history that they convey as they roll down the streets of San Francisco.

Following retirement, I planned to make transportation photography a full-time avocation. Then it dawned on me: There have been dozens of articles extolling the virtues and experiences of the F-Line, but no book has been written about how it came to be, why it works, etc. Additionally, it would be a good showcase for my photography, as well as that of other photographers.

Many of the anecdotes and situations described within this volume are derived from my own experience as a motorman, and sometimes I've chosen to write about them in the first person, or other times, simply as "the author." Along the way, I've called upon the memories of my peers as well–fellow operators, supervisors, maintenance workers, even managers. In this way, I trust that I can promote the human-interest aspect of the F-Line along with writing about the fascinating history behind what is the most successful new historic transit operation in the United States.

I have chosen to repeat certain circumstances several times within this book. For example, I discuss the 2009 remanufacture of four "Torpedo" PCCs in chapters 7 and 8. And I refer to Muni's "Iron Monster" B-Type 162, a significant and historical recent addition to the vintage car fleet, in many different places. Although this may seem redundant and repetitive, I believe that this will keep the reader focused on how, when and why events happened.

There are numerous other instances of this style of writing throughout the volume.

A note about references to Market Street Railway: There are *three* Market Street Railways in San Francisco's transit history. The first is the Market Street Railway Co. of 1893, one of the first electric streetcar companies in San Francisco. The second is the company created out of the ashes of United Railroads in 1921, lasting through the city's takeover on Sept. 29, 1944, and which gave San Francisco its patented "White Front Cars." Finally, there is today's F-Line booster organization, *Market Street Railway* (*MSR*), which has led the effort to bring historic streetcar service to San Francisco, and has supported Muni in maintaining the service.

To distinguish between the three entities, I have used the spelling out of "Market Street Railway Co." and its acronym "MSRy" to refer to the two companies which provided transit service, in normal typestyle, and *Market Street Railway* and its initials *MSR*, in *italics*, when I write about that non-profit organization. In this way, there should be no confusion.

In my enthusiasm in writing about San Francisco's F-Line, I have to remember that there was a lot of pain involved, insofar as construction delays, adverse political, managerial and operational decisions, questionable tactics, service snafus, etc., were concerned. In other words, I include the "warts and all." What successful enterprise doesn't have problems? Some of these problems can be attributed to "growing pains." Muni itself has been on the receiving end of scorn, and the butt of jokes (the late columnist Herb Caen called Muni the "Muniserable Railway," for example), for decades. But the average observer or rider will not normally notice such things as he or she boards an F-Line car. To most people, the F-Line is public transportation at its best and most attractive, and most colorful. And that's what the F-Line–and this book–is all about!

2012 is going to be a banner year in Muni's history. Already, big plans, led by the return of Muni's very first streetcar, Car 1, are being made to celebrate the Centennial of America's first large-scale publicly-owned transit system. This book will celebrate Muni's legacy with the tale of the most successful new historic streetcar line in the world.

Peter Ehrlich
Carmel, NY, April 8, 2012

Acknowledgments

AS MANY AUTHORS DO IN THEIR WRITINGS, I've done much reminiscing about my own experiences as a Muni and an F-Line operator. But I could not have written *San Francisco's F-Line* without the help, contributions, comments and input from many people.

First off, a big shout of thanks to the numerous photographers who have contributed photos and images for this book. Among them are Art Curtis, Doug Grotjahn, Mike Davis, Richard Panse, Joe Testagrose, Art Lloyd, the late Cameron Beach, Peter Straus, Rick Laubscher, John Pappas, Jeffrey Moreau, Don Jewell, the late Jack Smith, David Banbury, David Vartanoff, Richard Canino, Ethan Tam, Kevin Sheridan, Carole Gilbert, Michael Strauch, *Market Street Railway*, Jeremy Whiteman, the estate of Wilbur Whitaker, Elizabeth Krumbach, Salaam Allah, Steve Morgan, Pierre Maris, the late Joseph Saitta, Adolfo Echeverry, Mark Clifford and the LACMTA, and Matt Lee. Special thanks goes to Muni's Karl Johnson, who provided me with many photos, both his own and collected images, for this book. Added late 2013 in the 3rd edition: British photographers Kieran Cross and Gary Mitchell.

I was able to obtain high-quality images of San Francisco's early streetcar service from the archives of the San Francisco History Center unit of the *San Francisco Public Library*, most of which were used in Chapter 1, which traces early San Francisco transit history, before the F-Line was built.

Alan Fishel, of Long Beach, CA, was willing to provide me with many images of Muni's "Iron Monsters" and other streetcars in the 1950s and 1960s, taken by the late Ira Swett, one of the pre-eminent streetcar photographers of that era.

Environmental Vision, of Berkeley, CA, produced marvelous photographic renditions for the Golden Gate National Recreation Area's Draft Environmental Impact Report of March 2011 of what the future Fort Mason Extension could look like, and I would like to thank Patrick Shea of the National Park Service for allowing me to use high-resolution images of these for use in Chapter 7 of the book.

Nicolas Finck, Art Curtis, Peter Straus, Art Michel and Rick Laubscher all perused the original text drafts and submitted comments, changes, corrections and additions for me to make or include. Peter Straus, in particular, worked with me on timeline of the planning aspects for historic streetcar service, and forwarded me copies of two important and seminal documents: *San Francisco Tomorrow*'s "Market Street Streetcar Plan," and Gerald Cauthen's "A Surface Rail System for the San Francisco Waterfront." Both of these laid the groundwork for vintage car service in San Francisco. Thanks, Peter, for these documents, your comments, and your memories of the early days. Rick Laubscher, too, contributed much insight to how events leading to the Trolley Festivals happened.

Ron Niewiarowski and John Katz of the SFMTA staff gave me engineering drawings and other materials on the planning for the Fisherman's Wharf line and of upper Market, which I used in Chapters 2 and 4. Niewiarowski, in particular, was extremely helpful in straightening out the intricacies of the planning for an Embarcadero line. In addition, Jerry McGovern, the SFMTA librarian, assisted both Niewiarowski and Katz in preparing and photo-copying research materials for use in this book. Doug Wright, who was Niewiarowski's boss when both worked for the San Francisco Public Utilities Commission, contributed greatly to setting the timeline straight in Chapter 2. Thanks also to Murray Bond and Chimmy Lee of the SFMTA staff for permission to use the specially-designed 100th Anniversary logo, featuring Car 1.

Karl Johnson, from Muni Trolley Maintenance, gave me records on the disposal of Muni's original PCC fleet and other materials, which were very helpful for writing Chapter 8 and other chapters.

Thanks to Steve Morgan and Earl Hampton Jr., for submitting corrections for the Portland and New Orleans sections of Chapter 12, respectively.

Bruce Battles, of Menlo Park, CA, was most gracious for allowing me to use his "Ballad Of An F-Line Trip" takeoff on Gelett Burgess' 1901 ditty, "Ballad Of The Hyde Street Grip," which, in my mind, sums up the spirit of the F-Line perfectly.

I also wish to thank Alison Cant and Rick Laub-scher of the Market Street Railway, the F-Line support organization, for allowing me to use materials such as past issues of their newsletter, *Inside Track*, and other information from the blog on the MSR website. The back issues of *Inside Track*, in particular, helped me to lay the foundation for writing this book.

Thanks also go to Sam Garcia, the Muni Division Manager at the time the F-Line opened in September 1995, and to operators Tom Biagi, John Nevin, Lee Butler, Jr., Ed Fine, and the late Jack Smith, for their comments and reminisces. Jack, as my mentor, showed me how to operate a vintage car with style and grace, for which I will be eternally grateful. Without Jack's skills, expertise and friendship, I might have stayed a run-of-the-mill Muni operator.

Finally, I'd like to thank my father, Paul, for–at least, inadvertently–planting the railfan bug in me by taking me for long rides on New York's musical, wooden Third Avenue El trains when I was just a lad of eight years. When he was a kid himself, he loved the old trolley cars that ran all across his home turf, Brooklyn. Still hale at 90 years old in 2011, Pop also helped me rewrite passages so that they would appeal more to the average reader, and not just those in the transportation community. Thanks, Pop!

– *Peter Ehrlich*

Introduction

THROUGHOUT THE HISTORY of electrified urban public transport in the United States, there are a few events which truly stand out, and which also have affected and made a lasting impression on millions of Americans, as well as visitors from afar.

Some of these milestones include the perfection of the electric trolley car by Frank Sprague in 1888, which brought cheap and reliable transportation to American cities; his later invention of multiple-unit control for rapid transit trains, which led to the creation of elevated networks in Chicago, Brooklyn and Manhattan; and the opening of the first subway in Boston in 1897, followed seven years later by the first major subway system in New York. Other milestones included the opening of this country's first major publicly-owned street railway system in San Francisco in 1912; the development of the PCC streetcar in the 1930s; the new wave of subways in San Francisco, Washington, Atlanta and Los Angeles starting in the 1970s; and finally, the renaissance of surface electric urban rail, which began in San Diego in 1981, after streetcar technology had all but died out in America.

To this list, one must certainly add San Francisco's wonderful and colorful F-Market & Wharves historic streetcar line.

To be sure, the F-Line is not the first of its kind. That honor belongs to the St. Charles Streetcar line in New Orleans, whose olive green trolleys have been plying the line since 1924, earning it National Historic Landmark status (the line itself was established in 1835). The F-Line was also not the first new permanent historic trolley route constructed and integrated with a city's transit system; the nod here goes to Seattle's Waterfront Streetcar in 1982, joined by Dallas in 1989 and Memphis in 1993. (Actually, Detroit's Downtown trolley line was the first, in 1976, but it was abandoned in 2003.) And it was not even the first city to introduce colorful streetcars; witness Pittsburgh's multi-colored PCCs in the 1970s, where one writer remarked "I can't think of a better pastime than to watch the colorful trolleys go by." (Ironically, the same man who instigated Pittsburgh's flamboyant PCC trolley liveries was the one who later became general manager of Muni during the Trolley Festivals–Harold H. Geissenheimer.)

But its origins in the Trolley Festival years of 1983-1987, its unique international fleet and colorful liveries, its extension to Fisherman's Wharf in 2000, and its high ridership and frequent service have made the F-Line the most successful and influential historic transit operation in the country.

Indeed, transit and civic officials from across the United States and all over the world have descended on the F-Line to study why it works and how such a relaxing reminder of a more genteel time can be made to work in their own cities. The evidence continues to mount. Since 2001, Kenosha, Tampa and Little Rock have built and opened new, low-budget historic trolley systems, while Dallas, Memphis and New Orleans have extended theirs.

But the principal reason for the F-Line's runaway success is that it was conceived as a major transit line in a city that already enjoys high transit ridership. Figures from the 1970s and 1980s show that San Francisco had the second-highest *per capita* transit ridership in the United States, after New York City. The fact that the F-Line is a rail service was enough to spark a 43% increase in ridership over the bus service it replaced in 1995. Its acceptance, from its very first day of operation on September 1, 1995, and its quick assimilation into the fabric of everyday life and public transportation, is a tribute to the way it was planned from the very beginning.

Another aspect of the F-Line's success is that it serves four distinct markets: commuters, short-trip discretionary riders, residents, and tourists. A survey conducted during the Trolley Festival years showed that ridership was split in thirds between locals, Bay Area residents and people from outside the area. Clearly, this was a recipe for success! And the Trolley Festivals only operated from May to October. The F-Line operates 20 hours a day, seven days a week.

Re-instituting heritage streetcar lines isn't the only tool in American cities' efforts to improve transportation by bringing back rail transit. The light rail transit (LRT) renaissance began in 1981 in San Diego (and in two Canadian cities–Edmonton and Calgary–before that). By 2011, LRT had been introduced to 16 more American cities, and in virtually all of them, ridership has boomed as Americans rediscover the pleasures and efficiencies of electric rail transport. Many of these new systems also mix historic streetcars on their light rail tracks, either full-time or on weekends, and for special occasions. Many of the original LRT systems have expanded significantly, and at least three more cities will introduce light rail over the next five years.

The light rail building boom has even extended to cities that never completely abandoned the streetcar, such as Boston, Cleveland, Newark, Philadelphia and San Francisco.

The third way that streetcars have returned to cities is with the application of the low-budget, smaller-scale modern streetcar. Portland is the leader here, establishing a modern, entirely street-running line in 2001. The friendly, low-floor Czech-built trams have set off a building boom throughout their service area as residents move closer to clean, efficient and comfortable rail transport. Two other Pacific Northwest cities, Tacoma and Seattle, have since opened similar small-scale, modern trolley lines, and Tucson, Washington, Dallas and Cincinnati havce joined the linst.

This is an amazing turnaround for the United States, especially when one considers that after World War II, cities were literally tripping over each other in their haste to get rid of "old-fashioned" trolley cars, thinking that buses and freeway building would be the solutions to their transportation problems. For many observers, this was called the great "transit holocaust" as city after city succumbed to the temptation to replace what worked well with something that appeared to be an improvement. But when gridlock and air pollution started to choke our cities, and residents began leaving in droves, searching for a better "American Dream," clearly something else was needed, and civic leaders turned to what had worked in the past—clean, quiet, comfortable and efficient rail transportation.

San Francisco was very lucky. Some might say that its civic leaders were smart. In reality, they were just as eager to get rid of the streetcar, too. Heck, back in 1947, the city fathers wanted to scrap the cable car lines! (Look where that got them—among other things, a National Historic Landmark designation!) But it took many inspired people, both in and out of government, to change attitudes and show the world that those genteel "old-fashioned trolley cars" do indeed have a place in today's modern, bustling world. And San Francisco is, and will continue to be, a much better place for it.

When the average commuter uses public transportation in America, he or she thinks of it as a boring, sometimes uncomfortable, but necessary, routine. San Francisco's F-Line—or any trolley line, for that matter—proves the opposite, that a ride on public transport can be an exciting experience, part of the fun of exploring a city. The F-Line has taken public transportation and transformed it into a magical experience.

So step back in time and come take a ride on the F-Line!

2012 is San Francisco Muni's 100th Anniversary year. The City celebrated the 50th in 1962 with the reappearance of Old Number One, the first publicly-owned trolley for a major city. There was also a celebration for the 75th Anniversary in 1987, and it was a summer-long Trolley Festival, including Car 1 in its fleet of vintage cars, running practically every day. The 100th Anniversary, with a rebuilt Car 1 as its centerpiece, promises to be an event where Muni, and its innovative F-Line, can shine, showing the world again that San Francisco was indeed "The City That Knows How."

This pedestrian-only plaza at the 17th Street and Castro terminal of the F-Line was created in 2009 and made permanent in 2011. *Peter Ehrlich*

The Ballad Of An F-Line Trip
By Bruce Battles

This is a new version of a poem written by Gelett Burgess in 1901 entitled "Ballad Of The Hyde Street Grip." It was written for, and printed in, the *Market Street Railway*'s blog dated January 21, 2009.
URL: http://www.streetcar.org/blog/2009/01/the-ballad-of-an-f-line-trip.html

The author has kindly given me permission to reproduce this version of the ballad. The original can be found in the book "Cable Car Days In San Francisco," by Edgar Kahn (published by Friends Of the San Francisco Library, 1940).

The hills are slanting steeply, and you hope the brakes will hold -
The curves up on the J-line will make your blood run cold!
There's not much time for schmoozing, and little chance to yak,
As soon as you get to Castro, it's time to start heading back!
Your car is always crowded - they're packed in hip to hip!
There's at least 300 boardings, on every F-line trip!

Go easy there on Beach Street, where the track is near the curb,
And watch her at Pier 39 - that loop's a real tight curve!
Everywhere pedestrians, Pedi-Cabs, bikes, and cars,
Be careful of the tourists, when they're coming out of bars!
Giving lots of directions - you can never make a slip,
You feel like you're a Tour Guide, when you make an F-line trip!

There's the air brake and controller, air whistle and the gong,
You'd best know how to use 'em, or you'll soon be going wrong!
Shut her off through "special work," or the pole will draw an arc -
The Line Department hates it when they see that great big spark!
Embarcadero is a speedway - you can hit her up a clip
Taking tourists to the Wharf, on another F-line trip!

From Fisherman's Wharf to the waterfront, the Ferry Building too,
Then swing past Herman Plaza, as Market comes in view!
Past the Hyatt Regency, the Palace, and Kearny Street,
Your car is really filling up - there's not one empty seat!
You pass the crowds at Powell Street - they're waiting for the grip,
And you're glad you're on Electrics, as you make an F-line trip!

A trolley fan from Boston, where PCCs still run,
Can take a trip to Mattapan, and think that it was fun.
A guy from Philadelphia, (they sold us some PCCs),
Can go and ride 15-Girard, and glide along with ease!
But Philly'd give his Cheesesteak, and Boston - well, man, he'd flip,
For a chance to ride out Market on an F-line trip!

Oh, the lights are in the Castro - will the parties never end?
Hear those PCC cars leaving, as they squeal around the bend
From Seventeenth onto Market, as they try another stint
To hit the dip at Church Street, and then go past the Mint.
Down the hill above Valencia, you can really let her rip,
As you try to make your schedule on an F-line trip!

When the theaters are closing, and the crowds are on the way,
The farebox gets real busy, as you near the end of day.
The wait on Jones near Beach Street is very seldom still
As the tourists are out strolling, and looking for a thrill!
But the beacon on Mount Sutro through the rolling fog does rip
As the hush of midnight's broken by another F-line trip!

This book is dedicated to all the F-Line operators and other Muni employees,

both past and present,

who make it happen on a daily basis,

and to Senator Dianne Feinstein of California,

who made it possible in the first place,

when she was Mayor of San Francisco.

San Francisco's F-Line

By Peter Ehrlich

This is the final form of the famous Ferry Building Loop as it appeared on February 15, 1939, a month after Bay Bridge train service began and much streetcar activity rerouted to serve the new Transbay Terminal. Market Street Railway "White Front" cars and Muni "Iron Monsters" are circling on two of the three tracks. The innermost loop has been taken out of service. Today's F-Line passes here on The Embarcadero.
San Francisco History Center, San Francisco Public Library collection

Chapter 1 - Before The F-Line

"San Francisco,
Open your Golden Gate,
You let no stranger wait outside your door..."
– sung by Jeanette MacDonald, 1936,
written by Gus Kahn, Bronislaw Kaper
and Walter Jurmann

SAN FRANCISCO–America's Favorite City. The City that Knows How. The City by the Bay. Those are just some of the contemporary descriptions of what has become one of the most colorful and vibrant cities in the world–a city sought out by thousands of travelers for its climate, scenery, vistas, food, romance and ambiance.

Born in the 1700s, founded by the Roman Catholic missionaries who built dozens of missions all along the California Coast, San Francisco, practically overnight, became a thriving metropolis because of the 1849 Gold Rush. Its natural port became an instant gateway to Asia, Central America and South America, and cemented San Francisco as the financial center of the West, as thousands of people migrated westward. The opening of the country's first transcontinental railroad in 1869 hastened its development.

Horse Cars and Cable Cars

AS NEW RESIDENTS poured into the "Barbary Coast," it became necessary to move the masses up and down Market Street, which had been laid out as a broad northeast-southwest thoroughfare, and into the hills and valleys in downtown and outlying areas. The first rail-borne transportation on Market Street, in the form of horse cars, began running in 1860, starting an unbroken stretch of 122 years of rail service on an American main street (except for the period following the 1906 Great Earthquake, of course). Steam-powered trams and trains provided transportation into some of the northwest areas of the city, with some also running on Market Street.

On August 1, 1873, Andrew Hallidie, a transplanted Scotsman, introduced a mode of public transport which would become San Francisco's signature: the cable car. His invention came out of desire to eliminate the hazards and cruelty of operating horse cars on steep hills, after watching a team of horses stumble and get dragged by the car rolling backwards down the hill. He opened the Clay Street Hill Railway on September 1, 1873.

Practically overnight, the cable car became *the* mode of public transport in the city. Besides covering the "Seven Hills" (the northeastern quadrant), cable cars made it onto Market Street.

But the cable car's limitation was that it had a top speed of about nine miles per hour (although this speed varied in some cities). While that was good enough for hilly lines and those running through congested areas such as downtown San Francisco, residents using transportation reaching into the outer areas demanded more speed. This is why steam trains and steam dummy cars–locomotives where passengers could sit around the engine's perimeter–operated to Ocean Beach and other areas in western and southern San Francisco instead of cable cars.

The Making Of A Streetcar City

IN THE 1880s, A NEW FORM of propulsion was being developed for street railways–the electric trolley car, or streetcar, which drew power from an overhead wire to drive motors and returned the current through the rails. Although there were other inventors, Frank J. Sprague perfected a working electric trolley system, using a 600-volt D C system to power electric motors mounted on the axles of small, boxy railcars. His first successful installation took place in Richmond, Va. in 1888. Although initial installations were rudimentary, the cars could reach speeds that were not possible with any horse car or cable car. Best of all, they were pollution-free–no soot from coal or manure from horses. Street railway companies all across the United States took notice and quickly built similar electric systems, in many cases converting lines from cable propulsion which had opened just a few years earlier!

The first electric system in San Francisco was the San Francisco and San Mateo Railroad (SF&SM),

This was the original Ferry Building as it appeared in 1889. Very long cable cars assigned to Market Street are being turned on the turntable or are waiting their turn or loading for their outbound trips. Other cars from the Sacramento/Clay and Union Street lines sit at the north end.
San Francisco History Center, San Francisco Public Library collection

Geary Street, California Street and Union Street companies continued their independence, but two of these would later be taken over by Muni in the 1910s.

Even though new electric lines were springing up all over San Francisco, not a single one ran on Market Street. That's because a city ordinance banned overhead wires on the city's premier boulevard. URR cajoled, pleaded with, and allegedly bribed, city officials to repeal the law, all for naught. That would change as a result of something cataclysmic that occurred at 5:13 a.m. on April 18, 1906.

The Great Earthquake and Fire; Muni Opens

ON THAT DAY, THE Great Earthquake and Fire ravaged the city, including much of the street railway and cable car system. Rebuilding began immediately, with electric car service restored to Fillmore Street just nine days later. URR ordered 200 new and larger double-truck cars from St. Louis Car Company and arranged to have 50 more diverted from an order with American Car Co. intended for the Chicago City Railway. More importantly, the "no-wires-on-Market Street" ordinance was waived, and later repealed, permitting electric car service on San Francisco's premier boulevard.

which started operation in 1891 on a somewhat convoluted route from Steuart and Market via Steuart, Harrison, 14th, Guerrero, 30th, Chenery and San Jose Avenue to the "Top Of The Hill, Daly City." The Metropolitan Railroad followed a few months later with a new electric route between Market and Eddy Streets and Golden Gate Park. Small cars with only two axles were used on both routes. Muni's car 578(S), built for the original Market Street Railway Company in 1895, is typical of the small cars constructed in this period. As electric traction systems developed, larger and improved streetcars with four axles and trucks on both ends were introduced.

The first consolidation of San Francisco's transit routes took place in 1893, resulting in the first Market Street Railway Company, which was controlled by Southern Pacific Railroad interests. The new company converted many horse and cable car lines to electric traction, but the SF&SM remained outside its purview–at least for the time being. The consolidation included the Powell Street and Clay Street cable car lines, but not the California Street Cable Railroad lines.

The final consolidation occurred in 1902 with the creation of the United Railroads Company (URR). This time, SF&SM came under URR's aegis, along with the Sutter Street lines. The

Preserved car 578(S), built for the first Market Street Railway Co. in 1895 and pictured on the new T-Line in 2008, is typical of the small, four-wheel streetcars constructed during the first years of electric traction. *Peter Ehrlich*

Market Street scenes from the 1900s

(*top left*) Looking east from 6th Street. Two United Railroads cable cars are passing Powell Street, in 1904, with the landmark Flood Building under construction. The Flood Building survived the Earthquake and Fire and today houses the offices of the non-profit trolley booster organization Market Street Railway. (*top right*) Market and Granton March 31, 1906. In less than three weeks, the calamitous earthquake and fire would lay to ruin virtually everything in this picture. (*bottom*) Three years later, in 1909, electric streetcars ruled Market Street. The Union Trust Bank building, now a Wells Fargo office, is at Grant Avenue on the left. One of the new trolleys from St. Louis Car Co. heads inbound.
All photos, San Francisco History Center, San Francisco Public Library collection

Meanwhile, pressure was building to create a new municipally-owned streetcar system. This developed out of growing public dissatisfaction with URR because of its refusal to expand service into outlying districts clamoring for public transportation, as well as strikes and post-Earthquake scandals alleging corruption involving URR officials. In December 1909, after a string of defeats at the ballot box, the electorate passed a bond issue enabling the City to purchase and modernize the Geary Street cable line. Construction started in June 1911, and the large cable cars of the Geary Street, Park and Ocean Railroad turned on the turntable at Kearny Street for the last time on the night of May 5, 1912.

Forty-three new streetcars, called "A-Types" or "Arnold" cars due to their design by transit consultant Bion J. Arnold, were to be delivered to the new Muni carbarn at Geary and Presidio Avenue by December 8, 1912. The award was made to a local builder, W. L. Holman Company, which had constructed cable cars for San Francisco and interurban cars for the Oakland, Antioch and Eastern, an interurban serving the East Bay and reaching all the way to Sacramento, ultimately becoming part of the Sacramento Northern. Unfortunately, Holman had difficulties with the contract, and ultimately went bankrupt before the full order was completed. It did manage to deliver 10 finished cars in time for a December 28, 1912, opening. Today's Car One was one of these streetcars. The company was able to complete ten more A-Types before shutting its doors

for good. The last 23 cars were completed by nearby Union Iron Works.

The People's Road

DESPITE MAYOR "SUNNY JIM" ROLPH's plea to the citizens of San Francisco to "get the cars going all right first and toot our horn afterward," a crowd of about 50,000 was on hand to greet the new Municipal Railway that afternoon. All ten of the first cars were surrounded by a wildly enthusiastic citizenry. Some 20,000 people rode the new cars on that first day, and even more the day after, which was a Sunday. This nearly matched the ridership now experienced on today's F-Line.

The first two new Municipal Railway streetcar lines were the A, which ran from Geary and Kearny Streets to 10th Avenue and Fulton Street, across from Golden Gate Park, and the B, which continued out to 33rd Avenue. The B ran as a shuttle until February 10, 1913, when it became the trunk line and the A became a shuttle. Four months later, the B was extended to Ocean Beach and to the Ferry Building. But this had to wait until all 43 cars were delivered.

Between 1914 and 1928, Muni expanded greatly, adding 10 more streetcar lines, 191 more streetcars (including B-Types 130 and 162, on Muni's vintage car roster), and a few feeder bus routes, while United Railroads did nothing to expand into outlying areas of the city or improve service.

The "Roar Of The Four"

THE BEGINNING OF THE four-track era on Market Street dated back to before the turn of the century, when the Sutter Street Railroad built alongside the tracks of the first Market Street Railway. The city's last horse cars traversed this route. Starting in 1913, the City arranged for its Geary lines to link up with these tracks at Sutter and continue down to the Ferries Loop.

The next section of "four tracks on Market" opened in August 1917, when the J-Church line began service. At that time, J cars operated via Geary, Van Ness, Market, and Church. But more was to come. The K-Market route, which ran through the new Twin Peaks Tunnel from the developing West Portal district, added outside tracks between Castro and Church and from Van Ness to Geary in 1918. San Franciscans would now hear the famous "Roar Of The Four" over the next three decades, as thousands of streetcars sang and rattled their way up and down Market Street, motors humming and howling at a feverish pitch. To many, it was sweet music. San Francisco had joined New Orleans, Cleveland (a short segment), and Richmond, Virginia, as the only American cities to boast four streetcar tracks on their main streets.

Nowadays, there are six tracks on—and under—Market Street, starting with the F-Line on the surface, Muni Metro on the top subway level, and BART on the lower level. That shows how intense public transport has always been on Market Street.

Market Street Railway Succeeds URR; The "White Front Cars"

BY 1918, UNITED RAILROADS was in dire straits. Faced with competition from Muni, two bitter strikes in 1907 and 1917, public dissatisfaction and finally a disastrous 1918 wreck on the remote Visitacion Valley line, which was blamed on conversion to one-man operation of the cars assigned to that line (and subsequent passage of an ordinance requiring streetcars to run with two-man crews), URR had no choice but to reorganize. Out of its ashes came the second Market Street Railway Company in February 1921. Nearly five years later, control of MSRy passed to Standard Power & Light Corp., who brought in the Byllesby Engineering and Management Corp. to manage the transit company. Byllesby, in January 1926, introduced a feature on its streetcars which would become the company's signature for the rest of its corporate life: The "White Front Car."

The "White Front Car" was simply that: the car ends were painted white, and were

The A-Types were Muni's first streetcars and served San Francisco for 39 years. Car 36 operates on the original F-Line, the F-Stockton, opened in 1914. In the late 1940s, when this picture was taken, line F was extended across Market Street to the Southern Pacific (Depot over a portion of the old Market Street Railway's 20-Ellis route.
Tom Gray, San Francisco Public Library collection

Armistice Day, 1918. In this view from 6th Street, Market Street is bedecked with American flags celebrating the end of World War I. The "Roar Of The Four" is in full swing with United Railroads and Muni streetcars everywhere. But while Muni would continue to expand, United Railroads had only three more years of existence, and was subsequently reorganized as Market Street Railway.
San Francisco History Center, San Francisco Public Library collection

The Ferry Building Loop

SAN FRANCISCO'S FERRY BUILDING, designed by famed San Francisco architect A. Page Brown and built in 1898, is the most famous transit icon in California, and has survived two major earthquakes virtually unscathed. In the heyday of ferries and streetcars, it was the second-busiest transportation center in the world, after London's Charing Cross Station.

All Market Street lines terminated in a loop in front of the Ferry Building. A two-track loop was built following electrification after the 1906 Earthquake and Fire. This was enlarged to become a three-track loop after Muni's K-Line began service on Market Street in 1918. At peak operating periods, up to 250 cars per hour traversed the three Ferry Loop tracks.

But there was more to the Ferries Terminal than just the Market Street Loop. URR and MSRy cars from Mission Street and other South of Market lines terminated in a five-track stub just south of the loop. The terminals of Muni's original E-Union Street line (a former Presidio & Ferries line which Muni took over in December 1913) and the private company's 16-Third & Broadway, were located north of the loop. The Sacramento-Clay cable car line, which was rebuilt after the quake, also had a loop here, adjacent to the E-Line terminal. To top it off, the State Belt Railroad's steam locomotives chuffed by with cuts of freight cars.

With the opening of the San Francisco-Oakland Bay Bridge in 1936 and the Golden Gate Bridge a year later, the number of ferries calling at the Ferry Building dwindled considerably. The opening of the East Bay (later Transbay) Terminal Loop at First and Mission on January 14, 1939, cut the number of streetcars operating to the Ferries in half. The innermost loop track was removed from service at that time. Following the Muni/MSRy merger in 1944, the number of car lines gradually shrank to the point where all of them could be routed to the Transbay Terminal. The last rail operation to the Ferries was with a chartered PCC on November 25, 1951, more than two years after regular streetcar service ended.

Of course, streetcars began calling at the Ferry Building again when the Fisherman's Wharf Extension of the F-Line opened on March 4, 2000. But a landscape architect's 1998 design proposal to partially re-create the old Ferry Loop was eventually rejected in favor of a much simpler and less aesthetic plan. [See Chapter 6.]

adorned with dash lights. MSRy claimed that this was a major safety enhancement, and received a patent for its efforts. But it changed the face of San Francisco's transit, especially when comparing its cars to the somber gray colors of Muni's streetcars.

MSRy also introduced the "California Comfort Car." 250 of these wood-and-steel cars were cranked out by the company's 1907-vintage Elkton Shops from 1923 to 1933. All of these new cars had leather seats, something previously unheard of in San Francisco. Clearly, MSRy wanted to put a positive PR spin on its service, something its predecessor had never done. Car 798, currently under restoration by the Market Street Railway (MSR) non-profit group, is the sole survivor of this class of streetcar.

MSRy also upgraded its famous 40-Line interurban to San Mateo, built a new 31-Balboa line (opened in 1932, the last new San Francisco streetcar line until the F-Line came along 63 years later) and started San Francisco's first electric trolley coach service. On the minus side, it lost its most scenic service, the California Street line's Land's End extension in February 1925 due to a landslide; the line was never rebuilt.

"The Roar Of The Four"

No phenomenon in San Francisco's streetcar history was as famous as the daily operation along Market Street's four tracks. United Railroads and Market Street Railway trolleys held down the "Inside Track," while Muni's gray "Battleships" had to operate on the outside. The symphony that was the "Roar Of The Four" endured for nearly three decades. (*above*) A Market Street "White Front" 31-Line car turns onto Market Street off of Eddy Street in 1937. (*below*) On the second weekday of service to the new Transbay Terminal–January 17, 1939–an endless trolley traffic jam stretched out Market Street in this view from First Street. *Both photos, San Francisco History Center, San Francisco Public Library collection*

Consolidation!

DURING THE DEPRESSION, Market Street Railway Co. was hard hit by falling revenues. It attempted to revive one-man streetcar operation, first by getting the city government to allow such operation, followed by buying up several relatively modern streetcars from Eastern and Midwest systems. For a while, this worked well, until the ugly

With its "Eclipse" fender drooping, Market Street Railway "California Comfort Car" 827, which was home-built in MSRy's Elkton Shops in 1926, heads outbound at Market and Mason in 1944. Muni absorbed MSRy later that year, and cars such as 827 would soon be on their way to the boneyard, as Muni proceeded to obliterate any trace of the two railways' competitive existence. *Ira Swett collection, courtesy of Alan Fishel*

specter of the URR's 1918 Visitacion Valley wreck involving a one-man car reared its head, and voters reaffirmed the City's two-man ordinance in 1939. Defeated, MSRy abandoned some lines to buses before World War II broke out, only to have to resurrect trolleys on at least one route due to wartime gas and rubber restrictions. Muni, meanwhile, was thriving.

Along with some streetcar lines that got bused, two cable car routes and the unique Fillmore Street Counterbalance line, a funicular where one car going downhill on Fillmore between Broadway and Green Streets pulled another car upgrade, were also replaced. (From Green Street to the flat Marina District, the electric cars assigned to this route used normal electric traction.) The Counterbalance and the system's only standard gauge cable car line, Castro Street, succumbed to buses on April 5, 1941, and the city's very first cable car line, Clay Street (paired with Sacramento Street) followed a year later.

As MSRy's rolling stock and physical plant continued to wear out due to heavy use and deferred maintenance, it became clear that the City was going to have to eventually take over MSRy service, although voters had turned down six previous attempts. The seventh time was the charm: On May 16, 1944, the voters approved a buyout for $7.5 million, and Muni officially took over MSRy on September 29.

There were few immediate changes other than Muni being forced to paint the ex-MSRy "White Fronts" to avoid paying royalties, and the first fare increase in Muni's history, to 7¢, matching what MSRy had charged (today, the fare is $2.00). But Muni began the process to eradicate the MSRy from the public consciousness by repainting cars, buses, car houses, and other infrastructure. One of the first projects was to remove the outer rails on Market Street from Valencia to Castro, which was done in 1945. Many already-derelict ex-MSRy trolleys were scrapped in 1945 and 1946. A few former MSRy cars were reassigned to Muni lines C and H. Some got the new "Muni Wings" livery (which today is worn by ex-Philadelphia PCC 1050 and B-Type 162, and will soon reappear on "Torpedoes" 1006 and 1008 and "Baby Ten" 1040, when those three PCCs return from rehab by Brookville Equipment Company in 2011/12).

To continue total replacement of the life-expired ex-Market Street Railway physical plant and rolling stock, five general obligation bond issues and two related measures were approved by the voters in November 1947. The $11.5

Two 1911-built ex-MSRy "Haight Street Jewetts," assigned to Muni's C-Line, meet on Market near 1st Street in 1948. A brand new "Torpedo" PCC precedes car 471. Like the Jewetts, all the small buildings in this photo have disappeared.
Interurban Press/Peter Ehrlich collections

million raised by these bond issues, plus $5 million previously raised, funded purchase of motor buses and electric trolley coaches, ten new PCC streetcars (the 1006-1015-series "Torpedoes") and partial modernization of 64 Muni B, K and L-types (including B-Type 162, which returned to Muni in 2003 from a museum), and reducing the four tracks on Market Street to two. Although some lines bit the dust before 1948, the bulk of conversions of ex-MSRy rail lines to rubber-tired vehicles occurred between June 1948 and July 1949. By 1950, there wasn't a single ex-MSRy "White Front" streetcar in service.

A special note about why Muni invested in a large electric trolley coach fleet: First, they were superb hill-climbers, and second, they used cheap City-owned and generated Hetch Hetchy hydro-electric power. San Francisco still maintains the largest trolley bus system in the United States. An example of the trolley coach's hill-climbing ability manifested itself when Muni's E-Union Street line was converted to electric trolley bus (ETB) in 1947. E-Line cars had to use the gentler grades on parallel Vallejo Street between Van Ness Avenue and Larkin Street because Union Street was too steep for normal rail adhesion vehicles—a time-consuming matter. The replacement trolley buses instead zipped up the steep Union Street grades between Van Ness and Larkin, then the steepest grade for trolley coaches in the world, with ease and in silence, and their dynamic brakes helped keep the downgrade speeds low.

Retrenchment Continues

AFTER TOTAL REPLACEMENT of MSRy's former streetcar routes, Muni continued rail-to-rubber conversions of its own lines in the 1950s. Five lines, including the oldest, the B-Geary, were converted to buses or trolley coaches between 1950 and 1956.

Now it was Muni's turn to be hamstrung by the City's 2-man streetcar ordinance, the same one that led to MSRy's demise. Buses and trolley coaches, of course, weren't covered by this restriction, and Muni even substituted buses on its rail services (except the K-Line from West Portal to downtown) at night and on weekends through most of the Fifties.

In addition, the cable car lines were coming under fire. Muni, which bought out the California Street Cable Railroad and its three routes in 1952, wanted to dispose of them as soon as possible. But a fired-up electorate, led by local socialite Friedel Klussmann, stymied the City at virtually every turn, although the City pulled a sly trick by pretending that the "Hyde Street Grip" would be protected if the voters approved a 1953 measure that would actually shrink the then-existing system to half its size. Ultimately, three lines were saved, which continue to this day, as the cable car became the city's number 1 icon, and caused thousands of visitors leave their hearts in San Francisco every year.

Even after the purchase of 25 more PCCs in 1951-52 (the last domestic order for PCCs), repeal of the 2-man streetcar ordinance in 1953, and

Two Images at East Portal

East Portal of the Twin Peaks Tunnel, at Castro Street, was a rather simple affair. Like the more ornate West Portal (opposite page), it succumbed to subway construction in the 1970s. (*above left*) Muni B-Type 130 exits East Portal in 1957. Today, car 130 is an F-Line star. (*above right*) Just moments later, PCC 1105, one of the first of 66 PCCs leased from St. Louis in 1957/58 to replace the "Iron Monsters," approaches Castro Street. *Both photos, Ira Swett, courtesy of Alan Fishel*

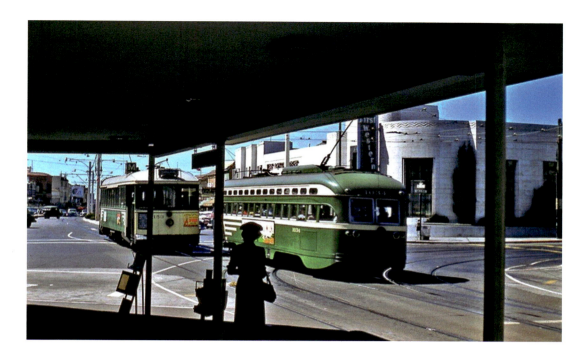

San Francisco Streetcars in the 1950s – West Portal

West Portal has always been one of the great street railway junctions in America. West Portal Avenue itself was created along with the opening of the Twin Peaks Tunnel in 1918, and from the outset, it served an upscale and growing business district. Three streetcar lines served West Portal, beginning with the K-Market (now K-Ingleside). The L-Taraval, whose streetcars turned right once they left the tunnel, was added in 1919 with shuttle cars, becoming a through route in October 1923. Both the K and L lines competed directly with United Railroads. Last to be added was the M-Ocean View, which began as a shuttle in 1925. Full or partial through service began in 1927. (*above*) In 1957, B-Type 153 meets PCC 1034 just outside the tunnel. The handsome concrete bracket arm overhead wire support poles were a West Portal feature until the avenue was rerailed in the 1970s. (*below*) The impressive entrance to the Twin Peaks Tunnel was demolished in the late 1970s to make room for the West Portal Muni Metro Station. "Iron Monsters" 159, a B-Type, and K-Type 170 meet at the Portal during their last full year of service, 1957. *Both photos, Ira Swett, courtesy of Alan Fishel*

abandonment of Geary Street lines B and C in 1956 (the C-California had been cut back to 2nd Avenue and Cornwall in 1950), Muni still had 68 2-man streetcars (referred to as "Iron Monsters" or "Boxcars") on its roster to cover the five remaining rail lines–J-Church, K-Ingleside, L-Taraval, M-Ocean View and N-Judah, joining the 40 modern PCCs and "Magic Carpets" which had been quickly converted to one-man operation. But PCCs were no longer in production, and Muni was prohibited by the City Charter from purchasing used vehicles. So a lease arrangement with St. Louis Public Service Co. was negotiated in 1957 for 66 PCCs built in 1946 to replace the remaining "Iron Monsters." Turnback wyes were added to two lines, which didn't have turning loops at both ends, to accommodate the single-ended PCCs. The first ones arrived from St. Louis in 1957, and on May 9, 1958, the "Iron Monster" era ended when K-Type 181 pulled in from the L-Line for the last time. (Two other K-Types, 171 and 178, exist at streetcar museums, and 178 operated in San Francisco from 1981 through 1985, on lease from the Western Railway Museum.) After the restriction on purchasing used transit vehicles was lifted, four more PCCs were

San Francisco Streetcars in the 1950s – Market Street

(*above*) "Torpedo" 1011 and a slew of "Boxcars" are visible in this scene looking east from 11th Street. In one of the worst preservation travesties of all time, the beloved Fox Theater movie palace was allowed to fall to the wrecking ball in 1963, five years after the "Iron Monsters" vanished. ☻ (*below*) Looking east toward Castro Street and along Market, we see K-Type 187 and B-Type 154, plus a "Baby Ten" PCC, at East Portal, also in 1957. Today, the F-Line terminates on 17th Street alongside the gas station. Redlick's "17 Reasons Why!" Furniture was a local institution located on 17th Street, in the Mission District several blocks east. *Both photos, Ira Swett, courtesy of Alan Fishel*

(*left*) Muni's last 2-man crew, motorman Tony Marelich and conductor Albert Flieger, pose in front of K-Type car 181 at the Transbay Terminal on May 9, 1958. A special dash sign was created to commemorate the last run of the "Iron Monsters." *Art Curtis*

acquired from St. Louis in 1962 to replace the 1939 PCC-style "Magic Carpets," and the previous 66 cars were also purchased outright at that time.

With one-man streetcars now in place, night and weekend rail service was restored to four of the five lines. Saturday daytime service also returned to the M-Ocean View. But night and Sunday rail service on the M-Line would have to wait until the 1980s.

BART and Muni Metro

THE "ROAR OF THE FOUR" was a fact of life in San Francisco for three decades. But as early as 1932, there were dreams of building a subway under the city's premier street. (An earlier Jules Verne-type vision for a subway and tunnel under San Francisco Bay was talked about in 1911.)

But would a subway be merely a San Francisco phenomenon, or would it be part of a broader regional approach? Starting in 1939, electric interurban trains from the East Bay and even from places like Sacramento reached into San Francisco over the new San Francisco-Oakland Bay Bridge. But continued traffic pressure on the Bay Bridge eventually forced the Key System's Bridge Railway to close in April 1958, and this rail link connecting both sides of San Francisco Bay was lost forever.

The region's business leaders, concerned about growing traffic congestion caused by workers migrating to the Bay Area during and after World War II, began talking about an underwater tube with subway trains, even as the Bridge Railway was operating. By 1951, a commission had been created by the state to study transit needs. Its final report came out in 1957, and BART (officially, the San Francisco Bay Area Rapid Transit District) was formed, composed of San Francisco, Alameda, Contra Costa, San Mateo and Marin Counties. The latter two withdrew from the District in 1961 for financial and other reasons, leaving the other three county governments to recommend that a $792 million bond issue be submitted to the voters for approval in November 1962. With 60% voter approval required, it passed–barely. (Much later, San Mateo County bought its way back into the District, and as a result, BART now operates to San Francisco International Airport.)

The stipulation for San Francisco's approval was that a four-track, two-level subway was to be built under Market Street. The top level was intended for Muni streetcars, while regional rapid transit trains, similar to those in New York and Chicago, would occupy the lower level. Construction in the East Bay began in 1966, and work began on the Transbay Tube the same year. Construction of the subway under Market Street, including cut-and-cover excavation at the sites for Montgomery, Powell and Civic Center Stations and the Muni-only Van Ness Station, commenced in July 1967 and was finished by 1970. During station construction, Muni streetcars were guided around the work on "shooflies" resting on wooden timbers. No excavation was required between stations, as the tunnels were bored through.

BART began its subway service in San Francisco in 1973, but only between Montgomery "Montgomery Street Station in the Financial District" and Daly City. The following year, BART started through service from San Francisco to the East Bay. As envisioned by the engineers who built BART, its trains were sleek and fast, computer-controlled, and capable of speeds up to 70 mph, unheard of in the subway world up to that time, but common among electrified commuter railroads. In the East Bay, BART was essentially that–a commuter railway, albeit a very fancy one. Later, a station at Davis/Beale Streets, called Embarcadero, was added and excavated, but this didn't require any streetcar track deviations. But it did bring up the necessity of deciding how to turn the streetcars around. Muni's original plan had been to

BART was one of the first new-generation rapid transit systems in the United States. Service in the East Bay began on September 11, 1972, and trains began running from San Francisco under the bay in 1974. The shovel-nose "A" cars, like this one at Civic Center Station in 1980, became a Bay Area icon. *Doug Grotjahn*

17

BART used simple cut-and-cover excavation to build the Muni Metro subway west of Van Ness. A PCC runs alongside the excavation zone just past Gough Street in November 1971. *Peter Ehrlich*

simply run PCCs with low-level platforms and left-hand running. This would have required a turning loop somewhere in the lower Market area. Then it dawned on Muni and the City that this would be an opportunity to replace the aging PCC fleet by buying new double-ended, larger capacity cars with high-level platforms, requiring on-board steps that changed heights for street running. After several years of debate, BART forced the issue, and Muni would have to go with how BART configured the subway—even though a loop would be more efficient operationally.

West of Van Ness, simple cut-and-cover for the Muni Metro Subway under Upper Market was all that was needed, and streetcars ran on each side of the excavation. But to get around construction of Church and Castro Street stations, a detour was necessary. The solution was to run cars the normal route to Market and Duboce, then make a right turn onto Duboce, the route of the N-Judah (with the street closed to traffic, as Duboce Portal was part of the construction) to Church Street. From there, N cars would continue out their normal route, but all other lines would turn left at Church, cross Market, and K, L and M trolleys would turn right at 17th Street for new trackage, called the 17th Street Detour, which linked up to the 1918-vintage Twin Peaks Tunnel. The excavation at Castro Street Station led to some very interesting track arrangements, with outbound PCCs crossing the west end of the station work on the roller coaster-like "Collingwood Elevated" and descending a steep grade into the tunnel. All this added several minutes of running time to the PCC runs and required purchase of 11 used PCCs from Toronto, but the tracks were never restored to Market Street between Duboce and Castro after the work was done. But the legacy of the 17th Street Detour remains as the access route to and from today's F-Line by pullout and pull-in cars. (The rails returned to Upper Market beginning in 1993 during the construction for today's F-Line.)

Ordering Replacement Streetcars

AS MENTIONED, THE CONFIGURATION of the inner subway terminal gave Muni an opportunity to replace the PCCs. The problem was that no streetcars had been built in the United States since 1952. In the early 1970s, Muni hired Louis Klauder & Associates, a design consulting firm, to draw up specifications for a new subway-surface streetcar for Muni's portion of the subway, called Muni Metro. Bids, however, came in at 66% above engineering estimates, and no contract was awarded.

It was about that time that the United States Department of Transportation got involved. There were four cities that were looking for new streetcars to replace their PCCs, and USDOT came up with a specification for a "United States Standard Light Rail Vehicle," or SLRV. The only bidder was Boeing-Vertol, a manufacturer of helicopters and a newcomer to transit car building. Boeing produced five prototype cars, three in Boston colors, and two in the new Muni Landor two-tone orange and white livery which Muni had adopted in 1975. Two cities—Philadelphia and Cleveland—dropped their interest in the project, claiming that "unique local requirements" precluded ordering a standardized car. One of these, Cleveland, had even tried out a Boston LRV. The two remaining systems, Boston and San Francisco, ordered a total of 275 SLRVs between them.

Because streetcar technology had been dormant for over 20 years, Boeing and USDOT basically had to start from scratch. The systems engineering approach to the design of the PCC had been long forgotten. The result was an over-designed trolley with a plethora of redundant systems, intended to make a fail-safe product, that in actuality was prone to failure. Boston, which received the first 135 cars, had trouble from the start, with brake and propulsion failures, door hiccups, and other annoyances that plagued operation, making the cars no better than the battered PCCs they were intended to replace. Muni had no better luck, and the high-low step requirement was simply another headache to worry about.

Boeing-Vertol "United States Standard Light Rail Vehicle" 1215 poses at Van Ness Station on December 28, 1983. On February 18, 1980, the N-Judah became the first line to serve the Muni Metro subway, but on weekdays only. Seven-day subway service would not happen for another two years and nine months. The Boeings' career on Muni spanned only 23 years, a rather short life for a railcar. *Peter Ehrlich*

Although weekday rail service through downtown San Francisco was now entirely underground, PCCs continued to soldier on, serving all five lines on weekends. Perhaps it was because of budgetary reasons, or the need to gradually train operators and hire more station agents, but Muni decided not to offer seven-day Muni Metro service until the end of 1982. Muni did intend to retire the PCCs, however, by September 1981, replacing them with buses until seven-day service started. But a severe diesel bus shortage forced the agency to continue running the old green trolleys (some had been painted in Landor orange) for another year. The last day of streetcars on Market Street—the last main street in the United States with trolleys—was September 19, 1982. It was the end of 122 years of rail operation on Market Street. Or was it?

But the die was cast, and Muni's 100 Boeings began arriving in 1979. (Thirty more were added in 1983, after Boston refused them.) Enough Boeings were on hand to convert weekday service on the N-Judah line from PCC to LRV operation on February 18, 1980—nearly seven years after BART service began—and to route it via the new Muni Metro subway. Muni converted the other four lines to LRV operation gradually; all weekday service became subway-surface operation on June 17, 1981, when LRVs replaced PCCs on the J-Church line. This gradual phase-in of subway service was a practical way of introducing the public to it, while giving Operations staff the means to work out operational and logistical kinks. Credit is due the Muni Service Planning department to phase in Muni Metro service, rather than making the conversion in one fell swoop, as many officials within Operations had advocated.

A two-car N-Judah train emerges from the Muni Metro Subway on March 28, 1991. It would continue to rain on the hard-luck Boeings' parade for another ten years. The train on the left is on the siding because it probably failed in service. In the background, a vintage car is undergoing restoration by *Market Street Railway* volunteers at Mint Yard. *Peter Ehrlich*

Last Day of PCC Service In San Francisco

September 19, 1982

It was a bright, sunny day, but hearts were heavy as many San Franciscans believed that this day would mark the end of 122 years of streetcar operations on Market Street and the friendly cars would be gone forever.

(*facing page, top*) K-Type 178, then on lease from the *Western Railway Museum*, pulls out of the ancient Geneva Carhouse for service on the J-Church line [see Chapter 2] as PCC 1158 awaits its turn. (*bottom*) Old Number 1, also assigned to the J-Line, stops for passengers at Powell Street. (*this page, top*) PCC 1125 poses on last-day operation at Market and Duboce. (*center*) At Judah and 16th Avenue, with the landmark St. Ann's of the Sunset Church and UCSF Medical Center behind. (*bottom*) "Baby Ten" 1038, in "Landor" two-tone orange and white, works a last-day charter at Judah/46th Avenue. All photos, Peter Ehrlich

(*below*) A last-day flier. Peter Ehrlich collection

PCC Storage and Scrapping

(*right*) Muni retained 38 PCCs for possible future use. They were moved over to Pier 70, and later to Pier 72. This 1984 shot features a bunch of "Baby Tens" and "Torpedoes" 1009, 1014 and 1011. 1014 later migrated to Australia, and 1009 and 1011 are at Brookville in 2012 being rehabbed for service. *Peter Ehrlich*

(*left*) After the PCCs Muni intended to keep had been moved to Pier 70, scrapping of other cars began. Landor-liveried PCC 1167 is being tipped over in Geneva Upper Yard in January 1983. *Mike Davis*

Geneva Carhouse Demolition

The demolition of the red brick United Railroads-era Geneva Carhouse shed, which dated to the 1890s, began in 1982, after all the retired PCCs had been moved to storage at Pier 70 or across the street for scrapping.

(*above*) Demolition of the shed. (*right*) Only one window in the east wall remains in this shot. January 1983. *Both photos, Mike Davis*

1932

1932 was the last year of the full original Muni system.
Line terminals shown in RED.

Maps of the Muni System - 1932 and 2007

●

(*left*) In 1932, the Muni rail system reached its peak. The N-Line was the last major line to open, and the map on the left shows all routes before abandonment of the A-Line, Muni's first route, on December 5, 1932.
(Not included: The three Panama-Pacific International Exposition routes, or the experimental O-Line.)

●

Not shown: Market Street Railway Company streetcar lines, or Muni bus routes.

●

During the 1940s and 1950's Muni rail routes shrank to just the J, K, L, M and N lines. The E-Union was abandoned in 1947; the D and H in 1950, the original F-Stockton in January 1951, and finally, the B-Geary and C-California routes were replaced by buses on December 29, 1956.

●

It would be 63 years before Muni expanded its rail system with the opening of the F-Market historic streetcar route on September 1, 1995.

●

Maps drawn by Peter Ehrlich; base map from Rand McNally Corp.

(*right*) This map includes the changes since 1980. Muni Metro opened on February 18, 1980. The M-Ocean View was also extended from its original Broad and Plymouth terminal to Balboa Park Station that year.

●

In 1991, the J-Church was also extended to Balboa Park via San Jose Avenue. The F-Market, of course, began service in 1995, and was extended to Fisherman's Wharf on March 4, 2000.

●

Muni Metro subway service was extended to King and 4th Streets/ Caltrain Depot by 1998.

●

Finally, the T-Third Street route began operation in 2007.

●

The carbarns were Metro Center (Green Light Rail Division), Geneva Yard and Metro East, replacing Geary and Potrero Divisions.

●

Future extensions call for the E-Embarcadero line to open in 2013; the F-Market and Wharves to reach Fort Mason, and the new Central Subway, now under construction, with a 2016 opening.

●

Not shown: BART or Caltrain.

2007

In 2007, the T-Line opened, and was through-routed with the K. Existing lines are in GREEN; terminals and future lines, in RED.

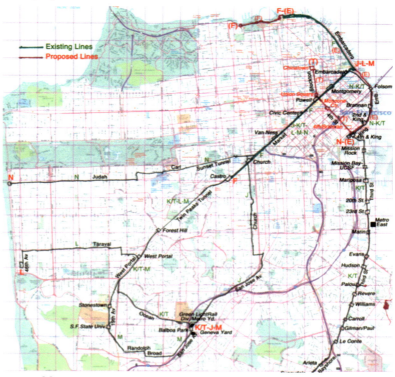

The PCC Car:
An American Success Story

THE PCC STREETCAR is considered to be the finest streetcar ever designed using a systems engineering approach. The idea was born in 1929 when a consortium of street railway presidents met to design a new car that would compete with the private automobile. The streetcar of that day was perceived by the public as being old, slow, noisy and uncomfortable, and Americans were deserting them in droves for shiny new automobiles. Thus was formed the Electric Railway Presidents' Conference Committee (ERPCC).

Out of this consortium, a new, streamlined, quiet car with leather seats and improved lighting was designed from the ground up. Dr. Clarence Hirshfeld, formerly of Detroit Edison and an outsider to the street railway industry, was hired to head the design team. He and his assistants examined all aspects of streetcars of that day—the motors, trucks, braking, suspension, ride quality, interior design, lighting and air comfort. From their exhaustive research came a new vehicle that could "float" in traffic, keep up with automobiles, and whisk passengers in comfort and safety. The new car's appearance was an Art Deco-influenced design, something which had almost never been seen on an urban rail transit vehicle up to that time, and fit in with the streamliner craze introduced by the railroads in that era. A new right-angle-drive hypoid gearing ensured a quiet ride. The trucks and wheels were cushioned with rubber throughout, and rode on roller bearings. The motors were completely redesigned to match the hypoid right-angle-drive: there were four motors wired at 300 volts and set up in

(above) Although Pittsburgh was the first American city to run a PCC in revenue service in September 1936, Brooklyn became the first to introduce a fleet of these modern trolleys–the most successful American streetcars designed from a systems engineering approach. Brooklyn 1001, the first of 99 cars from St. Louis Car Co. to enter service in October 1936, is approaching Coney Island on Route 68-Coney Island Avenue shortly before that line was abandoned in 1955. *Joe Testagrose/nycsubway.org collections* (below) Brooklyn's legacy is represented today on Muni by F-Line PCC 1053, shown here with sister 1055 (Philadelphia) at Judah and 9th Avenue on a test run in 1994. *Peter Ehrlich* (facing page) Pioneer PCC 1001 has been lovingly restored by the *Shore Line Trolley Museum* in East Haven, CT to its 1936 Brooklyn and Queens Transit appearance, and it's posing here on that museum's Stony Creek trestle in 2008. *Richard Panse*

pairs. The underfloor drum controllers ranged from 99 to 250 points of power, rather than the 8-10 points found on most standard streetcar controllers. Acceleration was 4.75mph per second; full emergency braking, 8-9 mph per second, and balancing speed was 42 mph, all rates that were far greater than anything experienced before. Dynamic braking was the principal component of the brake system, assisted by air-operated tread or drum brakes and, in emergencies, magnetic track brakes. The motorman operated the car with pedal controls, similar to an automobile.

The key to the PCC, and the feature which provided the Transit Research Corp., ERPCC's successor, with funding to continue improving the PCC, was in the new lightweight trucks, built by Clark Equipment Company (Clark B-2 trucks) and St. Louis Car Co. (St. Louis B-3 model). These provided royalty payments from PCC purchasers, who, in essence, operated the PCC under license from TRC. Purchase and use of the ERPCC-designed resilient wheels also provided a constant flow of royalty payments to TRC.

The ERPCC produced a couple of prototype cars, and the first production order, for 100 cars, was delivered to Brooklyn in October 1936, although Pittsburgh had already placed one car in service. By 1938, nearly a dozen cities, including Pittsburgh, Baltimore, Los Angeles, San Diego, Chicago, Washington and Philadelphia. had the streamliners in service, and ridership on routes using the PCCs soared. St. Louis Car Co. and Pullman-Standard, of Worcester, MA, were the builders, while old-line carbuilder J. G. Brill decided not to join in production of the PCC. Brill produced a similar, but less successful, competing car design and ultimately left the business.

The systems engineering design of the PCC also made it adaptable to purchasers who needed longer, wider or shorter cars. For instance, PCCs for Chicago, Pacific Electric, Muni and Illinois Terminal were both longer and wider. Cars for Washington were one window shorter because of tranfer table clearance in several carhouses.

Chicago acquired the greatest number of new PCCs–683. Pittsburgh was next at 666, not counting the ten new home-built aluminum-bodied PCCs from the 1980s. Toronto, which purchased large numbers of used PCCs, had 744–more than anyplace else. The smallest fleets were on the Illinois Terminal running out of St. Louis, with just eight cars; Johnstown, PA, where 17 cars operated from 1947 to 1960–the smallest U. S. city with PCCs; Montréal, with 18 cars; and El Paso, with 20 ex-San Diego PCCs. Muni, which started with 10 double-enders in 1948, ultimately rostered 116 PCCs in the postwar era up to 1982 [see *Muni And The PCC* sidebar in this chapter] and, since 1992, has purchased 25 PCCs and rebuilt them for F-Line use, and those plus eight of its own postwar cars are in daily service or are being remanufactured [see Chapters 4 through 8].

Starting in the mid-1940s, the all-electric PCC supplanted the air-electric car, and a new standee-window body design was crafted. By the time PCC production ceased in 1952, with San Francisco receiving the last order, nearly 5000 PCCs had been manufactured for the North American market.

In the 1950s, as systems using PCCs abandoned operations, a booming used-PCC streetcar market developed, with many cities adding to their fleets and hastening scrapping of older cars. San Francisco was one of these, obtaining 70 PCCs from St. Louis starting in 1957. Another example was in Newark, New Jersey, whose used PCCs from Minneapolis, placed in service on the famous Newark City Subway in 1954, were the only ones they ever owned. (Eleven of these came to San Francisco more than 50 years later.)

PCC technology was also exported to Europe, where Belgium and the Communist Bloc countries, under license from Transit Research Corp. (TRC), were the principal producers and operators. (TRC was the name taken by ERPCC after the first

25

PCCs around the United States

Pittsburgh had more PCCs than anywhere else except Chicago; Chicago's PCCs were longer and wider and had more doors; and Washington's cars were one window shorter.

(*this column, top to bottom*) Chicago's PCCs, besides being longer and wider, also had triple-stream rear doors. Brand-new PCC 4309 has just entered service on the Clark Street line in August 1947. Muni's car 1058 represents Chicago. Washington's PCCs were one window shorter because of carhouse clearances. 1495 is at Friendship Heights in 1959. Muni 1076 models Washington's paint scheme. Washington purchased 20 pre-PCCs in 1935. 1053 was the sole survivor of this group; it's on a fantrip in 1959. 1053 went to a museum in 1962, but was lost in a devastating fire in 2003. *All photos, Joe Testagrose collection*

Pittsburgh totaled 678 PCCs, spanning 64 years of operation. (*this column, top to bottom*) PCC 1614 rolls up Grant Street at 4th Avenue in downtown Pittsburgh in summer 1970. *Joe Testagrose* Until Muni's F-Line came along in 1995, Pittsburgh's PCCs had the most colorful liveries, thanks to Harold Geissenheimer, who later came to Muni. 1735 and 1744 lay over at Simmons Loop on the Library line in 1984. Of note: The last Pittsburgh PCCs ran on the Drake line in 1999. *Peter Ehrlich* PCC 1713 was later rebuilt and returned to its original red-and-cream hourglass paint scheme. It's at Wood Street Station in 1987. PCCs ran in the downtown Pittsburgh subway for a few years after it opened in 1985. *Peter Ehrlich*

Los Angeles operated PCCs on two systems: The Los Angeles Railway, whose narrow-gauge PCCs ran from 1937 to 1963; and Pacific Electric, where three-car trains of PCCs ran for a little over ten years. (*above left*) The last three "Big Ps," which were 108" wide, still in Los Angeles Transit Lines (LATL) "Fruit Salad" colors, line up at Vermont and Monroe on the V line shortly before system abandonment at the end of March 1963. (*above right*) 3163, in Los Angeles Metropolitan Transit Authority (LAMTA) paint, rolls past First and Main in March 1963. Los Angeles-liveried cars on Muni: 1052 (LARy 2-tone yellow), 1080 (LATL) and 1061 (Pacific Electric). *Both photos, Joe Testagrose collection* (*bottom*) Pacific Electric and Los Angeles Railway PCCs shared trackage on Broadway in downtown L. A., albeit with different track gauges. PE used standard gauge; LARy, 3'-6." PE quit running on Broadway in 1955. *Ira Swett, Alan Fishel collection*

production cars made their American debuts in cities across the land.) PCCs were also built in Spain and Italy under license. Brussels 7037, now in the San Francisco fleet, was a typical Belgian PCC, built by Ateliers de La Brugeoise of Brugge, Belgium in 1952. La Brugeoise also constructed PCCs for France and The Netherlands. The ones for The Hague were patterned after the St. Louis Car. Co. body style, but outfitted with picture windows. Undoubtedly, had American PCC production continued beyond 1952, similar cars would have rolled on the streets of American cities.

The systems engineering success of the PCC was applied to rapid transit technology by TRC. The most notable application of this manifested itself in Chicago, where 570 of its PCC surface cars were scrapped and reincarnated as "L" cars, joining 204 similar cars built new. This enabled the Chicago system to modernize its ancient elevated lines, but at the cost of ridding the Windy City of its surface streetcar network, one of the largest in the world. Other PCC-specific rapid transit cars were produced for New York City and Boston, and certain aspects of this technology was also found in cars built for Cleveland.

It is safe to say, though, that had the United States embraced a pro-transit policy in the 1950s instead of continuing its love affair with the automobile, PCC production would have continued for many more decades, improving all the time. But because the technology was allowed to fall dormant, when it came time to build new cars for existing lines and open new light rail systems, the systems engineering approach and standardization imbued in the PCC design and production had been lost forever. Today, each new system has its own different rolling stock and "unique local conditions," which the PCC had been designed to sidestep.

Yet even today, the PCC's legacy can still be experienced in San Francisco, Boston, Philadelphia and Kenosha, Wis., in regular service. Overseas, they still run in Belgium and the former Communist Bloc countries. That is a testimonial to its success!

Muni And The PCC—1939 to 1982

ONE OF THE SUCCESSES of the ERPCC (and the TRC, or Transit Research Corp. that succeeded it) was the program of royalties collected from the use of patents of ERPCC-designed equipment, such as trucks, wheels and body design. These royalties enabled TRC to continue research to improve the PCC. But one of the arcane sections of San Francisco's City Charter ruled out any royalty payments to any company. So, in 1939, Muni couldn't buy PCCs. It did, however, order five cars which had a PCC-style carbody. Numbered 1001- 1005, they were nicknamed "Magic Carpets" for their smooth acceleration, braking and riding quality. For all practical purposes, they could have been considered PCCs, as they had the same motors and electrical controls. In fact, three of the cars rode on Clark B-2 PCC trucks, and royalties were paid to TRC. A significant difference was that they used hand controls instead of pedal controls found on PCCs. This feature earned them another sobriquet, "One-Arm Bandits." Actually, the royalty payments were disguised in the purchase price.

The "Magic Carpets," whose official designation was C-Type, were based initially at Potrero Division and assigned to the L-Taraval line. When Potrero was renovated as a trolley coach barn in the 1940s, they moved to Geneva Carhouse, where they continued to work the L-Line. These cars were retired in 1960. "Magic Carpet" 1003 is preserved at the Western Railway Museum.

As part of the 1940s modernization program to obliterate the Market Street Railway consciousness from the streets of San Francisco, Muni, in 1948, was able to order 10 Presidents Conference Committee (PCC) cars from St. Louis Car Company. Cars 1006-1015 were double-end, all-electric cars which had the basic prewar, no standee-window body style of the five "Magic Carpet" cars received in 1939. They were dubbed "Torpedoes" by the operating crews. Officially, they were classed as D-Types. (Three of them now run on the F-Line every day, with four more slated to return from remanufacturing in 2012.) An earlier plan to buy 317 PCCs to re-equip about a dozen routes was shelved.

This purchase came about because the "no-royalty" restriction had been repealed by the voters, and Muni was now free to buy PCCs outright. The D-Types' first assignment was on the N-Judah line. They also worked the B-Geary route since they were initially based at Geary Carhouse. Like the "Magic Carpets," the "Torpedoes" boarded passengers through the rear door during the two-man era.

The next order, placed in 1951, consisted of 25 standard single-end all-electric PCC cars from St. Louis Car Co. These were numbers 1016-1040. Car 1040 was the last PCC built for an American street railway system. (In 2009, 1040 went to Brookville Equipment Co. in Pennsylvania for remanufacturing, and it returned in 2011.)

Before placing this order, Muni tried to get St. Louis Car Company to produce a postwar single-end design with standee windows and doors at each end (as it had done for Chicago). But the builder rejected the proposal, and Muni had to settle for the standard offering.

The "Baby Tens," as they were nicknamed, were initially assigned to line B-Geary, but were transferred almost immediately to Geneva Carhouse, a pre-1906 Earthquake facility built by the San Francisco and San Mateo Electric Railroad, for service on the K-Ingleside route (originally named K-Market). Passengers boarded through the center door and paid the conductor, who sat opposite the doors.

In 1953, the two-man ordinance was finally repealed by the voters, and Muni immediately converted its 40 modern cars to one-man operation. In the case of the "Magic Carpets" and "Torpedoes," the doors on one side were blocked off or covered with sheet metal, but the operating controls on the #2 end were retained for backup movements. Starting in 1957, after a wye was installed at 30th and Church on the J-Church line, the "Baby Tens" were shifted there, but did work the other four routes. The "Torpedoes" usually worked the three "Tunnel" lines K, L and M.

All 40 cars were 108" wide. Cars 1001 through 1015 were 50'-5" long, while the "Baby Tens" were the standard postwar PCC carbody length of 46'-5⅜". In terms of width, the 1016-1040 group were identical to cars manufactured for Minneapolis/St. Paul and the "Big Ps" (class P-3) for Los Angeles Transit Lines. (Some 55 years later, some of the Minneapolis cars would join Muni's fleet.) The "Magic Carpets" arrived in the 1939 blue and gold "World's Fair" livery; the postwar cars received Muni's new and handsome late '40s verdant green and cream "Wings" pattern. Like all San Francisco streetcars, front and rear poles were the norm even on single-end cars, since Muni required them for backup moves. This arrangement was also found on PCCs in El Paso.

Now that the two-man ordinance had been dumped, Muni management was desirous of getting rid of the last of its crew-operated "Iron Monsters," over 80 of which dated to 1914. But there was a new problem: money for acquiring new streetcars and

(*above*) The "Magic Carpets" (cars 1001-1005) arrived in 1939. 1002, on the original F-Stockton route, is passing a cable car in 1939, just after they were introduced to revenue service. Columbus and North Point, in the distance, was as close as Muni got to the Wharf before the F-Line was extended in 2000. *Arthur Lloyd, Cameron Beach collection*

(*below*) "Torpedo" 1012 passes 17th and Castro in September 1973. Originally double-enders, they were converted to single-end status by blocking off the doors on one side, but they retained their control pedals for backup moves. *Peter Ehrlich*

"Magic Carpets" and early PCCs

Muni showed interest in obtaining modern cars, but was hamstrung by 1930s-era City Charter restrictions, which did not permit acquisition of true PCC cars until the restrictions were repealed in the 1940s. Muni did purchase five "Magic Carpet" cars in 1939, which, for all practical purposes, could have been classified as PCCs as they had some PCC components. The ten 1948 double-end "Torpedo" purchase and the 1951/52 25-unit "Baby Ten" order were the only new PCCs that Muni rostered.

(*below*) PCC 1018 was the third of 25 PCCs built on St. Louis Car Company's Job 1675, the last order for PCC cars in the United States. When Muni received these cars, the agency modernized the K-Market line and renamed it the K-Ingleside. *St. Louis Car Company photo, Art Curtis collection*

(*above*) "Torpedo" PCC 1013 is being tested outside the St. Louis Car Company plant in Baden, Mo. before delivery to Muni in 1948. These D-Types were Muni's first true PCC cars. *St. Louis Car Company photo, Art Curtis collection* (*below*) PCC 1040, the last of the 25 "Baby Tens" of 1951/52, survived the 1979/1982 scrappings and remained active into the early F-Line era, but was allowed to deteriorate badly until saved with the decision to include it in the contract with Brookville Equipment to rewire the 11 ex-Newark PCCs and the remanufacture the four Muni "Torpedoes." At Metro East in December 2009 just before it went to Pennsylvania. *Karl Johnson* [See Chapters 8 and 13 for pics of 1040 after its rebuilding and return to service.]

buses from the 1947 bond issues had run out. And the city was also faced with another Charter restriction, namely that no used transit vehicles could be purchased. Clearly, another way to get more modern cars needed to be found.

A possible solution was to negotiate a lease arrangement with suppliers. In 1955, Muni was able to scrap its oldest and most worn-out buses when it set up a lease deal with Mack Truck Co. to obtain 100 buses initially and 70 more each year for five more years. In addition to the phased replacement of worn-out motor coaches, this lease arrangement also permitted conversion of the B-Geary and C-California streetcar lines to bus at the end of 1956, allowing for the junking of about 50 B-Types. Could a similar setup be used for obtaining PCCs?

Starting in 1956, attempts in this direction were made to obtain used PCCs. Cars from San Diego and Vancouver were looked at and rejected because of general condition. Next, Muni attempted to lease 80 all-electric cars similar to the "Baby Tens" from Detroit, but were outbid by Mexico City. In addition, funding necessary to make immediate track changes on two routes–the J-Church and M-Ocean View, neither of which had loops or wyes–for additional single-end cars didn't pan out in 1956.

Success finally came the following year, when St. Louis Public Service agreed to lease 66 of its 1946-built 1700-series PCCs to San Francisco. They were regauged from St. Louis' unusual 4'-10" gauge to standard gauge, painted in Muni "Wings" livery in St. Louis, and shipped west. They also retained the odd left-foot power and right-foot brake pedal configuration, but since they ultimately became the majority fleet on Muni, many motormen preferred this arrangement. All of the cars, numbered 1101-1166 and dubbed "Eleven Hundreds" (or simply "Elevens") on Muni, were on the property by mid-1958, and the last "Iron Monster" ran on May 9 of that year. Four more 1100s, numbered 1167-1170, were purchased outright from St. Louis in 1962 to replace the "Magic Carpets." The "no-used-vehicle-purchase" Charter restriction had been scrapped by that time, and the other 66 "Elevens" were then purchased by Muni.

For the next 15 years, the fleet remained at 105 cars. In 1973, two developments forced Muni to acquire more used PCCs. First, car 1102 was lost in an accident when it was broadsided by a speeding gravel truck blowing through an uncontrolled intersection. The motorman was badly injured and had to take a disability retirement. The other, and more significant reason, was that excavation for the Muni Metro Church and Castro Street Stations, which were being built by BART, required setting up a streetcar detour off Market Street via Duboce Avenue, Church Street and 17th Street for cars on lines K, L and M. However, this also resulted in longer journey times. The first attempt to fill the extra vehicle requirements was simply to add buses for some rush hour runs on the N-Judah line, but when Sunset District residents protested over inadequate service even with the added buses, Muni was forced to turn to Toronto for eleven third-hand PCCs from that city's ex-Kansas City fleet. The "Torontos" began arriving in late 1973 and were pressed into service as trippers on the K-Ingleside and N-Judah lines after the trucks had been regauged from Toronto's odd 4'-10⅞" gauge. They received fleet numbers 1180-1190.

The "Torontos," which kept their maroon and cream paint as it was similar to the buses of that period (although they received the Muni ribbon logos found on Muni's General Motors diesel buses purchased in 1969), were narrow (100" wide) and were unpopular with most operators. They had a tendency to roll back severely on grades, tripping circuit breakers in the process. In addition, the bodies were falling apart from rust. Two of them never entered service. Most of the "Torontos" were retired after just two years of operation, and by 1978, only 1183 and 1190 were still in service. 1190 lasted another year, and eventually was given to the Western Railway Museum. In 2007, it was sold to a Kansas City group, which gave it a cosmetic restoration in Kansas City colors and placed it on display. Car 1183 went to the Illinois Railway Museum, which scrapped it several years later because of its rusty, deteriorated condition.

By 1977, with Muni Metro's opening still three

PCC 1103, the former St. Louis Public Service 1701, sits in St. Louis in 1957 after SLPS had performed work such as regauging the car and painting it in Muni "Wings." Although a base for the front trolley pole had been installed, the pole was not yet mounted. Ultimately, 70 of these cars came from St. Louis' 1700-series and would run on Muni for 25 years. *Peter Ehrlich collection*

Two legacies of the 17th Street Detour were the "Collingwood Elevated," built to move PCCs around the excavation for Muni Metro's Castro Street Station, and the purchase of 11 used PCCs from Toronto in 1973. (above) PCCs 1108 and 1160 negotiate the dipsy-do trackage at Castro Street on Sept. 18, 1973. Many "Muni Wings" cars remained painted this way to the very end. ☻ (below) Car 1188, ex-Toronto 4775, approaches Church and Market on April 1, 1974, outbound on the K-Line, which used the 17th Street Detour. Most of the "Torontos" didn't survive beyond 1976, but the detour remained in place until the end of the PCC era in 1982. *Both photos, Peter Ehrlich*

years away, Muni's PCC fleet was severely stressed, especially because of the situation with the "Torontos." Two "Torpedoes," 1012 and 1013, which had not run after 1974, because of electrical failures or wreck damage, had been officially retired, further reducing the active fleet. "Baby Ten" 1017 was also an early casualty. It had suffered wreck and electrical damage about 1976, but was repaired. Despite repairs, 1017 was very unreliable, and used as little as possible. Many times, rush hour runs were held in the barn due to equipment unavailability. All three retired cars were scrapped in 1979.

A program to partially rehabilitate 30 cars was announced in 1977. Although Muni claimed that they were rehabilitated, in actuality, all of these PCCs–28 "Elevens" plus "Baby Tens" 1038 and 1040– received only a cosmetic restoration and a new Landor paint job of "California Poppy Gold," "Sunset Glow" and white, the standard Muni vehicle livery since 1975. (Walter Landor and Associates, who designed the Muni paint scheme, was a San Francisco-based industrial design firm, with offices on the old ferryboat *Santa Rosa*.) Their interiors, too, were redone, with white walls and roof, and new tan upholstered seats. Mechanically and electrically, they were still unreliable, and it was a common sight to see an 1100 still in original Muni "Wings" livery tow a sister "Eleven" in orange and white that had failed in service. The last car to go through this "rehab" process, 1132, never again turned a wheel in revenue service following its release from Metro Center in 1979 despite its spiffy new paint job.

The weekdays-only conversion of line N-Judah to Muni Metro service in February 1980 finally eased the pressure on the increasingly derelict PCC fleet. By June 1980, weekday PCC requirements had dropped to filling just two lines–a K-Ingleside/L-Taraval shuttle, and the J-Church, as LRVs began subway operation to West Portal and St. Francis Circle, and the M-Line was bused because of a three-month track renewal project. In September, the L and M became the PCC shuttle as LRVs took over the full K route. By December, the L-Taraval was converted to LRV, leaving only the J-Church as an everyday PCC operation. This, too, succumbed on June 17, 1981. But because of various funding and manpower issues, Seven-day subway service remained elusive for another 15 months, and PCCs continued to operate on weekends and holidays.

The first major scrapping of PCCs took place at the beginning of 1981, when 23 "Elevens" met the torch. Thirteen of these had been "rehabbed" in Landor livery. Another four 1100s, all in Landor colors, were saved by museums.

Starting with the December 1980 conversion, Muni maintenance heads made a drastic policy decision to use only the 42 remaining GE-equipped 1100s as much as possible, as the General Electric controls were considered more robust, despite the Westinghouse controllers on the "Baby Tens" being easier to maintain. From this point on, up to the time PCC service ended for good, it was indeed rare to see a "Baby Ten" out on the street, and the remaining double-enders almost never made it out of the barn. One consequence of this policy was to place buses on the N-Judah on Saturdays. On Sundays, when the M-Ocean View was not in service, there were sufficient cars to deploy PCCs to the N.

Muni wanted to lower the guillotine on the remaining PCC service by September 1981, by running buses on all lines on the weekends until such time as budgetary and manpower issues could be resolved to operate seven-day Muni Metro service. But the diesel bus fleet was in no better shape than the PCC fleet, and, in fact, was much worse, with nearly half of the 500+ buses out of service. So this plan had to be shelved, and the remaining cars, battered but unbowed, soldiered on for the rest of 1981 and on into 1982.

September 19, 1982, was a warm sunny day, but hearts were heavy and tears were flowing as the PCCs made their last runs. Car 1108, still painted in original Muni "Wings" green, was the last scheduled revenue service car to pull in to Geneva Carhouse. However, in a surprise move, Ken Johnson, the motorman of 1121 (another "Wings"-liveried car), who later became a star F-Line operator, decided to make an extra unofficial trip on the N-Line. The very last car to pull in, at about 3:00 a.m. on the morning of September 20, was "Torpedo" 1006, chartered by the Northern California Railroad Club with Larry Bernard as motorman. It was *finis* to the first San Francisco PCC chapter.

In the months that followed, 10 "Baby Tens" and seven 1100s were scrapped. One by one, they were tipped over in Geneva Upper Yard and carted to Schnitzer Steel in Oakland on flatbed trailers. Four "Baby Tens" and two 1100s went to streetcar museums. The rest, including all seven of the "Torpedoes" (1008 was converted to a work car in 1982), were stored at Pier 70. Gradually, cars were sold off between 1982 and 1992 until only six D-Types, four of the 1016-1040 series, and eight ex-St. Louis PCCs remained on Muni property. The largest chunk of cars sold off–about 20–went to a man in South Lake Tahoe. Most of those that remain are still awaiting the call for possible rebuilding, pending available funding and a concerted effort to expand historic streetcar service in San Francisco. In the mid-2000s, some cars sold to private buyers were repurchased and returned to the property. Ironically, even the moribund Market Street Railway Co. proposed purchasing PCCs or similar streamlined cars in 1939, to compete with the "Magic Carpets." These would have harkened back to the "California"-style era of the early 1900s with open end sections. A drawing of such a streetcar is included in the late Charles Smallwood's book *The White Front Cars of San Francisco* (Interurbans Special 44, Interurban Press, 1978). This livery will grace one of the four remaining "Torpedoes"– car 1011–through a contract with Brookville Equipment Co. awarded in mid-2009.

(above) PCC 1163 was one of only 28 "Elevens" to receive a "mini-rehab" (actually, only cosmetic work) in 1977 and 1978, and were repainted the "Landor" colors of California Poppy Gold, Sunset Glow and white. This livery matched the Muni buses and trolley coaches of this era, but the PCCs got brown around the side windows, too. This one was one of the few "Landor" repaints to survive to the end of service on Sept. 19, 1982. It's passing beautifully restored Queen Anne Victorians on the J-Line on May 22, 1982. *Peter Ehrlich* (left) PCC 1162, which was wrecked just before the end of service in 1982, was being carted over to Schnitzer Steel in Oakland for final scrapping. It's leaving San Francisco in January 1983. About 35 of its sister Elevens survived the final scrapping, and some cars are still in storage at Marin Yard. *Mike Davis*

The PCC Era – 1958 to 1982

(*right*) Three "Baby Tens" and a gaggle of trolley coaches brighten this 1962 Market and Powell scene.

(*below*) Five years later, BART construction is about to begin, and the Telenews newsreel theater is about to meet the wrecking ball.
*Both photos,
Ira Swett, Alan Fishel collection*

(*bottom row, left*) "Baby Ten" PCC 1019 and "Torpedo" 1006, which was on a charter, lay over at the Ocean Beach loop of the N-Judah line about 1967. Both classes of PCCs were purchased new by Muni. Although the double-enders were first assigned to the N-Line when they arrived, they were not normally used there after the cars from St. Louis arrived. (*bottom row, right*) Two "Elevens" meet at Taraval and 35th Avenue in 1966. These ex-St. Louis cars still had their original rear drop windows. Both of these PCCs have been preserved, and 1170 will soon return to service in San Diego. *Both photos, Ira Swett/Alan Fishel collection*

Two Muni Anniversary events contributed to development of today's F-Line

(*top*) In 1962, Muni celebrated its 50th Anniversary by running its first streetcar, Car 1, on Market Street from the Transbay Terminal to 11th Street. The fare was a nickel–same as in 1912. *Ira Swett, courtesy of Alan Fishel*
(*bottom*) During Muni's 75th Anniversary and the 1987 Trolley Festival, ex-Oporto, Portugal 189 loads passengers at Pier 39 for the Festival's Embarcadero Demonstration. The huge boarding crowd has been replicated many times at the outbound Pier 39 stop on today's F-Line. *Peter Ehrlich*

Chapter 2 -
Planning for New Historic Streetcar Lines

*"...It would be an intolerable paradox...to spend $32 million
to create a great street and then promptly [relegate] it to
the role of carrier of tens of thousands of noxious automobiles and diesel buses."*

– *from the Market Street Streetcar Plan report
by San Francisco Tomorrow, 1971, advocating a historic
streetcar line on Market as part of the Beautification Plan*

Market Street Without Trolleys?

IT WAS HARD TO BELIEVE that after 122 years of street railway operation on America's last main street, that the rails would now be silent forever, and might soon disappear entirely. Market Street was now in imminent danger of being overrun by cars and trucks, like so many other conurbations across the land. In reality, however, planning for continued streetcar service on Market Street began over a decade before the end of PCC service on September 19, 1982. And according to Market Street Railway president Rick Laubscher, talk of using the old State Belt Railroad trackage for a historic streetcar operation along the waterfront began in the 1960s.

The Market Street Beautification Act

BEGINNING IN THE LATE 1960s, there was considerable debate about the future of the tracks after BART construction was finished. Most politicos, business people and other movers and shakers of the 1960s and early '70s dreamed of a Market Street without streetcars and even without buses and "no more unsightly wires," where the automobile would reign supreme. So once construction ended, BART laid "temporary" T-rail at the locations where subway station excavation had taken place, as officials certainly didn't want to install new permanent track only to have it be ripped up and scrapped once the streetcars had been banished.

To this end, voters in June 1968 passed the Market Street Beautification Act, which was a $24.5 million bond issue, which, once BART construction was completed, would create a *new* Market Street, dubbed the "Champs Elysées Of The West." New and broader sidewalks would be laid with red brick and lined with granite curbstones. New "Path Of Gold" lampposts would be installed that didn't need to be anchored, because they would no longer have to support overhead wires. Sycamore trees would be planted along the entire street between the Ferry Building and Van Ness, the extent of the project's scope. (West of Van Ness, a different kind of broadleaf Evergreen was envisioned, but that would come under a separate project.) The new Market Street would be a pedestrian's paradise with its broad, bricked sidewalks complete with granite curbstones–a place to leisurely stroll, shop and window-shop. Or they could hop a shuttle bus. But would they do that?

The intention was that once streetcars were gone and trolley bus lines rerouted or truncated, Market Street would be free of the "visual blight" from overhead wires forever. Cars would have the streets to themselves, unencumbered by those pesky buses and lumbering streetcars "that only got in the way." Not only would Market Street be rid of the tracks, but also the overhead wires used by trolley buses. All surface transit would be rerouted over Mission Street, or truncated where the lines entered Market Street, with everyone having to get off and take the subway. Muni Metro and BART would carry riders underground, and a diesel bus shuttle would operate up and down Market Street. At that time, transit officials also wanted to scrap San Francisco's extensive trolleybus system, claiming that new trolley coaches were no longer being manufactured.

All of this rejuvenation of San Francisco's main street was supposed to begin taking shape once subway excavation was complete in 1970. That was the dream, at least, in the eyes of the politicians and planners during that span of time, who were still clinging to the mindset that "cars are good, public transit is bad," a concept which has been roundly repudiated since by latter-day planners.

This conceptual drawing graced the cover of the *San Francisco Tomorrow* pamphlet "The Market Street Streetcar Plan," published in May 1971. Twenty old-style trolleys, either imported from Portugal or built new using PCC components, were proposed to serve the line, from the Ferries to Castro. *San Francisco Tomorrow drawing, courtesy Peter Straus*

The *San Francisco Tomorrow* Plan

Despite officialdom's rush toward a transit-free Market Street, there were voices, as early as 1971, suggesting that a historic trolley line providing service on Market Street would be a better, more attractive and productive approach. One of the first ideas came from a group called San Francisco Tomorrow, a non-profit organization concerned with keeping San Francisco a livable city through sustainable and environmentally-friendly policies, published a position paper in May 1971 titled "A Concept for the Market Street Railway Restoration." In the draft version, writer Gerald D. Fox proposed retention of the existing streetcar tracks; purchasing 20 old cars from Oporto, Portugal, or building new old-style trolleys using parts from the existing PCC cars, or a combination of both; building a new carbarn to house the fleet at Market and Octavia (at that time the Central Freeway still stood there); incorporating new track connections to permit cars to be moved to Elkton Shops (replaced by Metro Center in 1977); and modification of the Beautification Act to allow for retention of overhead wires by re-replacing the "Path Of Gold" lampposts with new anchored poles which could hold up span wires. The final version of the report omitted the Oporto car option.

One of the points raised in the report was that, according to San Francisco Tomorrow, it would be an "intolerable paradox...to spend $32 million to create a great street and then promptly relegating [sic] it to the role of carrier of tens of thousands of noxious automobiles and diesel buses."[1] SFT went further by suggesting that with streetcars continuing to occupy the center lanes, the curb lanes could be used for taxis, emergency and utility vehicles and bicycles, all without disrupting traffic. SFT estimated total costs to be $3 million in 1973 dollars, which would be reduced by $1 million when the savings from having to run buses was factored into the equation.

Then Muni Planning got involved. Muni's Planning Division was a new department, led by the energetic and progressive Tom Matoff, assisted by Peter Straus, who became Planning Director when Matoff moved on to another transit system. Both planners realized that not only were Muni riders not buying the idea of having to endure forced transfers, but they continued to enjoy their one-seat rides on their buses even after BART opened in 1973. (Muni Metro followed in 1980.) They determined that the monetary costs of rerouting or turning back electric trolley coach routes, while they would save money, were far outweighed by the

The first version of the 1971 *San Francisco Tomorrow* report, "The Market Street Streetcar Plan," called for importing a number of 1910s-vintage Oporto, Portugal trams, like No. 205, shown here at Batalha Guindais Castle in its native city in 2010. These American-design trolleys would fit the bill perfectly. Today, Oporto trams run in Memphis, Dallas and Yakima, and Muni is holding onto tram No. 189 for possible restoration. *Peter Ehrlich*

negative social costs of forced change. Still, as late as 1975, officials such as Supervisor John Molinari, who later became a backer of continued rail transport on Market Street, espoused removal of all overhead wires and the electric trolley buses (ETBs). By then, though, the tide was turning. Muni found a trolley coach builder located in Canada, and ordered a fleet of 343 new ETBs in 1974, which would replace the entire postwar fleet, which, in the late Forties, had dispatched all of the ramshackle ex-Market Street Railway Co. streetcars to the scrap heap.

By 1975, Muni Planning, under Matoff, had brought about a 180-degree turn with city officials regarding the "no overhead on Market Street" issue. Simultaneously, it swayed City officials such as Molinari and fellow Supervisor Dianne Feinstein. Feinstein (now a U. S. Senator), who was to become Mayor after the assassination of George Moscone in 1978, later championed the Trolley Festivals of the 1980s, and retention and rebuilding of the tracks on Market Street, which, of course, led to the F-Line. Matoff, Straus & Co. worked hard and diligently to overturn aspects of the Market Street Beautification Act to ensure the possibility of retaining streetcars and maintaining through trolley coach service. This made necessary the strengthening of the "Path Of Gold" light standards to support overhead wires.

It is noteworthy that the San Francisco Tomorrow streetcar concept was decades ahead of its time. Today, cities across the United States are rediscovering the streetcar, as officials visit, ride and study today's F-Line. The idea of using PCC components in old-style trolleys was later carried out in Portland, OR, while cars from Oporto now operate in Memphis, Yakima and Dallas. [See Chapter 12.]

Throughout the 1970s, the idea gained more credence and additional supporters. One of them was Maurice H. Klebolt, a travel agent and streetcar booster. He was a member of the Board of Supervisors-appointed CAPTrans transit advisory panel. He also formed several *ad hoc* committees, such as the "Committee To Acquire Trams From Melbourne," to drum up interest in vintage car operations among city officials and civic leaders. In 1978, he imported a tram from the just-abandoned Hamburg, Germany, system and paraded it around City Hall on a flatbed trailer, simply to make his point that streetcars needed to be retained.

Early Talk Of An Embarcadero Line, and the Cauthen Report to Dianne Feinstein

THE FIRST RECORDED MENTION of a possible Embarcadero historic trolley line was reported around

(*above*) *San Francisco Tomorrow* also proposed new old-style carbodies with PCC components, similar to Portland's 1988-vintage Council Crest replica streetcars. Note the PCC trucks. (*below*) Memphis operates a fleet of former Oporto trolleys on its Main Street line. *Both photos, Peter Ehrlich*

1974, when a report, dated May 28, 1974, and called "A Surface Rail System for the San Francisco Waterfront," was published by Muni engineer Gerald Cauthen, who prepared it for then-Supervisor Dianne Feinstein, who was President of the city Board of Supervisors at that time. (Because of San Francisco's unique designation as both a city and a county, the members of San Francisco's Board of Supervisors, who are officially elected as county representatives, act as a City Council would in other locales.)

This report, the first of its kind, focused on the eventual removal of the Embarcadero Freeway and the use of the State Belt Railroad tracks for a historic streetcar service, as part of the plan to return The Embarcadero to recreational use. It also stated that San Franciscans preferred less emphasis on the private automobile regarding transportation solutions. Under this plan, the replacement of the freeway would be by a surface roadway of moderate auto capacity, and peripheral parking in the southern edge of downtown. Those parking in these facilities would travel to more northern points along the waterfront by the streetcar. The service was to be of high quality and frequency, able to reach key destinations, and provide a one-seat ride from what is now Caltrain Depot (in 1974, the Southern Pacific Railroad–SP–provided the Peninsula commuter train service) past the Ferry Building, through Fisherman's Wharf and the tunnel under Fort Mason to the Marina District, and on into The Presidio, terminating at Crissy Field. Cauthen noted that The Embarcadero never had a truly "through" service, only a fragmented one. The route through the Wharf would be westward via Jefferson and eastward on Beach, much as it is today.

Success of the streetcar line would be in its ability to tie in with other Muni lines, BART, the Peninsula commuter trains, and the growing ferry services calling at the Ferry Building, and distributing the riders to key destinations. Cauthen proposed a moving walkway, approximately 1300 feet long, to connect the BART/Muni Metro Embarcadero Station with the Ferry Building. A similar one between Embarcadero Station and Transbay Terminal had been proposed by the State Division of Bay Toll Crossings. These "moving sidewalks" would be either partially or entirely underground.

As for the vehicles envisioned for the Embarcadero service, diesel and trolley buses were rejected outright because of the need to operate on a paved right-of-way. A diesel-powered streetcar was also considered, but this, too, was eliminated because of the on-board noise and pollution such a vehicle would create. Cauthen proposed rebodied and converted PCCs, much as what was considered for Market Street by San Francisco Tomorrow's 1971 plan. Cauthen had been the *San Francisco Tomorrow*'s president in 1971.

Cauthen emphasized that to make the streetcar service reliable, it must run on a private right-of-way for the major portion of its route. He proposed 15-minute headways with 5-7 cars, depending on where the northern terminal would be located, but if ridership really skyrocketed, up to 14 cars would be needed.

Already, there were plans to upgrade the State Belt Railroad trackage. As far as who would operate the service, it could be Muni itself, or Port Railroads, Inc., which took over operation of the State Belt from the State of California a few years prior. Maintenance of the fleet would have to be done under contract at the then-existing Southern Pacific Bayshore Shops, or by Muni at their Elkton Shops. As there was no planned physical connection to any Market Street

The report by Muni engineer Gerald Cauthen to Supervisor Dianne Feinstein in May 1974 advocating an Embarcadero historic streetcar service included this picture of a United Railroads 1300-class car. Like the *San Francisco Tomorrow* report three years earlier, Cauthen proposed installing PCC components on similar new carbodies. *United Railroads*

trackage, cars would have to be trucked to either Elkton or Bayshore. Either method would have been a terribly cumbersome affair, but at the time the report was written, there was no easy alternative.

The report also noted that this streetcar service could eventually be extended southward f Depot to points in China Basin and destinations in the planned Mission Bay Redevelopment area. Today, this is part of the new T-Third Street Muni Metro line, which opened in 2007, and the idea of running vintage trolleys to the Union Iron Works Historic District has been floated. [See Chapter 7.]

The report laid out the city Department of Public Works plans for a replacement roadway, which in part consisted of an underpass between Howard and Washington Streets. In one of the more amusing points in the report, the city's Traffic Engineer's initial response to a paralleling streetcar line next to the roadway "can only be described as 'anguished'."[2] Cauthen dismissed this concern ably by stating that there would be little difficulty, provided that the roadway be held to a reasonable width.

Cauthen found that the costs of building a streetcar line were quite reasonable, compared to the cost of building a new freeway. He estimated the total capital costs, including constructing new streetcars and construction and rehabilitation of track, at $11.6 million in 1976 dollars.

Feinstein became enamored of the Embarcadero idea, and in 1977, met with a Mr. F. D. Snell of the Melbourne & Metropolitan Tramways Board (Australia), as well as other San Francisco officials, for the purpose of acquiring two of their iconic W2 trams for San Francisco. Had this occurred, it would have coincided with a parallel acquisition by the City of Seattle for a Waterfront line there (which opened in 1982). The "Committee To Acquire Trams From Melbourne" put out a press release announcing this meeting.

Despite the gaudy "Committee" moniker and Supervisor Feinstein's enthusiasm, no Melbourne trams were purchased. Later, however, one W2 tram ultimately came to the Bay Area and the Western Railway Museum, where it ran in the first four Trolley Festivals on Muni tracks before it was moved to its home at Rio Vista Junction, Calif. Still later, Muni did acquire two W2s, one of which is in daily F-Line service.

In 1979, with strong urging from Muni's Planning Department, the Northern Waterfront Survey, an official City Planning document, recommended a vintage trolley line from SP (now Caltrain) Depot all the way to Fort Mason. (The City's Planning Department had originally favored a "mini-train." This had been based on, in part, by the 1972 visit of Alan Pegler's restored "Flying Scotsman" steam train, which ran on The Embarcadero.) This proposal gained a route name in Muni's Short Range Transit Plan of 1979-1984: the E-Embarcadero.

The 5-Year Plan 1979-1984

THE 5-YEAR PLAN 1979-1984 was the culmination of the Muni Planning Division's efforts to bring about a formal policy endorsement by the San Francisco Public Utilities Commission, Muni's governing body, of the concept of establishing historic streetcar service in San Francisco.[3] Led by planners Tom Matoff and Peter Straus, it defined a formal route from the Southern Pacific Depot to Fort Mason; it presciently proposed fleet alternatives that could include new old-style streetcars, historic and genuine Muni "Iron Monsters," vintage cars from other cities, or PCCs. (The mix of cars on today's F-Line reflects this far-sighted vision.) Essentially, the Five-Year Plan embodied Gerald Cauthen's vision from a few years before, and when the SFPUC adopted the Five-Year Plan on April 3, 1979, operation of historic streetcars became official SFPUC policy. It's hard to imagine now, but in the context of the times, asking the Commission to take this action was a difficult and momentous step.

Although the Five-Year Plan focused on an Embarcadero line, the planners had, in their minds, the idea of ultimately returning streetcars to Market Street as well. Subsequent Short Range Transit Plans, as early as 1981, proposed this in the form of an F-Market & Wharves route as a combined Embarcadero/Market Street service.

Overall, the Five-Year Plan was a blueprint for change in many aspects of how Muni conducted itself, focused on reconfiguring its then largely downtown-oriented radial system along multi-destinational grid principles. Significantly, the E-Line, and later the F-Line, were not conceived as isolated tourist or secondary transit services, but rather as integral components of Muni's general purpose service plan, a key contributing reason for the subsequent success and high ridership of the F-Line by riders with varied trip purposes—residents, workers and visitors. This trend will continue with the addition of E-Embarcadero line service, now likely to happen in 2014.

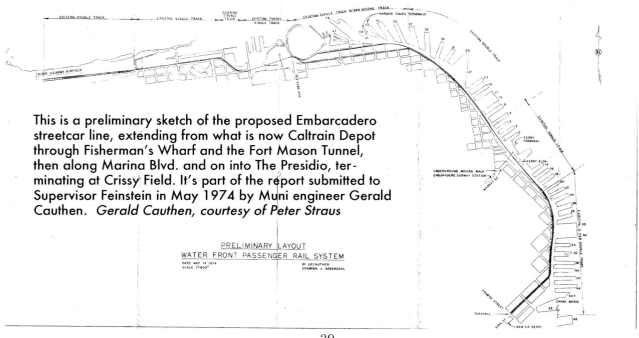

This is a preliminary sketch of the proposed Embarcadero streetcar line, extending from what is now Caltrain Depot through Fisherman's Wharf and the Fort Mason Tunnel, then along Marina Blvd. and on into The Presidio, terminating at Crissy Field. It's part of the report submitted to Supervisor Feinstein in May 1974 by Muni engineer Gerald Cauthen. *Gerald Cauthen, courtesy of Peter Straus*

The I-280 Transfer Fund

BACK IN THE EARLY DAYS of the federal Interstate Highway program, the California Department of Highways (predecessor to CalTrans) had espoused construction of new freeways everywhere, including San Francisco. Interstate 280 was envisioned as a ring route tying into the Golden Gate Bridge (but not the Bay Bridge and I-80) and, as such, would make a freeway ring around the Bay Area. To do this, highway planners planned a freeway all the way along The Embarcadero across Fisherman's Wharf and through the upscale Marina District to the Golden Gate Bridge, then north and east across the Richmond-San Rafael Bridge and then down through western Berkeley and Oakland. Well, when the plans for double-deck elevated "monster walls" hit San Franciscans, the Great Freeway Revolt of 1959 erupted. The state had also proposed a Panhandle Freeway, which would have destroyed part of the Haight-Ashbury and Golden Gate Park. Both the Marina and Panhandle Freeways were stopped cold, and the state was soundly beaten. It had to settle for partial structures built west of Civic Center and along the central part of The Embarcadero to Broadway. The southern part of I-280 was built in 1966, however, and its north end was at Third and King streets. It never was envisioned to connect with the Bay Bridge.

However, ever since the Embarcadero Freeway opened in the 1950s, civic leaders and citizens started to push for its eventual demolition, as it really had become a blight on the Waterfront, ending, as it did, far short of its intended destination and acting like a great wall, blocking views and inhibiting recreational improvement. By the late 1970s, the clamor to remove the freeway intensified.

The question then was asked: what to do with the Federal funds allocated to build I-280 along The Embarcadero? Around 1971, the federal Urban Mass Transportation Administration (UMTA) changed the rules to permit jurisdictions to use these funds for other transportation purposes, as a result of a change in Federal law by Congress. The first instance of this reallocation of funds occurred in Boston, and was also carried out in Portland, Ore. This allowed San Francisco officials to plan for an improved

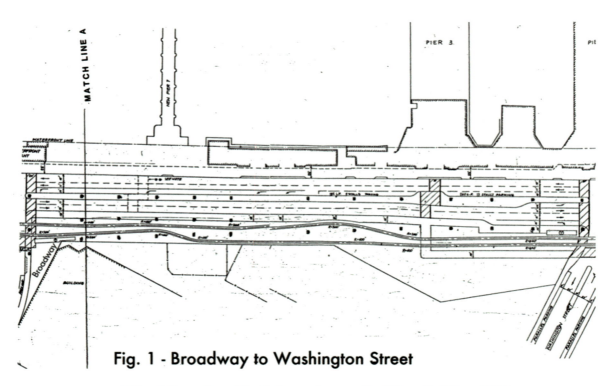

Fig. 1 - Broadway to Washington Street

F-Line Schematic on The Embarcadero north of Ferry Building, 1988

These drawings, shown on these two pages, show how the F-Line and the Embarcadero Roadway would look between the Ferry Building and Broadway, with the Embarcadero Freeway still in place. In 1986, voters rejected a 1985 measure passed by the Board of Supervisors to demolish the structure, so the project engineer, Ron Niewiarowski, created these plans showing freeway support pillars (black squares), weaving tracks, and side-of-the-road trackage. The last drawing also shows a track plan for Steuart Street with a northbound right turn switch for cars to head back to The Embarcadero, which was not adopted. Not shown is the treatment north of Battery Street, where the tracks move into a center median. Of course, the Loma Prieta earthquake doomed the Embarcadero Freeway, and today's F-Line and The Embarcadero Promenade and Roadway, with magnificent vistas for pedestrians and streetcar riders, are the happy result.
San Francisco Public Utilities Commission drawings, courtesy of Ron Niewiarowski

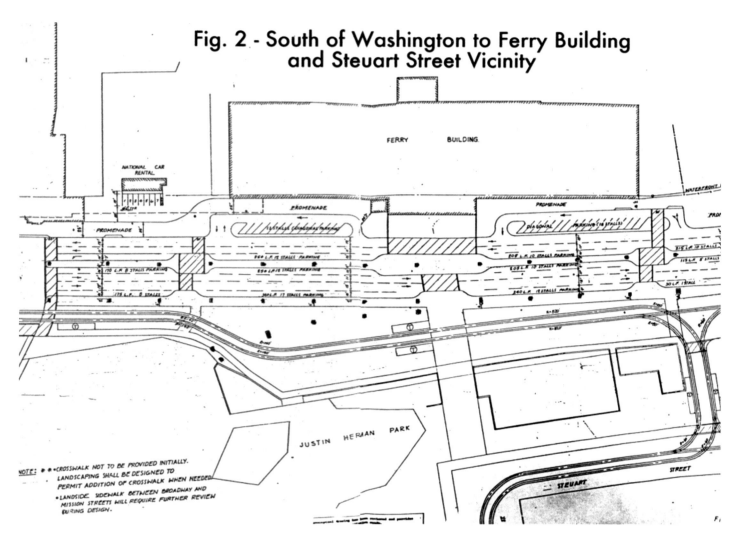

Fig. 2 - South of Washington to Ferry Building and Steuart Street Vicinity

Embarcadero boulevard, which included a streetcar line. Most of the money transferred from building I-280 was earmarked for constructing this roadway; the rest eventually was used toward building the Muni Metro Turnback, which extended Muni Metro east and south from Embarcadero Station, and was completed in 1998. Like the F-Line, the proposed E-Embarcadero streetcar line was considered an eligible project.

The I-280 Transfer Fund did require city officials to take the normal steps in preparing to reallocate money earmarked for the freeway. An Environmental Impact Report/Environmental Impact Statement (EIR/EIS) had to be issued and approved by Federal officials at the Urban Mass Transportation Administration (UMTA). Doug Wright, who was an UMTA official at the time of the I-280 Transfer Fund program in the late 1970s, later came to Muni as Deputy General Manager of the SFPUC to work on the City's end of the transfer project and led the resulting I-280 Waterfront Transportation Program. He was assisted by SFPUC staffer and engineer Ron Niewiarowski as the engineer assigned to shepherd the Embarcadero streetcar project (as well as the Muni Metro Extension (MMX), the F-Line/MMX Track Connector, and the E-Line stops along the MMX, and the MMT) through the conceptual design and approval process, as well as the I-280 Transfer Fund work. A portion of the funds that came from the withdrawn money was termed the I-280 Concept Program.

Doug Wright, who grew up in Portland, OR, came to UMTA when his boss, Neil Goldschmidt, who had been Portland's mayor during the cancellation and reallocation of the monies earmarked for the Mt. Hood Freeway there, was appointed Transportation Secretary by President Jimmy Carter. In 1980, after Carter had been defeated for re-election by Ronald Reagan, Wright knew he'd be out of a job, so he called for a "meeting of the minds" to get I-280 Transfer going in a lame-duck session, and all parties–Gov. Jerry Brown of California, Lawrence Dahms, director of the Metropolitan Transportation Commission, and Mayor Dianne Feinstein–to get the project going. Otherwise, the approval process would take many more years under what was perceived to be an unfriendly-to-transit bias in the Reagan

Administration. A Draft EIS/EIR was completed and submitted to the U. S. Department of Transportation in 1984, but it was decided to discontinue the EIS work and by 1985, the city had certified the environmental document as the Final EIR. Approvals also came from CalTrans and the Metropolitan Transportation Commission (MTC), a regional agency covering the nine Bay Area counties which acted as a clearinghouse for all local and regional transit projects. The Embarcadero streetcar line was considered the locally preferred alternative.

Urgency to Get Historic Streetcars Running On Market

BY 1979, IT BECAME OBVIOUS that the subway would open soon and the streetcar lines would leave the surface tracks and run underground. While planning for an Embarcadero route continued, movement toward getting a historic line up and running shifted away from The Embarcadero back to Market Street as a more practical–and a more urgent– way of showcasing the rolling treasures of the past in public service. As February 18, 1980, the date for the opening of Muni Metro, approached, the cries became louder and more frequent, despite the "temporary" tracks now in place. As already mentioned, more and more officials realized that the "no transit on Market" policy would be a disastrous one, and maybe there could be a place for a post-subway-conversion streetcar line, after all. Still, attempts to make this possible would have to wait for four more years and one cable car shutdown to pass.

Modifying the voter-approved Market Street Beautification Act also required several Board of Supervisors resolutions. The first of these passed in 1978, and called for continued operation of electrically-powered transit vehicles (streetcars and trolley coaches). The second resolution was approved in 1979 and this prevented the SFPUC, overseer of Muni at that time, from removing streetcars from Market Street prior to the opening of Muni Metro.

There were two crucial Board resolutions passed in early 1981. First, the Board authorized the SFPUC to conduct a Market Street Design Planning Study to investigate retaining streetcar service permanently. This would require changes to the 1968 Beautification Project. A short time later, the Board requested SFPUC to institute a temporary historic streetcar shuttle service between Civic Center and The Embarcadero and Fisherman's Wharf during the impending systemwide cable car shutdown, which was going to occur in 1982.

The Board's 1983 resolution became the linchpin to make permanent changes to the 1968 Beautification Act. Four lanes of transit, retention of boarding islands and the streetcar tracks and operation of a historic streetcar line were formally adopted. The SFPUC was ordered to develop an operating plan for historic streetcars.

Meanwhile, many private citizens became involved in the transformation of the Beautification Project, too. Earlier in this chapter, mention was made briefly of Maurice H. Klebolt. Klebolt, a native of Illinois, was a hard-core railfan and traction enthusiast, whose interest in electric transport dated back to the 1950s, when he organized many fantrips through his Illini Railroad Club over the fast-shrinking Illinois Terminal Railroad interurban system, whose final passenger runs occurred in 1956. Following Illinois Terminal's closure, he also organized trips on the Chicago, North Shore & Milwaukee and Chicago, Aurora & Elgin interurbans.

Maury (as he was known to his friends) later moved to San Francisco and opened a successful travel agency. But it was in his capacity as a member of CAPTrans, the citizens' advisory panel on transportation matters to the Board of Supervisors, that he was able to forge important liaisons with key city officials–influential contacts that would later prove to be most helpful with regard to the retention of streetcars on Market Street. Although his style of influence was considered brusque and bombastic by his detractors, he was able to sway officials to achieve his goals, the result of which was the first of five Historic Trolley Festivals in 1983. In addition to his day job and his work on behalf of continuing streetcar operation on Market Street, he became a part-time Muni operator in 1981.

One of Klebolt's friends was Muni operator Jack Smith, considered by many to be the finest and most knowledgeable historic streetcar operator at Muni from the 1960s through 1990s. Smith learned his craft from his father, who was one of the first black

Car 1 has just backed out of the 11th Street Wye on the first day of free shuttle service on Market Street, April 18, 1981. Running alternate Saturdays during the spring and summer, this operation was a harbinger of better things to come. Note the F-Route sign in the signbox. *Peter Straus*

motormen hired during World War II by Muni's competitor, Market Street Railway Company. When he was a boy, Smith would ride with his dad, who worked night runs on Sutter Street. When it was time for him to have his "lunch," he'd turn to his son and say, "Run the car," at night, no one was wiser. Later, Smith was associated with Pacific Electric in the Los Angeles area and became an operator for Muni in 1963, working as a gripman, PCC operator, vintage car motorman and LRV operator. He retired on December 28, 1994 (coincidentally, Muni's birthday) with honors. Fellow historic car motorman John Nevin, quoted in a *San Francisco Chronicle* article on Smith's retirement, said of Jack Smith, "Muni will fill his position, but they'll never fill his shoes."[4] [See Chapter 9.]

Klebolt and Smith worked within Muni, along with such people as Planning Director Peter Straus and SFPUC General Manager Richard Sklar, to start the free shuttle service with Old Number 1, Muni's first streetcar, in 1981, and the weekend revenue operation using Cars 1 (A-Type, built 1912) and 178 (K-Type, vintage 1923) on the J-Church line in 1982. 178 was on lease from the Western Railway Museum. Working with Geneva Division Manager Don Cameron, Smith, Klebolt and the author forged schedules for the J-Line vintage operation. The two cars ran most weekends in 1982 from the July 4 holiday weekend through the end of surface rail operation on September 19. On that first holiday three-day weekend, with virtually no notice to the public, the cars were packed with riders all day long.

1982: Vintage Cars on the J-Line
(*below*) A-Type 1 and K-Type 178, running in revenue service, meet at Church and 24th Streets. *Peter Straus*

On the first and second nights, the two cars were stashed on the inbound "East Portal" track inside the old Eureka Station of the Twin Peaks Tunnel. This was possible because buses had taken over all other streetcar runs that particular weekend. On other weekends, Cars 1 and 178 pulled out and pulled in through the Twin Peaks Tunnel, just as the PCCs did.

Following the end of PCC service in 1982, Smith and Klebolt turned their attention to the now-idle tracks on Market Street and the void left by the cable car system reconstruction. Would it be possible to have an alternative summertime operation with streetcars? The obvious conclusion was an emphatic "Yes!", but numerous city officials still had to be convinced.

It helped that Dianne Feinstein was mayor, and an enthusiastic supporter of historic streetcar operation, and had been since the Cauthen Report was published. It also helped that Muni's new General Manager, appointed by Feinstein in late 1982, was Harold H. Geissenheimer, a dyed-in-the-wool railfan and career transit official who had previously held positions in Pittsburgh, where he introduced the wild and colorful paint schemes carried by the Steel City's remaining PCC cars, and Chicago, where he was manager of rail operations. While in Chicago, he initiated the Chicago Transit Authority's acclaimed Bicentennial livery on that system's rolling stock, which included PCC-derivative rapid transit cars [see *PCC: An American Success Story* sidebar in Chapter 1]. Geissenheimer was appointed to succeed retiring General Manager Curtis Green, who had started his career with Muni as an operator and had risen through

On the first weekend of vintage car service on the J-Church line in 1982, cars 1 and 178 were kept at Eureka Station overnight. Operators prepare for pullout along the inbound Eureka Portal track on July 5, 1982. This was part of the 17th Street Detour created in 1973 during construction of the Muni Metro subway. *Peter Ehrlich*

the ranks and was beloved among the rank and file. Klebolt and Smith pitched their idea to Geissenheimer, who approved the plan enthu-siastically. Meanwhile, the city's Chamber of Commerce and the San Francisco Convention and Visitors Bureau, concerned with a loss of tourist revenue due to the cable car shutdown, became involved. Independently of Klebolt and Smith's work, Rick Laubscher, a Bechtel Corporation public relations executive and member of the Chamber, was working on a similar idea to line up private sector support and act as a liaison toward securing funding for a Historic Trolley Festival. Laubscher, who was born and raised in San Francisco and a regular J-Church line rider for many years, also had a number of political connections through his work as a TV reporter and as PR director for Bechtel, a respected multinational engineering firm with headquarters in San Francisco. But his work with getting the Chamber on board, and its own pitch to Feinstein, was instrumental. Support from the late John Jacobs, then the Chamber's president, was also crucial. Time, too, was a critical factor here. The cable car lines were being shut down for a 19-month rehabilitation.

So separately, both Klebolt and Laubscher approached key members of the Board of Supervisors and Mayor Feinstein, who would have to vote on and sign legislation appropriating government funding for the scheme. Approval came relatively quickly. Only Supervisor Louise Renne voted against the Trolley Festival legislation; on the first day of the 1983 Trolley Festival, after seeing the colorful cars and the parade and the enthusiasm, she admitted to Rick Laubscher that she had made a mistake. (It was Laubscher who came up with the name "San Francisco Historic Trolley Festival.") [Chapter 3 explores the Trolley Festivals in greater detail.]

The bureaucracy within Muni was another matter. There were still many officials in relatively high positions at both Muni and the SFPUC who were opposed to streetcars, and fought hard to prevent any surface rail transit from ever returning to Market Street. However, with Mayor Feinstein at the helm, and with Geissenheimer on the scene, that was that. In the words of Rick Laubscher, all "internal Muni resistance was bulldozed aside."[5] Rudy Nothenberg, the General Manager of Public Utilities who succeeded Richard Sklar, was one such individual. After the 1983 Trolley Festival began, he became an avid supporter.

Another organization which became part of the planning and development process was Market Street Railway, a group which was established in 1976 by Muni Planning Director Peter Straus and others for the purpose of saving a 1950 Marmon-Herrington trolley coach from the scrapper's torch. Its mission broadened with the imminent demise of surface streetcar operation, and grew with the nascent idea of the Trolley Festival. Maury Klebolt was already a director of this group, and Rick Laubscher joined the MSR Board, and later became its president. There now was a voice supporting historic streetcar operation in San Francisco that would have a wide range of influence over the next three decades. [You'll read more about *MSR* and its influence in the *Market Street Railway: Promoting Museums In Motion* sidebar to Chapter 5.]

Working With The Wharf Merchants

THE SUCCESSFUL EFFORTS to get streetcars to return to Market Street culminated with the 1983 San Francisco Historic Trolley Festival. The 1983 Festival was so popular that it was held four more times, even after the cable cars returned to service in 1984. [Trolley Festival operations are described in detail in Chapter 3.] With trolleys running up and down Market Street, a new chapter was being written. The line even got a name: The F-Market and Wharves. This name first appeared in Muni's 1981-1986 Short Range Transit Plan.

In 1985, the "I-280 Concept Program Staff Recommendation," authored by Doug Wright, went to the Board of Supervisors for approval, recommended both the E and F-Lines for institution. To quote from the report: "As the Municipal Railway intends to operate 'vintage trolley vehicles' on the E and F Lines, it is clear that this service will not only be important to those who live and work along the waterfront corridor, but it will also provide an attractive means of transportation to the thousands of tourists who would be attracted not only to the destinations served but also to the trolley vehicles themselves."[6] In fact, it was a joint effort, with the Port of San Francisco, the SFPUC, the Redevelopment Agency, and the Department of City Planning. Dean Macris, Planning Director at that time, was particularly supportive at the policy level. The Board, by an 8-2 vote, endorsed the plan. This included demolishing the Embarcadero Freeway, although that was by a separate, but related, vote on November 5, 1985. Again, the vote was 8-2.

But in June 1986, a problem surfaced when voters approved two initiatives to *not* tear the Embarcadero Freeway down, in direct response to the Board of Supervisors vote to demolish this eyesore on an 8-2 vote. One of the Supervisors on the losing end of the vote, the late Richard Hongisto, decided to take the matter to the voters with these initiatives. This act of defiance, which grew out of fears that the freeway removal would result in gridlock, led city officials, both elected and appointed, to threaten that there would be no E-Line built! Nevertheless, conceptual design continued, and Niewiarowski came up with a contingency set of plans and drawings which incorporated working a streetcar line around the freeway support pillars in the vicinity of the Ferry Building and side-of-the-road running on the alignment of the existing State Belt Railroad tracks between Washington Street and Battery Street, instead of a center-of-the-roadway right-of-way.

Further up the Embarcadero, there was still much work to be done. The principal hurdle was to convince the Wharf merchants and restaurant owners that a streetcar line to Fisherman's Wharf would be viable, good for business, and a fun way for tourists to get there. Even after the Trolley Festivals showed the rest of San Francisco how exciting a new and extraordinary kind of transit service could be, and the 1987 Embarcadero demonstration at the end of that year's Festival proved that a Wharf trolley service would be viable [see *The 1987 Embarcadero Demonstration* sidebar in Chapter 3], many Wharf interests remained unconvinced. It took nine months of considerable neighborhood outreach and many meetings between Niewiarowski, acting as F-Line Wharf Extension project engineer on behalf of Doug Wright, and organizations such as the Fisherman's Wharf Merchants Association, the Fisherman's Wharf Port Tenants Association, and even the Telegraph Hill Dwellers Association, to agree to the basic Wharf streetcar alignment concept. Niewiarowski developed the Jefferson/Jones/Beach alignment based on a variety of considerations, including semi-exclusive transitway or transit only lanes, traffic circulation, on-street parking, underground seawall structural issue, commercial and sport fishing concerns and other Wharf merchant issues. Sixteen different alignments were proposed, and one by one, they were rejected. The final two contenders were a terminal loop in front of Piers 43 and 45, and the terminal on Jones Street between Jefferson and Beach. The fruits of Niewiarowski's efforts were rewarded on July 14, 1988, when directors of both Wharf associations, in a joint meeting, unanimously voted to endorse the Jones Street terminal and the Jefferson/Beach track alignment. A month later, and as part of the development of the Transportation Expenditure Plan for the half cent sales tax that was eventually passed as Proposition B by a vote of the people in San Francisco in November 1989, the Fisherman's Wharf Citizen's Advisory Committee gave unanimous consent in an April 24, 1989, letter to the City Planning Commission and the Board of Supervisors Transportation Committee, with copies to Mayor Art Agnos and the president of the SFPUC. The FWCAC "urged adoption of the F-Line [Wharf Extension] as a priority project and inclusion in the Transportation Expenditure Plan," citing broad-based support not only from Fisherman's Wharf entities, but all across the city. The letter further urged that the project receive full funding.

It was in this manner that the Jones and Beach loop, with inbound cars running on Jefferson and outbound trolleys on Beach, became the "locally preferred alternative," to use the jargon dictated by official planning and environmental documents. Even with the approval of the Wharf merchants, there were still some minor matters to be resolved, such as surface treatment of the trackway, and design and placement of the stops, handicapped ramps and the line poles and bracket arms supporting the overhead wire, and other details. But the major hurdle had been overcome.

With Wharf interests on board, it seemed that getting the F-Line to Fisherman's Wharf was a slam-dunk. Yet, there still were people who doubted its viability and questioned its need, despite all the positive actions taken in the last years of the decade. It took an earthshaking event to lay those doubts to rest.

References:

1. Market Street Streetcar Plan, *San Francisco Tomorrow* (San Francisco), p. 2.
2. Cauthen, Gerald P. *A Surface Rail System For The San Francisco Waterfront,* San Francisco, May 28, 1974, p. 13.
3. San Francisco Municipal Railway 5-Year Plan 1979-1984, *San Francisco Public Utilities Commission* (San Francisco, adopted April 3, 1979), pp. 81, 209-212, 218-224.
4. *San Francisco Chronicle* article, Dec. 29, 1994, by Carl Nolte.
5. Letter from Rick Laubscher to Peter Ehrlich, March 1, 2011.
6. Wright, Douglas L., "I-280 Concept Program Staff Recommendation," *San Francisco Public Utilities Commission, City & County of San Francisco* (San Francisco, 1985), p. 13.

Today's F-Line is the happy result of major planning started in the 1980s. *Peter Ehrlich*

Trolley Festival motorman Lee Butler, Jr. waves out the front window of Car 1 at the Transbay Terminal. Old Number One, Muni's first streetcar, was built in 1912, and is decked with bunting to celebrate the Democratic National Convention, which was held in San Francisco in 1984. *Peter Ehrlich*

Chapter 3 - The Trolley Festivals

*"...The old trolley cars on Market continue
to be the most entrancing transit
that has operated around here in years.
Fun to ride and watch, especially the
'Iron Monster' on a foggy day, emerging from
the past, flashing into the present and then
fading away, like all its noisy
brothers and sisters..."*

– Herb Caen, from a 1985 column
in the San Francisco Chronicle

Cable Cars Shut Down Too

AS MUCH AS SAN FRANCISCANS would miss streetcars on Market, it was the cable cars that were the city's No. 1 icon, and one of the biggest draws for visitors, which would also be shutting down. The system, however, had not been significantly revamped since 1957, and much of the trackage and other infrastructure dated back to reconstruction after the 1906 Earthquake and Fire.

In the meantime, the cable cars had achieved National Historic Landmark status and protection from further truncation by amendments to the City Charter, stemming from public anger over the drastic system cutbacks in the 1950s. But the aging and crumbling physical plant caused many failures and temporary service disruptions. One of the most severe occurred when one of the bull gears of the cable winding machinery at Washington-Mason Cable Car Barn and Powerhouse failed in 1979. Engineers rigged a temporary solution using the remaining bull gear, crossing their fingers that this quick fix would hold on until the system could be completely renovated. It did. Simultaneously, plans were engineered to deliver a completely new (except for the cars themselves) cable car system–new rails, winding machinery, sheave pits, pulleys and other infrastructure and hardware. Washington-Mason Division (the cable car barn at Washington and Mason Streets, which had been the Ferries & Cliff House Railway's barn, originally built in 1887, and rebuilt after the 1906 Earthquake and Fire) was also to be reconstructed and made seismically sound. Federal, state and local funds were used for the rehabilitation.

Coincident with the end of streetcar service on Market Street, it was the shutdown of the cable car network on September 21, 1982, for a 20-month, $60 million rebuilding project, that inadvertently led to an eventual about-face with regard to the now-dormant tracks on Market Street, although [as described in Chapter 2] this about-face was already moving forward. But, for 20 months, visitors would have to endure a city without "little cable cars climbing halfway to the stars." What could be done as an alternative?

Gathering a Truly International Fleet

THE EVENTS LEADING UP TO the 1983 Trolley Festival, and the people who made it possible, have already been described in Chapter 2. [Also, see sidebar in this chapter.] Once the plan got the green light, the details still had to be worked out and finalized. The first steps were to establish a route and obtain vehicles. The People's Car–Old Number One– was the logical choice as a nucleus for an interesting and varied fleet. Two of Muni's PCCs, "Baby Ten" 1040 (the last PCC built in America) and "Eleven Hundred" 1128, were chosen to represent the modern era of Muni streetcar operation. 1128 was taken a step further when Muni General Manager Harold H. Geissenheimer ordered it to be painted in its original St. Louis Public Service livery and to carry its as-built fleet number, 1704. But more cars were needed.

Maury Klebolt contacted Paul Class of Gales Creek Enterprises in Glenwood, Ore. and arranged a lease of two single-truck deck roof trolleys native to Oporto, Portugal, which were built by legendary American carbuilder J. G. Brill (patterned after that company's semi-convertible design) and had

The reconstruction of the cable car system between September 1982 and June 1984 pushed civic leaders to develop an alternative transportation attraction in 1983, which resulted in the San Francisco Historic Trolley Festival. Work on the California line near Hyde Street is well along in this December 30, 1983, photo. The crossover will be used for California cars pulling in via Hyde and Washington Streets to reach the 1887-vintage Ferries & Cliff House Railway carbarn, which was also being made earthquake-resistant as part of the system reconstruction project. They will coast across to the outbound track and then turn right on Hyde, where they will again "take rope." *Karl Johnson*

them brought down from Oregon. A 1903 Brill trolley from the somewhat associated Oregon Electric Railway Historical Society museum also migrated south. Number 503 was a car that had run on Portland's scenic Council Crest line until 1950. A typical one-man standard streetcar, native to Milwaukee–number 978–came west from a Wisconsin museum. A deal to bring out New Orleans 934, which had just received a complete overhaul, fell through when a pair of standard-gauge trucks could not be located in time. Atlanta 948, undergoing restoration at the Shore Line Trolley Museum in Connecticut, was also considered.

But Klebolt wanted to make this Trolley Festival a truly international affair. He got the Government of Australia to donate a typical classic 1920s-era Melbourne W2 tram, 648, for the Festival. This tram would later become part of the Western Railway Museum collection at Rio Vista Junction, CA. From WRM itself came Blackpool, England's 1934-vintage open-top "Boat" tram 226, as well as Muni "Iron Monster" 178, which was already on the property. And Klebolt's own Hamburg "Red Baron" 3557, which he had purchased in 1978, was put into the shop for overhaul and preparation for service. Rick Laubscher, a Bechtel employee and a member of the San Francisco Chamber of Commerce (who later became a Market Street Railway director), was responsible for bringing the Boat tram down to San Francisco.

To help with the funding, nearly all of the trolleys got sponsors. Portland 503, for example, was sponsored by Embarcadero Center; PCC 1704, by St. Louis-based brewery Anheuser-Busch and its local beer distributor; "Iron Monster" 178, by San Francisco jeans maker Levi Strauss; etc. Blackpool "Boat" 226 was Bechtel's car.

The route was selected next. It was decided that the terminal was to be 17th Street and Castro, which would serve as a strong neighborhood anchor. Trolley Festival cars would use the 17th Street detour route established in 1973 to route streetcars around excavation for Church and Castro Street stations. A crossover was installed just east of the intersection for changing ends. PCCs and other single-end streetcars, however, would have to operate out the J-Church line to 30th and Church, which had a wye to turn cars.

The Castro District was beginning to blossom as the largest and most influential gay/lesbian neighborhood in the United States. It had always boasted a strong transit ridership from the beginning, being located at the east end of Muni's Twin Peaks Tunnel. Castro Street Station on the Muni Metro Subway was the most heavily used station outside of downtown. It was only natural, then, that this would be the outer terminal. The tracks extended across the intersection and into the Twin Peaks Tunnel to allow cars to be moved to and from Metro Center for heavy maintenance.

The double-track private-right-of-way section on Duboce Avenue was selected to be the Trolley Festival light maintenance facility, and a pit track for inspections was constructed. The inbound track would be used for storage of cars not needed for service, while the outbound track was utilized for movements in both directions, protected by a block signal setup. There were crossovers at the west end of the yard, which became known as Mint Yard, and on Market opposite the famous Mint Bar, where Klebolt, Jack Smith and others would sometimes repair for libations after work. A trailer was brought in to serve as the division "office."

The schedule called for seven cars operating five days a week between 10:00 a.m. and 6:00 p.m. with Tuesday-Wednesday off, so service could be covered by simple 5-day work assignments. Headways were set at every 15 minutes. Five cars were 2-man double-enders, with the traditional motorman/conductor crew, although in practice, the guys switched roles each trip. Two cars, the single-enders, were one-man operated. Most of the operators who signed on the Trolley Festival runs were long-time street-car veterans, but a few came over from cable cars because of that division's shutting down for the duration of the rebuild project.

The process of moving the fleet of vintage cars between Geneva Yard and the Mint storage area was quite arduous, and had to be done after the subway closed down at night, so there was no interruption to Muni Metro service. Even so, the cars had to travel in packs, and care had to be taken to make sure that overhead wire clearances were negotiable. This was especially true with the Blackpool "Boat," whose ultra-long trolley pole would occasionally make contact with the wire at points other than the current collection "harp."

With vintage car veterans Jack Smith and John Nevin handling the training of operators (no longer possible under current-day employee classifications and work rules), and manager Carl Barton overseeing the operation, assisted by inspector Rino Bini, Muni and city officials gave the green light for a June 22, 1983, opening. The rails on Market Street were once again about to feel the clank of steel wheels rolling on them!

1983–First And Foremost!

ON JUNE 22, 1983, in keeping with the tradition begun by long-serving Mayor "Sunny Jim" Rolph, Mayor Dianne Feinstein piloted Muni's venerable Car One inbound from Van Ness Avenue, leading a parade of nine old and colorful trolleys from three continents, to the cheers of residents, visitors and transit fans. The streetcars' pedigrees ranged from 1900 to 1977, the newest being Muni's own Boeing LRV 1213, with poles affixed and reassigned to the Trolley Festival fleet for the duration, and the oldest being line car 0304, which had been converted from a 1900-vintage passenger car by United Railroads around 1910. Preserved Marmon-Herrington trolleybus 776 from 1950, and a restored 1930s-vintage Key System bus, brought up the rear. The 1983 San Francisco Historic Trolley Festival was in full swing!

From the outset, the new service was called the F-Market and Wharves. This designation first appeared in Muni's 1981-1986 Short Range Transit Plan, which was prepared by the Muni Planning Division staff under the direction of Planning Director Peter Straus. Signboxes with the insertable letter "F" appeared on Muni's Old Number One and leased K-Type 178, and later on B-Type 130. The PCCs had rollsigns with "F-Market" designations.

Why "F"? That question has been asked often. Well, the proposed Embarcadero service was line E-Embarcadero, and "F" was the next letter in the alphabet. Apparently, Muni planners didn't simply want to pick up where names of Muni original lettered lines ended, at "R-Howard," its designation for a trolleybus route that was created in 1941. So they decided to recycle certain letters, and wanted to reserve letters "A" through "D" in case the original Geary Street lines ever returned as rail routes. Since "E" could easily represent "Embarcadero," logic prevailed. The original lines E and F were E-Union and F-Stockton, which quit in 1947 and 1951 respectively; both were replaced by electric trolley coaches. The fact that the new E and F lines would cross the terminals of the original E and F helped affirm the decision. The first terminal of the F-Stockton was Stockton and Market; that of the E-Union was the Ferry Building. After Muni took over Market Street Railway, the F-Stockton was extended across Market Street.

Despite the 15-minute headways and no service on Tuesdays and Wednesdays, the first of what ultimately became five Trolley Festivals was, in many ways, considered the best. It was fresh in the

Many of the Muni workers who helped to restore Muni's 1914-vintage B-Type 130 to passenger service pose in front of the glistening streetcar on July 25, 1983, outside of Metro Center. 130 was brought back exactly 25 years after its first revenue service career ended. *Peter Straus*

49

minds and hearts of the residents—a new concept in public transportation. It was innovative. It was colorful, what with streetcars painted in virtually every hue across the spectrum. And it showed what could be possible. It embodied "The City that Knows How!" attitude, a philosophy that was just becoming prevalent in all aspects of life in San Francisco. A rider waiting for a streetcar would never know what to expect, which car would be the next to arrive. That sense of surprise continues on today's F-Line.

Innovative? Most certainly. Here was a historic trolley operation on a main street in a major city. New vintage car operations had already commenced in Detroit and Seattle, but neither was a major addition to their city's public transport picture (although Seattle's Waterfront Streetcar was fully integrated with the bus system there, insofar as fares and transfers were concerned). Being on Market Street, the Trolley Festival cars quickly became a fully accredited part of the intense surface transit operation that had been in place for over 120 years.

Colorful? Without a doubt! The array of different liveries was a cheerful contrast to the standard Muni "Landor" colors of white with a broad two-tone orange stripe at waist level worn by buses, trolley coaches and LRVs. The colors featured were gray and maroon (Muni 1), blue and gold (130), green and cream (178 and the Blackpool "Boat"), red and cream (Portland 503, PCC 1704 and Hamburg 3557), and yellow or brown and cream (the two Portuguese single-truckers). Only PCC 1040 and Boeing 1213 remained in "Landor" livery. This cornucopia of colors would become a feature of the future F-Line.

Even as city government waxed enthusiastic about the new Trolley Festival concept, not everyone was on board. Many people who resided in the Castro District were opposed to the return of surface streetcars. A petition signed by 180 residents, mostly people who lived on either 17th Street or Hartford Street (just a stone's throw away from the terminal) was sent to the Board of Supervisors opposing the "tourist trolley." In addition, many Castro District merchants were skeptical and afraid that "straight tourists and gawkers" would inundate "their" district, and were suspicious of "downtown" (aka the Chamber of Commerce). To counter this, Market Street Railway (by that time, Laubscher had joined the group and Klebolt was already a director) allowed the Castro merchants to design their own posters and promotional materials. Of course, the Trolley Festival turned out to be a big win-win for them.

To keep public interest fresh, more cars were added to the fleet mix as the Festival grew in popularity. Several months before the June 22 kickoff, the orders had been given to restore Muni B-Type 130, a 1914 jewel of a streetcar which Muni converted to a work car after its passenger-carrying days were over in 1958, back to passenger service. Over 50 employees in Muni's maintenance and crafts ranks worked virtually around the clock to get the old girl back in revenue service. Motors were checked. The seats, which had been removed by Charlie Smallwood, the man who saved 130 from the scrapper back in 1957, were brought back from storage and reinstalled. The roof received new wood and canvas. The interior mahogany woodwork got a new coat of dark varnish, representing its original appearance. The wiring, controls, brakes and other accessories received a thorough makeover. Finally, on July 25, Trolley Festival Maintenance leader Karl Johnson piloted 130, sparkling in Muni's 1939 World's Fair livery of blue and gold, through a banner at Metro Center to a cheering crowd of maintainers, officials and trolley fans. All the employees who had helped bring the B-Type back to life posed with the car, and a party ensued. 130's second career had begun!

The other trolley made operational in 1983 was Hamburg 3557, which had been built in 1954 and retired in 1978, when Hamburg closed down its last tram line—one of the very few German cities to abandon trams. It was a single-end car, like the PCCs, and it featured a cassette music system. Riders would listen to German polkas and other folk music as the tram sped down Market Street. The first operator to run the car in service was the man who had brought it over "across the pond" and who had paraded it around City Hall in 1979 for befuddled city officials to see—Maury Klebolt.

During the 1983 Trolley Festival, Muni brought the Festival cars to other neighborhoods. Oporto 122 meets Boeing 1269 on the L-Taraval line on August 13, 1983. *Peter Ehrlich*

There were other service wrinkles which simply added to the interest and charm of the Trolley Festival. For the annual Gay Pride Day in late June, Car 1 ran a special schedule on the N-

1983 – First and Foremost!

(*this column, top*) The Portuguese pair–single-truckers 189 (assembled in 1929 in Oporto from parts supplied by J. G. Brill) and 122 (Brill, 1912) lay over at 17th and Castro Terminal on July 10, 1983. *Peter Ehrlich* (*center*) The elegant Victorian-era 1903 Council Crest Brill from Portland is leaving the outbound stop at Powell on July 24, 1983. *Jeffrey Moreau* (*bottom*) "Iron Monster" 130 was added to the Trolley Festival in mid-summer. It's at 4th Street on Sept. 17, 1983. *Peter Ehrlich*

(*this column, top*) The iconic Melbourne, Australia W2 trams, in production since 1923, have become popular in America, where they ran in Seattle and New Orleans, and still operate in Memphis, Dallas, San Jose and northern Minnesota. San Francisco's first W2, 648, was leased from the Western Railway Museum. It's at Gough Street on July 1, 1983. *Peter Ehrlich* (*center*) 189 turns onto Market from Fremont on July 31, 1983. *Don Jewell* (*bottom*) The most improbable Trolley Festival car was Boeing LRV 1213, up from the Muni Metro Subway for the duration. It lays over with 1912-built Car 1 at 17th and Castro on July 4, 1983. *Peter Ehrlich*

Judah from the Beach to Church and Duboce, turned right, and ran to Castro Street, picking up riders attending the event. And the "Boat" tram was part of the parade on Market Street, too.

On a few weekends in August, Muni, at MSR's urging, introduced Trolley Festival cars to other city neighborhoods. Muni A-Type 1 and Oporto 122 operated between St. Francis Circle on the K/M lines through the upscale West Portal shopping district and out the L-Taraval line to the Zoo. Occasionally, some of the single-end cars would run through the N-Line's Sunset Tunnel out to the 30th Avenue and Judah wye.

On September 18, 1983, a day before the end of the Festival, there was a Photo Day. The festivities began at Mint Yard in the morning by posing the three Muni "Iron Monsters" in front of the yard. Then Oporto 189 and Muni B-Type 130 ran out to the Ocean Beach loop on the N-Line. Finally, the Blackpool "Boat" and the other Portuguese single-trucker, 122, climbed the J-Church grade in Dolores Park for pictures at the scenic skyline overlook at 20th Street. Historic Marmon-Herrington trolley coach 776 ran on the 8-Market all day long, which it had done countless times during its illustrious career. But as an extra attraction, 776 also added part of the brand-new 24-Divisadero line, climbing Castro Hill to 26th Street. This route had been converted from diesel bus to trolley coach only a month earlier. (Until 1942, this was a cable car route.)

Every Trolley Festival featured a Photo Day, sending streetcars out to unusual locations. The 1983 Festival's Photo Day–Sept. 18, 1983–shows (*top right*) the lineup of the three Muni "boxcars" at Mint Yard; (*center*) Three vintage cars at the Ocean Beach end of the N-Judah line; and (*bottom left*) Oporto 122 at a favorite photographer's spot at the top of the grade on the J-Line in Dolores Park. *All photos, Peter Ehrlich*

Photo Day was essentially a day of appreciation given to the fans, and thanking them for their support. With the variety of services offered, it was hard to figure out where to go next to get interesting shots. Different incarnations of Photo Day would be a regular feature in subsequent Festivals.

On the last day, September 19, the cars made their rounds as normal. At the end of the day, they terminated in Mint Yard, and all went back to Metro Center as a parade, actually waiting until the end of the evening rush hour. From this point, leased cars Oporto 122 and Portland 503 returned to their owners (122 was later sold to the McKinney Avenue Transit Authority in Dallas). The three trams leased from the Western Railway Museum remained on the property, as did Oporto 189, which was purchased by Muni while the Festival progressed. LRV 1213 had its poles removed and dove back into the subway.

Milwaukee 978 never entered service. It had suffered a broken back, probably incurred during loading in Wisconsin and, as a result, was considered unsafe to use. This was a disappointment, because it was a one-man car, and one of the reasons Muni wanted the car in the first place was to keep platform costs down (akin to the desire by street railway companies in the 1920s). It returned to Wisconsin in late October.

The 1983 Historic Trolley Festival, despite its short duration and long headways, was considered a beyond-anyone's-dreams success. It captured the hearts and thoughts of both ordinary people and those in the transit world.

But Muni was not done. Even though the 1983 Trolley Festival was over, Geissenheimer decided to allow weekend "Mini-Festivals" to continue through the Christmas season and on into January 1984. Four cars—two double-enders running to 17th and Castro, usually the Melbourne car and one of the "Iron Monsters," and two single-end trolleys to 30th and Church or 30th and Judah—did the honors. This permitted half-hourly service on Market Street. It also led to the planning for the next Trolley Festival.

1984–Serving the Democratic National Convention

EVEN THOUGH MANY PEOPLE inside and outside Muni were making plans to launch a repeat of the successful 1983 Trolley Festival, there were some who thought this would be an unnecessary extravaganza, considering that the cable cars would be returning, and that trolleys on Market were no longer needed. Nevertheless, the core cars were still on the property, and this suggested that The City prepare for a repeat event. Accordingly, planning continued.

During the off-season, Klebolt, Laubscher & Co. were busy prevailing on international governments to donate trams as gifts or at very low cost to San Francisco as gestures of goodwill, which would be repaid by advertising the host countries on board the trolleys. One such gift came from the Comune di Milano, and the Italian government, in the form of a typical Milan "Peter Witt," car 1834. This car was one of a fleet of 502 such trams built in 1928/29 to an American design. No. 1834 had signs on its side noting that it was a gift from the people of Milan to the people of San Francisco. Although it arrived in 1983, it was too late for use in that year's Festival. But Metro shop workers prepared it for service in 1984 anyway. (1834's presence, and its ease of operation and maintenance, would later play a pivotal role in the future, as we will see.)

Another country to provide a streetcar was Mexico. A Veracruz historian, aiming to convince his city of the value of restoring streetcars as a visitor attraction after closure of the system in 1981, approached Muni officials to bring a streetcar to San

The Veracruz, Mexico car debuted in the 1984 Trolley Festival. Mech-anically, it wasn't quite ready for service, so in the June 7 Opening Day Parade, it was towed by Muni B-Type 130. *Peter Ehrlich*

Francisco. The plan was agreed to, and the move was assisted by the Mexican Federal Railways, and a lovely 4-wheel single-end open streetcar, No. 001, nicknamed the "Mexican Jumping Bean" due to its loose suspension and resulting bouncy ride, debuted in the 1984 Trolley Festival.

And Muni was preparing another car of its own for service: "Torpedo" PCC 1006, the first of 10 double-end PCCs built for Muni in 1948 as their first true PCCs. It was cosmetically restored in its original "Muni Wings" paint scheme, but it could still run only as a single-ender. Full restoration as a double-end car would come the following year.

Rounding out the 1984 fleet were Muni A-Type 1, B-Type 130, K-Type 178, Blackpool 226, Oporto 189, Melbourne 648 and PCCs 1040 and 1704.

As in 1983, Mayor Feinstein was motorman of Car 1 in the Opening Day parade on June 7, 1984, which began at Transbay Terminal instead. This time, there were 13 trolleys in the parade, including Boeing LRV 1213, which stayed in the Trolley Festival for a week until it was needed to ease a car shortage in the subway.

Again, the crowds cheered the arrival of the trolleys. Motorman Ed Fine, a Trolley Festival veteran since 1984, recalled that the ladies "were out blowing kisses at us and giving us bouquets of flowers."

The Veracruz car carried a mariachi band. Mechanically, it wasn't quite ready for service, so it was towed behind "Iron Monster" 130, a task the B-Type had performed countless times during its 25 years as a Muni work car. Hardly anyone cared or even noticed the difference.

In 1984, as in 1983, the streetcars didn't operate on Tuesdays or Wednesdays. But enough cars

1984 – Serving the Democratic National Convention

(*this column, top*) The Western Railway Museum's Blackpool, England "Boat" tram 226 served the first two Festivals. At Market/Sansome, August 3, 1984. (*center*) Car 1, Muni's first streetcar, rolls up Fremont Street after leaving Transbay Terminal on July 22, 1984. (*bottom*) Milan "Peter Witt" 1834 joined the F-Line fleet in 1984 and is signed for the N-Judah line heading to Ocean Beach. All single-end cars operated on the N-Line in 1984. Taken on August 13. *All photos, Peter Ehrlich*

(*this column, top*) Melbourne 648 traverses a portable cross-over on 17th Street heading to Castro during a J-Church line rerailing project as a Boeing LRV passes inbound. July 27, 1984. (*center*) Veracruz 001 and Milan 1834 were newcomers to the 1984 Trolley Festival. Both cars are switching back at the 11th Street Wye on August 11, 1984 *Both photos, Peter Ehrlich*

Muni K-Type 178, built in 1923, lays over at Transbay Terminal as Grumman bus 4040, on a "Farewell to the Grummans" bus fantrip, pulls up behind it. The motorman, the late veteran vintage car operator Jack Smith, walked back and snarled, "Get That Bus Off My Track!"
All in good fun. June 10, 1984. *Peter Ehrlich*

1985 – Seven Days A Week

(*left*) During the 1985 Trolley Festival, "Moveable Music" was featured on Friday afternoons on board Blackpool "Boat" 228. Members of the local Red Garter Band serenaded passengers up and down Market Street. On July 26, 1985, the Boat passes inbound Portland 503 at First Street. *Peter Ehrlich*

(*above*) PCC 1704, representing St. Louis, crosses Van Ness on May 30, 1985. As in 1984, single-end cars operated outbound to the N-Line. (*below*) Hamburg 3557, the "Red Baron," wyes back at the Judah/30th Avenue wye on October 12, 1985. *Both photos, Peter Ehrlich*

(*this column, center*) Looking down on Car Number One, outbound at Market/2nd Street, from the private park installed atop the old Crocker Building at Montgomery and Post Streets, which had been reduced to just two floors in the late 1960s. October 12, 1985. K-Type 178 heads out Market past 7th Street on June 23, 1985. Car 1 is inbound in the background. This was 178's last summer in San Francisco, and it returned to its owner, the Western Railway Museum, at the end of the '85 Festival. *Both photos, Peter Ehrlich* (*right*) One of the Photo Day lineups at Mint Yard featured a trio of deck-roof cars grouped at the front of Mint Yard. Portland 503, Veracruz 001 and Oporto 189 mug for the camera on September 29, 1985. *Peter Ehrlich*

The oldest streetcar in public transit service today is 1895-built 578(S). Patterned after the double-end cable cars of the period, 578(S) passes its cousin—a Powell cable car—at the foot of Powell and Market on July 4, 1985. *Peter Ehrlich*

were available to provide 12-minute headways, a significant improvement. The outer terminal for single-enders, now up to five cars, became Judah and 30th Avenue on the N-Judah line. The single-end Veracruz car was used mostly on weekends as an extra-service car, running only between the Transbay Terminal and 11th and Market.

Unlike 1983, there were no special runs on the K, L or M lines. But the 1984 Democratic National Convention was held in San Francisco that year. So for one week in July, seven-day service was offered for the first time.

The last-day parade had most cars running from Transbay Terminal, with unassigned cars at Mint Yard joining the parade there. This time, well-wishers cried, with the hope that there would be a third Trolley Festival. Weekend service, similar to what had operated the year before, continued through New Year's Day 1985.

The 1984 Trolley Festival was significant in that it proved that heritage streetcars could coexist with the iconic cable cars. Clearly there was a place for both.

But the most important aspect of the 1984 Festival was that it reinforced the dream for a permanent historic streetcar line in San Francisco. Most of the credit can be given to Mayor Dianne Feinstein and her enthusiasm for the Trolley Festival operations. She worked hard to transcend the political, logistical and financial hurdles necessary for a permanent surface streetcar line, and ultimately was successful. Today's F-Line is a testimonial to her legacy.

1985–Seven Days A Week

IN 1983, THE TROLLEY FESTIVAL route had an official name: the F-Market. The PCCs had rollsigns with F-Market designations and the "Iron Monsters" carried metal "F" signs in their rooftop signboxes already. But in reality, the name "F-Market and Wharves" first appeared in the 1981-1986 Muni 5-Year Plan publication. When the 1985 Trolley Festival began, this designation appeared on Muni maps, brochures and other documents for the first time.

The fleet mix began to change significantly in 1985. Gone was the Western Railway Museum's Blackpool "Boat," 226. Replacing 226 was another "Boat," number 228, which was making its second foray on U. S. rails (it ran in Philadelphia for the Bicentennial in 1976) and was purchased outright from Blackpool. The Veracruz car was on hand

The signature slogan for the 1985 Trolley Festival was "Joy Ride!", and car cards with this phrase were carried inside every Festival car, and on the flanks of B-Type 130, which is passing K-Type 178 as it heads out to the N-Judah line. 178 has just made an inbound trip from Ocean Beach and is turning onto Church Street to head to the normal 17th and Castro terminal. August 31, 1985. *Peter Ehrlich*

The only time a two-car train of Boeing LRVs ever operated on the surface of Market Street was on August 25, 1985, when a San Jose transit enthusiast chartered Boeings 1212 and 1213 and ran the train up and down Market Street several times. Here at 2nd Street, the chartered train of "new" streetcars passes 1914-vintage Muni 130 running in regular service – odd, to say the least! *Peter Ehrlich*

The 1985 Trolley Festival was the only one to offer seven-day service. Its theme was "Joy Ride!", and advertisements and car cards with this phrase were carried on board most of the fleet. Headways were still every 12 minutes, with single-enders continuing to run out the N-Line. The other significant feature, which carried over to the 1986 and 1987 Festivals, was that it began much earlier (mid-May) and concluded later (mid-October).

Another notable event during the 1985 Festival happened on August 25. A two-car train of Boeing LRVs, consisting of cars 1212 and 1213, both outfitted with trolley poles, was chartered to run up and down Market Street for several trips. This was the only time a train of LRVs ever ran "upstairs." It was odd to watch a charter with newer cars pass ancient trolleys in regular transit service, to say the least. Normally, the opposite would be the rule.

The 1985 Festival proved that seven-day service could be operated on a vintage trolley line. It also showed that even 19th century streetcars had a place in making the Festival the success it was.

for a second year, and the elegant Portland Council Crest trolley, car 503, came down from Oregon to make an encore appearance. "Torpedo" PCC 1006 was finally made a true double-ender, and "Baby Ten" PCC 1040 had its Landor orange/white replaced with a fresh coat of original "Muni Wings" green and cream. The *W*estern Railway Museum's Muni K-Type 178 stayed on for yet another season, as did Melbourne 648.

But the most notable car to see service in 1985 was Muni's oldest possession, 1895 "Dinky" 578, returning home from loan to the Western Railway Museum. This car, originally owned by the first Market Street Railway Company, was a single truck, California-type trolley with lever hand brakes, open ends and enclosed center section, similar in appearance to the cable cars of California Street. 578 later received an "S" suffix, on paper only, to distinguish it internally from Japanese car 578, which arrived in 1986 and was called 578(J). This car, which for many years had been ex-MSRy work car 0601, had first been restored in 1956 to commemorate the 50th Anniversary of the '06 Earthquake and Fire. For its 90th birthday, Muni shop forces made it operational once again and gave it a fresh coat of mustard yellow and cream paint. It ran mostly on weekends and holidays, but, like the Veracruz car, only between Transbay Terminal and 11th Street. Car 578 is, arguably, the oldest electric streetcar in passenger service for a public transit agency in the world.

1986–All Cars on One Route

IN ORDER FOR Trolley Festival service to be more consistent and reliable, it made sense that all cars should operate on the main route to 17th and Castro. Routing the single-enders out the N or J lines would occasionally result in service gaps, especially if the trouble-prone Boeing LRVs broke down on the N or J lines.

To make this possible, it was necessary to install a wye at 17th and Noe Streets. In the spring of 1986, Muni's Track Department got authorization to remove the switch points and special work from the M-Ocean View line's Broad & Plymouth wye, a 1957 installation that was no longer needed, and re-lay them at 17th and Noe. The work was finished just before the opening of the 1986 Trolley Festival.

As in past years, Mayor Feinstein operated the first car. But this year, there was a different trolley at the head of the May 19, 1986 Opening Day Parade. The car was Kobe/Hiroshima 578(J), a 1927 two-tone green car with a silver roof presented to Muni by the Japan Railway Corporate Assembly. It had green plush longitudinal seats and a generally cheery interior.

1986 – All Cars on One Route

Installation of wye switches at 17th and Noe was the principal change to Trolley Festival operations in 1986. The special work was removed from the Broad and Plymouth wye on the M-Ocean View line and reinstalled by Muni track crews. This allowed single-end cars such as Hamburg 3557 to run up to 17th and Castro, although they had to run backwards up the last block. Both photos were taken on June 9, 1986. *Peter Ehrlich*

(*above*) Another wyeing single-ender at 17th and Noe. Cars could back-pole out of the wye and up 17th Street. June 6, 1986. (*below*) An inbound telephoto view, taken June 6, 1986, depicts Melbourne 648 approaching 7th Street. *Both photos, Peter Ehrlich*

(*left*) On Parade Day, May 19, 1986, Kobe/Hiroshima 578(J) has just passed under the Central Freeway. Other parade cars and historic Marmon-Herrington trolley coach 776 follow. In 1986, this car had a single long trolley pole, but two shorter poles were later mounted on each end. *Don Jewell* (*right*) Oporto 189 has also ducked under the Central Freeway, but is heading inbound at Gough Street. September 26, 1986. *Peter Ehrlich*

1987 - All Good Things Must End

(*this column, top to bottom*) "Iron Monster" 130 stops at Market and Kearny/Geary Streets on the Fourth of July 1987. Lotta's Fountain, where dozens of San Franciscans gather every April 18 to commemorate the 1906 Earthquake and Fire, stands in the foreground. Kobe/Hiroshima 578(J) and Milan 1834 pass at Market and Montgomery Streets on the same day. The Japanese car now has both front and rear trolley poles. PCC 1006, a true double-end car since 1985, passes the construction site of the San Francisco Centre shopping mall at 5th Street on May 16, 1987. *All photos, Peter Ehrlich*

(*this column, top to bottom*) Muni's Blackpool, England "Boat" carries 75th Anniversary banners as it heads outbound at Montgomery Street on May 16, 1987. PCC 1040 passes vintage Marmon-Herrington trolley coach 776 at Van Ness on September 3, 1987. Both are painted in Muni "Wings" green and cream. (The VW van alongside 1040 belonged to Muni motorman Jack Smith.) The Moscow/Orel single-end tram 106 was the Opening Day Parade leader in 1987. Much later that day, May 14, 1987, the 1912-vintage tram, "From Russia with Love," crosses Gough Street enroute to 17th and Castro. *All photos, Peter Ehrlich*

The 1986 Trolley Festival introduced a new international streetcar to the fleet–Kobe/Hiroshima 578(J), which Madame Mayor Dianne Feinstein is piloting during the traditional Opening Day Parade, May 19, 1986. *Peter Ehrlich*

578(J)'s career in Japan spanned nearly six decades. Originally a Kobe car, 578(J) and its sisters were sent to Hiroshima to rebuild that war-ravaged city's tram system. It was set up for Japan's left-hand drive streets. What would normally be the front door became the rear door in San Francisco, and there was also a center door for alighting passengers. Both doorways were narrow, and had two steep steps to climb, making for slow boarding and alighting. Coupled with having just two motors, 578 (now called 578(J) to distinguish it from 578(S), the 1895 "Dinky") was the slowest car in the fleet. Nevertheless, motormen Jack Smith and William "Chip" Palmer, who normally were assigned Car 1, would take 578(J) instead. This would give Smith the opportunity to wisecrack that on days when he took out Old Number One, it was because he wanted "More Steam!", as Car 1 was considered to be the fastest two-man historic streetcar in the fleet. (Jack Smith was also a lover of steam locomotives.)

578(J) was the only new car added to the heritage fleet in 1986. Melbourne 648 was still being leased from the Western Railway Museum, however, but the museum's Muni K-Type "Iron Monster" 178 had returned home.

With all cars now running out to 17th and Castro, it was now possible to schedule seven cars at 10-minute headways. But there was a down-side. With seven runs (3 two-man car assignments and one 1-man) out of 12 given Saturday-Sunday off, this resulted in six-day service, and the day with no service, therefore, had to be Sunday. The railfan community grumbled, but in order to keep the best operators, it was necessary to provide certain runs with weekends off. No longer would a 25-year man like Jack Smith accept Tuesday-Wednesday off. The runs were also paid actual platform time starting in 1986, instead of eight hours plus lunch pay regardless of the hours spent on the streetcar. (One of the concessions from the union back in 1983 was to allow runs to be paid eight hours plus lunch, regardless of run length, as a way of making the Festivals more affordable.)

Another perk for 1986 Trolley Festival operators was addition of 32 minutes of "Rail Pay," paid at time and a half, matching that of LRV and cable car operators. [See Chapter 9.]

1987–All Good Things Must End

BY THE TIME THE 1987 Trolley Festival rolled around, the operators had had some great experiences under their belts, and the public was quite pleased with this new concept in public transport. And the intended result–a permanent Market Street historic streetcar line–was well on its way to happening, as funds had started to pour into Muni's coffers to get started on the tracklaying. The influx of money actually began in 1986.

But as long as Dianne Feinstein was mayor, there would be one more Trolley Festival. And so it was that one last Festival took place in 1987. Coincidentally, this was also the year Muni celebrated its 75th Anniversary. Most of the cars wore special 75th Anniversary logos on their ends.

Another new streetcar was chosen to lead the 1987 Opening Day Parade. This car was Moscow/Orel 106, a single-truck, single-end car "From Russia with Love," aka "A Streetcar Named Desire for Peace," a term given by the Soviet Union Consul-General, Valentin Kamenev. This tram, which was built in 1912 reportedly by a German carbuilder, came to San Francisco with Maury Klebolt's help and was presented to The City by Consul-General Kamenev in a decorative ceremony at Transbay Terminal on January 27, 1987. It had actually arrived in 1986, but the Metro Center shop force had to regauge the tram from its Russian gauge of 5'-6" to standard gauge before it could run on the streets of San Francisco. 106 had steerable axles (axles that could pivot independently of each other) because of its long wheelbase; but this was not a new feature for San Francisco. Previously, Muni's Union Street "Dinkies," which ran on the original E-Line from 1921 to 1947, had such a feature, riding on Brill "Radiax" trucks.

Madame Feinstein again piloted the car, but a Muni employee had to stand next to her to work the "leftist" brake valve (meaning that the brakes were applied by moving the air handle to the left, instead of to the normal right; it was later changed over to eliminate confusion). The only other new car in the fleet was Melbourne W2 496, replacing identical tram 648 which returned to its owner, the Western Railway Museum. 496 was purchased outright from Australia. 1987's Opening Day Parade fell on May 14.

Of course, there was a Photo Day, as in earlier Festivals. The last day, October 16, was a somber and sad event, as the cars gathered at and left Transbay Terminal for the last time and progressed slowly up Market Street in almost funereal procession. This time, the ladies wept as the motormen ran their trolleys outbound. Indeed, there would be nothing like the family atmosphere and camaraderie that the five Trolley Festivals brought to Muni and to San Franciscans.

Fittingly, that evening, the operators were honored by Maury Klebolt and MSR for their work with a lavish dinner at a Church Street restaurant. Klebolt, despite his brusque exterior, was truly a gentleman to the end.

Another new car for the 1987 Trolley Festival was Muni's own Melbourne W2, 496, which replaced sister 648. It's passing the fountain at United Nations Plaza on July 4, 1987. *Peter Ehrlich*

Despite the sadness of the last day of the last Trolley Festival, the future held bright. The money was now all in, and the tracks would see a near-complete facelift beginning in 1988, which would ultimately bring back to San Francisco a permanent trolley line on Market Street.

Operationally, the 1987 Festival mirrored 1986. The work and schedule assignments were the same, all cars went to Castro etc. But there was one event that set it apart from all the other Festivals, and this was a demonstration service on The Embarcadero in the Festival's waning days. It laid the cornerstone for the most successful historic streetcar service to come, some 13 years later. [The Embarcadero Demonstration is described in a sidebar section in this chapter.]

The dedication of the "Streetcar Named Desire for Peace," as Soviet Consul-General Valentin Kamenev (right) proclaimed Moscow/Orel 106, occurred on January 27, 1987 at Transbay Terminal. Mr. Kamenev reads the proclamation as Muni General Manager Bill Stead, Superintendent of Maintenance Rich Rogers, Trolley Festival "Godfather" Maury Klebolt and Mayor Dianne Feinstein look on. The 1912-built tram became a big hit during the 1987 Festival. *Peter Ehrlich*

61

Opening Day Parade, 1983

The parade for the first Trolley Festival in 1983 was the only one where cars paraded east on Market Street.

(left)
The first Blackpool "Boat," 226, is festooned with balloons as it follows Wonderful One down Market at Powell.
June 22, 1983.
Peter Ehrlich

Oporto 122 crosses Powell Street during the 1983 Trolley Festival Opening Day Parade on June 22, 1983. It's followed by a vintage automobile and Muni K-Type 178. *Peter Ehrlich*

1987 Opening Day and End of Festival Parades
These two images were typical of those from other Festival years.

Opening
Day
Parade
1987

(*above*) The 1987 Trolley Festival Opening Day Parade featured newly-restored 1938-vintage "Baby White" bus 062, famed as one of the three Coit Tower buses that lasted in service until 1975, making them the longest-lived motor coaches in Muni's history. 062 is about to be passed at Market and 10th Street by identically-liveried green-and-cream streetcars 1006 and 1040. May 14, 1987. *David Banbury*

Last Day
Processional
1987

(*right*) By contrast, the last day processional was a somber and sad affair. The parade of vintage cars, seen here at Market and 6th Street, took its time to return to Geneva Yard. Although there would be no more summertime Trolley Festivals, their presence cleared the way for a permanent historic streetcar line in San Francisco just eight years later. October 16, 1987. *Peter Ehrlich*

The 1987 Embarcadero Demonstration

A huge crowd waits for the departure of 1895 MSRy "Dinky" 578(S) on October 10, 1987, under the Embarcadero Freeway, which, two years later, would be badly damaged by the Loma Prieta Earthquake and ultimately torn down. Oporto, Portugal 189 will follow about 20 minutes later. This successful demonstration helped to get the F-Line to Fisherman's Wharf built. *Peter Ehrlich*

ONE OF THE ORIGINAL ideas for a historic streetcar line in San Francisco, beginning in the 1970s, had been to build a line along The Embarcadero, the city's waterfront boulevard, which stretched from Fisherman's Wharf in the north to Mission Bay in the south and flowed past the Ferry Building. Until the 1950s, The Embarcadero served a bustling port, where freighters and ocean liners regularly called. To serve the intensive movement of goods, the State Belt Railroad of San Francisco, owned by the State of California, which also owned the port at that time, ran a railroad along the entire length of the roadway, with turnouts servicing the many finger piers and port-side industries, such as coffee roasteries, breweries, and the like. This railroad also served Fort Mason and the Presidio of San Francisco, running through a tunnel under Fort Mason itself. But during the 1960s, the Port of Oakland, with its inland location, modernized facilities and easy access to the transcontinental railroad network, usurped most of the maritime business, and both the Port and the railroad fell into decline. Ultimately, California transferred both entities to the city. The State Belt Railroad served its last North Waterfront customer, a brewery off Francisco Street near Fisherman's Wharf, in 1983, and the last use of the trackage north of the Ferry Building occurred in 1985 when a RailFair Expo was held in the shadow of Telegraph Hill.

For a long time, the ever-imaginative and energetic Maury Klebolt had eyed the idle rails for a chance to test the theory that a streetcar operation to Fisherman's Wharf was economically viable. Muni actually jumped the gun with a limited Battery Street (Levi's Plaza)/Pier 39 service for a RailFair display in April 1987, when car 578(S) was used as a shuttle service with a diesel generator in tow. Accordingly–and building on the weeklong RailFair operation–he pitched a trial run between the Ferry Building and Pier 39.

Klebolt succeeded with his pitch. Late in the 1987 Trolley Festival, Muni management and city officials agreed to a demonstration service. It was to begin in mid-September for a five-week period, and operate on Fridays and Saturdays only.

For the test, the two smallest vintage cars in the fleet–1929 Oporto, Portugal 189 and 1895 MSRy "Dinky" 578(S)–were trucked down to the tracks below the Ferry Building. They were provided with diesel generators on flatcars coupled to the southward-facing ends of the cars.

The test entailed 20-minute headways between terminals. The service was scheduled between 10:00 a.m. and 6:00 p.m., similar to regular Trolley Festival hours of operation. Passengers would only be allowed to board and alight at the Ferry Building, under the Embarcadero Freeway; at Embarcadero and Battery Streets (Levi's Plaza); and opposite Pier 39. For the duration, the trolleys were stabled at the Northeast Sewage Treatment Plant at Kearny and North Point, where there were enclosed access tracks. This facility jokingly became known as "Sewer Division."

The first day of operation was Friday, September 18. Folks started lining up early to try out this special service. Each car carried twice its normal capacity or greater, and the pair of fareboxes on each car had to be emptied out by the Fare Collections Department several times a day, such was the crush of dollar bills inserted by the passengers.

Despite occasional problems, such as a brake glitch affecting 189, and an accident where a car tore off one of 578(S)'s running boards (Klebolt arranged to fix the step and the car was back in service the next day), the experiment proved to be an overwhelming success. Even with two-man crews, the operation reportedly produced the best revenue-to-expense ratio in Muni's history! There would no longer be any doubt in anyone's mind that a streetcar service to Fisherman's Wharf would pay huge social and financial dividends to San Francisco. But it would take an earthquake to make it a reality.

Klebolt, ever the adventurer, took liberties while the cars were down on The Embarcadero. One night, after the close of service, he, with Jack Smith and Supervisor Kenny Rodriguez, took 578(S) westward to Taylor and Jefferson, the heart of Fisherman's Wharf, as far as the rails would go. In fact, the car left grooves in the pavement! Another time, he and Smith operated it south of the Bay Bridge. According to Trolley Festival vet Ed Fine, Klebolt would have taken the car all the way down to Bay Meadows Race Track in San Mateo if there had still been a track connection to the Southern Pacific!

The name given to the trial operation, of course, was E-Embarcadero. By 2014, there will likely be a permanent E-Line running between Fisherman's Wharf and Caltrain Depot, fulfilling a

The 1987 Embarcadero Demonstration

(*top*) 578(S) passes Coit Tower and Telegraph Hill. Diesel generators propelled the cars. (*center*) The two cars meet on State Belt Railroad trackage near Battery Street. (*bottom*) After hours, 578(S) rolled into the heart of Fisherman's Wharf on a test run. *All photos, Peter Ehrlich*

dream spanning over four decades and complementing the F-Line.

Four Who Made It Happen

THE TROLLEY FESTIVALS OF THE 1980s galvanized San Francisco and the transit world with their innovations and their ability to change the city's attitude from the brink of eliminating the streetcar from one of the main streets of America to bringing about a permanent rail line that would inspire government officials and ordinary citizens all over the world. But this "mood swing" might never have happened without the efforts of four principal players involved within and outside government.

These four people are Mayor Dianne Feinstein, who was mayor from 1978 through 1987; Maurice H. Klebolt, a travel agent, trolley fan and citizen transit advocate; Rick Laubscher, a former TV reporter who was associated with the San Francisco Chamber of Commerce, employed by Bechtel Corporation, and is now president of F-Line booster organization, Market Street Railway; and Harold H. Geissenheimer, a career transit official who became Muni General Manager in 1982.

Maury Klebolt

MUCH HAS ALREADY BEEN WRITTEN about Maury Klebolt in Chapter 2. Suffice it to say that his methods, while decidedly unorthodox, got things done and made things happen. Whether it was purchasing a tram from Germany and parading it around City Hall or calling in favors from politicians or obtaining streetcars from all over the world for the Trolley Festivals, Maury was a force to be reckoned with. Already a successful travel agent, his enthusiasm for Muni led him to become a part-time operator in 1980, and, in that capacity, he became the only part-timer to be trained on the historics. He was also a member, and later a director, of Market Street Railway.

Maury cajoled. He bullied. He turned people off. But his overwhelming spirit in pursuing the big picture–the return of streetcars to Market Street–was his driving force, his *joie de vivre*, if you will. With his connections, he kept on working to add international trams to the fleet, whether it be Italy, Japan or the Soviet Union. His work made a lasting impression on not only the Trolley Festivals, but the F-Line as it is today. Sadly, Klebolt passed away in 1988 from a sudden heart attack. But without a doubt, he was the Godfather of the Trolley Festivals.

Rick Laubscher

RICK LAUBSCHER, A FOURTH-GENERATION San Franciscan with a passion for "putting history to work" as valuable contributors to his hometown's economic vitality, served as volunteer project manager for the first San Francisco Historic Trolley Festival. He helped grow a tiny non-profit group, Market Street Railway, into a 1000-plus member organization that played a key role in winning approval and funding for a permanent historic streetcar operation, the F-Line. He currently serves as board chair and president of the organization. He also heads a strategic communications consulting firm, Messagesmith, served as the founding chair of The City Club of San Francisco, a landmark social club quartered in the historic Art Deco Stock Exchange Tower, and has served on the boards of the San Francisco Chamber of Commerce, San Francisco Planning and Urban Research (SPUR), and San Francisco Beautiful.

Before forming his current company, Rick was a public relations executive at Bechtel, the San Francisco-based global engineering and construction company, and worked as a journalist for NBC television affiliates in San Francisco and San Diego, and for KSFO Radio in San Francisco. He holds a Master's Degree in Journalism from Columbia University, New York, where he won a Pulitzer Fellowship. (*Bio supplied by Mr. Laubscher.*)

Harold H. Geissenheimer

HAROLD H. GEISSENHEIMER was born in 1928 and worked in the transit industry for practically his entire life. In the transit industry, his most notable contributions were as Rail Operations Manager in Pittsburgh, where he oversaw repainting of Pittsburgh's remaining PCCs in wild and colorful paint schemes; in Chicago, where repainting of Chicago's vast "L" rapid transit fleet in Bicentennial liveries was an accomplishment; and in San Francisco, where he was appointed General Manager of Muni in 1982 by Mayor Dianne Feinstein.

Under Geissenheimer's watch, the Trolley Festivals started and continued even after he left the post in 1985. He was one of the very few managers among American transit systems who was also a railfan. After leaving Muni, he joined consulting firm LSTS, and continued as a rail transit advocate and consultant until his death in 2010.

Dianne Feinstein

DIANNE FEINSTEIN, WHO WAS MAYOR from 1978 through 1987, is a native San Franciscan, born in 1933. She was elected to the San Francisco Board of Supervisors in 1970, where she served 2½ terms. In 1978, following the assassination of Mayor George Moscone, her colleagues on the Board appointed her

Mayor, and was re-elected twice, serving to the end of 1987. Art Agnos succeeded her as Mayor.

It was during her tenure as Mayor that she helped get the Trolley Festivals running, oversaw reconstruction of the cable car system from 1982 to 1984, and laid the groundwork and worked on gathering the funding for the permanent F-Line.

She was elected U. S. senator from California in 1992 to fill a vacant seat, and was re-elected four more times to six-year terms.

It is fair to say that without Dianne Feinstein's hard work, enthusiasm and diligence, the F-line might never have happened. (*Bio supplied by Senator Feinstein's office.*)

(*above*) Sen. Dianne Feinstein. *Steve Jurvetson via WikiMedia* (*below*) Harold H. Geissenheimer (right, with predecessor General Manager Curtis Green). *John Pappas*

(*above*) Maurice H. Klebolt, in front of his tram, "Red Baron" 3557. *Karl Johnson collection* (*below*) Rick Laubscher. *Rick Laubscher collection*

The placement of the first Canary Island palm trees along the F-Line Upper Market section, controversial as they were, was just another excuse for a party. On April 30, 1993, neighborhood residents and officials gather at Market and Noe/16th Street to bless the first palms. *Karl Johnson*

Chapter 4 - Rebuilding The Tracks

"I love the [palm] trees. I think they upgrade the look of the street a lot."

– Eddie Hahn, an ex-Air Force staff sergeant, commenting on the installation of the palm trees on Upper Market in conjunction with F-Line construction, quoted in the San Francisco Chronicle, May 14, 1993

The Facelift Begins

AS MENTIONED IN THE PREVIOUS CHAPTER, Mayor Feinstein, the enthusiastic backer of the Trolley Festivals, and her Chief Administrative Officer, Rudy Nothenberg (an inveterate transit rider), worked quietly behind the scenes to secure funding for a permanent historic streetcar line. The official title of this project, and the recipient of the accumulated funding, the "Market Street Transit Thoroughfare," and the first manifestation of this project occurred on August 7, 1985, with the institution of four sets of trolley coach wires. Local wags quickly dubbed this phenomenon "The Hiss Of The Four," owing to the sounds of the wires that the trolley bus current pickup shoes made as the coaches sped along the street, and a takeoff of the "Roar Of The Four" way of life on Market Street decades earlier. This setup resulted in service patterns where inbound transit lines with a Ferries destination used the inside wires, while those terminating at the Transbay Terminal were assigned to the curbside wires east of 8th Street. In the outbound direction, trolley coaches that turned off Market before reaching 9th Street–lines 5-Fulton and 21-Hayes (31-Balboa became a trolley coach route in 1992)–utilized the outer set, and buses on the Haight Street routes and the F-Line were given the "inside track." An anomaly with this setup was, of course, that F cars would have to turn off for the Transbay Terminal from the "inside track" at First Street.

The first of four track replacement projects occurred in 1988 during the administration of Mayor Art Agnos. Agnos, while generally supportive of the permanent return of streetcars to Market Street, and who also worked hard to secure funding and plans for much of the Fisherman's Wharf Extension and the F-Line/Muni Metro Extension connection for a future E-Line, was not nearly as enthusiastic as his predecessor in actual trolley operation. Maury Klebolt had supported Agnos' opponent, John Molinari, in the 1987 mayoral primary, and he had to change his *modus operandi*. (Although some MSR board members privately supported Molinari over Agnos, the organization, a non-profit, by law could not endorse either candidate.)

Phase One consisted of installing a new crossover west of Market and Fifth Street, and generally replacing all the worn-out sections of girder rail that remained between the cut-and-cover excavations for the BART/Muni Metro Montgomery, Powell and Civic Center stations that had been completed back in 1970. (Ordinary T-rail had been laid at the station sites at the time, because the plan in that era had been to get rid of the tracks.) Most track work was completed by November 16, 1988, and on that date, with Trolley Festival Supervisor Kenny Rodriguez, city engineers and other officials looking on, PCC 1006, B-Type 130 and Moscow/Orel 106 tested the crossover successfully. The street was repaved in time for the 1988 Christmas shopping season.

During the planning and conceptual engineering phase, in 1984, the question arose as to how to treat the trackway at stops. Would the tracks weave to accommodate islands, or would the lane paralleling the islands have to be adjusted to remove some sidewalk space? Neither idea was really palatable, but the final solution did result in keeping the tracks straight, with sidewalk cutbacks at some locations to allow for the streetcar islands which had to be a specific width to allow for wheelchair access. The granite curbstones were replaced at intersections such as 5th Street and 6th/Taylor Streets.

Phase Two; MSR Regroups

WITH MAURY KLEBOLT'S untimely death from a second heart attack in October 1988, MSR lost one of its principal voices in support of trolleys. He had actually, however, lessened his involvement and

Phase One consisted of installing a new crossover at Market and 5th Street and replacing worn-out rail elsewhere. Here, on a rainy November 16, 1988, Muni officials look on nervously as "Torpedo" 1006 tests the installation. *Peter Ehrlich*

Nearly a year later, a new turnout was installed at Market and First Street, and a trailing switch at Market and Fre-mont, as part of Phase Two of the F-Line rerailing. This time, Muni chose Moscow/Orel 106, which was a two axle tram with steerable axles, to perform the test. September 25, 1989. The straight track would be linked to the Fisherman's Wharf Extension trackage in 1998.
Peter Ehrlich

After the special work at Market and First was tested by Moscow/Orel 106 on September 25, 1989, Market and Fremont was tried out next. The car "From Russia with Love" is sitting on the straight track, which eventually would be extended eastward and tied into the route to Fisherman's Wharf. But that would come over 10 years later. *Karl Johnson*

took an important long-term step by leasing the Duboce Yard (Mint Yard) from Muni for $1 a year so it could carry out some of its car restoration projects, as well as assisting Muni in its own endeavors.

Phase Two, carried out in September 1989, consisted of placing new switches at First and Fremont streets, with track stubs extending east on Market. Nine years later, these stubs were connected to tracks extended down to Steuart Street as part of the Wharf Extension.

The mini-Trolley Festivals, typically, consisted of MSR chartering up to four cars—two single-end and two double-end—and operating them in the daytime on a holiday such as Memorial or Labor Day. Most times, all cars ran to 17th and Castro, with occasional trips out the J or N lines. By 1991, however, MSR ran out of money to continue this practice, and in

activism within MSR after suffering his first heart attack a year earlier. With regular Trolley Festivals out of the question because of track reconstruction and financial concerns, the group had to be content with sponsoring mini-Trolley Festivals on special days such as holidays and the Fridays after Thanksgiving for several years.

Nevertheless, the organization continued its constant pressure on city government to expedite construction and the startup of permanent historic streetcar service. Simultaneously, MSR, along with Muni planners, began to solicit support from Fisherman's Wharf interests and neighborhood groups toward eventual extension of the line to the Wharf and Northern Waterfront. [See Chapter 2.] It also

Typical scenes of the mini-Trolley Festival days sponsored by Market Street Railway. (*above*) Melbourne W2 496 running on the N-Judah line on May 31, 1993. (*left*) A meet at Church and 24th Streets on the J-Line with Milan 1834 and Muni 130 on July 5, 1993. *Both photos, Peter Ehrlich*

1992, San Francisco was experiencing a severe financial crunch. It was just as well, because Phase Three was about to begin.

But there were three last hurrahs: On Labor Day Weekend in 1991, MSR took advantage of the just-opened J-Church Extension from the J's traditional 30th and Church Terminal out to Balboa Park and Metro Center, through the Bernal Cut and San Jose Avenue, by running a "Z-Excursion" service with three cars operating on an hourly headway. This magnificent 15-mile run, the longest in San

The Z-Line and the Market Street 100th Anniversary "Race"

During the track reconstruction period, there were several notable events where streetcars could use existing trackage: the Z-Line weekend in 1991, and the 100th anniversary of electric streetcars in San Francisco. (*left*) Car 130 heads out the Z-Line enroute to the Zoo via the newly-opened J-line Extension on September 2, 1991. *Peter Ehrlich* (*facing page, top*) For the 100th Anniversary on April 25, 1992, streetcars ran inbound on both tracks!At Market and 10th Street. (*bottom*) The ceremony was held at Market and 5th Street. *Both photos, Y. Maeda, Karl Johnson collection*

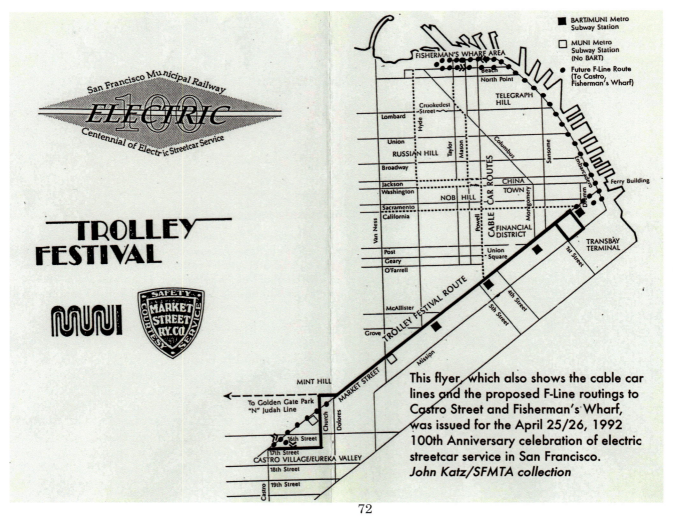

This flyer, which also shows the cable car lines and the proposed F-Line routings to Castro Street and Fisherman's Wharf, was issued for the April 25/26, 1992 100th Anniversary celebration of electric streetcar service in San Francisco. *John Katz/SFMTA collection*

Francisco's historic streetcar history, essentially replicated the old Market Street Railway Company's 12-Mission and Ocean route, which ran from the Ferries out Mission, Onondaga Street, Ocean Avenue and Sloat Blvd. to the Zoo. The Z-Line covered Market Street, the J-Line and its new extension, the K-Line and the L-Line. This was an extra-fare service pegged at $5.00, with discounts to card-carrying MSR members.

Then on October 19, 1991, Muni and MSR sponsored a regular F-Line preview service in conjunction with the annual meeting of the National Trust for Historic Preservation that weekend.

Finally, on April 25 and 26, 1992, Muni celebrated the Centennial of Electric Streetcar Service in San Francisco. This operation also re-enacted—for a few minutes, at least—the old "Roar Of The Four," which was the hallmark of San Francisco trolley operations from 1918 to 1947. Beginning from Market and Duboce, Muni staged and ran several cars, with inbound cars occupying both tracks! Then the cars "raced" each other, much as United Railroads/MSRy and Muni cars did back in the day. This was indeed a sight to behold! The commemoration ceremony was held at Market and 5th streets. After the ceremony, the trolleys continued to "race" each other as far as the still-existing crossover west of First Street, when the cars on the outbound track were able to switch over to normal operation. (Later, the crossover was removed, under Phase Three.)

Phase Three-
Rails Return to Upper Market

ON MARCH 13, 1992, bids for Phase Three—the return of rails to Upper Market, between Duboce and Castro Streets—came in at $13.36 million, considerably lower than estimated. This project returned rails to Upper Market, which had been ripped up in 1973 due to Muni Metro Subway construction.

Although the return of rails to Upper Market was never controversial by itself, deciding on the eventual terminal loop was. Many people wanted the F-Line to replicate the turning loop of the then-in-existence 8-Market trolley bus, via Castro, 18th Street, Collingwood and 19th Street. But this would have entailed running trolleys on narrow, congested streets such as 18th and Collingwood. Others advocated for cars to cross Castro, unload on the far side where the tracks ducked into Twin Peaks Tunnel, and loop south on the short Diamond Street block between 17th Street and Market, and back to Market, with a nearside terminal on the inbound track.

The winning choice was also the simplest and most logical to construct: a terminal at 17th and Castro, with outbound cars swinging over to the inbound (eastbound) track and laying over there. This had been the terminal during the Trolley Festivals. This choice also proved to be a boon to the neighborhood, as it kept trolleys off Market Street and Castro Street as they took their layovers. A sharp curve leading from the terminal brought streetcars back onto Market for their inbound trips. The tracks leading to the Twin Peaks Tunnel were retained, and have been used for occasional emergency and after-hours car movements, but not since 2004.

Many years later, in 2009, the 17th and Castro terminal was turned into an auto-free zone, and tables, chairs and plants have been set up, turning this space into a pedestrian-friendly "piazza." In 2010, permanent fixtures replaced the temporary ones. [See Chapter 10.]

Phase Three also covered the installation of the one-way track south along Noe Street, and new switches at 17th and Noe for cars heading west to the 17th and Castro Terminal, and east for pull-in cars. A right-turn switch from northbound Church Street to eastbound Market was also included in this contract.

Another feature of Phase Three was highly controversial. This was the decision to place Canary Island palm trees in the center median of Upper Market Street. Purists complained that palm trees were better suited to Los Angeles and Southern California than the more temperate climate of San Francisco, and they most certainly had no place on Market Street, San Francisco's main drag. Ignored was the fact that Dolores Street, which begins at Market Street, is lined with Canary Island palms for its entire length, a little over two miles.

The anti-palm tree faction wanted to use some other kind of tree that would stay green all year. But after the trees were planted and their lush vegetation began to fill out, the controversy died down. Canary Island palms have since been planted along Muni Metro Extension (South Embarcadero) and the F-Line's Wharf Extension. The author was one of those who was skeptical of the palm tree scheme at first, but came to appreciate their presence.

To minimize neighborhood disruption caused by construction, one block at a time, and one direction at a time, was under work at any given point for the duration of the Phase 3 project. This procedure was also practiced during the Phase 4 construction, which followed almost a year after Phase 3 was finished.

On May 7, 1994, PCC 1051, painted in the "Muni Simplified" green and cream scheme first used in 1963, tested the Phase Three tracks. Its appearance produced smiles and cheers from passersby and questions about why the F-Line was not yet in service.

Phase Three Construction Progress

Two images of the rebuilding of the 17th Street and Noe trackage, taken in the summer of 1993. (*above*) Workers lay the turnouts. The switch to the left leads to the J-Line for pull-ins; the track to the right will lead to Castro. (*below*) About three weeks later, the area has been completely paved. *Both photos, David Vartanoff*

Reconstructing the 17th and Castro tracks was well under way in summer 1993. The track curving to the right in the upper part of the photo leads to the Twin Peaks Tunnel. *David Vartanoff*

Phase 3 returned tracks to Market Street between Duboce and Castro, absent since 1973.

(*left*) The complex Market and Church intersection, where the F-Market and J-Church lines cross, is being laid out in this August 22, 1993 view looking west. The trackage west of here has already been completed, the palm trees are in place, and the overhead wire configuration, which includes "inside track" trolley coach wires, is up. The turnout on the left will enable F cars to join the line if they are late pullouts or have done emergency looping via Noe, east on 17th and north on Church. *Peter Ehrlich*

Testing and initial PCC service

Following the arrival of the new PCCs, each one had to undergo a rigorous burn-in test period before Muni would accept them for service. This program continued through 1994. In 1995, Muni introduced the cars to the public by providing a free shuttle service on weekends operating on the outer ends of the J-Church and N-Judah lines.

Two vignettes during the testing phase: (*left*) PCCs 1061 (Pacific Electric) and 1058 (Chicago) head outbound onto the K-Ingleside line at St. Francis Circle on January 22, 1995. (*below*) 1055 (Philadelphia green/cream) and 1053 (Brooklyn) sit at the 11th Street Wye as 1061 (Pacific Electric) sneaks in behind them. May 1, 1994. *Both photos, Peter Ehrlich*

Three scenes from the free pre-F-Line weekend demonstration service in 1995: (*left*) Both Muni green and cream PCCs loop at Ocean Beach on Aug. 22. (*below left*) 1062 (Louisville) speeds through the J-Line Bernal Cut private right-of-way under the Highland Avenue Bridge on April 23. (*below*) The Sunset District is often known as the "Fog Belt" because its summertime fog lingers when other parts of San Francisco get to bask in sunshine. The towers of the St. Anne's of The Sunset Church are barely visible behind outbound PCC 1057 (Cincinnati) at Judah/16th Avenue. August 20, 1995. *All photos, Peter Ehrlich*

Two scenes of the track rebuilding at Geneva Yard. (*left*) A crane sets up the north ladder tracks on August 5, 1994. (*right*) Some of the new F-Line PCCs are visible in this July 26, 1994 shot, along with Oporto 189, Line Car 0304 and the remains of a derelict LRV. *Both photos, Peter Ehrlich*

PCCs arrive; Rewiring Geneva Yard

WHILE ALL THE TRACKWORK was laid or renewed, other necessary infrastructure work had to be done to get ready for opening the F-Line. One of the other projects was a complete rewiring of Geneva Yard so that the new ex-Philadelphia PCCs, which were beginning to arrive, as well as the LRVs used for Muni Metro, could be stored at Geneva Yard. The overhead had to be made both trolley pole and pantograph compatible. In addition, some of the tracks had to be reconfigured.

The 14 PCCs, all ex-Philadelphia and remanufactured by Morrison-Knudsen of Hornell, NY, were delivered starting on September 3. 1993 with delivery of car 1055, painted in Philadelphia green and cream, with the last ones arriving on January 19, 1994. The option "Torpedoes" on this contract, which went to Hornell on the same day, were returned to Muni in 1995. [See Chapter 8 for a more thorough description of the PCCs remanufactured by Morrison-Knudsen.]

Each PCC underwent rigorous acceptance testing and burn-in, operating over all extant Muni lines (except, of course, for the F, which wasn't ready). The first three PCCs to be accepted—1055 (Philadelphia green/cream), 1060 (Newark) and 1062 (Louisville)—were displayed at Mint Yard on New Year's Day 1994, after which they all ran to Transbay Terminal, back out Market and then out the N-Judah line, which was doable because Phase Four construction, between 11th Street and Duboce, had not yet begun.

After all of the ex-Philadelphia PCCs had been accepted, Muni began operating a free service on the outer ends of the N and J lines in April 1995. Seven cars, running together in groups of two or three, operated on most weekends through August 1995. This was a way of introducing the new cars to San Franciscans, and the service was well-received and well-liked by the public.

Phase Four–Bureaucratic Frustration Replaced by Speedy Construction

PHASE FOUR, THE CONTRACT to replace the "temporary" and seriously deteriorated trackage between Duboce and 11th Street, including rebuilding the 11th Street Wye, proved to be an exercise in bureaucratic frustration. It was planned to award the contract for Phase Four reconstruction, a relatively simple, straightforward project, in early 1993. But the award was delayed three times. In one instance, the unsuccessful bidder filed a protest. Another time, just hours before the contract was to be executed, the City Attorney blocked implementation because he objected to the contract's language. On the fourth try, contractor Stacy & Witbeck was given the "Notice to Proceed" in November 1994. Again, the contract price was well under estimates–$9.2 million.

Stacy & Witbeck worked feverishly to meet a September 1 deadline for F-Line startup imposed by Mayor Frank Jordan, an enthusiastic F-Line backer. In early August, the reconstructed 11th Street wye trackwork, the contract's most complex, work, was set down and the intersection paved in just days, with minimal disruption to bus service.

Testing of Phase Four track began in July 1995, and starting on August 24, 1995, F-Line cars began simulated service runs according to schedule assignments and as part of the training of F-Line operators. This also allowed for operators of Market Street buses and motorists to become acclimated to the presence of the new streetcars.

Phase Four Track Reconstruction Scenes

Phase 4 replaced the temporary and badly-deteriorated trackage between Van Ness and Duboce.
Rebuilding of the 11th Street wye was included in the contract.

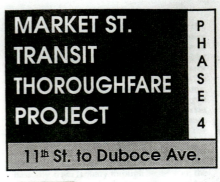

(above) This photo looks east from McCoppin Street. The inbound rails are being laid, but work has yet to be done on the outbound side. February 13, 1995. (below) Crews reconstruct the Market and Duboce intersection. A direct connection to Duboce Junction, where the J-Church and N-Judah lines emerge from the subway, and to Mint Yard, was maintained. The subgrade for the planter boxes, which will hold the palm trees, is also under construction. April 3, 1995. Both photos, Don Jewell

A four-page brochure detailing the scope and impacts of the Phase 4 F-Line track construction project was printed up by Muni and given out to hundreds of transit riders, shopkeepers and other businesses in the affected area of the construction. (The other pages of this flier follow on subsequent pages.) *John Katz collection/SFMTA*

(*right*) During the summer of 1995, 11th Street was closed to traffic to allow for a staging area for the complex trackwork necessary to replace the 11th Street Wye. This shot was taken on July 14, 1995, and one of the wye curves has already been fabricated. *Peter Ehrlich*

Even though the track was ready for Opening Day, September 1, 1995, there was still much to be done. Temporary wooden guard rails were fitted to the concrete handicapped ramps until permanent metal railings could be installed. And much of the landscaping, brickwork and other masonry finish was still incomplete.

The presence of the new, colorful PCCs on Market, as before, drew widespread acclaim and eager anticipation of great things to come. A new and exciting chapter in San Francisco rail transport was about to begin!

Just days before the F-Line opened, Muni operators ran the new PCCs on the line to get accustomed to its operating characteristics. Here at Market and Duboce, PCC 1052 (Los Angeles) is about to pass a sign stating that federal funds were used to build the line. The palm trees had just been installed. August 26, 1995. *Peter Ehrlich*

(*below*) An F-Line stop marker and a billboard announcing the opening of the F-Line. (*right*) 1053, representing Brooklyn, the first U. S. city to operate a fleet of PCCs, poses at 5th Street, with the Flood Building above. Although this scene dates from 2011, it could have just as easily been 1995, when the F-Line opened. *Both photos, Peter Ehrlich*

79

Duboce to Van Ness - Engineering Drawings

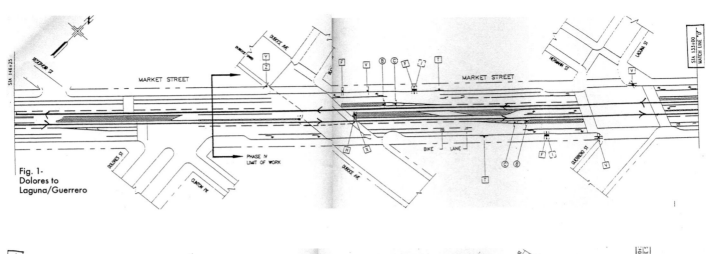

Fig. 1 - Dolores to Laguna/Guerrero

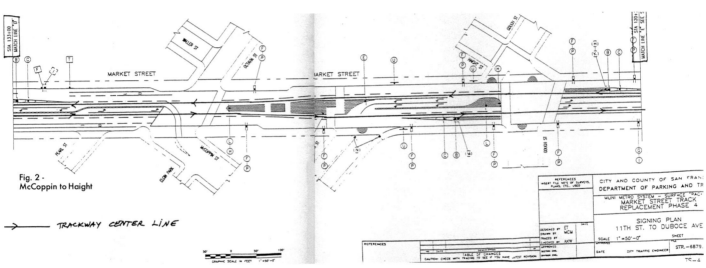

Fig. 2 - McCoppin to Haight

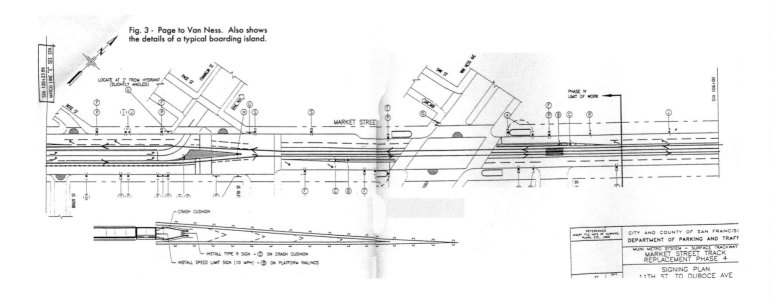

Fig. 3 - Page to Van Ness. Also shows the details of a typical boarding island.

Phase 4 Engineering Drawings and Flier

(*facing page, top to bottom*) The engineering drawings for Phase 4. Figure 1: Dolores to Laguna/Guerrero (although the sketch shows trackage to Dolores, which had been completed under Phase 3). Figure 2: McCoppin to Valencia/Haight Streets. Not shown: the Central Freeway, which had been damaged by the 1989 Loma Prieta Earthquake but was still standing in the early 1990s; it was removed in stages between 1997 and 2003. Figure 3: Page Street to Van Ness Avenue. A typical approach to a boarding island, showing crash baffles and other protective fixtures, is also depicted. SFMTA

(*this page*) Other pages of the Phase 4 Flier distributed to businesses, shopkeepers and transit riders affected by Phase 4 construction. Page 2, *right*; Page 3, *below*; Page 4, *below right*. John Katz collection/SFMTA

PROJECT PURPOSE

For nine months, from early January to early October 1995, construction will take place for the **Market Street Transit Thoroughfare Project, Phase 4**. Encompassing the mid-section of Market Street from 11th Street to Duboce Avenue, this final phase of the project is the missing link whose construction will allow the S.F. Municipal Railway (Muni) to begin service on its colorful F-MARKET historic streetcar line.

Improved traffic flow and beautification of middle Market Street is also part of the project's scope. Additionally, parts of lower Market Street will see minor construction, for the installation of new overhead wire (from 8th to 11th Streets) and new wheelchair-accessible boarding islands (see map inside for locations).

At the end of construction in October, service on the brand-new F-MARKET line, Muni's first new streetcar line in 67 years, will begin from Market & Castro Streets to the Transbay Terminal, replacing the 8-MARKET trolley bus line. (There has been limited historic streetcar service since the 1980s on lower and middle Market Streets, during summer festivals, special events, and some holidays.) F-line streetcars will run approximately every 10 minutes, from about 6:30 am to 12:30 am, seven days a week.

The F line is also in the process of being extended to run along The Embarcadero from Market Street to Fisherman's Wharf, as part of the city's Waterfront Transportation Projects. In the late 1990s, when these projects are scheduled for completion, service on the full F MARKET & WHARVES can begin, directly connecting upper and middle Market neighborhoods with the downtown core and the northeastern waterfront all the way to Fisherman's Wharf. The historic F line will serve as an important transit link for the busy Market and Embarcadero thoroughfares, and will be an attractive rail alternative to the crowded cable car and underground Muni Metro systems.

The F line will operate with 17 rehabilitated vintage PCC (Presidents' Conference Committee) streetcars designed in the 1930s—considered among the sturdiest and most reliable transit vehicles ever made, and the same type of car that ran in S.F. from the 1940s to the early 1980s—as well as other vintage cars in Muni's collection, including cars from Italy, Japan, and Russia. The PCCs are painted in colors representing U.S. transit systems that used to run PCCs, such as Boston (orange, cream, silver, red), Cincinnati (yellow, gray, green), and S.F. (green, cream). The colorful old rail vehicles will be both a visual delight and a practical transit option for traversing key corridors of the city.

PROJECT DESCRIPTION

Phase 4 construction will include:
- replacement of existing deteriorated streetcar tracks with new tracks
- partial street reconstruction, including new

Car 130 of the vintage F-MARKET fleet

paving, modest sidewalk reshaping (for safe traffic lane and boarding island widths), and some utility relocation
- modification of traffic controls, such as the addition of turn lanes and the addition of a traffic signal at Valencia Street (for improved traffic flow)
- installation of medians, some landscaped with Canary Island palm trees (palm trees as far east as Valencia Street, and medians as far east as 12th Street)
- consolidation of streetcar and trolley bus overhead wire in a center alignment (as far east as 8th Street)
- installation of boarding islands that are wheelchair-accessible, as mandated by the Americans with Disabilities Act (ADA) (see map—as far east as Transbay Terminal)

A total of 13 palm trees will be planted as part of Phase 4, in locations allowed by the complex streetscape (see map). Plaques containing poetry will be embedded in the 11th-to-Duboce accessible boarding islands through the efforts of the S.F. Art Commission.

CONSTRUCTION IMPACTS

During construction, at least one lane of **traffic** in each direction on Market Street will always be maintained. During weekday morning and evening rush hours, two traffic lanes in the direction of rush-hour traffic will be kept open. Detours of auto traffic are not anticipated; temporary turning restrictions may be necessary at times, and signs will be posted. Access to **deliveries and driveways** will be maintained; please call Henry St. Stevan (552-1976) to alert him to any special needs. **Parking** usually will be restricted on the blocks on which the contractor is currently working. **Work hours** will generally be on weekdays from 7:00 am to 4:00 pm, though some **weekend and night work** (8:00 pm to 6:00 am) will be necessary to perform track and overhead wire construction at complicated intersections. Major track **construction is set to begin** near the western end of the project, on Market between Duboce Avenue and Guerrero Street, and in general work east block by block. The other work (overhead wire, street surfacing, traffic control, median, and boarding island work) will follow as soon as possible. Basically, from January through September, the main Phase 4 project area will be under intensive construction, with only some respites for each block. Diesel buses will have to be substituted for electric trolley buses on **Muni lines 6, 8, 21, 47, and 49** during some periods of construction, particularly for intersection work. Also, some lines may be temporarily rerouted or have some of their stops temporarily discontinued in the project area; signs will be posted.

QUESTIONS

Muni's Capital Engineering Department is managing this project. Questions or comments may be directed to Muni staff:
· Don Chee, Project Manager, 554-1823
· John Katz, Project Planner, 923-6149
· Hannah Silverman, Community Affairs, 923-6160, or 949 Presidio, Rm 238, SF, CA 94115
· Henry St. Stevan, Construction Inspector, 552-1976

Continued on back panel

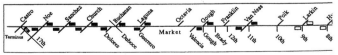

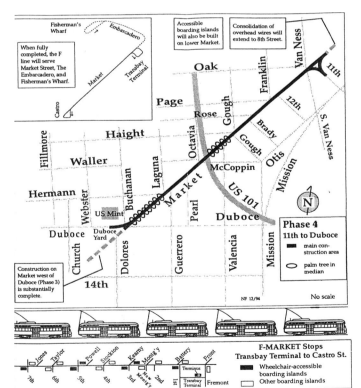

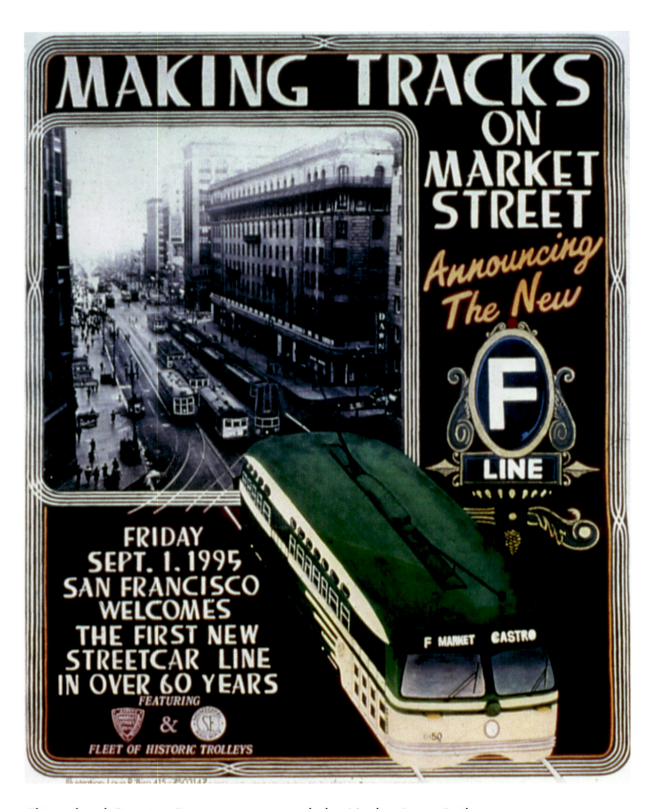

This stylized Opening Day poster was made by *Market Street Railway* to commemorate the beginning of San Francisco's new F-Market historic streetcar service. *Market Street Railway*

Chapter 5 -
The F-Line Opens!

"The day that we made the F-Line a reality...was an exciting and momentous day for Metro and the Municipal Railway...The cars pulled out of the yard and were put on display on Market Street. The media, rail buffs and San Franciscans lined up along the route [and] took pictures of the parade of vintage cars...The small group of dedicated operators who were trained and then assisted in the training of [other] operators for the vintage cars deserve a lot of the credit. A job well done by these operators and I take my hat off to them...I would also like to commend the Training Department, the dispatchers, inspectors and Muni Maintenance...for making these cars ready to roll on Opening Day."
-— Sam Garcia, Green Light Rail Division Manager on Opening Day, Sept. 1, 1995

A Glorious Sight!

THE DREAMS OF MANY SAN FRANCISCANS– transit workers, politicians, railfans and the general public–came true on September 1, 1995, when motorman Walt Thomsen gave two toots on the whistle of the former Blackpool, England Boat Tram, notched up the controller and led a 20-trolley parade from Market and Second Streets. The procession of trolleys marked the opening of San Francisco Municipal Railway's fabulous new F-Market historic streetcar line, and the return of surface rail transit to San Francisco's premier thoroughfare.

Following the Boat Tram was PCC No. 1050, sparkling in its 1952-vintage green-and-cream "Muni Wings" paint, the first of 14 newly-remanufactured ex-Philadelphia PCCs that would provide everyday service on the new route.

The parade lineup consisted of 12 of the 14 new ex-Philadelphia PCCs and just about every available vintage trolley and work car on Muni's roster. Trailing 1050 was Boston 1059, followed by a vintage car, then one or two more PCCs arranged in order by cars representing East Coast companies and agencies to those of Western systems which had used PCCs, interspersed with another vintage car. Two PCCs in Muni green and cream–1051, a new F-Line car, and 1040, the last PCC built in the United States, brought up the rear.

To accommodate the parade, Market Street, between First Street and Montgomery, was closed to all traffic. A "reviewing stand" was erected on 2nd Street just off Market, where Mayor Frank Jordan, Sam Francisco Public Transportation Commission (SFPTC) General Manager Phil Adams and other Muni and Market Street Railway dignitaries made their speeches and then boarded the trolleys for the first outbound trip.

As the colorful Art Deco streetcars rolled up Market, with many returning downtown to usher in regular service, bystanders and residents gushed "Beautiful!", "Fantastic!", and other accolades. Herb Caen, in his column a few days later, wrote, "The vintage streetcars now running up and down Market Street are a glorious sight." In just days, the F-Line quickly became part of the fabric of the city, with residents and Muni riders taking the cars into their hearts like new additions to the family.

The Market Street stretch of the F-Line was the first phase of an all-surface streetcar line that was eventually extended northward along The Embarcadero to Fisherman's Wharf. The 3½-mile, $55 million starter historic streetcar line was San Francisco's first new trolley route in 63 years.

That this line made it into operation, 13 years after the supposed end of Market Street trolley service is nothing short of a miracle–one performed by a dedicated group of trolley supporters working with Muni management and local, state and Federal officials.

Settling Down

AFTER THE PARADE, most of the vintage cars, and some of the PCCs, pulled in. Basic weekday service was identical to the 8-Market trolley coach service the F-Line replaced. Weekday headways were every 15 minutes; rush hours, 9 minutes; nights, 20 minutes. On Saturdays, 12-minute service was provided, while on Sundays, a car would come every 15 minutes. As a hedge, Muni continued running the 8-Market trolley bus line through January 1996.

The lineup for F-Line Opening Day on September 1, 1995 stretched from Market and 2nd Street to east of Sansome. It was a glorious day for San Franciscans, as streetcars returned to its premier street permanently. *Peter Ehrlich*

(The trolley coaches on the 8-line had replaced the old Market Street Railway streetcar route of the same number in July 1949.)

In reality, Muni management, without an inkling of how popular the F-Line would become, was rather conservative in setting the schedule for the colorful new cars, and based its schedule on past service levels, with no room for improvement. Soon, every weekday daytime PCC was carrying standing loads between the Castro District and downtown. Passenger boardings were up 43% over the previous trolley bus service.

But the F-Line cars were also a big relief to frustrated Muni Metro riders, who constantly experienced lengthy delays caused by the troublesome Boeing LRV (light rail vehicle) trains serving the subway. Most people seemed to want to continue to commute by subway, a service that opened in 1980. Many Castro District riders, however, simply preferred the genteel rides aboard the comfortable cushion-seated PCCs over the sardine can conditions of Muni Metro. The author worked the morning rush hour for many years and would wait for his departure time at 17th and Castro and watch the string of riders get off connecting buses. The "sheep" would shuffle in line from the bus into the subway station. But the folks opting for the F-Line would run excitedly across the street, smiling and waving all the way, as the friendly PCC beckoned them on board with open doors.

For normal morning rush hour service, nine minutes was a decent enough headway. But when the subway "took a dump," in the words of insiders, suddenly a "mushroom cloud" of people would rise from Castro Street Station and "blow over" to the F car, and the line was quickly overwhelmed.

Going home, there were fewer standing loads than in the morning, despite regular and frequent service. This was because outbound subway service was generally faster, since Muni Metro trains had left the clumsy Embarcadero Station stub-end terminal that was the source of most inbound delays.

Occasionally, there were delays caused by F-Line car breakdowns. When that happened, cries of "Bring Back The 8 Line!" were heard. In general, though, no one really wanted to go back to trolley bus

Although the F-Line had already been in operation for two weeks before this image of PCC 1058 (representing the Chicago Transit Authority) was snapped, there was still much work to be done, such as replacing the wooden handicapped ramp railings with permanent metal fixtures. The masonry at this boarding island at Market and 3rd Street was also unfinished. September 14, 1995. *Peter Ehrlich*

This view of Market Street looking toward the Ferry Building was taken from the lower deck of the now-demolished Central Freeway, nine days after the F-Line opened. Inbound car 1054 (Philadelphia "Cream Cheese" silver/blue/cream) is approaching Franklin Street while 1061 (Pacific Electric) is stopped at Van Ness. The way this shot was taken was amusing and clever. There were small pockets on the right side of the lower roadway where a motorist could move a disabled vehicle out of the way of the usually bumper-to-bumper traffic. I used one of those, propped up the hood, frowned and wrung my hands in despair. When the two PCCs appeared, I snapped my picture, let down the hood and worked my way back into traffic. *Peter Ehrlich*

service, when a ride on the rails was smoother and much more pleasant.

Even though the F-Line opened on September 1, 1995, much infrastructure work remained to be completed. For example, temporary wooden guard rails were mounted on the handicapped ramps on lower Market Street at places such as 3rd, 8th Streets and Van Ness Avenue. Several granite curbs had not yet been put in place, and the bricklaying at some islands hadn't been completed. Nor had route information signs and stanchions been installed. Some minor adjustments to the track and the overhead wire needed to be made as well. But for all intents and purposes, the F-Line was becoming accepted as part of the public transit system.

More Exotic Cars

THE 1990 AMERICANS WITH DISABILITIES ACT dictated that the new F-Line PCCs were required to be available to wheelchair users. Each car carried a folding aluminum platform, which the operator could deploy at handicapped ramps for wheelchair users. They were carried in a cabinet behind the operator's seat. The operator would spot the front door at the ramp, get the platform out, open the doors, load or unload the patron needing assistance, and once that was done, pull up to the regular platform to complete boarding. The procedure would, in most cases, take less than a minute. Each PCC had two tip-up seating positions near the front of the car for wheelchair users.

Ramps were built at every F-Line stop from Van Ness west, and at "Key Stops" elsewhere on Market—the already-existing portion of the line. [See Chapter 7.] At one outbound and three inbound stops, space considerations forced installation of more cumbersome, trouble-prone and time-consuming mechanical lifts.

Technically, being a new line, every vehicle was required to be accessible. Occasionally, however, one of the non-accessible streetcars pulled out in tripper (rush-hour-only) service. Among them were Trolley Festival PCC veterans 1704 (St. Louis) and "Baby Ten" 1040. To one F-Line regular, 1040 earned the sobriquet "The Limo," because of its smoother acceleration, better ride and double seats throughout. (The ex-Philly PCCs tended to have difficult-to-control low-speed acceleration.)

In mid-September, another Trolley Festival star, and the first non-PCC to see service—Milan "Peter Witt" 1834—made it out for tripper service. But this car was different. It had a portable ramp, so it could carry wheelchair users. 1834's appearance on the streets introduced a refreshing new color to the fleet—orange. One Sunday, the four cars on the line were three green and cream PCCs and the Milan car, and its operator wisecracked, "Well, I had to break up the all-green monotony on the line today!"

For the first time in San Francisco since 1951, two streetcar lines crossed each other when the F-Line opened for service. This is Market and Church, where the F-Market crosses the J-Church. A Boeing LRV heads inbound as Milan "Peter Witt" 1834, PCC 1050 and an 8-Market trolley coach await their signal. October 17, 1995. *Peter Ehrlich*

This fisheye view looking out the front windows of Milan 1834 captures PCC 1057 (Cincinnati) heading inbound at Market and 11th Street on October 18, 1995. The quaint Italian phrase inscribed on the top corner window, *"Non Parlate Al Guidatore E Che Non Deve Essere Distratto Dalla Manovra"* loosely translates to the standard Muni admonition on every streetcar and bus: "Information Gladly Given But Safety Requires Avoiding Unnecessary Conversation." *Peter Ehrlich*

Service Expansion, of Sorts

OSTENSIBLY, HAVING 14 PCCs on the property, with a need to assign nine cars for weekday service, gave the Muni Trolley Maintenance staff a good-sized "float" for inspections, running repairs and preventive maintenance. A service change affecting the subway about a month after F-Line startup made this more of a challenge than expected.

In October 1995, the Muni Metro Subway needed to be shut down in late evening for nearly three years for installation of a new communications-based automatic train control system, called ATCS, for a new fleet of LRVs which would be entering service starting in 1996. When implemented, ATCS would permit automatic operation of trains in the subway. After 10:00 p.m, buses replaced trains on four of the five lines. But a new wrinkle kept one line all-rail: On the J-Church line, PCCs covered the late evening service! Since F-Line cars used the J-Line to pull out and pull in, this was

One of the late-night PCCs assigned to the J-Church line to finish off service in the evening because of the subway shutdown due to new signaling installation stops at Fremont and Market on February 5, 1997. Buses worked the four other Muni Metro lines affected by the subway closure. This state of affairs lasted until mid-1998, but provided 10-minute rail service headways at night on Market Street for the duration. *Peter Ehrlich*

really a no-brainer. Inbound J PCCs operated to Church and Market and turned right. Outbound cars assigned to the J went to 17th and Noe, turned left instead of right, and went back to Church Street. This was also the pull-in route for F cars.

This setup meant that eight cars were required for service after 10:00 p.m.–three for the regular F, and five more for J-Line runs. This put extra demand on the shop to make sure that there would be enough PCCs available to handle night service, as well as the routine maintenance functions, especially preventive maintenance, and preparation for the next morning's rush hour. The schedules called for 10-minute frequencies from Transbay Terminal to 17th and Noe and inbound from Market and Church, with alternating F and J cars. The special night service continued until August 1998, when major changes to Muni Metro operations were implemented following completion of the ATCS project.

A small improvement on Sundays, matching it to Saturday service, occurred in mid-1997. But weekday service didn't improve until September 1998, and it took a major service disaster to bring this about (described later in this chapter).

Torpedoes and Vintage Cars

IN DECEMBER 1995, A NEW PCC joined the F-Line fleet. But this car was an original San Francisco PCC, not an ex-Philadelphia rebuild. This was car 1007, one of ten double-end "Torpedoes," or D-Types, built for Muni in 1948, and the first of three from this class remanufactured by Morrison-Knudsen under a contract option. The "Torpedoes" were 108" wide and 50'-5" long, had doors in the front and rear, befitting their double-end configu-ration, and could carry about 20% more passengers than the Philly cars. These cars were also smoother riding and their acceleration was easier to control than the other PCCs, owing to their St. Louis B-3 trucks and General Electric motors and controls.

In their heyday, they were considered "Cadillacs" by some operators.

1007 arrived in a very unusual paint scheme–the same silver, dark gray and red carried by the brand new Breda LRVs, which quickly got dubbed the "Stealth" livery, because of its tendency to become

Two of the three Muni "Torpedoes" rehabbed by Morrison-Knudsen in 1995 pass at Market and Laguna Streets on February 13, 1996, shortly after they returned to Muni. In the background, the eyesore Central Freeway double-deck structure, which was weakened but not closed by the 1989 Loma Prieta earthquake, was torn down in two stages. Its complete removal in 2003 allowed for the return of the spectacular view down Market Street for the first time in 45 years [see Chapter 13]. *Peter Ehrlich*

The F-Line in Its Early Days

(clockwise from top left) Just days after the F-Line opened, PCCs 1054 (Philadelphia 1938 silver) and 1062 (Louisville) pass at Market, Noe and 16th Streets. Mission Dolores is off to the right. The Kansas City car turns at Noe and 17th Street to head to Castro. The track on the right (which turns left) is used for pull-in cars, and the one in the foreground is used by pullout cars. September 3, 1995. PCC 1052, modeling the attractive 2-tone yellow of the Los Angeles Railway of 1937, passes under the despised Central Freeway. Despite this blight on the horizon, the Ferry Building is visible in the distance. December 25, 1995. 1057 (Cincinnati) plays peek-a-boo among the Canary Island palm trees on upper Market. Also Dec. 25, 1995. Milan 1834 and PCC 1057 meet at Market and 2nd Street on Christmas Day 1995. The use of the Milano as one of the four streetcars assigned to Sunday and holiday service was a Yuletide treat for F-Line riders. All photos, Peter Ehrlich

The F-Line quickly blended into the fabric of San Francisco's public transit picture. The introduction of the colorful streetcars resulted in a 43% ridership increase over the old 8-Market trolley coach service, which the F-Line replaced.

(*above*) This October 14, 1995, image, taken with a fisheye lens, shows the lively Castro neighborhood as well as the F-Line terminal on 17th Street. The landmark Castro Theater anchors the neighborhood. The tracks in the foreground lead to the Twin Peaks Tunnel. In 2009, the terminal area was converted into a "pedestrian-only" zone. (*below*) The Rainbow Flag flies over the entrance to the Muni Metro Station at Castro, and is a symbol of gay pride. A PCC has just turned onto Market Street after leaving 17th and Castro Terminal. Wisps of San Francisco's trademark fog still hover over Twin Peaks in this late morning view on May 31, 2005. *Both photos, Peter Ehrlich*

nearly invisible on typical San Francisco foggy days. The second "Torpedo," 1015, had a more prosaic livery–the green and cream of Illinois Terminal Railroad, an interurban railroad that operated throughout the state of Illinois, and which used identical PCCs on a suburban line from St. Louis to Granite City, Ill. The third car was 1010, dressed in Muni's 1939 World's Fair colors of blue and gold, a livery also represented by vintage car 130.

The addition of the three "Torpedoes" to the active fleet helped to ease the pressure on maintenance staff to field enough cars to maintain service requirements exacerbated by the need to assign extra J-Church cars at night.

Following the introduction into regular service of Milan "Peter Witt" 1834, one of the vintage cars, there was much desire among MSR members and directors, some operators, and fans, to get other historic streetcars, including such jewels as A-Type 1 and B-Type 130, out on the street and in F-Line service. These efforts were stymied by the realization that precious few operators were qualified on vintage equipment. Muni management was perceived by some people as being more intent on making Muni Metro run more efficiently, pouring more resources into its operation, rather than dealing with a popular upstart route. In fact, some people regarded Muni's attitude as one of treating the F-Line as a stepchild. There were plenty of F-Line operators, though, who were interested in getting trained, but there were no resources available to train them.

Nevertheless, a few operators, working with Division Manager Sam Garcia–an enthusiastic backer of the F-Line since opening day–came up with a spring 1996 scheme to use some extra board operators as conductors for rush hour trippers with vintage cars. For a few weeks, exotic cars like Blackpool "Boat" 228, Melbourne 496 and the two Muni original "Iron Monsters" delighted regular riders.

On an unseasonably warm February 14–St. Valentine's Day–in 1996, the temperature hit 80°, and the author, with the blessing of Division Manager Garcia, found a conductor and pulled the Blackpool "Boat" tram out. With MSR director Rick Laubscher on board, a bystander on Fremont Street, puzzled by the presence of this unusual tram, asked, "Why is this car running?" Without missing a beat, I said, "It's the Love Boat!"

Later, in 1997 and 1998, there were interested operators available to work as conductors. Management would allow them to forego the second half of their Muni Metro run to allow a two-man car to go out on the F-Line. Even one inspector pinch-hit as a conductor!

The most frequently used vintage car, of course, was one-man-operated "Milano" 1834. It even made some nighttime runs.

On July 22, 1998, "Iron Monster" 130 made a trip on the last run at night. This occasion marked both the birthday and the retirement of veteran Trolley Festival motorman Tom Biagi, a 30-year Muni operator who personally took Number 130 under his wing and lovingly cared for it, even after the end of the Trolley Festivals. His regular assignment was as a "burn-in" motorman for the new Breda LRVs, but on his final day of work for Muni, he asked for, and got detailed to, Run 162, the last nighttime F-Line run. He pulled his PCC in to Geneva Yard and pulled out 130 for the last trip, using a volunteer conductor.

Politics, The Castro and The City

ALTHOUGH NEARLY EVERYBODY loved the F-Line, there were always detractors, as in other aspects of city life. One of them lived on 17th Street right by the Castro Terminal. This misanthrope allegedly threw eggs and tomatoes at the cars while they were laying over. But in 1997, he got the city Board of Supervisors involved in how and where F-Line cars made their terminal layovers.

In the beginning, the line had 10-12 minute layovers at both the Transbay Terminal and 17th and Castro, which is standard operating practice on transit lines everywhere in the country. By getting elected City government officials to interfere with operations, this individual managed to force Castro layovers to just 1-2 minutes, with excessively long layovers at Transbay Terminal. This unfortunate situation resulted in general line management problems such as those caused by outbound traffic delays. Frequent bunching of cars and irregular service became routine. Thankfully, when the Fisherman's Wharf Extension opened a few years later, cooler heads won out over NIMBYism and normal terminal breaks were once again the rule. ("NIMBY" is the acronym for "Not In My Back Yard," where residents of an affected area try to block planning for and building new rail lines, new roads and other public works projects and improvements everywhere.)

The F-Line was also much involved in the 1995 mayoral race, between incumbent Frank Jordan, on whose watch the F-Line was launched, and challenger Willie L. Brown, Jr., whose campaign literature featured an F-Line PCC at Castro Street. Brown, who was a very shrewd politician and was California's assembly speaker for many years, clearly knew how to pick a winner. It helped lead him to victory in the election.

But was the F-Line becoming too popular? In the minds of some Castro District leaders, yes. The F-Line was bringing in new hordes of "straights, out-of-towners, gawkers and other troublemakers" into "their" private enclave, which happened to be the largest gay/lesbian community in the United States. Others, however, especially the Castro District Merchants Association and other business leaders, welcomed the increased business brought in by the colorful F-Line trolleys. One 20-year business owner's quote, in an article in the *San Francisco Examiner*, stated simply that "the F-Line is the best thing to ever happen to this community."

Citizens Keep the Cars Clean

ONE OF THE REASONS the F-Line won over the hearts of Muni riders was due to the general cleanliness of the cars. This can be attributed to Market Street Railway's all-volunteer program of sweeping the cars at the 17th and Castro Terminal.

Led by the late MSR director Art Michel, every day, a volunteer would ride out from Mint Yard to 17th and Castro and sweep the cars out from end to end during the operator's layover. Newspapers and litter would be removed. Gum deposits on the floor would be scraped off. Even the windshields would be cleaned. And the volunteers always brought a supply of soda and bottled water for the operators. This volunteer effort was much appreciated by the riders, and some were recruited into the program this way. The operators, of course, were very supportive. Most of them would make their own efforts at terminals to rid cars of trash. The F-Line cars, arguably, were the cleanest fleet of Muni vehicles in the city.

Of course, every car was cleaned at night in the yards by regular Muni car cleaners. But when MSR director Dave Pharr was the "boss" of Mint Yard, he would regularly schedule thorough car-washing by having extra cars brought in by maintainers on Saturdays. He and other yard volunteers would scrub the car from head to toe, steam-clean the floor, and have the car ready for a "cutout" and give it to an operator at Market and Duboce. The passengers would be transferred, the riders would continue to the Castro in a fresh car, and the second car would be pulled into the yard for its treatment. Sadly, this practice has stopped since Pharr's untimely death in 2003.

More Frequent Weekday Service Finally Added

THE 15-MINUTE WEEKDAY daytime levels were a sore point for those who wanted improved service to match demand from riders. In 1998, an acute operator shortage affected the F-Line and Muni Metro alike and had a further impact on weekday service. Part of this was due to a no-overtime policy, but there simply weren't enough operators to cover all runs, and use of RDO (regular day off) operators would have only been a drop in the bucket anyway. One problem was that run pay for F-Line runs lacked a feature known as "rail hazard pay" or "LRV pay" [see Chapter 9], which was 32 minutes added to the run paid at time-and-a-half, a benefit built into the contract with the Transport Workers Union, Local 250-A, since the subway opened in 1980. This resulted in low-seniority operators assigned to F-Line runs, and some of these folks did not have the interest or the passion for vintage equipment. Coupled with the heavier traffic and harder work associated with F-Line operations, it was commonplace for operators to "hit the sick list." Others were reassigned from time to time by management to Automatic Train Control System (ATCS) testing, further exacerbating the situation.

Weekday service finally increased in September 1998. But it was because of the most disastrous service event ever to befall a public transit agency in U. S. history: the infamous Muni Metro Meltdown.

On August 24, 1998, Muni management made several drastic changes to Muni Metro service. It activated the communication-based ATCS signaling system, installed under a contract which had been awarded to Alcatel Corporation back in 1995; it instituted two-car, one-operator trains on the N-Judah line and extended the line to Caltrain Depot via the Muni Metro Extension along the South Embarcadero; and it started turning trains back in the Muni Metro Turnback area just east of Embarcadero Station. Additionally, "Proof-of-Payment" was adopted on every light rail line (but not the F-Line). Confusion and pandemonium reigned. Riders accustomed to boarding an inbound train from Montgomery or even Powell to get a seat for the outbound ride were suddenly forced to get off at Embarcadero and reboard outbound service. The resulting overcrowding at Embarcadero Station reached dangerous levels. Sunset-bound N-Line riders, thinking they'd

Art Michel, the leader of *Market Street Railway*'s volunteer car-cleaning program, polishes the front windows of Car 1015 at 17th and Castro. This effort to keep F-Line cars clean is greatly appreciated by riders and operators alike. February 13, 1996. *Peter Ehrlich*

be on their way home, wound up watching the Bay Bridge come into view instead. These were immediate inconveniences to riders.

But the worst aspect of the meltdown was the state of the Muni Metro fleet at the time of the changeover. Although there were 52 Bredas and 59 ATCS-equipped Boeings, about 30 soon-to-be-retired Boeing LRVs were left out of the ATCS upgrade program, and their presence in the subway caused extensive communication failures, causing more delays and inconveniencing riders. The author, assigned an N-Judah run that first fateful day, stated that it took him 17 minutes to travel between Embarcadero Station to Folsom Street Station on the surface, a distance of only a half-mile!

After three days of this mess, Muni top brass made two immediate decisions to try to ease the pain.

One was to retire all unconverted Boeings immediately. This improved subway service a little, but led to overcrowding because there was now a severe shortage of available equipment. The second was to add five "temporary" weekday F-Line runs. Muni was able to accomplish this because there was a surplus of F-Line cars. This created 7½-minute headways at most times in midday, and five-minute rush hour service. This "temporary" additional service ultimately lasted until the last day of operation to the Transbay Terminal, March 3, 2000.

Some observers lay the blame to this fiasco squarely on the engineers who designed and implemented ATCS, and the managers who rushed the system into service. Unlike the carefully phased introduction of Muni Metro service eighteen years earlier, all of these changes occurred simultaneously, with predictably disastrous results.

Gradually, however, the ATCS hiccups became less and less frequent. In February 1999, Muni suddenly announced that the five supplemental F-Line runs would be eliminated because the subway "was now running so well that they weren't needed any more." When word got to the operators, several of them, the author included, banded together to fight this withdrawal. Leaflets were printed up at private expense warning riders of management's plan and urging them to call, write and e-mail the Mayor's Office and the Muni General Manager to overturn this hasty and ill-advised decision. On the first day the fliers were distributed, as if on cue, Muni Metro "took another dump" at Castro Station and frustrated riders boarded waiting F cars—and this time, there were plenty of them!—and soon Mayor Willie Brown, Jr. announced that these "service cuts" weren't going to happen. Everybody said, "Thank God for the F-Line!" A big debt of gratitude and much praise was heaped on the F-Line operators who were there during the riders' time of need. And so the increased weekday service was there to stay.

Valencia Grade and First Street

UNLIKE MOST NEW AMERICAN light rail and streetcar lines and systems that have opened since 1981, the F-Line on Market Street operates as a traditional streetcar line–that is, entirely in city streets, in mixed traffic, with no private right-of-way or grade separation. While that adds to the charm, it also makes it susceptible to traffic congestion and line delays, and increases the potential for accidents.

PCC 1062 is crossing Valencia Street at the bottom of the Valencia Grade. Although this scene was taken in 2007, it shows the alignment inbound F-Line operators have had to contend with since the F-Line opened in 1995, weaving their streetcars from the center of the street to a lane on the right, dodging motorists who are attempting to head to Franklin Street and northward, all the while rolling downgrade. The potential for accidents here is high. A safer solution might have been to create a raised right-of-way on the left, running all the way to Franklin Street. *Peter Ehrlich*

Two F-Line locations that have always been accident-prone are the inbound downgrade between Laguna/Guerrero and Valencia Streets, called the Valencia Grade, and First Street between Market and the Transbay Terminal. When I was an operator, I termed these places "Waterloos," such as where Napoleon "met his Waterloo," the battle that finally defeated him and his army. Both became accident magnets due to the way they were engineered, or, in the case of First Street, re-engineered. In reality, they could–and should–have been designed differently to cut down on the potential for accidents.

Leaving the stop at Guerrero, F-Line cars have to descend about a 6% grade. At the same time, auto traffic comes onto Market northward from Guerrero Street. At Octavia Blvd. (formerly McCoppin Street), traffic heading to Franklin Street conflicts with streetcar movements by having to cross the track, which curves gently right across two traffic lanes and straightens out at Valencia Street, the bottom of the grade. Streetcar motormen have to operate very slowly here, ringing the gong constantly to deter motorists from swerving in front of the streetcar. (If I had a PCC, I'd use the outside PA system to warn motorists to be careful–"Think Safety.") One of the worst things a motorist can do is to suddenly swerve into a streetcar lane and stop. Too often, it ends up as a rear-ender. Now if the dynamic brakes fail on a PCC or the Milan car's brakes are too slack due to

The trackage on 1st Street, between Market and Mission Streets, dated to 1939 and was considerably worn out even during the Trolley Festival years, when this 1985 photograph of Oporto 189 was snapped. Rush hour traffic exacerbated the situation, when lines of stopped automobiles heading to the Bay Bridge would block streetcar traffic. *Peter Ehrlich*

First Street was a completely different story. This trackage dated to 1939, the "Roar Of The Four" era. The tracks were initially used by Market Street Railway "White Front Cars," as a continuation of the "Inside Track." They stayed through the reduction of four tracks to two in the 1940s and into the PCC era and continuing through the Trolley Festivals. Up to this point, the streetcars always had a lane of their own. But sometime between 1987 and 1995, in anticipation of eventual track removal, City traffic engineers re-striped the lanes so that the lane immediately to the right of the tracks got moved leftward, actually encroaching on unimpeded streetcar operation there. Coupled with the worn out rails, which had never been replaced, and thus reduced stopping ability, many sideswipe accidents between cars and streetcars have occurred.

worn out brake shoes, multiple-vehicle collisions can happen, and have happened here.

This was an engineering design flaw. What should have been done was to keep the tracks on the extreme left until past Franklin and then raise them between Valencia and Franklin to keep automobiles off, similar to what had been done on the N-Line in the Inner Sunset, or on The Embarcadero. But F-Line operators have to live with this mistake, and be extra careful. Actually, such a design was considered, and ultimately rejected by City engineers and officials.

Evening rush hour traffic was especially problematic on First Street, with scores of vehicles backed up trying to get on the Bay Bridge, whose entrance was several blocks away. Operators had to use the outside PA system to get motorists to move over in their lane. One evening, the author, operating a PCC, was trying to get people to their buses at Transbay Terminal, and a white Toyota was blocking his path. So I called out on the PA, "Attention, lady in the white Toyota. You're over the line. Please move to the right." Nothing happened. So I raised my voice a little, and repeated the command. Again, nothing. Finally, in the most booming voice I could muster, I shouted, "THIS IS GOD TALKING! LADY IN THE WHITE TOYOTA! YOU'RE OVER THE LINE! MOVE TO THE RIGHT!!!" She moved, and I zipped on by and got my passengers to Transbay amid lots of cheers and applause.

Streetcar Named Desire Arrives

ONE OF THE WAYS the Trolley Festivals kept things interesting was by adding different new trolleys every year. In the same way, the F-Line, by introducing new cars from time to time, and by running the historic streetcars periodically, maintained this tradition.

After a trip from New Orleans to San Francisco, which some likened to a CIA operation due to controversy caused by the car leaving the Crescent City [see Chapter 8], New Orleans 952 arrives in the City By The Bayon September 6, 1998. It debuted with a gala ceremony twelve days later. *Peter Ehrlich*

The most significant addition to the F-Line Fleet during the first years occurred when New Orleans 952, the "Streetcar Named Desire," entered service in September 1998. All through 1997 and early 1998 MSR had been trying to obtain Detroit

Peter Witt 3865, put up for sale by the Henry Ford Museum in Detroit, where it had been since its retirement in 1954. At the museum, it was a static exhibit, but could be made operational again with a minimum of effort and funding. 3865 was a splendid example of a type of American streetcar that was produced between the 1920s and the PCC era, and its acquisition would fit in nicely with MSR's living history concept for historic streetcars in San Francisco. Plus, it was a one-man car.

Hopes were dashed when the Ford Museum directors, while acknowledging and respecting MSR's (and ultimately Muni's) intention to operate the car, voted instead to sell the car to the Illinois Railway Museum in Union, Ill, to keep it in the Midwest.

MSR then turned its attention to New Orleans, where three Perley Thomas streetcars had just been idled due to broad-gauging of the Crescent City's Riverfront Line. Could San Francisco obtain one of these?

Delicate negotiations between transit officials of both cities, and mayors Willie L. Brown, Jr. and Ernest Morial, took place during 1998, and in August, it was announced that car 952 would arrive in time to kick off a new San Francisco Opera production of the Tennessee Williams play, *A Streetcar Named Desire*.

952 was introduced to San Francisco with a decorative ceremony at 17th and Castro on September 18, 1998. For a day, San Franciscans celebrated the new historical addition to the city's unique and colorful trolley fleet and forgot about the Muni Metro Meltdown that had occurred nearly a month earlier.

A special operator was picked to make the inaugural run of New Orleans 952. He was Joe Certain, a native of New Orleans whose career as a motorman began on the St. Charles line. He later moved to San Francisco and became a Muni trolley operator, participating in several of the Trolley Festivals. Another New Orleans native and Trolley Festival veteran, Lee Butler, Jr., acted as conductor.

The following day, a Saturday, 952 was assigned to a regular run by special request, and performed ably. Two other Trolley Festival veterans, Ed Fine and the author, were the motormen.

The desire to bring another historic streetcar to town had now been fulfilled. But it was the last new car to be introduced into service during the first five years of the F-Line.

On the "Streetcar Named Desire"'s first day of San Francisco service, 952 passes PCC 1058 at Market and Grant. Sept. 18, 1998. *Peter Ehrlich*

Last Run to Transbay Terminal

THE OLDEST AND THE MOST DECREPIT track in San Francisco in regular use was the loop to the Transbay Terminal via First and Fremont Streets. It had been in daily use since January 14, 1939, by Market Street Railway Co. and Muni cars of all kinds. It was originally a double-track loop to match the four tracks on Market Street. As rail service dwindled in the 1940s, the outside track (the one in the center of the street, used by Muni cars) was removed. The terminal ramp, across Mission Street, featured three tracks, with the one closest to the building entrance used by Muni, the one furthest away by Market Street Railway Co., and the center track by both. Track 3–the Muni-only track–was removed some time in the 1940s, but the other two remained in use, with the erstwhile center track available for emergencies. It stayed this way until the east switch on Fremont was removed, making the center track a stub-end breakdown track only.

Upstairs, trains of the Key System, Sacramento Northern and the Southern Pacific-owned Interurban Electric Railway whisked passengers across the lower deck of the San Francisco-Oakland Bay Bridge to all East Bay cities. Sacramento Northern commuter and interurban trains brought riders to the growing suburbs east of the Oakland Hills and as far away as Sacramento, Marysville and Chico.

Unfortunately, both SP/IER and Sacramento Northern folded their passenger operations before the outbreak of World War II, leaving Key System to soldier on until April 21, 1958.

When the bridge opened, autos traveling in both directions used the top deck, and commercial vehicles shared the lower deck with the trains. After

Transbay Terminal F-Line Memories

(*right*) PCC 1053, representing Brooklyn, NY, the first American city with a PCC fleet, lays over on the Transbay Terminal ramp on September 16, 1995, two weeks after the F-Line opened. Streetcars called here from 1939 to 1982 and during the Trolley Festival era, and occasionally in the early 1990s while the F-Line was being built. *Peter Ehrlich*

(*below*) The Art Moderne-style Transbay Terminal (as spelled out on F-Line PCC rollsigns) was also known as the East Bay Terminal, but its official name was the Transbay Transit Terminal. AC Transit, Golden Gate Transit and Greyhound buses loaded inside the Terminal where, from 1939 to 1958, electric interurban trains called. In this image from Mission Street, PCC 1054 lays over in 1998. (*right*) Although F-Line cars ended regular service to the Transbay Terminal starting on March 4, 2000, the loop was occasionally used for emergency switchbacks. The last day of such use was August 8, 2000. Milano 1834 lays over for the last time on that day. The loop trackage was pulled up later that month, and in late 2010, the Transbay Terminal itself bit the dust. *Both photos, Peter Ehrlich*

The last official run from the Transbay Terminal occurred at 12:50 a.m. on March 4, 2000. 1051, the last scheduled car, and chartered trolleys 1010 and 130, all in Muni liveries, close out 61 years of operation to this important transportation hub. *Richard Canino*

130. The three trolleys represented three different eras of streetcar service to the Transbay Terminal. Thus, in the wee hours of March 4, 2000, the trio brought the curtain down on 61 years of rail service to one of San Francisco's most important transportation centers.

As a postscript, there were a few instances when blockages on lower Market caused F-Line cars to detour and switch back via the Transbay loop. The last such occurrence happened on August 8, 2000. 1923-vintage work motor C-1 then made a ceremonial last trip over the line on August 15. But just three days later, work crews began pulling up the loop tracks on First and Fremont streets.

After cessation of streetcar service, trolley coaches on lines 5-Fulton and 6-Parnassus, and motor coaches on lines 38-Geary and 38L-Geary Limited, continued to use the ramp until the Terminal was closed in August 2010.

the tracks were removed, traffic flow on the Bay Bridge was altered to allow San Francisco-bound traffic on the upper deck, with eastbound traffic using the lower deck. (The rationale behind this arrangement was obvious. After all, the San Francisco skyline is a glorious vision, and was even in 1958!)

Until the Transbay Terminal was demolished in late 2010, AC Transit (serving the East Bay), Golden Gate Transit (to Marin and Sonoma Counties) and Greyhound buses used the lanes inside the terminal, and SamTrans buses, operating to Peninsula locations, loaded outside.

The official end of streetcar (and F-Line) service on the Transbay Terminal Loop arrived on March 3, 2000. PCC 1051, one of the ex-Philly cars painted in San Francisco green and cream, was fittingly chosen to be the last revenue service car. But the Northern California Railroad Club chartered both San Francisco streetcars that were dressed in 1939 blue and gold livery, representing the year Transbay Terminal opened: PCC 1010 and "Iron Monster"

The end for the 1939-vintage Transbay Terminal came in August 2010, with removal of the bus approach ramps. On December 10, 2010, a pile of rubble sits where Muni PCCs and "Iron Monsters" called for 61 years, and the wrecking ball will soon attack the Art Moderne-inspired main structure. *Ethan Tam*

While there was a lot of history attached to this important loop, and many people mourned its abandonment, the fact remained that the tracks were too worn out and the city too uninterested in keeping the Transbay streetcar loop in service. The Transbay Terminal itself was allowed to deteriorate, with most of its East Bay commuters now arriving by BART under Market Street. The terminal, the Muni transit ramp outside, and its elevated approach and exit ramp all succumbed to the wrecking ball starting in August 2010.

The dream of making it an important transportation center again, with high-speed trains and an electrified Caltrain anchoring transit, combined with a new and vibrant retail marketplace beckoning weary travelers, will come to fruition in perhaps a decade from now, and construction of this new terminal began in 2011. But it's doubtful that streetcars will ever call here again.

But a vibrant new chapter in the history of the F-Line was about to be written: the return of electric streetcar service to Fisherman's Wharf!

In this remarkable panorama, taken with a 400mm lens from the top of Twin Peaks in early October 1995, a month after the F-Line opened, PCC 1056 (Kansas City) is turning From Market into Noe Street, closely followed by car 1060 (Newark-PSCT). The photographic possibilities offered by the F-Line trolleys are endless! *Peter Ehrlich*

Market Street Railway: Promoting Museums In Motion

PCC 1007 passes the front door of the San Francisco Railway Museum, run by the non-profit group *Market Street Railway*. The genuine Wiley "Birdcage" traffic signal "dings" Go. *Peter Ehrlich*

THE RUNAWAY SUCCESS of San Francisco's F-Line can be directly attributed to the attitude within government, and with interested, involved citizens wanting to get the line built and the job done. Much of the momentum to run the F-Line can be credited to the work of a unique non-profit group, Market Street Railway (MSR).

Taking its name from San Francisco's original Market Street Railway streetcar system, MSR was formed in 1976 to save a 1950 Muni Marmon-Herrington trolley coach from destruction. Early in the 1980s, it gained a Board of Directors and assumed more of an advocacy role to promote historic streetcar service. Directors such as Rick Laubscher and Maurice Klebolt worked on plans for the Historic Trolley Festivals of the eighties. Their efforts included acquiring streetcars and generally supporting Muni in every way possible, from keeping the cars clean, to initiating restoration of some streetcars, to supporting day-to-day operations.

But MSR's biggest behind-the-scenes efforts lay in advocating and pushing for building a permanent historic streetcar line in San Francisco. Its first goal was to establish the F-Line from Transbay Terminal to Castro Street. It lobbied hard for city officials to obtain the necessary local, state and Federal funding to make the line a reality. MSR's efforts paid dividends the moment Motorman Walt Thomsen gave two toots on the Boat Car's whistle at Market and Second to kick off the F-Line on September 1, 1995.

But MSR was never a group to simply rest on its laurels. Even as the original F-Line got underway, it was pushing for funding to obtain streetcars for the Fisherman's Wharf extension. Here, again, the group was successful, and the line to the Wharf began service on March 4, 2000.

Meanwhile, under the guidance of President Rick Laubscher, MSR was developing a broad membership base, bringing in cash and volunteers for a variety of projects, such as partially restoring two PCCs, setting up a regular program of sweeping the cars out at Castro Street during the day, and in general, supporting the hard-working operators in the process. In 2005, the opportunity to set up and operate a transportation museum presented itself with the building of the Hotel Vitale on the site of the old Muni trolley bus turnaround at Steuart and Mission Streets. As part of the city approval process for the hotel to use the former terminal, MSR was given a 66 year, rent-free, 1000-square-foot space, located in the northwest corner of the hotel, and in 2007 opened the San Francisco Railway Museum. Exhibits were created depicting streetcar life in San Francisco, which could be changed out periodically. Volunteers reconstructed a replica of an end of one of Market Street Railway Company's 100-series "Haight Street Jewetts," complete with motorman's controls, where kids can play streetcar. The museum also offers transit-related items for sale—DVDs, T-shirts, pictures, posters and much more. The original store manager, John Hogan, was always cheerful, and greeted people with a smile and regaled visitors with tales about the history of the streetcar in San Francisco, and was especially good with children. The museum is just steps away from the F-Line car stop at Don Chee Way and Steuart Street. John left in 2012.

As mentioned, early on during the F-Line's existence, MSR volunteers would sweep out the cars at the Castro Street end of the line. This was a chance for the volunteers to interact with the operators and get the pulse of the operation. MSR has brought in volunteers from organizations working with developmentally challenged individuals to help clean the cars, and it gives these folks a sense of purpose. Some of them will not only clean the cars out but will clean the windshields. Their efforts are greatly appreciated by the operators, who are offered soft drinks or bottled water.

MSR has also worked hard to obtain streetcars for Muni to restore and operate. Cars such as Market Street Railway Co. 798, Johnstown 351, New Orleans 952 and 913, Muni B-Type 162 and a number of PCCs were acquired in part with funds raised from MSR members.

This is the MSR volunteer Christmas decoration crew after they finished work on Milano 1818 in November 2007. *Peter Ehrlich*

MSR also has an extensive outreach program to bring in new members, donations, volunteers, and interest and support. Every October, it has a display at the Castro Street Fair, usually on board Muni's oldest streetcar, the 1895 "Dinky."

Every year, at Christmastime, some cars are fully decorated inside and out—usually Milano 1818, painted two-tone green, and New Orleans 952. In addition, wreaths are affixed around the headlights of most other trams. They help bring seasonal cheer to Market Street and all along the line.

MSR has a web site: www.streetcar.org, and a blog, complete with histories of all F-Line streetcars and cable cars, and much more. It publishes a newsletter, *Inside Track,* four times a year, puts out a *Museums In Motion* calendar each year, containing images by noted photographers of F-Line cars and cable cars.

MSR volunteers constructed a full-size replica of an old Market Street Railway Co. "Haight Street Jewett" with actual controller and brake stand, where children can play "motorman." The museum also has historical displays and sells collectibles such as T-shirts, DVDs, calendars and posters. It's open Tuesday through Sunday. *Peter Ehrlich*

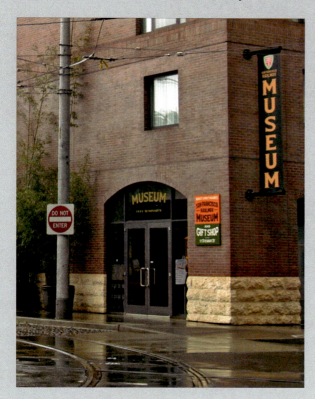

The museum is located at Don Chee Way and Steuart Street, in the *Hotel Vitale. Peter Ehrlich*

The dream of hundreds of San Franciscans to return electric rail service to the heart of Fisherman's Wharf, which last saw streetcars in 1941, and whose last service passing close to the Wharf ended in 1951, began in the decade of the 1970s, and reached fruition on March 4, 2000. Ten years later, 24,000 riders a day have taken F-Line streetcars to and from Fisherman's Wharf, one of the premier visitor attractions in the United States, aboard trolleys such as Muni's classic B-Type "Iron Monster" 162, passing the heart of the Wharf at Jefferson and Taylor Streets on June 16, 2009. Car 162 itself was a five-year restoration project carried out by both Muni and its non-profit support organization, Market Street Railway, and it's because of a fleet of vintage trolleys like 162 and other historic gems, as well as the everyday fleet of sleek PCC cars and sturdy Milan "Peter Witts" that make the F-Line the most exciting historic streetcar line in the world. *Peter Ehrlich*

Chapter 6 - Bound For Fisherman's Wharf

"I told my wife that Muni finally did something right. I'd like to thank the people who did this."

–Marina resident Jud Hurley,
as reported by MSR's Rick Laubscher
in Inside Track, after the F-Line
opened to the Wharf

At Last! Trolleys to the Wharf!

AT 5:42 a.m. ON SATURDAY, March 4, 2000, at 17th and Castro, PCC No. 1053 (ironically painted for Brooklyn, NY, the first transit system in the U. S. to operate a production fleet of PCC cars) became the first streetcar to carry revenue passengers to the new Jones and Beach terminal at Fisherman's Wharf. A new era in rail transit in San Francisco had begun. The dream, which took over two decades to realize had finally come true! One could now take a fun ride aboard a rolling symbol of living history to one of America's premier visitor destinations. Up in heaven, Maury Klebolt must surely have looked down on the scene, grinning from ear to ear.

"F-antastic!" was the one-word headline on the front page on Market Street Railway's spring 2000 issue of its newsletter, *Inside Track*. The lead article inside the newsletter, written by MSR honcho Rick Laubscher, gave a detailed description of the excitement embodied throughout San Francisco and the entire Bay Area for the opening of the F-Line's Fisherman's Wharf Extension.

Nine heavily-loaded PCCs and the Melbourne W2 tram kicked off the first day of service along the gleaming new Embarcadero Roadway. Unlike the opening of the F-Line four years and six months earlier, there was no fanfare or civic celebration by Muni to open the line. That would come later, in the dedication of the entire Embarcadero Roadway, of which the F-Line Fisherman's Wharf Extension was a chief component. But it didn't stop the citizenry from celebrating on their own, as that first car, number 1053, left 17th and Castro with a "swinging load."

In the ten years since it opened, the extension to Fisherman's Wharf has made the F-Line the most famous historic streetcar line in the world (matching New Orleans' St. Charles streetcar, which has been in service since 1835). It has been ridden by millions of tourists and San Francisco residents, studied by scores of transit officials, checked out by city governments desirous of building streetcar lines for their own cities, and praised in dozens of newspaper and magazine articles.

The opening of the F-Line to Fisherman's Wharf brought trolleys back to terminate there for the first time since 1941. In Chapter 2, we saw how planning for an Embarcadero line to and from the Wharf (as well as the Market Street portion of the F-Line) began in 1971, and how the 1989 Loma Prieta Earthquake was the catalyst to hasten construction. Now we'll see how it was built.

Building the Line in Phases

LIKE THE ORIGINAL F-LINE, the 2½-mile long Fisherman's Wharf Extension was built in phases. Don Chee, an enthusiastic backer of the F-line and its trolleys, was the Muni engineer who served as project manager in charge of constructing the Fisherman's Wharf Extension. Picking up from the planning and conceptual engineering work by Muni's Ron Niewiarowski on track alignment and car stop locations, the scope of his work included these items and others such as the surface treatment of the trackway to a limited form of signal preemption. Both Chee and Niewiarowski had to work closely with the city Department of Public Works here, since DPW was the lead agency in charge of the $50 million Embarcadero Roadway Project. Chee had also been the project manager, and Niewiarowski the project planner and conceptual engineer, for the Muni Metro Extension (MMX) along the South Embarcadero and King Street to Caltrain Depot, where today's N-Judah and T-Third Street light rail routes now operate, and where E-Embarcadero vintage cars will eventually tread.

As with Phases 3 and 4 of the Market trackwork and MMX, the Embarcadero portion of the

The different phases of Wharf Extension construction

(*left column, top*) Workers lay "faux" Belgian block along the trackway near Powell Street. (*left*) Along Jefferson Street near Taylor. The 32-Embarcadero bus line the F-Line will replace was ill-defined and infrequent. (*bottom*) Con-struction of the line between Taylor and Jones streets. *All photos, Peter Ehrlich*

(*above*) The Pier 39 Loop installation was a separate con-tract required as part of the approval to build the Pier 39 aquarium and its garage. February 16, 1996. *Peter Ehrlich*

(*above*) Completed trackwork along Beach Street. Note the decorative bracket arms for supporting the trolley wire, which hadn't yet been strung up in this November 17, 1998 shot (*below*) Embarcadero and Broadway was the contract division point between Phases One and Four. The overhead wire is tied off, as construction on Phase Four didn't begin until two years after the work from Broadway to North Point was completed. Note the stones embedded in the right-of-way to deter motorists. *Both photos, Peter Ehrlich*

PCC 1075 (Cleveland) stops at Embarcadero and Washington on July 19, 2007. Unlike Upper Market, where placement of Canary Island palm trees was controversial, those planted along The Embarcadero faced little or no protest. Coit Tower's on the left. *Peter Ehrlich*

extension was lined with Canary Island palm trees. When these trees were first proposed for placement along Upper Market in 1993, there were howls of consternation from purists who objected that such trees, which in their minds were suitable for Los Angeles, were completely out of place in temperate San Francisco. As the trees settled in and had a chance to let their lush vegetation fill out, public criticism died down and now they are well received by the public. So by the time the F-Line and MMX were built, there was no outcry regarding planting palm trees along The Embarcadero.

Don Chee lived long enough to see his dream come true. Sadly, he passed away in 2002. In honor of his accom-plishments, the little "street" for trolleys only, which cuts between Steuart Street and The Embarcadero at the south end of Justin Herman Plaza (and alongside the San Francisco Railway Museum, run by MSR), is named Don Chee Way, and Milan car 1893 is also dedicated to him. (Not many civil servants get a street named in their honor!)

The trackage eastward from First and Fremont Streets to midway down Steuart Street, fronting Justin Hermann Plaza, was built quickly, and was finished by the end of 1998, and a Northern California Railroad Club Christmastime charter that year featured this short segment as part of its excursion. This short segment was a separate contract from other phases of the F-line project. This track segment was built as the last part of the original F-Market project, which was a transit guideway replacement of the 8-Market trolley coach line; however, these new tracks would not be used in revenue service until the entire F-Line Embarcadero Extension was built in four phases.

Phase One covered the stretch from Broadway to North Point streets, and was mostly complete by the end of 1996. This was a two-track private right-of-way in a median strip. The pavement treatment in the median is of two types. Between Broadway and Battery/Lombard streets, small stones were embedded in the concrete in a lengthwise fashion to deter errant motorists from driving on the trackway. From Battery northward to North Point, smoother, but lightly pebbled and distinctive concrete paving was used, because it was intended to have buses from a line that partially paralleled the F-Line travel on this portion of the line, which was tested but never implemented. However, whenever Muni has to operate motor coaches on the F-line, or for the July 4th fireworks at the Wharf or other street closures affecting trolley service, it routinely operates them on both types of right-of-way. Two-globe blue street light standards, which supported the trolley wire, lined both edges of the trackway, and these became a signature of the entire Embarcadero Roadway.

The trackwork in Phases Two and Three, the Fisherman's Wharf loop via The Embarcadero, Jefferson, Jones and Beach Streets, was finished in 1998, and tastefully-designed light poles and bracket arms for the trolley wires were completed in 1999, as were the handicapped platforms. The railings of the platforms were reminiscent of the original New York subway's elevated platforms from 1904. Phase Two actually covered only the inbound track between

On the first day of service on the F-Line Fisherman's Wharf Extension–March 4, 2000–PCC 1063 speeds along The Embarcadero past Houston's Restaurant with a good-sized crowd on board. This is also the stretch of the private right-of-way that was intended to be paved for use by buses from a paralleling route, but was never implemented. *Peter Ehrlich*

Construction at the Ferry Building

(facing page, top) Sections of the Embarcadero and Don Chee Way special work are laid out like puzzle pieces at Ferry Plaza on October 22, 1998. *(bottom)* Don Chee Way was nowhere near ready on October 15, 1999, but four cars were towed through this construction zone just a week before, enroute to display at the Wharf for the annual Navy Fleet Week festivities. A January 18, 2000, deadline was not met, and the route finally opened on March 4. *Both photos, Peter Ehrlich*

The distinctive curved-glass-roof shelters were placed at all Wharf Extension stops except the Ferry Building during late summer 2000 and were unique to this line. Chicago 1058 stops at Embarcadero and Sansome enroute to Castro on September 15, 2011. *Peter Ehrlich*

North Point/Embarcadero and Powell, and included an emergency storage track/turnback loop track at the east end of the Pier 39 garage, and this track, which had been conceptually engineered by Niewiarowski at the time of Pier 39's application to build an aquarium and to expand its garage, would allow for a disabled streetcar to be stored off of the revenue track, and was built when the Pier 39 aquarium and garage expansion was constructed. Phase Three included the rest of the inbound track along Jefferson Street to Jones, and the outbound track along Beach Street and back to North Point, as well as the remainder of the emergency turnback loop track located east of the garage. It is interesting to note that on the first day of F-Line operation to Fisherman's Wharf there was a fire at a Wharf restaurant and the emergency loop track was immediately put into good use for an hour or so to keep service to the Wharf area running.

Bronze poetry plaques were affixed to the concrete platforms at Wharf stops. This one's at Sansome and The Embarcadero. Similar stone poetry plaques grace some stops on the original F-Line west of Van Ness. It's part of the trend toward "Art In Transit" which has become commonplace among new American light rail systems. *Peter Ehrlich*

In Phase Four–the Mid-Embarcadero alignment between Broadway and Folsom Streets– the city Board of Supervisors got involved. They were required to select from several designs for the plaza in front of the Ferry Building. One of these was a proposed grand loop similar to the "Roar Of The Four" days, where trolleys could go anywhere just by traversing a circle. This proposal, and some others, also advocated putting the northbound lanes of auto traffic underground. The design ultimately picked by the supervisors was the least aesthetically pleasing of all of them. It called for a broad concrete-and-granite expanse with London Plane trees and precious little other vegetation in between northbound and southbound lanes, with the F-Line tracks running along the east edge of the plaza. Frankly, though, the Board really didn't have much choice, because of the restrictions posed by the presence of Justin Herman Plaza Park (described in the next paragraph). But it was one of the most contentious battles to go before the Board of Supervisors.

The Ferry Loop was also constructed during Phase Three, as was the two-block connector between Mission and Folsom streets for the future E-Embarcadero line. Because it was not possible to build tracks through Justin Herman Plaza Park at the foot of Market Street, streetcars had to run halfway down Steuart Street and cut over to The Embarcadero via short, trolleys-only Don Chee Way. This alignment was recommended over a longer route via Mission Street. From here, streetcars could turn left to head toward the Wharf, or right for service to Caltrain Depot. The loop from Steuart and Don Chee Way via Steuart and Mission was in one direction only. A more versatile plan for a second loop track, suggested by MSR officials, was rejected. (The proposal to have the line run straight through Justin Herman Plaza was turned down because the plaza is considered a park, and it was argued that the Federal Government would have rejected that plan.)

Phase Four was mostly complete by the end of 1999. Although the trackwork was finished by October, installation of the overhead wire was lagging behind.

The stone treatment of Mid-Embarcadero trackage differed significantly from the stretch north of Broadway. Here, stones were embedded in an up-and-down position, and any motorist who even dared to try to drive onto the tracks was in for a rude shock! The city definitely wanted the Mid-Embarcadero private right-of-way to be the exclusive domain of rail cars! (Despite this washboard surface, buses, either subbing for, or adding to, the streetcar service, have to endure this stretch occasionally.)

Retired Muni Chief Inspector Art Curtis, now a MSR director, remembers early on, before the F-Line began service to Fisherman's Wharf, when he first proposed operating motor coaches for the Fourth of July fireworks, and some Muni officials said, "Oh, no. The buses will break up the stones and concrete." Curtis, who was always a service-oriented Muni employee throughout his distinguished 40-plus year career, replied, "We have two choices. First, we can run them at a reduced speed of 10 mph. Second, we could operate them on the Embarcadero Roadway but we'd need between 30 and 60 motor coaches in order to maintain adequate service headways to meet the passenger demand, because they would be caught in the gridlock on Embarcadero."[1] So Muni ran them on the right-of-way, first at 10 mph, and later at 35 mph, the track speed limit, and there was no damage to the trackway whatever.

First Streetcars Reach the Wharf; Setting a Date

ALTHOUGH WIRES WERE still not erected between Mission and Broadway, the overhead on the Wharf Loop was energized, permitting the first visit of trolleys to Fisherman's Wharf since 1941, when Market Street Railway Co.'s 15-Line bit the dust (not counting the old Muni F-Stockton route, which skirted the west edge of the Wharf area). On October 8, 1999, cars 1, 130, PCC 1015 and new Milan "Peter Witt" 1556 were towed up to Bay Street by Muni's venerable work car C-1, outfitted with a diesel generator. The occasion was to celebrate the completion of the Wharf loop and for the annual Navy Fleet Week festivities. It would still be five months before regular service was to commence. While the other cars returned to the barn, 1556 remained behind at Jones and Beach, the new Wharf terminal for the F-Line, and served as an MSR information booth, as well as showcasing the soon-to-enter-service Milano fleet.

It was hoped that service to the Wharf would begin by the last Christmastime of the 20th century, as work crews hastened to string up the wires in the Mid-Embarcadero area and perform touch-up work. But issues involving traffic signals, electric power capacity and reliability, streetcar signal pre-empts, and training of operators, set the opening date back twice, first to January 22, 2000, and finally to March 4.

A New Fleet for Wharf Service

IN 1998, MUNI MANAGEMENT recognized that more cars were needed to provide respectable service on the Fisherman's Wharf extension. But foot-dragging and yanking of funding for other purposes by the Muni Capital Projects and Finance departments ruled out getting more PCCs from Muni's idled and stockpiled original fleet rehabbed in time.

Enter Muni General Superintendent of Rail Transportation Ken Rodriguez. Rodriguez, a native of the Philippines, and a 27-year Muni veteran, started as an operator and worked his way up through the ranks, becoming Trolley Festival inspector and manager for several years. He had observed the performance of Muni's Milan "Peter Witt" 1834–nicknamed the "Pumpkin" because of its orange hue–on Market Street, seeing first-hand that it performed well mixed in service with the PCCs. He then approached Breda, the builder of Muni's new LRVs, and the Milan transit agency, Azienda Trasporti Milanesi, with the idea of trying to obtain additional Peter Witts for San Francisco. Negotiations between The City and Milan were successful, and in November 1998, ten "Ventotto" (so named to mark the year of their birth, 1928), arrived at the Port of San Francisco, along with one for parts only. One by one, they were brought over from Pier 80. Number 1859 was first to arrive at Metro Yard, on November 24, 1998. [For a complete description of the Milanos, see Chapter 8. See also the *Milan's Icons: The Peter Witt Trams* sidebar in this chapter.]

Two Milanos were quickly brought up to operating condition, but the Muni bureaucracy and the California Public Utilities Commission (CPUC) ordered many modifications to be made in preparing them for service. These included installing new and brighter headlights and regauging and reprofiling the wheels to fit the San Francisco rails. The cable car shop crew added seating for eight more passengers and one of the seats was a tip-up seat for wheelchair users. They did a masterful job, matching the original wooden Milan seats. Car 1793, still carrying Italian ads, was the first to operate in its new city, and ran in training service for many months. As mentioned, number 1556 was the first to be displayed to the public, during the annual Navy Fleet Week celebration. Credit for the big push to get the Milanos ready for service went to new General Manager Michael Burns, a veteran transit manager brought in from Philadelphia.

Three cars—1793, 1515 and 1859—went into revenue service within days of the opening of the F-Line to Fisherman's Wharf. 1556 followed in April. Gradually, others were brought online. As of fall 2002, nine of the ten cars were in operation, and the last car, 1807 (originally 1507), once considered as a parts car, made its debut in October 2004.

Riders Quickly Overwhelm the Trolleys

THE NINE PCCs ASSIGNED on March 4, 2000, were overwhelmed with joyful riders that Saturday, and Muni's historically overly-cautious service pattern plans proved to be dreadfully inadequate. Manager Kenny Rodriguez, riding a VIP charter with Melbourne 496 at Ferry Plaza, quickly ordered the operators to return to the Wharf with a revenue load. Later in the first week, F-Line Supervisor Steven Clark went into action and worked with the Green Division dispatchers to secure up to five more shuttle cars every weekend day to handle crowds from the Ferries to the Wharf, operating on an as-needed basis. The new Milanos covered most of these shuttle cars.

Weekday service proved to be as badly designed as the weekend schedules. The Scheduling Department based its service to the Wharf on the old 32-Embarcadero bus schedule, whose infrequent departures and general lack of visibility the F-Line replaced—one of the positive benefits of having a visible, permanent rail line in place. As such, Scheduling reasoned that more cars would be needed between the Ferries and Castro, so during rush hours, only every other car was sent to the Wharf. This proved to be a big mistake. The resulting 12-minute headways caused most cars to pass up passengers trying to reach the Ferry Building for their boats home in the afternoon, while most riders going home to the Castro District were now using the now-improved Muni Metro Subway service instead of the F cars. Night service was every 15 minutes with only six cars. (With the popularity of the F-Line growing almost exponentially, the problem of afternoon pass-ups on The Embarcadero continues today, even with more frequent headways.)

With the June 2000 signup, a tenth car was added to the base service, and schedules were lengthened to reflect actual travel times from Jones and Beach. This allowed for 10-minute headways. The short turn runs were eliminated, and all cars now ran the entire route. Five cars were assigned as trippers. But four shuttle cars—usually three Milan cars and one two-man vintage car—were in place to handle overflow loads on the Embarcadero portion of the line. A seventh car was added to nighttime service. The regular deployment of a two-man historic

A huge throng of riders tries to board already-overcrowded Milano 1807 at the Ferry Building on October 9, 2004. This scene is repeated daily as ridership on the F-Line has soared, approaching 24,000 riders a day. *Peter Ehrlich*

streetcar was the first time Muni had ever made these cars available on a consistent basis, but they were not given any specific schedule. Scheduled vintage car operation would come later.

The Embarcadero Roadway dedication was held on June 16, 2000. It's hard to believe that this beautiful civic promenade, with multi-hued, living history conveyances whisking the masses to the Wharf, was the result of one of the closest and most fought-over battles at the Board of Supervisors to destroy its predecessor roadway. But no one is complaining now.

2001: First Major Improvement

JANUARY 2001 SAW A MAJOR IMPROVEMENT in service and scheduling. 15 cars were now assigned, permitting 8-minute basic headways and 6-7-minute rush hour intervals, with two extra tripper cars. Three shuttle cars, all with two-man vehicles, were provided—the first time regularly-scheduled vintage car service was implemented. On weekends, there were 14 basic service PCCs or Milan cars, and two shuttles. Even with this improvement, cars were still overcrowded and passing people up south of Pier 39 in the evening rush. This trend was to continue for the next ten years and hamper room for improvement.

The patronage trends on the new line were fascinating. During the early days of the Wharf Extension, the F started attracting a large number of passengers who previously used paralleling bus routes but who found the trolleys faster and more comfortable. The F-Line is also credited with opening up the Fisherman's Wharf and Northern Waterfront areas to residents—people who would not consider riding a bus to the Wharf. This is borne out by the author, who has operated all the bus lines

Daily Vintage Car Service Becomes A Reality

The dream to have Muni's unique fleet of heritage trams operating every day came true when the Fisherman's Wharf Extension opened for service on March 4, 2000.

(*right*) B-Type 130 is approaching Washington Street in this September 8, 2004 shot. (*below*) The flagship of the fleet–Muni's Wonderful One, its very first streetcar, built in 1912–approaches Broadway on its very first trial run since returning from rehab by Brookville Equipment in Pennsylvania on February 24, 2011.
Both photos, Peter Ehrlich

(*above*) Melbourne W2 496 passes inbound PCC 1061 (Pacific Electric) at Embarcadero and Greenwich on July 21, 2006. (*below*) Muni's oldest trolley, Market Street Railway 578(S), vintage 1895, heads outbound at North Point on May 26, 2005. *Both photos, Peter Ehrlich*

(*above*) New Orleans 952 rounds the corner at Embarcadero/Beach/Grant heading for Market Street in this view looking east from the Pier 39 Garage pedestrian overpass. The Bay Bridge looms overhead.
May 30, 2006, *Peter Ehrlich*

penetrating the Wharf area at one time or other, and observed that the ridership was at best a seated load on all of the lines. Yet the lines of people waiting for the cable cars at Powell and Market are still as long as before. Clearly, the F-line has attracted a significant chunk of new riders. In February 2001, in the depths of the off-season for tourists, well over 19,000 riders a day were carried on F trolleys, and during the summer of 2001, this level went over 20,000 a day, more than the entire daily ridership of the nearby Santa Clara County light rail system that year and matching the number of people who rode Muni's first streetcars back on December 28, 1912. The tragic events of September 11, 2001, caused ridership to dip a bit in 2002, but in 2011, crowded cars are still the rule and daily ridership is now estimated at 24,000.[2]

The City's fiscal and manpower policies during the 2003-2006 period didn't help the situation, either. Under Mayor Gavin Newsom, who was elected in 2003, a "no-overtime" policy was instituted for all city departments, including Muni, and many cars, trains and buses never left the yards because the policy would not allow dispatchers to assign RDO (regular day off) operators to open runs (RDO operators would get paid time-and-one-half). The same policy led to a hiring freeze, and by 2007, the agency was well over 100 operators and dozens of mechanics short systemwide.

Despite the internal Muni and municipal manpower problems, the F-Line has garnered, and continues to receive, much positive publicity, with large numbers of local, national and international TV networks and stations doing documentaries on the colorful trolleys. The line has achieved international acclaim. Thousands of photographs of the trams are taken by people who have no real interest in public transportation, but who wish to document their San Francisco experience with another symbol of the city—and a bus just doesn't cut it for them!

To many visitors, the F-Line represents two sides of an "Iron Triangle." They will ride the Powell cable cars from downtown to the Wharf and the F-Line back, or vice versa. This way, they can sample and enjoy two different rides on the rails, as well as not having to pay another $6.00 cable car fare for the return journey. The F-Line fare is only $2.00.

Nevertheless, Muni must continue to take the necessary actions to ensure that the line doesn't become a victim of its own success. With 24,000 riders a day, it has to do a better job to meet demand than it has so far. Slowly, the agency is working on ways to meet the demand. Weekend service was increased in 2007. In late 2011, more daytime runs were added, seven days a week, with the latter improvement resulting in 22 scheduled cars, and five-to-six-minute headways.

The Need for More Trolleys

AS EARLY AS 1996, and even before the F-Line opened in 1995 (according to internal Muni documents), it was recognized that more cars would be needed to expand service. The addition of 10 Milanos helped for Fisherman's Wharf service expansion, but more cars are desperately needed. [The frustrations with regard to attempts to get the four remaining double-ended "Torpedo" PCCs and up to four "Baby Tens" rebuilt are discussed in Chapters 5, 7 and 8.] Accidents, too, have taken their toll on the F-Line fleet. PCC 1056 (Kansas City), which rear-ended another PCC at Pier 39 loop in 2001, didn't return to service until early 2007. Another PCC, 1060 (Newark), wrapped itself around a light pole at Market and Steuart on November 6, 2002. Two years later, the same operator involved in the 1060 mishap was operating a Breda on November 16, 2004, when he rear-ended PCC 1054, which had stopped on the J-Line's San Jose Avenue right-of-way during a shop test. His speed was estimated at 35 mph. The rear of 1054 was demolished, and it became the first ex-Philly car to be retired, and it also put in place new notification procedures and announcements from Central Control to operators on the J-Church Line. In 2006, Chicago PCC 1058 rear-ended a trolley coach at Powell Street and finally emerged from the Geneva body shop some four years later, but in the process, 1058 lost its CTA green and cream—The Windy City's last paint scheme—in favor of a repaint in Chicago's more famous original postwar "Green Hornet" livery of Mercury Green and Croydon Cream with a Swamp Holly Orange belt rail. PCC 1061 (Pacific Electric), sidelined since the beginning of 2010 with braking and electronics issues, triumphantly returned to service in December 2011. Minor accidents and propulsion/braking issues sideline various cars for short periods of time.

Accidents have also put many of the Milanos out of service for extended periods of time at various intervals. In late 2011, three of them were sidelined with accident damage. Only one of these returned to service in 2013.

But a bright light and the promise for service improvements manifested itself with the purchase of 11 former Newark, N.J. PCCs in 2003, which were given a mini-rehab the following year by Brookville Equipment Co. Four of them entered service in 2007, and a fifth in 2009, adding still more colors to the beautiful F-Line fleet. This also permitted an improvement in weekend service by adding two more cars to the line and reducing daytime headways to every 7 minutes. Unfortunately, it was discovered,

Ferry Building layover

At Ferry Plaza–Embarcadero and Don Chee Way–vintage cars hang out between trips, other cars switch back to change direction, and even minor repairs are performed.

(*above*) Cleveland 1075 and Zürich-hued PCC 737 (ex-Brussels) meet at Ferries layover in 2007. (*below*) Vintage cars are banked south of Mission Street during the Brussels car's welcoming ceremony at the Ferries, June 4, 2005. *Both photos, Peter Ehrlich*

(*above right*) Looking from the Hotel Vitale, A Milano lays over at Ferries. (*right*) New Orleans 952 and Washington 1076, October 17 2010. Both Photos, *Peter Ehrlich*

Occasionally, an "interloper" will appear at the Ferries. On May 12, 2004, a Breda, on a training run, pulled up to Embarcadero and Mission behind Car 1, resting between trips. This was possible because the overhead wire is pantograph-compatible. *Peter Ehrlich*

Sometimes, it is necessary to bank F-Line cars at the Ferry Building, usually because of disruptions affecting the J-Church line, its pullout, pull-in route. One such instance occurred on January 4, 2008, with PCCs and Milanos laid up for the night on the E-Embarcadero line trackage between Mission and Howard streets. *Kevin Sheridan*

Views from the Top

Images of F-Line Cars on the Wharf Extension taken from elevated locations

(*left*) Looking northeast from One Market Plaza, we see inbound PCC 1052 (Los Angeles) meeting a new Milan car, 1793, on April 18, 2000, six weeks after the Wharf extension opened. (*below*) New Orleans 952 stops at the inbound Pier 39 stop, busiest stop for people heading to the Wharf. About 50-60% of the riders will begin their Fisherman's Wharf experience here. May 30, 2006. *Both photos, Peter Ehrlich*

(*above*) Los Angeles 1052 stops at Beach and Mason in this view looking west from the Pier 39 Garage. The Longshoremen's Hall is partially to the left of the trolley; the Ghirardelli Square Clock Tower and Fort Mason are in the distance. June 19, 2005. (*right*) Twilight is disappearing and The Embarcadero is ablaze with light as cars 1059 and 1818 exchange passengers at Ferry Plaza. The Milano will run to the Wharf, while the PCC will switch back inbound to outbound and head to Castro Street. August 22, 2010. *Both photos, Peter Ehrlich*

embarrassingly, that these cars needed complete rewiring, something that was never carried out in Newark over their 47-year career there. These wiring problems, which produced symptoms such as rear doors opening mysteriously while the cars were moving, did nothing to alleviate pressure to keep the fleet running. Brookville got a contract to rewire the cars, and the pilot car, 1071 (Minneapolis/St. Paul), and most of the rest of the "Brookvilles," as Muni refers to them, returned by early 2012. The last unrewired car went to Pennsylvania on January 16, 2012. [For details on the ex-Newark PCCs, see Chapter 8.]

Choke Points: What to Do About Them?

F-LINE RIDERSHIP, as mentioned, has been going through the roof. There are some stops where there are so many people waiting to board an F-Line streetcar that they spill over to the curb or off the island.

Inbound, the heaviest boardings are at Market and Fourth Street, in the middle of the retail shopping district; Market and Main, where patrons exit the BART and Muni Metro Embarcadero Station, and the Ferry Building, where dozens of ferries from the East Bay, Vallejo and Marin County bring folks to shop, eat at San Francisco's fine restaurants and ride F-Line cars to continue their public transportation experience in The City by the Bay. Outbound, the single heaviest stop is in the afternoon and evening at Beach and Stockton, opposite Pier 39.

The problem with stops such as the Ferry Building or Beach and Stockton is that the cars are already filled with riders who boarded further up the line. Then patrons waiting along The Embarcadero get passed up. For workers trying to catch a specific ferry to go home, this causes them to miss their boats.

To partially solve the Pier 39 and Embarcadero problems in the evening rush hour, the author, who is no particular fan of buses, nevertheless suggested that Muni's Kirkland Division, which abuts the Beach and Stockton stop and is a motor coach base, assign certain evening rush hour Richmond Express runs to pull out to Beach and Stockton or even the Beach and Jones Terminal, pick up riders, and deliver them to Market and California (Embarcadero Station), then they would be in place to move over to their Richmond Express service. They have to travel this route anyway for this pullout trip, so why not press them into service? This suggestion has been ignored. Unfortunately, this solution won't be possible when Kirkland's buses move to the new Islais Creek facility, near the Central Waterfront, sometime in 2014. But when the E-Embarcadero line begins in 2014, this will help to alleviate the situation.

Another, more Capital Project-intesive suggestion was broached by MSR Wharf service opened This was to build shortly a loop afger from the Market an Fifth Street via 5th Street North (across Hallidie Plaza), Eddy and Mason, then back onto Market for some short turn cars to begin picking up at Fifth and Market to return to the Wharf. Simultaneously, MSR urged Muni to connect the overhead wire over the 5th Street crossover to make this turnback more useful. Again, nothing became of this idea, but within the last two years, MSR has been pressing for something to be done, which makes perfect sense–although engineering tests of the strength of the 5th Street North "overpass" need to be carried out to determine whether this street, actually a bridge, can support streetcars. A variant of the loop could be via Taylor, reverse flow on Turk for a block to Mason, and an S-curve back onto Market.

Then there is the problem of how to handle huge crowds of passengers, yet still collect all fares. Frequently, some operators will simply open all the doors (especially on the three-door Milan cars) and implore people to board through every door, whether they had a cash fare, pass or transfer. The alternative is to have everyone board through the front, fumble with dollar bills and the balky fareboxes and tie up the stop for three minutes or more. The worst offending stop here is Market and 4th Street, since other bus lines using the safety island are affected.

Operators and others have suggested two possible solutions: First, assign loaders at busy stops to collect fares, or to at least board riders who have Fast Passes, Clipper Cards (the new SmartCard technology which is replacing paper passes in 2011), Visitor Passports or valid transfers. Second, install ticket vending machines at places such as Market and Fourth, Market and Main, Ferry Building and Beach and Stockton. Management has taken these ideas under advisement.

Another partial solution being considered at Muni would be to make the F-Line a "Proof-of-Payment" line, like the Muni Metro routes. While this would permit passengers holding fare media such as Passports and transfers to board any door, this would still not solve the service delays caused by riders paying cash fares. This happened in 2012.

Everyday Vintage Car Service a Reality

WITH THE OPENING OF THE F-LINE to the Wharf, for the first time, a regularly-scheduled service with Muni's fabulous historic fleet became an everyday occurrence. Now Muni could show off such gems as Wonderful One (Muni A-Type 1), Iron Monster (Muni B-Type 130, and 162 since 2009), The Streetcar Named Desire (New Orleans 952), The

Wonder Down Under (Melbourne W2 496), and especially the Blackpool Boat (228). A dedicated schedule for the vintage cars was instituted in January 2001, Starting at 6:15a.m, with others following at 7:15 a.m. and 10:00 a.m, vintage cars delighted morning commuters on their pullout runs over the J-Line and F-Line, then entered Wharf Shuttle service. Many years later, all vintage car schedules were changed to pull out in late morning, to better serve ridership demand.

A gaggle of giggling girls looks out of the rear window of PCC 1052 at the Milan car behind it.
Peter Ehrlich

For many years, Motorman Walt Thomsen, the self-proclaimed "Captain Of The Boat," thrilled riders with his piloting of the Boat Tram in weather as low as 40º! He was immortalized in a series of cartoons drawn by the late Phil Frank in the comic strip "Farley," published only in the *San Francisco Chronicle*, which featured the Boat car. Walt retired in 2002 with honors. Sadly, Walt passed away in 2010.

The author, who was sometimes called the "Mayor Of The F-Line" by some fellow operators because of his expertise in F-Line operations and his ability to clear line delays, was a vintage car motorman for almost five years until he retired in mid-2005. He was the last throwback to the Trolley Festival era.

The Shuttles were designed to fill in when runs were missing or the Ferry Building stop got overloaded with prospective riders. Usually, they ran only on the Embarcadero portion, but occasionally would be sent all the way to 17th and Castro. When I was a vintage car motorman, I always enjoyed running the occasional trip to Castro to break up the routine. However, the cars perform better and endure less wear and tear if they are kept on the flat Embarcadero portion of the line.

Nevertheless, there were some detractors, both among the platform employees, and managers within Muni, and outside observers, who complained that these crews didn't do any work. One operator called them the "Shuttle Bums." Other people complained about the perceived extra-long layovers "enjoyed" by the crews. In reality, there were times when things were running smoothly enough and the crowds at the Ferry Building were manageable. But the crews were always on the watch for when they were really needed, such as during a line delay or when a particular ferry arrival would disgorge enough passengers to warrant a trip to the Wharf. And of course they were always subject to inspector's orders.

In late 2003, Muni modified the runs to operate to Market and 11th Street, as a way of exposing the cars to Market Street riders while attempting to improve service. In reality, this did little to help, because they were no longer available to scoop up a big load of riders at the Ferry Building when they were really needed. After a few years, the runs to 11th were discontinued and the cars reverted to an Embarcadero-only operation, but for a while in 2010, the schedule was adjusted to send all the vintage cars to 17th and Castro on all trips.

And then there were problems with management's role in how the operators were detailed to the shuttles. Most operators signed on the shuttles because that was their choice. Yet dispatchers, with the blessing of the Green Light Rail Division manager, would routinely reassign them to other F-Line runs or even Muni Metro runs to cover "the needs of the service," and sometimes not a single vintage car would be out on the streets. In late 2007, this philosophy changed because the motormen and conductors would regularly refuse reassignment, but in 2011, service patterns have reverted to the way it was before 2007.

Starting with Melbourne 496 in 2005, Muni started a program of upgrading the vintage cars to make them more compatible with the rest of the fleet. A new low-voltage power supply was installed to operate radios and VETAG (Vehicle Tagging System) switch and signal controls. This equipment was also placed on Blackpool 228 and New Orleans 952, as well as on B-Type 162, which joined the vintage fleet for service in 2009 following a five-year restoration. Muni A-Type 1, recently restored by Brookville Equipment Co., also has VETAG. B-Type 130 will be the next to receive this CPUC-mandated equipment, which will also allow vintage cars to run on the E-Line in the future. According to the SFMTA 2008-2027 Short Range Transit Plan, everyday E-Line service will now start in 2014, but it also operated on some weekends for the America's Cup Finals, which were held in San Francisco between July and September 2013. [See Addenda, page 280.]

References:

1. Letter from Art Curtis to Peter Ehrlich, Jan. 8, 2011.
2. Ridership statistics taken in Summer 2008 show 12,235 inbound riders and 11,864 outbound riders, for a total of 24,099. (Source: SFMTA Ridership tables, July-August 2008.)

Milan's Icons: The Peter Witt Trams

Two Milanese icons: The Duomo, the spiritual center of Milan, located right in the "Centro Storico," or central Milan, and the Peter Witt tram, a Milan fixture for 85 years. Nicknamed "Ventotto," for the year of their birth (1928), these American-style streetcars still ply Milan streets in 2012, making them the oldest trams in regular service in Europe. Car 1723, passing here on March 16, 2008, is painted in two-tone green, a scheme that lasted four decades and was reputedly made famous by Benito Mussolini. *Peter Ehrlich*

IN 1926, ITALY HAD JUST CONVERTED to right-hand drive. Simultaneously, Milan's vast tramway network was becoming much too dependent on small trams pulling trailers, a labor-intensive operation.

Faced with a need to modernize its fleet, Milanese officials studied the American Peter Witt design. In 1912, Peter Witt, a Cleveland traction commissioner, designed a large-capacity, front entrance and center exit streetcar, which made riding safer and fare collection better. Passengers boarded at the front door, sat or stood in the area between the doors if they hadn't yet paid their fare, paid the conductor, who was stationed ahead of the center door, and were then able to sit facing traffic in the rear of the car. The conductor controlled the rear door operation. The Peter Witt streetcar operated in Chicago, Detroit (781 cars there!), Cleveland, Buffalo and dozens of other cities. (They also ran in Philadelphia, but the curmudgeonly Mitten management refused to pay royalties, so they were called the "Eighty-Hundreds" there.)

Two prototype Peter Witts were built for Milan in 1928, giving them the sobriquet "Ventotto," for year of their birth. After some minor modifications, Azienda Trasporti Milanesi (ATM), the Milanese transit agency, placed an order with six different Italian carbuilders for 500 Peter Witts, and these began arriving in 1929 and 1930.

In the 1930s, ATM began improving their Peter Witts, concentrating on passenger flow. The most significant change was addition of a rear door. There were now three doors for entrance and exit.

The Peter Witt fleet suffered greatly during World War II. All but one were rebuilt. But major attrition didn't occur until about 1976, when 100 new

One of the Peter Witts to migrate to America was 1859, shown passing Piazza della Repubblica on March 18, 1998. 1859 was the first Milano to be delivered to Muni Metro Center. *Peter Ehrlich*

Muni acquired 11 trams–10 "Revisione Generale" and one non-rebuilt–for its F-Line, following receipt of tram 1834 in 1984. Two cars went to San Jose.

The future for the Peter Witt in Milan is cloudy. In 2011, Witts were assigned to just five lines. The "Ventotto" are the oldest regularly-scheduled tram fleet in Europe. To be sure, they are using 1928 technology in a 2013 world. The need to accommodate disabled riders, which most European Union countries have adopted as law, as has the United States, with its ADA law, and similar laws in Canada and Australia, dictates eventual total replacement of these durable trams. But for now, the Peter Witt remains a symbol of Milan, and should stay that way through the third decade of the 21st Century, if all goes right.

Jumbotrams arrived. Still, the status quo was maintained for another dozen years. In the early 1970s, the Witts were converted to pantograph operation, and in the process, lost their conductors. ATM went to a prepaid ticket system, common to most systems in Europe. The motormen no longer had to handle fares.

Beginning in 1988, and lasting through 1992, 250 of the best "Ventotto" were selected for a major upgrade, called "Revisione Generale." Electric door buttons replaced the air valves; passenger emergency door release switches were installed, and most electrical components were made low-voltage with a battery system. The rest were scrapped–many in 1990 after Metropolitana Linea 3 (subway) opened, or offered to tramway museums, but the last "non-revisione" cars didn't succumb to the torch until 1999.

Today, about 150 Peter Witts remain in service. Their original livery, which appeared on the first 125 cars to be delivered, was yellow and white. Between the 1930s and 1970s, the Witts–and all other Italian transit vehicles–wore two-tone green, ostensibly on the orders of fascist dictator Benito Mussolini. In the 1970s a national "Italian Standard Transport Vehicle Orange" was adopted, but this rule has been relaxed, and most transit operators in Italy have now adopted their own liveries. In Milan, the new Eurotrams and Sirio low-floor models have reverted to 2-tone green. Beginning in 2007, many "Ventotto" reappeared in the 1928 yellow and white scheme.

In the 1990s, Peter Witts began to migrate to America. Gomaco Trolley Company, of Ida Grove, Iowa, imported six complete Peter Witts and parts from about 100 cars, including wrecked "Revisione Generale" trams, to its Iowa plant. Also, in 1998,

(*above*) Starting in 2007, Milan has been repainting many of its Peter Witts in heritage 1928 livery of yellow and white. 1673 passes the world-famous La Scala Opera House in 2008. (*below*) ATM has also converted a pair of "Ventotto" to restaurant trams. 1970 passes through Piazza Cordusio on the evening of March 25, 2009. *Both photos, Peter Ehrlich*

(*left*) Peter Witt 1818 is in Milan, being prepared for shipment to the United States and a new career. October 1998. *Karl Johnson collection* (*below*) "Ventotto" 1521 and other trams rest in Deposito Messina (Messina Depot) on Oct. 19, 2002. This is the largest of the five tram depots in Milan, and because of its many skylights and resulting bright interior, is considered to be the "Cathedral of Traction." *Peter Ehrlich*

Illuminated Peter Witts in Milan and San Francisco

The simple, straightforward lines of the Milan "Peter Witts" lend themselves to easy illuminated decoration. (*above left*) In March 2011, Milan's transit agency decorated tram 1847 with all-over lights to celebrate the 150th anniversary of Italy's independence from Austria. It's parading in Piazza Cordusio on March 17, 2011. The colors underneath the illumination represent the Italian flag. (*above right*) 1847 is reflected in the windows of a Sirio low-floor tram at Piazza Castello on March 20, 2011. Both photos, Peter Ehrlich

Witts in San Jose and Iowa

(*above*) The use of illuminated Milan Peter Witts is— as of July 24, 2011–not limited to their native city. Muni's yellow-and-white 1811 got the illumination treatment, along with the street lights, in a Christmassy streetscene re-creation at the Ferry Building for a shoot for the movie *The Five Year Engagement*, a comedy released in 2012. Carole Gilbert

There are two other places in the United States where Milan "Peter Witts" operate, albeit sporadically: San Jose and Mt. Pleasant, Iowa. (*above*) Milano 1945 loads passengers during the annual Midwest Threshers Reunion in Mt. Pleasant, held every Labor Day weekend. For five days, 1945 and other streetcars run on Muni-like frequencies. (*left*) San Jose's Valley Transportation Authority 's Milano 2001 was converted to a double-ender. At Civic Auditorium during the APTA Light Rail Conference, October 11, 2006. The car usually operates at Christmastime. *Both photos, Peter Ehrlich*

There are two likely expansions of historic streetcar service in the works, and when implemented, will fulfill dreams which have been brewing for over 40 years.

(*above*) The E-Embarcadero started weekend service in August 2015. It uses double-end cars like PCC 1007, shown at King and 4th Street during an official E-Line demonstration service on August 31, 2008. Weekday service was added in April 2016. *Peter Ehrlich* (*below*) The Golden Gate National Recreation Area (GGNRA) is actively pursuing plans to extend the F-Line from its Fisherman's Wharf terminal through the old State Belt Railroad's Fort Mason Tunnel into the Fort Mason Center, on the east edge of the Marina District. This is a conceptual photo of how a possible South Terminal at Fort Mason would look, with the Golden Gate Bridge in the background. In the March 2013 "Record Of Decision," a plan for a North Loop (shown on Page 124) was selected instead.
Environmental Vision/National Park Service

Chapter 7 -
Expansion In The Works

"The [Fort Mason F-Line] extension has the important benefit of reunifying the pieces of Fisherman's Wharf by rebalancing transit access between its eastern and western portions. After studying several possible east-west alignments...Beach Street was selected as the route for environmental and historic preservation reasons. Among other advantages, this allows the placement of streetcar stops in both directions directly opposite the Hyde Street cable car turntable, providing a mini-transit hub to visitors wishing [to] explore the Wharf area.
The streetcar tracks alone provide a clue to visitors getting off the cable cars that there's something to see where the tracks lead..."
– from Market Street Railway blog dated June 20, 2009, by Rick Laubscher
http://www.streetcar.org/blog/2009/06/reunifying-the-wharf.html,
accessed August 5, 2011.

WITH THE OPENING of the F-Line in 1995 a *fait accompli*, historic trolley supporters and Muni planners were now able to set their sights on future extensions and expansion of service.

It was all agreed that the next expansion of service was to the Wharf area, and this was described in the previous chapter. But what about realizing the original 1970s-era dream–namely an all-Embarcadero vintage car line?

There was no question that an E-Embarcadero vintage streetcar line would be viable. That was proven during the 1987 Trolley Festival with the demonstration between the Ferry Building and Pier 39 [described in *The 1987 Embarcadero Demonstration* sidebar in Chapter 3].

Ever since the F-Line was extended to the Wharf, countless riders and baseball fans have asked trolley operators how to get to AT&T Park, the wonderful new San Francisco Giants baseball stadium that opened in 2000 (back then, it was called Pacific Bell Park). Almost to a person, they'd get turned off when the operator told them they couldn't ride the colorful trolleys directly to the ball park and would instead have to transfer to the N-Judah or T-Third Street Muni Metro subway train at Embarcadero Station. When the E-Line eventually becomes a reality–likely to happen in 2014–this problem would be solved forever.

Muni Metro Runs First E-Line

AS IT TURNED OUT, the first E-Embarcadero streetcar service began on January 10, 1998, not with vintage cars, but with Muni Metro Breda LRVs. This was the first use of the Muni Metro Extension (MMX) along the southern part of The Embarcadero, which was then beginning to develop with new apartments, office complexes and condominium projects. AT&T Park, the new baseball stadium, was also built there.

The route began at the east end of Embarcadero Station and came to the surface at Folsom Street at what is called Ferry Portal. The trains made high-level platform stops at Folsom/Harrison Streets, Brannan Street, 2nd and King, and 4th and King/Caltrain. Service was daily, but only between 6:00 a.m. and 8:00 p.m. This was also the first application of the new Automatic Train Control System (ATCS) automated signal and train control system in the subway.

The MMX trackway was built similarly to that of the F-Line to Fisherman's Wharf. The rails were set in concrete studded with stones to deter motorists from driving on the tracks. Curb treatments, medians and planter boxes for vegetation consisted of faux-Belgian Block concrete bricks, the same ones applied to Upper Market and the Wharf Extension. Canary Island palm trees lined both sides of the trackway.

The Muni Metro version of the E-Line continued until August 22, 1998, when the N-Judah Muni Metro line was extended over MMX to Caltrain Depot.

As mentioned, the opening of the Muni Metro Extension has spurred considerable development and new construction along its entire route–well into the hundreds of millions spent to construct new apartment buildings, office complexes and condominium developments. This tremendous economic growth has served to transform a rather gritty industrial district into a viable and thriving community, anchored by AT&T Park. This is indisputable evidence how a permanent rail line, while costlier to build than simply providing bus service, can be an economic boon to a city.

Preparing for E-Line Vintage Operation

IN THE MEANTIME, construction of the last component of the Wharf Extension trackage–the rails

The first regular service with the E-Embarcadero designation was operated as a Muni Metro route between Embarcadero Station and King and 4th Street/Caltrain Depot. Breda 1428 pauses at Folsom Station on May 17, 1998. This service continued until August 22, when the N-Line was extended to Caltrain Depot. *Peter Ehrlich*

idea of what a vintage E-Line service could be like.

A number of other historic streetcar charters and special movements have since run out MMX. One notable trip featured "Torpedoes" 1007 and 1010 sandwiching New Orleans 952, which ran for the Electric Railroaders' Association convention on September 5, 2004.

In 2003, Muni took another step toward an eventual startup of the E-Line, when it awarded a contract to build low platforms at every MMX station. Although the high-level platforms for Muni Metro trains were located in the center median between the tracks, those for the low-level E-Line cars, with their right side doors, required platform placement on the outside. As with other F-Line stops, every between Howard and Folsom Streets alongside both sides of Ferry Portal—was finished in 2000 and was included in the Mid-Embarcadero phase of F-Line construction. This was the final link that would make an all-vintage car E-Line possible. Tests with PCC 1007 and a couple of Breda LRVs to check automatic operation of the switches at Folsom Street were performed in late June 2000. Although successful, there was no immediate need to use these switches, and for a while, they were spiked for the straight move into the subway and the VETAG electronic controls deactivated.

The first public rides with vintage cars took place under Market Street Railway auspices on July 13 and 14, 2001, as a demonstration service. Cars 1, 578S and 228 did the honors, but because there was no place for riders to get off the streetcars at 4th and King, it was set up as a round trip, originating and ending at Embarcadero and Don Chee Way. But it gave riders an

Market Street Railway sponsored the first public rides aboard vintage trolleys on what will become the south end of the E-Embarcadero historic streetcar line—a route first proposed in the 1970s. Muni A-Type 1, built in 1912, has passed under the Bay Bridge and is approaching Brannan Station on July 14, 2001. *Peter Ehrlich*

platform has a handicapped ramp per ADA (Americans with Disabilities Act) requirements. The work was completed by mid-2004, but as this is being written, they remain unused.

Missing: Cars and Cash

WITH THE PLATFORMS in place and the track connection at Folsom installed, it seemed that all was ready for an E-Line startup in 2004. However, this was not to be, for two principal reasons: lack of available double-end streetcars, and budget constraints.

At the start of the 2004-2005 fiscal year, Muni was faced with the need to institute systemwide service cuts, which affected virtually every part of the city, including the F-Line. The vintage car shuttles were on the chopping block, too, but were saved by intense political pressure from the Fisherman's Wharf Merchants Association and other trolley supporters, including MSR.

New Orleans 952 uses the E-Line low platform at King and 4th Street/Caltrain Station during the Sunday Streets E-Embarcadero vintage car demonstration on August 31, 2008 – one of two Sunday Streets celebrations held in 2008, when the northbound lanes on The Embarcardero were closed to auto traffic and opened for walkers, bicyclists and skaters to enjoy. *Peter Ehrlich*

But beyond the financial problems was the daunting physical evidence that there were simply not enough double-end trolleys available. There were the three "Torpedo" PCCs and four vintage cars available, but this was an insufficient number for the proposed everyday service. Additionally, the vintage cars lacked various electronic appurtenances such as a low-voltage power supply system for radios and VETAG switch and signal controls, necessary for operation over the MMX.

Ironically, a temporary solution for early startup of E-Line service could have happened in 2001. At that time, Muni management was hell-bent on ridding the system of its remaining Boeing LRVs. Some people, both within and outside Muni, proposed saving a modest fleet of 8-10 Boeings to begin the E-Line. With their moveable steps, they could use the high platforms on the MMX and the low platforms of the F-Line Fisherman's Wharf Extension. And the wire was pantograph-compatible. But this idea never saw the light of day due to the political demands from the Wharf merchants and other lobbying groups that all rail service to the Wharf must be provided with rail vehicles "older than 1955." The last Boeings ran on the J-Line on December 31, 2001, and were cut up for scrap a few months later.

To Loop, or Not to Loop?
That is the Question

2004 CAME AND WENT, and so did 2005, 2006 and 2007, without any E-Line service startup. The reasons were many: No cars. No money. No operators available. Each year, the executive directors of the SFMTA (San Francisco Municipal Transportation Agency, successor to SFPTC), first Michael Burns and then Nathaniel Ford Sr. expressed a desire to begin at least a limited service, but these pronouncements were just that: talk.

Nevertheless, some progress has been made. In 2005, Melbourne W2 496 became the first vintage car to be outfitted with the LVPS (low-voltage power supply) system and VETAG, followed by New Orleans 952 and Blackpool "Boat" 228. Muni B-Type 162, then in the process of being restored, was the next. Car 1, which returned from remanufacturing at Brookville Equipment Co. in Pennsylvania at the end of 2010, was outfitted with the LVPS system while at Brookville. The others were scheduled to be retrofitted by 2012, as were the four "Torpedoes" being remanufactured at Brookville. Having all of these cars available will permit a 2013 startup.

Lack of money also precluded construction of a turning loop at 6th and King, which would make the necessity of running the E-Line with double-enders a moot point. Although the idea has been considered in the 2008-2027 SFMTA Short Range Transit Plan,

Vintage Cars along the Proposed E-Embarcadero and MMX

Muni Metro Extension (MMX) opened in 1998 and is served by Muni Metro lines N-Judah and T-Third. Occasionally, F-Line cars can bee seen on the route,. The permanent E-Line started in 2015..

right) Car 1 passes the San Francisco Giants baseball stadium–then called Pacific Bell Park–on July 13, 2001, the first day of public vintage car rides on MMX. (*below*) 1895-built "Dinky" 578(S) is returning from the Metro East Yard, where it was on display during the American Public Transportation Association Light Rail Conference. It's followed by a Breda train at King and 3rd Streets on June 1, 2008. *Both photos, Peter Ehrlich*

2008 Sunday Streets scenes: (*left and below left*) Embarcadero and Folsom, showing residents enjoying their car-free street, and vintage trolleys. (*above*) PCC 1007 leans into the curve between 2nd Street and Townsend along The Embarcadero on August 31, 2008. (*below*) Diners at a sidewalk café on King Street are enjoying more than food as they watch streetcars such as 1914 Muni B-Type 162 pass by on a Sunday Streets day, September 14, 2008. Perhaps they will ride the vintage trolley back to the Ferry Building. *All photos, Peter Ehrlich*

early implementation is unlikely.

A longer-range proposal has been espoused by MSR, which also involves a turning loop. This plan would extend the E-Line over T-Line trackage through the burgeoning Mission Bay redevelopment district, to a loop at 18th, Illinois and 19th Streets into the Union Iron Works Historic District. (See below.)

There were, however, two demonstration E-Embarcadero services that occurred in 2008, in conjunction with an environmentally-friendly, sustainable living idea sponsored by The City for residents to enjoy their city, entitled "Sunday Streets." Parts of Third Street, along the new T-Line, and the northbound lanes of The Embarcadero, were closed off and residents could walk, ride bicycles, roller skate and skateboard along these streets without interference from auto traffic. Urged by MSR and others, Muni used vintage car 952 and "Torpedo" 1007 on the first Sunday, August 31, and added Muni B-Type 162 and another "Torpedo" on the second closure two weeks later. The demonstration was hailed and cheered by residents. For the first time, the side safety islands on the MMX were used as passenger stops. "Sunday Streets" has been repeated several times since, expanding to other parts of the city, but sadly, there have been no further attempts to demonstrate the E-Line service.

The Torpedo Project

AS DESCRIBED IN CHAPTERS 5 AND 8, there was a desire among many people, both within and outside Muni, to get the four remaining double-end PCC "Torpedoes"–1006, 1008, 1009 and 1011–remanufactured, and specifications were written by Muni Fleet Engineering around 1997. (There were concerns about including 1009 in this program, as it had received the brunt of the fire damage in 1994, but it was finally included in the most recent bid package.) There was even a call to repatriate 1014 from the Sydney Tramway Museum, but this would have caused an ugly international incident over the terms of how 1014's presence in Australia was defined, and the idea was dropped.

A renewed push to get the double-end PCC rebuilding program back on track was made in 2004, and the specs were ready for bid in 2005. There were two bidders, but one was later disqualified for non-compliance after the bids were opened in early 2007. The other bidder, Brookville Equipment Co., was asked to submit two bids–one for straight rebuild with the original General Electric DC electrical components and rebuilt trucks, and a second bid with AC propulsion and brand new trucks similar to what Brookville supplied to 18 PCCs remanufactured for Philadelphia in 2003. With Fleet Engineering leaning toward the AC package, the question of fleet authenticity became a factor. If Muni went to AC for these cars, would it also do the same for the mid-life rebuild of the ex-Philly cars later on? With AC guts, some people were concerned that the F-Line fleet would no longer be a "heritage" fleet. This issue was resolved in favor of keeping DC propulsion and the original contract was allowed to lapse, and Muni engineers set out to work on a new bid package.

The second bid package, which also included rewiring of the 11 ex-Newark PCCs and the remanufacturing of car 1040, was advertised in 2009. This time, a successful conclusion was reached with the award of the contract to Brookville. The first "Torpedo" to reach Pennsylvania was 1008 in February 2010, followed by 1006 a few weeks later. The last car, 1009, left on June 25, 2011. 1008, the pilot car, came back in May 2012.

Even this contract featured something different: The double-enders' original General Electric controls were replaced by new Westinghouse-design drum controllers from Bombardier, which holds the Westinghouse PCC controller patents and designs and is willing to supply new propulsion packages. GE, on the other hand, has stopped making PCC controllers, and was no longer interested in doing so. This will be the first application of Westinghouse controllers to a double-end PCC since the Dallas double-enders built by Pullman-Standard in 1945. (The 11 ex-Newark cars also received new Westinghouse controllers.)

All of this wrangling added up to more delay in instituting the E-Line, and riders from Fisherman's Wharf will still have to transfer at Embarcadero Station to go to a baseball game. According to the 2008/2027 SFMTA Short Range Transit Plan, this should have happened in 2010, but actually happened five years later. When the startup of E-Line service does occur, even more cars may be required, because of the next expansion project in the pipeline.

On to Fort Mason

AFTER ABOUT A YEAR of service to the Wharf, people were beginning to talk about where the historic trolleys should call their next destination. The universal, and natural, choice was to build (or rebuild) tracks westward along Aquatic Park and through the old State Belt Railroad tunnel to Fort Mason.

Fort Mason is an army outpost that was established in 1863 as the Post of Point San Jose, as part of the West Coast defense network. Renamed in 1882, it became an important embarkation point for troops and supplies in World War II, and later the Korean War. Muni's H-Potrero trolley line, which

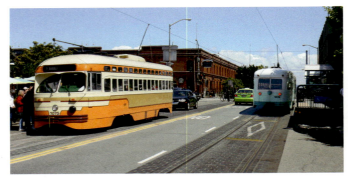 

The draft Environmental Impact Statement issued by GGNRA for the proposed Fort Mason Extension included these three photographic renditions of what the Extension could look like. (*top left*) At Beach and Hyde. (*top right*) Trackage through the west end of Aquatic Park approaching the Fort Mason Tunnel. (*right*) Possible loop arrangement at Fort Mason. *All photos, Environmental Vision/National Park Service*

ran on Van Ness Avenue, served Fort Mason until 1950, with its B-Type cars (augmented by ex-Market Street Railway 100-series "Haight Street Jewetts" after the Merger in 1944) signed for "U. S. Docks." But in the 1960s, its use diminished, its military activities shifting to the Oakland Army Base. In the 1970s, it became the headquarters for the Golden Gate National Recreation Area, and today its buildings house the Fort Mason Center's various non-profit organizations and cultural activities.

When Fort Mason was a military center, it was served by an extension of the State Belt Railroad, whose tracks ran along Jefferson Street, skirted Aquatic Park and through a single-track tunnel under the craggy bluff between Van Ness Avenue and Laguna Street, hard by the Marina Green. The tunnel was bored through in 1914, and tracks ultimately reached The Presidio. Trains continued into the Presidio Army Base, but the last trains ran through the tunnel around 1955. Therefore, any possibility of running streetcars through the tunnel depended on a full seismological evaluation of the bore. A preliminary investigation showed that it appeared to be structurally sound.

As mentioned in Chapter 2, it was suggested back in 1974, when original plans for an E-Line were broached, that the route reach Fort Mason. But with the planning for building the F-Line's Wharf Extension, a mid-Wharf terminal was selected, and further extension fell dormant for a while.

As noted earlier, the Fort Mason complex had become the headquarters of the Golden Gate National Recreation Area, and it was now attracting 1½ million visitors a year to its mix of performing arts venues, art galleries and associated functions. There are 40 non-profit organizations based at Fort Mason. Al Baccari of the Fisherman's Wharf Merchants Association (and a member of the MSR Advisory Board) began lobbying for the Fort Mason Extension, as there was little public transit service to Fort Mason, and, most especially, none from downtown. The tunnel was being preserved by the National Park Service as part of its GGNRA master plan for improved transit service to Fort Mason.

Another factor was that the businesses in the western part of the Wharf were underserved with the current F-Line terminal at Jones and Beach. They had only the Hyde Street cable car and two bus lines, neither of which operated on Beach Street. An extended streetcar along the State Belt Railroad tracks would solve that problem nicely. As this blog from Market Street Railway suggested, "The [Fort Mason] extension has the important benefit of reunifying the pieces of Fisherman's Wharf by rebalancing transit access between its eastern and western portions. After studying several possible east-west alignments...Beach Street was selected as the route for environmental and historic preservation reasons. Among other advantages, this allows the placement of streetcar stops in both directions directly opposite the Hyde Street cable car turntable, providing a mini-transit hub to visitors wishing (sic) [to] explore the Wharf area. The streetcar tracks alone provide a clue to visitors getting off the cable cars that there's something to see where the tracks lead..."[1]

The National Park Service issued a draft Environmental Impact Statement in March 2011, based on an extensive outreach program, including meetings, workshops and direct mailings begun in 2006. Part of this work involved a more thorough seismic assessment of the State Belt Railroad Fort Mason Tunnel, and, like the previous preliminary investigation, there appear to be no problems. However, the tunnel is too narrow for double-track operation, so single-tracking cars will be necessary. The final Environmental Impact Statement followed nearly a year later, in February 2012, and the "Record Of Decision" in March 2013. It included the "Locally Preferred Alternative" alignment along Beach Street, trackage at the west end of Aquatic Park connecting to the Fort Mason tunnel, and selected the North Loop at Fort Mason.

In the early stages of planning, Muni suggested that the extension become a continuation of the E-Embarcadero. For a time, however, the thinking was to continue the more-frequent F-Market from Jones and Beach to Fort Mason and have the E-Line terminate at Jones and Beach. In 2017, the pendulum has swung back to having E-Line cars run through the Fort Mason Tunnel instead, which has the blessing of MSR. Either way, more cars will be needed. [See Chapter 8.]

SFMTA and NPS estimate the cost of the extension to Fort Mason to cost about $53 million. Both entities are working on obtaining pots of money to build the extension.

In the meantime, San Francisco was selected to host the 34th America's Cup Finals, which took place on San Francisco Bay between July and September 2013. The City, headed by Mayor Ed Lee, who succeeded Gavin Newsom at the beginning of 2011 following Newsom's election as California's Lieutenant Governor, worked feverishly to develop transportation plans to move the estimated millions of race spectators, and of prime importance is to get the Fort Mason Extension up and running.

A controversial proposal by the National Park Service almost derailed the whole idea in 2015. NPS was considering a plan to move the Alcatraz Ferry boarding docks into Fort Mason. That roused the ire of District 2 Supervisor Mark Farrell, who represents the posh Marina District, who vowed that if NPS moved the boats into his district, he would fight it to the hilt, and the Fort Mason Extension would be a likely casualty as a result. Fort Mason is already inundated with workers and visitors, and having the Alcatraz runs would be ruinous. Fortunately, the Park Service changed its mind, and kept the Alcatraz boat boarding area back at Pier 31.

Muni's Old Number One, in E-Embarcadero service for Heritage Weekend, rolls up the Embarcadero Connector, between Folsom and Howard Streets and alongside the Muni Metro Ferry Portal, under a beautifully-mottled sky on September 26, 2015. This was the first year that regular E-Line service was provided for Heritage Weekend. *Peter Ehrlich*

**Finally! The E-Line
Begins Regular Service!**

AT LONG LAST, IN JULY, SFMTA announced that weekend service on the E-Embarcadero would begin on August 1, 2015, as part of a major, and continuing, overall system-wide service expansion that had actually begun in April. A dream for over 40 years was finally going to become a reality! San Franciscans would be able to ride a comfortable streetcar all the way from Fisherman's Wharf to Caltrain!

The startup of the E-Embarcadero was kicked off with the launch of the new Blackpool "Boat" tram, number 233, with Mayor Ed Lee, some members of the Board of Supervisors, and other dignitaries

Supervisor Scott Wiener, Mayor Ed Lee, SFMTA Executive Director Ed Reiskin (all in the center of the picture) and others kick off the E-Embarcadero with a ceremony in front of Blackpool "Boat" 233 and 1006 at the Ferries on August 1, 2015. Weekend service began this day. Weekday service was added nine months later. The Bay Bridge provides the backdrop. *SFMTA photo*

boarding at AT&T Park, and riding up to the Ferry Building.

Service hours for the new line, at least for the time being, were daytime only, from 10:00 a.m. to 7:00 p.m.

The schedule called for five of the seven "Torpedoes" to maintain a 15-minute service. This proved to be a little optimistic, however, because of delays at both the 4th and King end and at Fisherman's Wharf. At 4th and King, outbound cars had to wait through the clumsy light and switch operation cycle, before crossing to the low level platform on the west side of the intersection. In addition, the frequent N-Judah and T-Third Muni Metro trains would get in the way. Also, they often had to wait their turn to get into one of the switchback tracks at King and 6th, occupied by two-car N trains much of the time.

At the Fisherman's Wharf end, they would routinely be blocked by regular F-line service. However, for the most part, the kinks would get ironed out, and more steady service patterns would be the rule. MSR and riders had to be content with weekend service only for another nine months before weekday service would begin. The start day for 7-day service was April 25, 2016.

MSR is trying to negotiate a plan with Muni to have the vintage two-man cars operate on the E-Line regularly—at least on weekends—instead of just operating them during the annual Heritage Weekends. One of the impediments, as we have seen at other times during the operation of vintage cars, is the constant shortage of qualified operators.

G for Golden Gate Park

SHORTLY AFTER THE F-LINE was extended to Fisherman's Wharf, some people came up with an idea of building a line into the museum area in Golden Gate Park. This would be the G-Golden Gate Park historic streetcar line. Cars would run from the Ferry Building (or a rejuvenated Transbay Terminal loop) out the F-Line to Market and Church, turn one block north via the J-Line, then turn left and operate on the N-Judah out to Irving and 9th Avenue, then north and into the park, looping at the Music Concourse, hard by the new De Young Museum and California Academy of Sciences. It would not be expensive to build; the only new infrastructure required would be turnouts at Church and Market and trackage along 9th Avenue and in the park.

Some preliminary hearings were held concerning the concept, and considerable opposition came from the merchants along 9th Avenue, and from tour bus operators. So the idea has been quietly shelved for now.

The whole idea of streetcars in San Francisco parks has been controversial ever since John McLaren designed Golden Gate Park, transforming it from sand dunes to the jewel it is now. From the outset, he refused to allow any streetcar line into the park, especially not in the vicinity of the museums and the Music Concourse, off 8th Avenue in the Richmond District and 9th Avenue in the Inner Sunset. (However, the old 7-Haight line had a section of track running through the extreme southwest corner of the park so it could reach its Playland-at-the-Beach terminal.)

The Union Iron Works Loop

UNION IRON WORKS was a shipbuilder located off of Third Street and 18th/19th Streets in the Central Waterfront area south of Mission Bay. Nevertheless, it had streetcar-building expertise as well. In 1912, it completed the order for the new A-Type streetcars after original builder W. L. Holman went bankrupt, building 23 of the 43 cars. After Union Iron Works was absorbed into Bethlehem Steel in the 1920s, it received an order for 20 K-Type cars in 1923. Union Iron Works was in full gear throughout World War II and its workers arrived on Market Street Railway Line 16 cars for the duration, and even into the Muni era. Many of the Key System's Bridge Units of the 1930s were also built at the Union Iron Works site.

Milan "Peter Witt" 1818 has backed into the 19th Street leg of the future Union Iron Works loop, during a charter. This is what it would look like if E-Line cars were extended out here, with the possibility of using single-end cars. The old Union Iron Works cranes are in the background. May 26, 2009. *Peter Ehrlich* (A picture of car 162 using the 19th Street stub is on page 157 in Chapter 8.)

The cranes and original buildings still exist, and the district, just north of "Dogpatch," is now classed as the Union Iron Works Historic District. Eventually, the property will be rehabilitated and brought back to life.

There are the beginnings of a loop off the T-Line at 3rd and 18th and 3rd and 19th Streets. The intention, from the construction of Third Street Light Rail (the T-Line), was to allow for short turns on the T-Line as the Mission Bay Redevelopment Project gets built out. Completion of the loop for this purpose is still contemplated.

Then MSR joined in with its plan for historics. The idea from MSR and others is this: Completing the loop would allow for a natural off-line terminal for E-Embarcadero cars, and would not require exclusive operation of double-end cars. In addition, it would extend historic streetcar service to the burgeoning Mission Bay area. Sounds like a no-brainer, right?

Well, this became controversial when the Port of San Francisco, which owns the tracks along Illinois Street, barred Muni from completing the loop because, in its strange logic, "Freight trains will need the trackage to serve this area again." Port staff seemed unaware that the rails have already been severed seven blocks south for LRV access to the new Metro East carbarn, haven't been used since 1985, and are unlikely to ever see freight trains again. The Port never objected to those changes back in 2006. At any rate, the funding for completing the loop, once a priority for Muni and SFMTA, has fallen on the back burner. But a new push to obtain funding began in mid-2011.

The loop could still be built, however, with the costs borne by a developer of the Union Iron Works Historic District yet to be selected. In addition, the intention of the loop was to turn back T-Line trains terminating at the Mission Bay/UCSF Station adjacent to the new UCSF complex, much of which has already been built and is in use. The center could be served by N-Judah trains, which already serves UCSF Medical Center on Parnassus Avenue in the Inner Sunset District.

Ultimately, the Port relented, permitting SFMTA and Muni to start final engineering and prepare to finish the loop.

However, in 2015, a lawsuit to prevent the construction of the loop was filed by residents of the growing Dogpatch neighborhood, who contended that the loop's location between 18th and 19th would give the neighborhood short shrift in terms of service levels, with every other T train from Chinatown terminating there. They maintained that because of the growth of Dogpatch, a new environmental review and impact report was needed. The suit dragged on, and finally the judge in the case ruled against the petitioners.

SFMTA began construction of the loop in mid-2016, mostly moving utility installations. But it hopes to get the loop completed well before the Central Subway opens in 2019.

But where does that leave MSR's desire for E-Embarcadero cars to use the loop? Right now, it's in limbo. Several sources state that Muni doesn't want the E-Embarcadero cars to interfere with T-Third movements in and out of the loop, or anywhere on the T-Line for that matter, even by having the cars loop through Metro East Yard. This is an odd position, because already, there are N and T trains on South Embarcadero, along with E-Line cars, and, while there are physical issues with the infrastructure, such as at 4th and King which have nothing to do with the the type of vehicle, there are no rolling impediments.

If E-Line cars *are* extended out the T, low-level platforms will have to be built adjoining the stations. This does not to be an insurmountable problem. All of the T-Line stations are side-of-the trackway platforms, unlike those on the Muni Metro Extension, which are island platforms, where there are very real problems with people, not knowing where to stand for

E-Line cars, suddenly rushing from the high-level platforms to the E-Line low-level ones, and the potential for a tripping accident is high.

Into the Presidio?

LONG AFTER THE PROPOSED FORT MASON EXTENSION was broached and began to be studied, many people thought that the next logical step was to bring streetcars all the way to the Presidio. This is unlikely to happen, primarily because of considerable opposition among the wealthy and influential residents along Marina Blvd., and the realization that sources of funding may never be available, considering the climate regarding transit funding in the United States today. Still, it would make an already scenic streetcar line even more so, and the dreams first espoused in the early 1970s would be realized.

Why Are There No Vintage Cars on the N-Line?

WHEN THE F-LINE OPENED in 1995, PCCs would still occasionally operate on the N-Judah on charters or even in service. That changed in 1997, when Muni constructed handicapped ramps at "Key Stops" on existing streetcar lines–major transfer points or stops used by many people, such as UCSF Medical Center. This was a way of meeting Americans with Disabilities Act (ADA) requirements without building ramps at every stop. On the F-Line, this was done on the older Market Street portion of the line between 8th Street and Transbay Terminal.

One of the "Key Stop" locations where a ramp was built was the inbound stop at Judah and 9th Avenue, just before the line turns left (north). One day, Car 1 went out the N on a charter, and as it began the turn, there was a loud "crunch" as the right rear anticlimber struck the concrete ramp, which Bredas could clear–with an inch or so to spare. Single-end PCCs and Milan cars could also clear this easily, but not the 50'-5"-long double-end "Torpedoes," whose overhang was too great. Afterward, an attempt was made to shave back the ramp. Car 1 was then taken out and it cleared the ramp without any further problems.

However, when George Louie took over as Division Manager of Green Light Rail Division in 1999, he asked me "What is this all about?" as I was one of the few vintage car operators left at Green Division. So I explained the clearance problem with only the "Torpedoes" at 9th and Judah. Well, he must have misinterpreted my explanation, because within a few days, stickers appeared on the dashboards of all the PCCs and Milanos, which read "Do Not Operate On N-Line." Subsequent tests with PCCs and vintage cars proved he was wrong (except in the case of the "Torpedoes"), and MSR and others are trying to lift the ban. So far, with the N-Line having the heaviest patronage of any line, Muni certainly doesn't want any non-regular cars to run out there.

Double-end cars can, and have, gone out the N-Line through the Sunset Tunnel as far as the crossover at Carl and Hillway.

There was a funny anecdote involving the Muni bureaucracy about the handicapped ramp at 9th and Judah. In 2001, I had been appointed Division Safety Representative by the Union, and one of my tasks was to sit in on meetings of the Rail Change Control Board, which was just another useless function set up by the Muni bureaucracy to approve changes in rail-related infrastructure. So I asked a Muni engineer why the 9th and Judah ramp was designed in such a way so that vintage cars couldn't clear it. His response: "We thought that these cars would never have to run out there again."

But there's a different reason why B-Types 130 and 162 can't go out the N-Line. There is a long fire-suppression standpipe that runs the length of the tunnel alongside the inbound track. At the east end, the pipe would knock the car's roof signbox off. There are no plans to modify this pipe right now, but it may be done in the future.

Gimme Shelter!

UNTIL 1982, when Muni ceased PCC operation, its streetcars were always kept under cover at Geneva Carhouse. Following the demise of service, the historic carbarn shed was demolished. While Geneva Yard, sans cover, was renovated for use by LRVs and historic cars, the old cars would suffer during the rainy seasons.

For at least a dozen years after the F-Line opened, MSR and other interested parties advocated for some sort of covered storage to protect cars, especially those with canvas and wood roofs, such as the Milanos and most of the two-man vintage cars, from the elements. For several years, their desire was thwarted, first by design difficulties, and then by denial of funding. But MSR continued to press the issue. Finally, in 2008, the SFMTA approved a design/build contract to construct a six-track "Historic Streetcar Enclosure" over tracks 7-12 in Geneva Yard. When completed, all Milanos and the vintage cars would be stabled inside the shelter, while most PCCs, with their steel roofs, would be able to remain outside. Up to 30 cars could be stashed under cover when completed.

For some reason, work on building the enclosure didn't begin until early 2010. Finally, the shelter was completed in September, and cars were

After more than ten years of striving to get Muni's historic streetcars under cover, the new Historic Streetcar Enclosure was dedicated by SFMTA Executive Director Nat Ford Sr. (speaking in front of rehabbed PCC 1071) on December 2, 2010 as other Muni and SFMTA officials look on. The late Cameron Beach is standing behind Ford. *Rick Laubscher*

beginning to be stored inside shortly thereafter. The shelter was officially dedicated on December 2, 2010.

Another note about Geneva Yard: Until early 2010, when construction of the Historic Car Enclosure began, some of the tracks in the yard were used to store Bredas at night and on weekends. When construction began, these were "evicted" from Geneva Yard and moved over to the new Metro East barn, which opened in 2008. This allows for Geneva to handle historic car storage and maintenance functions exclusively. The yard will be needed for possible fleet expansion, anyway, so this was an extra benefit, and will continue to be this way for years to come.

In April 2011, Geneva Yard, a San Francisco streetcar facility since before the 1906 Earthquake and Fire, was renamed the Cameron Beach Historic Streetcar Yard, to honor SFMTA Director Cameron Beach, who died unexpectedly on March 18, 2011. Beach was a native San Franciscan and a lover of historic streetcars. He had also been a transit executive with the Sacramento Regional Transit District, where he served as Light Rail Operations Manager and Chief Operating Officer. He was a rare breed–someone who not only loved rail history, but also was a transit professional. For a while, Beach served as a MSR director and was also chairman of the Western Railway Museum board.

However, the use of the shelter for storing the regular F-Line fleet under cover turned out to be short-lived. In 2012, management, in a move that has not been satisfactorily explained to this day, ordered all the Milan Peter Witts to be based at Metro East. Ostensibly, this was a ploy to placate residents along the J-Church line, who complained about noise. The problem with keeping them at Metro East, however, once again exposes them to the elements, defeating the purpose of covered storage, and some of the canvas-roofed Milanos soon started exhibiting issues with mildew. Then, in 2014, a project to rerail Metro Yard forced the PCCs to join their Italian cousins at Metro East, so that some Bredas could use Cameron Beach Yard for storage. Management has pledged to move all the cars back to Beach Yard once the rerailing is complete, but that project is way behind schedule, and MSR is concerned that top brass will concoct another excuse not to make the move.

Extension into Fort Mason Stalled Again

IN LATE 2016, after about three years of inactivity, the SFMTA, the San Francisco County Transportation Agency (SFCTA) and the National Park Service began working together to try to get the stalled extension through the Fort Mason Tunnel and into Fort Mason back on track. For the record, the Environmental Impact Statement (EIS) was approved in 2014..

It had been hoped that money from a a grant—$1.9 million—from a program called FLAP, which doles out money for improved public transportation and general access to federal lands (such as the Golden Gate National Recreation Area, of which Fort Mason is a part—would come through. This would have provided some seed money to advance the project. But it was turned down. Part of the reason for its denial had to do with a change in the Federal government in 2017 from an administration that was friendly to public transportation projects to one that was perceived as being hostile, particularly to new rail projects. This was only one of the issues, however. The other issue was the Fort Mason Tunnel itself. Several years prior, inspection showed that it was structurally and seismically sound. Now, apparently, it needs $10 million in seismic upgrades before it can be used for rail–or other–purposes. (For example, the San Francisco Bicycle Coalition has long sought the use of the tunnel for a bike path.) The National Park Service and GGNRA have other issues that need financial attention, such as the rebuilding of the decaying Municipal Pier, part of the San Francisco Maritime National Historic Park, another NPS /GGNRA unit.

An interim solution might be in the making, however. In mid-2017, the leaders of the Fort Mason Center same to *MSR* with an idea that would at least extend the track into Aquatic Park up to the east end of the tunnel, which would be done anyway using the 2013 EIS as a basis. Either a stub-end terminal for E-Line cars, or a loop permitting any Muni historic vehicle, would be built, and a new, and level, "Peopleway" would be constructed for pedestrians, bicyclists and wheelchair users in kind of a semicircle around Black Point, the steepest part of Fort Mason, from Aquatic Park around to the Fort Mason Center at Pier 3. The "Peopleway" would begin at wherever the configuration of the streetcar terminal wold be located,

Three terminal options are being considered. Option A would be a a terminal at the foot of Beach Street. Option B would be an in-Aquatic Park terminal, following the approved route as set out in the EIS. up to the east end of the tunnel. Both of these options require double-end cars. The third option, Option C, would use a loop via a portion of Van Ness. Cars would drop passengers at the "Peopleway", and then loop around to the terminal stop in Aquatic Park. Having a loop would allow for single-end cars, as well as the planned double-ended E-Line cars.

Building this alternate terminal for E-Line cars would help improve schedule issues. Currently, with the shared loop at Jones and Beach, E-line cars are at the mercy of whatever is in front of them, and have to wait their turn. This throws the schedule out the window.

No official cost estimate has been made for this alternative project, but a rough estimate could be in

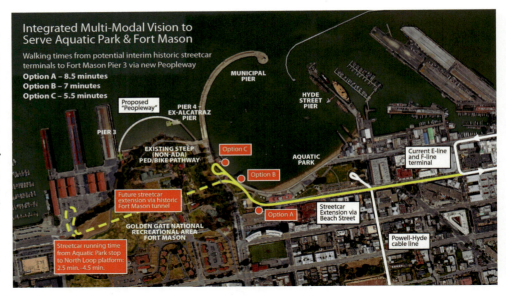

This is a conceptual graphic showing the three options for an interim Aquatic Park terminal for E-Embarcadero streetcars, until money to build the line through the Fort Mason Tunnel can be found. This includes the level "Peopleway" for walkers, bikers and people with wheelchairs to use to get from Aquatic Park to Pier 3. On the way, access to Pier 4, the embarkation point for prisoners to Alcatraz, may be included. *Conceptual graphic by Dave Dugan for Market Street Railway; used with permission. (Base map from Google Maps.)*

the neighborhood of $50 million. MSR, which is backing thee idea, is urging SFMTA to apply for any alternative sources of funds to get this proposal built. Hopefully, private philanthropies may also come forward to finance the project.

Proposed 7th Street Loop

THE F-LINE'S HEAVIEST LOADING begins at 5th Street, increasing at 4th Street and Main Street. Occasionally, cars have used the 11th Street wye to turn back for service. But that location—in addition to being a cumbersome maneuver, is also too far away for practical use.

MSR is lobbying The City and SFMTA to put in a loop turnback at 7th Street North, The loop would use McAllister, make a left onto 7th North, where cars would take their layovers, out of the way of traffic. When it's time to leave the loop, cars could then turn left to rejoin Market and start swallowing the crowds inbound. A switch for cars to turn outbound would be installed as well.

At presstime, there has been no further development on this rational and efficient idea.

Original O'Farrell, Jones & Hyde cable car 42, which was restored by Market Street Railway, is heading up Hyde Street as an inbound California car passes. The original O'Farrell, Jones & Hyde line, which was abandoned in 1954, crossed here and continued to Pine Street and made a left. So, for a brief moment, both Cal Cable lines were recreated! The parking lot on the right was where Cal Cable's carbarn stood. September 26, 2015. *Peter Ehrlich*

2014 and 2015 Cable Cars, Dinkies, Buses and Boats!

(*right column, top to bottom*) 2014 scenes: 1896-built 578(S), the oldest streetcar operating for a public transit agency in the world, is at Embarcadero/Sansome, heading for the Ferry Building. Special O'Farrell, Jones & Hyde cable car 42 crosses at California and Hyde. Up to 1954, both Cal Cable lines crossed here. A "second" debut of new Blackpool "Boat" 233 was made during the 2014 Weekend. Both Boats (233, left, and 228) are at the Ferries, "watching" PCC 1009 (Dallas) go by on a regular F-Line run. Later in the afternoon of November 2, No. 233 carries some special invited guests on its pull-in trip at Market and Church. (*below*) Working the historic trolley coach and bus loop, Marmon trolleybus 776 crosses Mason/Ellis. *All photos, Peter Ehrlich*

Heritage Weekends!

STARTING IN 2012, the use of vintage cars for regular service diminished greatly. There were several reasons for this. The principal reason was a lack of qualified operators available for everyday service. Another was the practice by division dispatchers and managers to reassign those same qualified operators to other runs, or even Muni Metro runs, based on the "needs of the service". Naturally, the leaders of MSR and other interested people became quite distressed. So Muni came up with another plan: Hold a "Heritage Weekend' once each year, so that people could enjoy the old stuff.

For the first three years, the first weekend of November was chosen to be Heritage Weekend. Treasures like Car Number 1, the two "Iron Monsters", 130 and 162, and the Melbourne car, provided service on the E-Line, which still wasn't officially open. In addition, Muni's fleet of vintage buses and trolley coaches operated. The rubber-tired fleet ran a special counter-clockwise loop service from Don Chee Way via Steuart, Market, Sutter, Mason, back to Market and back to D, which will come back as a St. Louis caron Chee Way. Vehicles such as 1950-vintage Marmon-Herrington 776, 1976-built Flyer trolleybus 5300, Baby White 042 (1938) and

2014 Heritage Weekend
The 2014 weekend took place on November 1 and 2.

Photos from the 2013 Heritage Weekend are on Page 321.

Another bus on the Mason Street bus loop: Baby White 042. *Peter Ehrlich*

GMC 3287, a 1969 product, were out for the riding public, with free rides to all.

Starting with the 2015 Heritage Weekend, there were two changes. First, the weekend was moved from the first weekend in November to the last weekend in September. Second, the 2015 Festival was the first to feature regular E-Embarcadero service.

The 2015 event was also the first to have the second Blackpool "Boat", 233, enter passenger service. 233, along with 228 and MSRy "Dinky" 578S, provided an unusual operation. They would operate between Don Chee Way and Pier 39. The procedure was this: When it became time for one of the cars to make a trip, it would pick up passengers on the *outbound* side of Don Chee Way, loop around the Hotel Vitale, and swing back onto The Embarcadero to go north. SFPD made it possible for cars to take their layovers on Mission Street by banning parking in front of the Audiffred Building.

From time to time, one of the double-end historics would make an unplanned trip out to Castro and back, taking a break from its E-Line duties.

The buses loaded on Steuart Street, alongside the San Francisco Railway Museum. 1941-vintage St. Louis Car trolley coach 506 was on display. To make it operational, it needs a new differential.

For the 2016 Heritage Weekend, Muni celebrated 75 years of providing trolley coach service by "recreating" the R-Howard/South Van Ness route, which opened in 1941. Coaches 776 and 5300 alternated every 45 minutes to make the run from Don Chee Way out to 26th and Mission. (This wasn't the first trolleybus route in San Francisco. That honor went to Market Street Railway Co., when it converted the 33-18th & Park [now 33-Stanyan, before that 33-Ashbury] line to trolley coaches in 1935.)

Another highlight was the appearance of newly-remanufactured PCC 1056 (Kansas City), which was brought over from Metro East by a shopman for a brief display at Ferries. 1056 was the first of the newly-rebuilt ex-Philadelphia PCCs.

The 2017 Festival, so far, is considered to be the best one yet. It was held earlier in the month of September, on Saturday and Sunday, September 9 and 10.

The 2017 event commemorated another milestone in Muni's history. 100 years earlier, Muni purchased its first motor coaches to expand service into places that its streetcar lines couldn't quite reach, such as the Jefferson Loop in the Marina District, connecting with the original F-Stockton line at Scott and Chestnut; and a cross-Golden Gate Park route from the terminal of the A-Line at 10th and Fulton into the Inner Sunset on the south side of the park.

Muni brought its newest historic bus down for display at Justin Herman Plaza, opposite the San Francisco Railway Museum, for the occasion. This was 1956 Mack 2230, which had its exterior cosmetic-ally restored. In addition, it was made fully operable. However, it still needs side windows and seats. Displayed next to it at the Plaza was brand new New Flyer Xcelsior 8853, which had a photographic exhibit inside depicting milestones in Muni's motor coach history.

The historic buses and trolley coaches got placed on a new route for 2017, too, essentially replicating the southern section of the rush-hour-only 41-Union between Mission/Steuart and Washington Square. In addition, Muni operated some of the historic motor coaches on the Friday before Heritage Weekend on line 7-Haight out to Golden Gate Park (the original outer terminal of the old trolleybus route). Featured buses were 1969 GMC 3287; 1975 AM General 4154; 1984 Flyer D901 4574; and 1990 Orion 9010.

A second commemorative was the 100th Anniversary of the J-Church line. PCCs 1051 (Muni Simplified) and 1060 (Philly "Cream Cheese") alternated trips from Don Chee Way out to the original J-Line terminal at 30th and Church, as did Car 1. 1914 "Iron Monster" 130 also made a trip out there, but was moved into other services because its appearance— last updated in 1996—was now decidedly ratty.

Heritage Weekends have proven to be a big success!

WITH THE E-LINE COMING ON BOARD in 2015, the addition of four more "Torpedoes" to the fleet, and the possibility of the extension into Fort Mason and south to Dogpatch, there is a lot to look forward to in San Francisco in the next few years!

References:

1. Blog from *Market Street Railway* website, "Reunifying The Wharf, Extending The F-Line To Fort Mason," June 20, 2009, by Rick Laubscher [http://www.streetcar.org/blog/2009/06/reunifying-the-wharf.html], accessed August 5, 2011.

2015 Heritage Weekend
Starting with 2015, Muni changed the Heritage Weekend dates to the last weekend in September — in this case, Saturday and Sunday, September 26 and 27.

Pullout scenes, under a beautifully mottled sky: (*left*) PCC 1009 (Dallas) rounds the corner of 3rd and Channel as an E-Line pullout from Metro East. (*right*) "Iron Monster" 130 passes Brannan Station as a Heritage Weekend pullout car. HDR images taken on the first day of the 2015 Heritage Weekend.
Both photos, Peter Ehrlich

2015 Heritage Weekend, continued!
All photos on this page by Peter Ehrlich.

(*above*) The Susan G. Komen Foundation's annual "Race for the Cure" (to fight cancer) took place simultaneously with Heritage Weekend on Sunday, September 27. The northbound lanes along The Embarcadero were closed off to traffic for the race. PCC 1076 (Washington), an F-Line pullout car, passes racers at Bryant Street. *Peter Ehrlich*

(*left*) MSR and Muni set up a chalkboard at the entrance to the San Francisco Railway Museum, announcing the departure times of streetcars and historic buses. (*blow*) PCCs 1071 (Minneapolis/St. Paul) and 1079 (Detroit) bracket 1896 "Dinky" 578(S) at Don Chee Way.

(*above* Operators Lan Lai and Shirley Hubbard are the bo'sun and captain of Blackpool "Boat" 233. (*below*) Dan Cohen, Jeremy Whiteman and the crew of MSRy "Dinky" 578(S) pose at Brannan Street.

(*right*) A little boy is having fun on Car 1.

More 2015 Heritage Weekend!

All photos on this page by Peter Ehrlich. A special guest joined Blackpool "Boat" 233 on Sunday: Emperor Norton! (One of the all-time notorious San Francisco characters from the late 1800s.) The Emperor poses with Motorman Melvin Clark at the Ferry Building (*left*) and with the crew at Pier 39.

(*below left*). (*below*) Boat 228 lays over on Mission Street as E-Line PCC 1011 passes by.

(*belowl*) Time to go home! Car 1 is making the turn at King and 4th Street (Caltrain Depot) and will head out to the Muni Metro East maintenance yard, where all cars were kept overnight on Saturday, September 26. Many cars call MME home, but others will return to Beach Yard after Heritage Weekend is over.

(*above*) Muni B-Type 130 passes the *Nuestros Silencios* sculpture set by the Spanish conceptual sculptor, Rivelino. This exhibit of 10 anthropomorphic bronze human figures, with mouths covered, has been displayed all over the world.

2016 Heritage Weekend

The dates for 2016 were September 24 and 25
All photos on this page, *Peter Ehrlich*.

(*above*) Car 1, a pullout from Beach Yard, passes PCC 1077 (Birmingham) at Steuart and Don Chee Way.
(*below*) Historic O'Farrell, Jones & Hyde cable car 42 leaves California and Drumm on the California line. #42 ran all weekend, and even made a trip out to Hyde and Beach, its old stomping ground! (See facing page.)

As in 2015, the Susan G. Komen Foundation's *"Race for the Cure"* (to fight cancer) coincided with Heritage Weekend. (*top photo*) Melbourne 496 passes runners at Brannan Station on the E-Line. (*second photo*) Car 1 passes the balloons marking the start of the race, and also PCC 1080 (Los Angeles Transit Lines) near the Ferry Building.

Muni also celebrated the 75th Anniversary of its first trolley coach route, the R-Howard/South Van Ness, which began service in 1941. (*below left*) 1941 St. Louis trolleybus 506, one of the coaches that opened the line, is on display on Steuart. (*below right*) 1950 Marmon-Herrington 776 poses at South Van Ness/18th, across from St. Charles Roman Catholic Church in the Mission District.

The 2016 Heritage Weekend was notable for a special event, commemorating both 125 years of Hyde Street cable car service, and the 75th Anniversary of Muni trolley coaches. For the occasion, original O'Farrell, Jones & Hyde historic cable car 42 was back on its "home rails" on the morning of September 24, 2016, later meeting up with Marmon-Herrington preserved trolley coach 776 at Hyde and Union.

Bringing back the "Hyde Street Grip": (*left column, top and bottom*) O'Farrell, Jones & Hyde cable car 42 poses at Hyde and Beach with gripman Val Lupiz and his conductor; cresting the Hyde Street grade. *Both photos, SFMTA* (*below*) 200 total years of transit history meet at Hyde & Union: Car 42, on its 'Home rails", and Marmon TC 776 on Line 41, Muni's 2nd trolley coach route. Muni started running trolleybuses in 1941; the "Hyde Street Grip"dates to 1881. *Rick Laubscher*

2017 Heritage Weekend

Muni changed the dates of the 2017 event to September 9 and 10. The major celebrations for 2017 were 100 years of Muni motor coach service, and 100 years of the J-Church line. This Festival was considered by many people to be the best one of them all!

The Pullouts!

(*left and below left*) 1896-built MSRy 578S at/past Brannan Street on the MMX. (*below*) A view of a Breda at Ferry Portal, as the Blackpool "Boat" 228 turns onto the Embarcadero Connector at Folsom Street. Three photos, Peter Ehrlich

137

The Buses!

The 2017 Heritage Weekend celebrated 100 years of Muni bus service.

The star of the show was nearly-completely-restored 1956 Mack 2230 (*right*), which was on display opposite the San Francisco Railway Museum. (*below and below right*) To its right was brand-new New Flyer Xcelsior 8853, which had an interior photographic display, covering 100 years of Muni buses. (*bottom*) Marmon-Herrington trolley coach 776 passes 2230. This could have been anytime between 1955 and 1968, when green and cream and Macks ruled the streets of San Francisco. *All photos, Peter Ehrlich*

The Mack was fully operable, and arrived on its own power. It still needs side windows and seats.

(*right*) Fruit Salad! PCC 1080 passes restored Key System bus 2103. Both represent former National City Lines properties. The bus, a 1958 ex-AC Transit GMC old-look, was brought over from the Pacific Bus Museum on Saturday, September 9. The PCC is painted as a Los Angeles Transit Lines car. *Peter Ehrlich*

2017 continued – More Buses!

All photos on this page by Peter Ehrlich.

On the Friday before Heritage Weekend, Muni operated a number of historic buses on the inner portion of line 7-Haight (which, until 2009, had been a trolleybus route.) (*right*) Here's 1969 GMC "Fishbowl" 3287 at Golden Gate Park. (*below*) 1990-vintage 30 foot Orion 9010, on pullout from Woods Division on Sunday, September 10 for the 41-Union Heritage Weekend loop service, pauses at Embarcadero/Brannan as PCC 1006 (Muni Wings) passes by inbound.

Scenes from the historic bus and trolleybus loop used during the 2017 Heritage Weekend

(*above right*) 1938 Baby White 042 is dressed in its period "Pumpkin" motor coach livery as it rolls downgrade on line 41-Union at Columbus and Pacific. (*below, left and right*) 1976 Flyer trolley coach 5300, one of the two historic trolleybuses assigned to this route, makes the extremely difficult turn at Union and Columbus (Washington Square). In the left photo, Saints Peter and Paul Roman Catholic Church provides the backdrop.

The other Muni 100th Anniversary commemoration celebrated during the 2017 Heritage Weekend was that of the J-Church streetcar line. Here are some scenes on the J-Line.

(*clockwise from top left*) PCC 1051 (Muni Simplified) is at Market/9th Street, headed for the J-Line. *Peter Ehrlich* Car 1's on the Dolores Park private right-of-way at everyone's favorite spot, 20th Street at the top of the grade. *Jack Demnyan* PCC 1060 (Phila. 1938 blue/silver/cream) is actually replicating the old method PCCs used to wye at 30th/Church by backing eastward through the intersection. *Richard Panse* 1051, on the other hand, is demonstrating the new method (since 1991) of wyeing single-end cars. Car 1 is inbound in the background at 29th Street. *Richard Panse*

Meanwhile, back at Don Chee Way, the Heritage Weekend Headquarters!

(*left*) Love of Three Oranges: 1859 (Milan), 1059 (Boston) and Baby White 042 compare their orange paint styles on Steuart Street, evoking the name of Prokofiev's satirical opera. *Peter Ehrlich*

140

Nighttime with the F-Line cars!

Although this page really has nothing to do with "Expansion In The Works", it's a way of "expanding" the reader's horizons in showcasing the beauty of nighttime streetcar service. These were all taken in 2017. *All photos on this page, Peter Ehrlich.*

(*this column, top to bottom*) Orange Milano 1815 faces the Ferry Building on Market at Main on September 7. The old SP Building's top floors are illuminated. 1814 is on the 4th Street Bridge, pulling in on September 11. HDR image. 1072 (Mexico City), also on a pull-in trip, is diagonally opposite AT&T Park and lit-up 24 Willie Mays Plaza at King/3rd Streets. Taken December 13.

(*this column, top to bottom*) 1071 (Minneapolis/St. Paul) stops in front of the illuminated Orpheum Theater on September 7. Milano 1814 is leaving 17th/Castro on a rainy September 11. 1057 (Cincinnati) leaves the Castro terminal, with illuminated flowers and a group of carolers. Photo taken December 15.

San Francisco's F-Line fleet is the most colorful and varied set of streetcars anywhere. Early on, a decision to have the PCCs represent other cities was a stroke of genius. PCC 1058, with the Ferry Building behind it, represents Chicago in 1947 colors. *Peter Ehrlich*

Chapter 8 -
The Colorful F-Line Fleet

*One man to another: "It's the fun, relaxing way to get to the Wharf.
You see much more of the city when you ride the streetcar."
"Yes, and no worries about parking," replies his friend.
"Everybody seems to have a good time on board the streetcar," adds the first gent.
"And they're so colorful."*

– *Conversation overheard by the author
on board an F-Line streetcar*

IN 1995, AS IN 1983 when the Trolley Festivals began, Muni's basic transit fleet colors were the 1975 Walter Landor-designed two-tone orange and white–specifically, "California Poppy Gold" and "Sunset Glow." PCC 1040, which ran in the Trolley Festivals, wore the Landor livery in 1983 and 1984. Introduction of the interesting and varied Trolley Festival cars made for a more colorful Market Street streetscape. The plans for a permanent F-Line would make this multi-hued addition to San Francisco's premier boulevard an everyday experience.

Selecting a Fleet

WHEN MUNI RETIRED its remaining fleet of PCC cars after the last N-Judah PCC pulled into the ancient Geneva Carhouse in the wee hours of September 20, 1982, it decided to retain about 55 cars–the eight remaining double-end "Torpedoes," ten "Baby Tens" and 37 of the ex-St. Louis 1100s, for "possible future use." Their battered bodies were trucked over to Pier 70 along the Central Waterfront and plunked down on the pavement. Later, the cars were shifted to Pier 72, with some moved inside. Gradually, cars were auctioned off, with a large chunk of them–20 in all–purchased by a South Lake Tahoe, CA man with a dream–to establish a rail line between that Sierra Nevada resort city and its airport, which was, coincidentally, his employer. Others made it to museums or other preservation venues. Ultimately, the cars retained by Muni included seven of the eight "Torpedoes" (car 1014 has emigrated to Australia), four "Baby Tens" and eight 1100s.

As federal and state funds poured in to rebuild the tracks on Market Street, management now turned to the question of what to use as an F-Line fleet. In 1988, the first post-Trolley Festival year, there were still five other North American systems operating PCC cars, and three of these had recently completed a general rebuilding program for many of their PCC trolleys.

Some people had alternative ideas, based on vehicles already in Muni's historic fleet. Melbourne, Australia, had just retired its famous fleet of W2 trams, some of which dated to 1923. And Milan, Italy, which rostered a large fleet of American-inspired "Peter Witt" trams, built between 1928 and 1930, had just embarked on a program to rebuild 250 cars–half of its original fleet, thus making many cars available for export.

Ultimately, though, the PCC–that unique American streetcar which was renowned as the best streetcar ever designed from a systems engineering standpoint–got the nod. [See *PCC Car: An American Success* sidebar in Chapter 1.] Now, the next question was: Which PCCs to use? Muni's own? Or some other city's cars?

With that in mind, Muni dispatched Trolley Festival foreman Karl Johnson and three other Muni maintenance officials on a three-city inspection trip. Cars in Toronto, Boston and Philadelphia were examined. In every city, the cars had been completely rewired–a very important consideration when compared to Muni's own PCCs, which had never had this done.

Body and structural corrosion was another important consideration. All the cars that were offered had some body rot due to the harsh winter climates they had to endure. Toronto's cars were rejected outright for this reason. Muni did not want a repeat of its own experience with 11 cars acquired from Toronto in 1973, which literally fell apart on the streets of San Francisco. Ultimately, Philadelphia won out over Boston as a source for F-Line cars as its cars had gone through a "General Overhaul" or "GOH" program by the Philly transit agency, SEPTA, in the early 1980s, and were all-electric cars. Boston's cars, while they had been through a similar refurbishing in the mid-1980s, were air-electrics. In addition, they had solid steel wheels, whereas the SEPTA cars still had the ERPCC-designed resilient wheels.

Interestingly, despite their battered appearance and general neglect, the bodies and

Philadelphia PCC 2122, one of 112 PCCs overhauled by SEPTA beginning in 1980, passes the old Reading Terminal at 12th and Market on Oct. 20, 1987. Six years later, 2122 became Muni PCC 1055. *Peter Ehrlich*

In 1990, ex-Philly PCC 2133 was purchased by Muni and used as a "guinea pig" to develop specs for rehabbing fourteen more cars for the F-Line. Here 2133, still in SEPTA paint, is passing Boeing 1290 near the end of the L-Line on a test run made on Aug. 31, 1990. The author was one of the test motormen, and, with other Muni operators and managers on board, we arrived at 15th Avenue and Taraval, and an elderly woman tried to board. So I opened the door and said, "I'm sorry, ma'am. We're not in service. We're visiting from Philadelphia." Everyone on the car roared with laughter, but the poor woman just shrugged her shoulders, gave us a sad smile, and returned to the curb. 2133, unfortunately, never went into the rehab program. *Market Street Railway* did start work on restoring it for possible revenue service, but Muni wouldn't certify it for operation. *Peter Ehrlich*

frames of Muni's own PCCs were actually in better shape due to the city's overall mild climate. This phenomenon was borne out when three "Torpedoes" entered the remanufacturing program in 1994 as Muni exercised a contract option. Less work and money was required to rebuild those cars.

Philadelphia PCC 2133, a 1948 product from St. Louis Car Co., and an early GOH recipient, was brought out to San Francisco in the summer of 1990 to act as a guinea pig for preparation of specifications for a rebuild contract. Muni then purchased 14 all-electric PCCs from SEPTA's 2100- and 2700-series for $12,000 apiece, plus two more for parts. These cars had Westinghouse motors and controls, and were narrow (100" wide). 2133, unfortunately, didn't enter the program.

In 1992, a contract was awarded to Morrison-Knudsen, a locomotive rebuilder with a solid reputation, but which had only recently entered the market for transit car manufacturing, to remanufacture the 14 PCCs from Philadelphia's SEPTA to as-new condition. The cost was $462,000 per car, with an option to rebuild more cars.

The cars were transported to Hornell, NY directly from Philadelphia, stripped to bare metal and rebuilt from the ground up. Motors and control systems were given a thorough overhaul. New sash replaced the schoolbus windows SEPTA had used. New seats were

On September 3, 1993, the first of Muni's new former Philadelphia PCCs, 1055, arrived in San Francisco. PCC 1055 is painted in Philadelphia's green and cream, which it wore throughout most of its 40+-year career in the City of Brotherly Love. Two years later, 1055 and its sisters opened service on Muni's new F-Line. *Peter Ehrlich*

mounted, including two sets of handicapped tip-up seats. A communications system, allowing operators to talk to each other during emergency tow or push movements, was included in the rebuild package.

The contract called for the first car to be delivered in September 1993, and on September 3, 1993, PCC 1055, the former Philadelphia 2122, proudly arrived in San Francisco from M-K's Hornell facility on a flatbed trailer truck, shining in its green and cream color scheme, complete with maroon belt rail, that it wore for three decades in the City of Brotherly Love. Deliveries followed about every 2-4 weeks through January 1994, when the last three arrived on the property.

Burn-in testing started almost immediately. As a way of introducing the new PCCs to riders, free weekend service on the non-subway portions of the J-Church and N-Judah started in April 1995 using seven cars, running in groups of twos or threes.

PCCs Represent Many Cities

FROM THE TIME BETWEEN Muni's takeover of the Market Street Railway Company in 1944 until PCC 1108 pulled into Geneva Yard for the last time in 1982, the reigning colors of San Francisco's streetcar fleet had been verdant green and cream with "Wings" pattern. Starting in 1963, trolley repaints adopted a cream stripe below the windows in a scheme known as "Muni Simplified," because advertising panels had covered up the "Wings." It was expected then that the new F-Line PCC fleet would continue the "Muni Wings" livery tradition. So why did 1055 arrive in Philadelphia green and cream?

The answer lies in a plan concocted by members of Muni's Planning and Community Affairs Departments. Credit Peter Straus, Muni Planning Director and founder of the non-profit *Market Street Railway*, assistant planner Duncan Watry, and Nicolas Finck and Jaimie Levin, who worked in Community Affairs, for the idea to honor other American PCC systems. Finck, a public information officer, former motorman and railfan steeped in transport history, Straus, Levin, and Carole Gilbert of the Muni Paint Shop chose a list of systems which could easily be replicated using Muni's existing paint palette. Over the objections of many people within and outside of Muni, including Phil Adams, who was Muni General Manager at that time, the plan was added to the specifications. Thirteen representative liveries were chosen by Muni personnel; the 14th–Brooklyn–was picked in a poll by the members of Market Street Railway and paid for by *MSR*, to honor the city with the first production order of PCCs in the United States. The first two cars–1050 and 1051–received Muni green and cream.

Here's the list:

- **1050** - Muni Wings (green/cream)
  ex-Philadelphia 2119
- **1051** - Muni Simplified (green/cream)
  ex-Philadelphia 2123
- **1052** - Los Angeles Railway (2-tone yellow)
  ex-Philadelphia 2110
- **1053** - Brooklyn (blue-green/silver)
  ex-Philadelphia 2721
- **1054** - Philadelphia (1938 silver/blue/cream)
  ex-Philadelphia 2121
- **1055** - Philadelphia (1947 green/cream)
  ex-Philadelphia 2122
- **1056** - Kansas City (black/cream)
  ex-Philadelphia 2113
- **1057** - Cincinnati (yellow, green stripes)
  ex-Philadelphia 2138
- **1058** - Chicago (green/cream)
  ex-Philadelphia 2124
  (later repainted original Chicago Mercury green/Croydon cream)
- **1059** - Boston (vermilion/cream)
  ex-Philadelphia 2099
- **1060** - Newark (gray/white)
  ex-Philadelphia 2715
  (later repainted like 1054)
- **1061** - Pacific Electric (red/orange)
  ex-Philadelphia 2116
- **1062** - Louisville (green/cream/black)
  ex-Philadelphia 2101
- **1063** - Baltimore (yellow, gray roof)
  ex-Philadelphia 2096

PCCs undergoing rehab at Morrison-Knudsen in 1992. Ex-SEPTA 2124 would become Muni 1058. The wide windshield divider strip was replaced with a narrower strip, more in keeping with the original PCC design and providing better visibility. *Karl Johnson*

A Panoply of PCC Paint Schemes

The last three of the 14 ex-Philly PCCs were all delivered on January 19, 1994. In the front is Brooklyn 1053; next is Los Angeles Railway 1052; and Boston Elevated Railway 1059 brings up the rear. *Peter Ehrlich*

The method of delivery was the same for every arrival of a new car. Here, "Philadelphia Cream Cheese" 1054, the second car to be finished, is towed off its specially-designed Silk Road Transport flatbed trailer by venerable Muni "Iron Monster" 130, a task this car had performed when it was in non-revenue status from 1958 to 1983. *Peter Ehrlich*

Each PCC underwent an extensive period of burn-in testing. In this shot taken on December 1, 1993, car 1060, in the first (but inaccurate) Newark, NJ Public Service Co-Ordinated Transport paint scheme applied to a Muni PCC, has just wyed back at West Portal Station and will head out the K-Line. (The accurate darker gray livery for Newark would appear some 13 years later on original ex-Newark PCC 1070.) *Peter Ehrlich*

All of the ex-Philly PCCs except 1061 (Pacific Electric) and 1053 (Brooklyn) were ready for the F-Line Opening Day Parade on September 1, 1995, arranged in order from Eastern system to Western system, except for "Muni Wings" 1050, which represented traditional San Francisco PCCs and was at the head of the lineup, behind the "Boat" car.

It should be noted that Messrs. Straus, Watry, Levin and Finck were not the first ones with the idea. Back in the Trolley Festival days, the idea of refurbishing a number of Muni's stored 1100-series PCCs in liveries representing American cities was discussed by Maury Klebolt and operators Jack Smith and Tom Biagi. Biagi came up with a copy of a book in his possession called *Traction Yearbook #2: The President's Car* (published by Traction Slides International), which showed cars from the many cities with PCCs. Smith and Klebolt presented a list of cars selected by Muni Trolley Maintenance head Karl Johnson, for possible rebuilding and repainting in other U. S. city liveries, along with the book, to Mayor Dianne Feinstein in 1986. The rebuilding of the Muni cars did not come to pass, however.

Because of the requirement to use Muni's existing paint palette (with the exception of Brooklyn), in some cases, the colors didn't exactly match those actually worn in certain cities. This resulted in loud outcries from railfan purists, but even those who had advocated a single Muni historic livery for the F-Line fleet, among them Karl Johnson and Rick Laubscher, quickly became enthusiastic converts. In the words of Karl Johnson, "It's easy to tell which car is coming down the street [from a maintenance standpoint]." The grumbles of the purists that "the colors are wrong" were offset by the rationalization that the average passenger couldn't care less if the colors are a little off, because they're colorful, different and attractive in their own right.

Cars 1052, 1054, 1055, 1056, 1057, 1058, 1060 and 1062 also received the chrome wings around the headlights, matching those used by several systems.

Nevertheless, there were several anomalies about the new F-Line PCC fleet. The green for cars 1050 and 1051 is not really the "verdant green" worn by the old PCC fleet, but darker. Los Angeles 1052 and Philadelphia 1054 represented paint schemes for those cities' air-electric PCCs that predated the arrival of all-electric cars. Chicago 1058 carried the later Chicago Transit Authority green and cream rather than the earlier, more famous Mercury Green and Croydon Cream with a Swamp Holly Orange belt rail livery. One can see that "Green Hornet" livery today on a Kenosha car, and in 2010, 1058 was repainted to match the Kenosha PCC following rebuilding from a serious accident in 2006. 1063's Baltimore yellow was really a lighter yellow than that worn by those that ran there until 1963.

1060, the Newark car, arrived painted in a lighter gray–a color found on Car 1–than that of the original 1954 Public Service Co-Ordinated Transport livery. 1060's wheels and trucks did receive the original "Ruby Slippers" treatment that graced the Newark PCCs when they were introduced to service there in 1954. Later, after 1054 was demolished in a disastrous November 16, 2003 accident when it was rear-ended on the J-Line's San Jose private right-of-way by a Breda traveling at 35mph, 1060, itself a previous accident victim, received 1054's Philadelphia 1938 silver, blue and cream, nicknamed "Philadelphia Cream Cheese"–the second F-Line PCC to receive a new paint scheme. (The original, and more accurate, Newark colors would return in 2006 on ex-Newark 1070.)

While the colors gracing 1056, the Kansas City car, are perfectly accurate, nonetheless the appearance of a car in Kansas City with standee windows would have caused the late Kansas City Public Service President Powell Groner to turn over in his grave. The original Kansas City all-electric PCCs were delivered with full-height windows because Groner "would have none of those little apertures on his cars!"[1] (The ex-Toronto PCCs that Muni purchased in 1973 began their operating life in Kansas City.) [See the *Muni and the PCC* sidebar in Chapter 1 for a picture.]

And then there is 1062, the Louisville Railway Company PCC. Of all the transit companies that ordered PCCs, Louisville had the dubious honor of never actually operating them in revenue service. After a few were delivered back in 1947, they were sold to Cleveland for buses and cash, with most of the 25-car order going directly from St. Louis Car Co. to the Cleveland Transit System.

Regardless of the exterior paint scheme of these cars, the interiors received the standard Muni PCC colors of dark green below the windows, and a greenish-white above the windows and on the ceiling.

There was some historical significance regarding why some cars represented certain cities, and this concerned the car's last two digits. For example, the "53" in Brooklyn 1053 commemorated the year the New York City Transit Authority, Brooklyn's last operator of its PCCs, was created–1953. 1054 was chosen to represent the 1938 silver, blue and cream "Philly Cream Cheese" PCC because there was a similarly painted car in Philadelphia, air-electric 2054. The other Philly representative, 1055, got its number to mark the year Philadelphia's famous Nearside trolleys were retired (1955). The "56" in the Kansas City car recalled that city's last PCC line, the 56-Country Club. The last two digits of

"Torpedo" 1007 is loaded onto a flatbed to be transported to Morrison-Knudsen for rehab under a contract option. The battered and graffiti-marred PCC, which had sacrificed its original "Golden Glow" headlight for the rebuilding of sister "Torpedo" 1006 in 1985, would return a swan! January 19, 1995. *Karl Johnson*

(*above*) "Torpedo" 1007's as-delivered livery was the same as the brand-new Breda LRVs, one of which passes 1007 at San Jose and Randall on December 30, 1996. The San Francisco skyline is off in the distance. (*below*) Before 1007 went to Benicia, CA for warranty roof repainting, Muni had decided to repaint 1007 as a Red Arrow car. Here's how it looked on March 31, 1997 before shipment to Benicia. *Both photos, Peter Ehrlich*

cars 1058, 1063 and 1061 marked the last year of streetcar operation in Chicago, Baltimore and on the Pacific Electric. On the other hand, the last two digits on one F-Line PCC mark a positive development: 1059. That's because 1959 was the year Boston's famous Riverside Line–a light rail prototype route–opened for service–using PCCs, of course.

In 2015, the Philly cars began getting their "mid-life" rebuild. (See later in this chapter.)

Contract Option For 3 Torpedoes

THE LAST THREE of the 14 ex-SEPTA PCCs were all delivered on January 19, 1994. Once all of them were unloaded onto Muni rails at Geneva, the three Silk Road Transport low-boys were moved over to Pier 72 to gather up three of Muni's own "Torpedo" double-end PCCs for remanufacture by Morrison-Knudsen under the contract option.

The three units originally selected for rehab were 1009, 1011 and 1015. However, just one week before they were to move to Hornell, homeless transients, who had long plagued the stored PCCs at the Pier 72 site, apparently set a fire that damaged 1009 and 1011. In their place, 1007 and 1010 were trucked east, along with 1015. The first car, 1007,

(*right*) All three "Torpedoes" line up at Transbay Terminal on August 31, 1998, ironically arranged in order of their entry into F-Line service. 1007 (Red Arrow) leads, followed by 1015 (Illinois Terminal) and 1010 (Muni 1939 blue/gold). *Peter Ehrlich*

returned in December 1995 and almost immediately entered service. 1015 followed a few weeks later. 1010, the third car, saw its first revenue operation in June 1996. (Nevertheless, 1009 and 1011 languished long enough to be included in the next PCC rebuild contract with Brookville Equipment Corp. in 2009.)

Although the "Torpedoes," being a double-end car, were mechanically and electrically a more complex car to rehab, the price tag per car was actually less than for the ex-Philly cars for one reason: the bodies and frames exhibited virtually no body rot because of their career operation in a drier and more mild climate. As part of their rebuilding, the "Torpedoes" were returned to their as-delivered true double-end operation for the first time since 1954.

The double-enders returned painted in new liveries, too, matching other properties with double-end PCCs or trolleys with PCC-derivative bodies.

    1007 - Muni Breda colors (dark gray/silver) (later repainted Red Arrow maroon/cream/black)

    1010 - Muni 1939 World's Fair (blue/gold)

    1015 - Illinois Terminal (green/cream)

Here, too, there were some anomalies. 1010 never wore blue and gold in its early career, but the similar-bodied "Magic Carpets" from 1939 (1001-1005) did. And 1007's "futuristic" Breda livery paint scheme, which was supposedly patterned after Muni's original 1912 gray/red paint scheme, was heavily criticized and dubbed the "Stealth" livery, because of the inability, on typical San Francisco foggy days and nights, to see the car. (Since 2003,

Shortly after the F-Line opened, Milan "Peter Witt" 1834 became the first non-PCC introduced into regular service. The pioneering Muni "Ventotto," assigned to a night run on November 8, 1995, lays over at 17th and Castro along with PCC 1051. *Peter Ehrlich*

the "Stealth Livery" has also been applied to all new Muni buses.) Muni took advantage of the opportunity presented by a 1997 roof repainting job performed by M-K under warranty to change its appearance to Philadelphia Suburban (Red Arrow) maroon and cream with a black roof.

Like the ex-Philly cars, the three M-K-remanufactured "Torpedoes" will be getting a mid-life rebuild by 2015.

Milan Peter Witts Add International Color

IN THE TROLLEY FESTIVAL chapter, we observed that one of the international trams donated to San Francisco was Milan, Italy "Peter Witt" 1834, one of 502 trams built for Milan in 1928-1930 and dubbed "Ventotto" in honor of the year of their birth, 1928. They were patterned after the very successful Peter Witt trolley design originated by a Cleveland traction commissioner back in 1912. The principal feature of the Peter Witt was a front entrance, center-exit streetcar, where passengers, once on board, either sat longitudinally or stood in the front area of the car, and paid a conductor stationed at the center door. Once they paid their fare, they could then ride in the rear of the car and face forward. This practice enhanced safety and eliminated fare evasion. It was also easy to convert Peter Witts to one-man operation, which, in the 1920s, was a very desirable goal of transit companies anxious to reduce operating costs. The door arrangement initiated by the Peter Witt was later carried over to the PCC. Many North American cities, such as Detroit and Brooklyn,

On November 24, 1998, tram 1859 became the first of ten Milan "Peter Witts" purchased in 1998 for the F-Line's Fisherman's Wharf Extension from *Azienda Trasporti Milanesi* to be winched down at Metro Yard. Most of the cars were made ready for service by spring of 2000, and, along with the PCCs, are the fleet workhorses. *Peter Ehrlich*

embraced the Peter Witt design, but San Francisco was not one of them.

In the 1930s, Milan modified its Witts by adding a rear door and installing perimeter seating throughout. This improved passenger flow. It converted its "Ventotto" fleet to one-man operation in the 1970s. Car 1834, thus, became one of the only one-man cars in Muni's international historic fleet.

Soon after the September 1, 1995 opening of the F-Line, the author, one of the first F-Line motormen, began taking 1834 out on afternoon trippers. (Trippers are runs that pull out for rush hour service, make a trip or two, and pull in.) At first this deployment was resisted by Muni's General

Peter Witt 1793 was the first operational "Milano." It's approaching Transbay Terminal on its first training run in August 1999, and the instructor is checking the rear truck for proper tracking as the tram negotiates the worn-out special work (dating to 1939). The car, still sporting its Italian advertising panels, has not yet had a front pole installed. *Peter Ehrlich*

Superintendent of Rail Transportation Ken Rodriguez, but he eventually relented, and 1834 went out on the line at least once a week. Gradually, Rodriguez and others in management noticed that not only was the sturdy Witt a reliable performer, but it could easily make the schedule allotted to the PCCs. Additionally, its presence on the streets of San Francisco delighted riders and passersby as well.

Beginning in 1996, Muni started replacing its problem-plagued Muni Metro Boeing LRVs with new cars built by Breda Costruzione Ferroviarie of Pistoia, Italy. Manager Ken Rodriguez was an active participant in the design of the Breda. Having also observed 1834's stellar performance and sensing that a fleet of Peter Witts would be a good fit for the F-Line while injecting a permanent international flavor, he approached Breda and Azienda Trasporti Milanesi (ATM, the Milan transit agency) with an idea of bringing over up to 10 more Peter Witts, which would be needed for the opening of the Fisherman's Wharf Extension. Breda was an enthusiastic backer of the plan, and Rodriguez, accompanied by Robin Reitzes of the City Attorney's office and John Callahan from the City Purchaser, flew to Milan in July 1998 to negotiate the deal. It was signed off by the San Francisco Public Transportation Commission (SFPTC, successor to the SFPUC's oversight of Muni) commissioners. The one-time purchase called for nine operational "Ventotto" which had undergone a "Revisione Generale" between 1988 and 1992, plus two cars for parts. The cost was $30,000 apiece for nine cars; $10,000 for parts car 1588 (which was later put into service); and no extra cost for "non-revisione" tram 1979, which was intended only as another source of parts. The cost of shipping was extra, as was the purchase of spare parts (between $3500 and $8000). The City arranged for a freight forwarder to bring the trams to the Port of Genoa, but Breda was most helpful in making the arrangements.

Milan's Peter Witt rebuild program embodied a complete rewiring of the trams, conversion of fuses to circuit breakers, installation of electric door controls and passenger emergency door release switches. 250 cars–half of the original "Ventotto" fleet–entered the program. The quality of the program was so good that 150 of these sturdy trams still provide daily service in Milan–the oldest fleet in Europe. [See *Milan's Icons: The Peter Witt Trams* sidebar in Chapter 6.] Some of the cars purchased by Muni were in service right up to the day they were placed on flatbed trucks and transported to Genoa, where they were loaded onto two ships bound for Texas. The journey to San Francisco was completed on rail. On November 24, 1998, tram 1859 became the first of the new Peter Witts to touch Muni rails when it was winched down in Metro Yard.

It took more than a year to get the Milanos ready for service. They had to be slightly regauged from Milan's 1445mm (4'-9") gauge to standard gauge (1435mm). The wheels needed to be reprofiled to the American conical tread standard. Front trolley poles were installed, and new sealed beam headlights meeting California Public Utilities Commission (CPUC) standards, were mounted. Muni carpenters from the Cable Car Shop did an exquisite job of adding two more seats, one of them a tip-up seat for wheelchair users, matching the new ones with the seats already on the car. 1793 became the first operational "Milano" and made some training runs in 1999 while still sporting Italian advertisements on its flanks. 1556 was displayed at Fisherman's Wharf during Navy Fleet Week in October 1999. 1793, 1515 and 1859 entered service in March 2000, the first month of operation to Fisherman's Wharf, followed by

Milanos Here, There and Everywhere

The standard "Milano" livery was orange. This color was known as "Italian Public Transport Vehicle Orange" and was worn by nearly every tram, trolleybus and motor bus in Italy since the early 1970s. 1814 and 1893 meet at Embarcadero and Greenwich, and the two Witts are handling passengers who have come to witness the *Queen Mary 2*, which called at San Francisco on February 5, 2007 on its maiden worldwide voyage.
Peter Ehrlich

In 2003, Muni repainted one of the "Ventottos" in original 1928 Milan colors of yellow and white. Car 1811 leads three orange sisters at the Jones and Beach terminal on May 25, 2005. In 2010, car 1807 joined 1811 as a yellow/white "Milano." *Peter Ehrlich*

The next "Milano" to be repainted in a color other than orange was car 1818, which debuted in the historic 1930 two-tone green, a scheme that lasted four decades, on November 9, 2007. Far from the F-Line, 1818 was photographed on a May 26, 2009 charter running on the T-Third Street line, at the UCSF-Mission Bay Station. AT&T Park, home of the San Francisco Giants baseball team, is off in the distance.
Peter Ehrlich

1556 and 1818 in April and May. Three of the remaining five Milanos–1911, 1795 and 1814, were in revenue service by the end of 2000, but 1888 (ex-1588, the erstwhile parts car) and 1807 (ex-1507), didn't enter service until 2002 and 2004, respectively.

The Milano fleet consisted of these cars:

1507 (later 1807, repainted yellow/white)
1515 (later 1815)
1556 (later 1856)
1588 (later 1888, repainted 2-tone green)
1793 (later 1893)
1795 (later 1895)
1814 (repainted 2-tone green)
1818 (repainted 2-tone green)
1859
1911 (later 1811, repainted yellow/white)

As mentioned, 1979, a "non-revisione" tram similar to 1834, was imported for parts only.

In 2001, to avoid a conflict with arriving Breda LRVs, the Milan trams not already numbered as 1800s were renumbered into the 1800 series. So 1507 became 1807, 1911 became 1811, etc.

The Milanos retain their quaint Italian-language interior markings such as "Uscita" (Exit), "Vietato Sputare" (No Spitting), etc. They came painted in the standard "Italian Public Transport Vehicle Orange" livery adopted by the Italian government in the 1970s. Accidents, however, gave Muni, at the suggestion of Market Street Railway, a chance to paint two cars in historic Milan color schemes. 1811 (ex-1911) received the attractive original yellow and white Milan colors which had been applied to its first 125 cars back in 1929. 1811 debuted in its new dress in August 2003. But it fell to 1818, which was rear-ended by a PCC on January 3, 2007, to wind up with the most famous Italian tram livery of all: the handsome and stately Benito Mussolini-dictated [reportedly] two-tone green. Three-quarters of Milan's "Ventotto" were delivered this way, and the yellow cars were quickly repainted. two-tone green reigned supreme in Italy for over four decades, and recently the government has relaxed the rules so that Milan, Rome and other cities have returned to two-tone green for their newest trams, or even completely different liveries. Starting in 2007, Milan itself began re-painting nearly all surviving Witts in yellow and white.

From time to time, ideas for painting some Milanos in American Peter Witt liveries surface, but given the high cost of repainting a streetcar, it's not especially a high-priority item at cash-strapped Muni. A scheme for a Cincinnati Peter Witt livery of orange and cream, for example, could easily be replicated

Milano 1807, just repainted in historic Milan yellow and white, shows off its PCC tow bar adapter socket and LED turn signals and taillights as it rests inside the new Geneva Historic Car Enclosure on December 10, 2010. *Peter Ehrlich*

because the Milan orange below the windows would be retained. A more rational idea has recently been espoused, which is to eventually have all three Milan liveries represented throughout the 11-car fleet, and as noted, a start has already been made with this effort, with cars 1807, 1814 and 1888 added. This plan would keep their interior Italian markings intact.

Muni maintenance has continued to improve the Milano fleet gradually. Whistles and repeater gongs were added in 2004 to meet CPUC requirements, and improvements to the motorman's cab heaters were also carried out. Most trams now sport LED turn signal and taillights, and a few have center door stepwell lights.

One thing that was not done by Muni in getting the Milano fleet ready for service was to install a backup controller. This means that a supervisor or other Muni employee must assist in backup moves in the yard or places such as 11th and Market. The pioneering Witt, 1834, does have one. When they are due for "midlife overhaul" at some point in the future, this may yet be done.

The Milanos, like the PCCs, became fleet workhorses. But a controversial move brought on by Muni engineers early on threatened to sideline the entire fleet. This was the application of composite brake shoes, replacing the traditional cast iron shoes. Intended for longer life, what they actually did was make it too easy for the trams to slide, causing flat spots on the wheels, and scoring the wheel tires, creating a horrendous, unnatural racket on the streets. This resulted in many complaints from residents, especially in the Castro District, and led to an outright ban on the cars staying out after 9:00pm. This, of course, forced on-street inspectors to juggle car assignments or, in extreme circumstances when no trades were possible, having operators pull in prematurely, resulting in loss of service at night. Finally, after receiving reports that Milan had tried composite brake shoes that exhibited similar problems, and after a month-long boycott by operators in late 2002 over their braking and noise, Muni maintenance threw in the towel and returned to cast iron brake shoes in mid-2003. Almost overnight, the clatter and the problems with scored wheels disappeared, and the only noise coming from the Milanos was the sweet music of the motors and gears. More recently, a different kind of composite brake shoe has been used on the Milanos, but some of the clatter has returned as a result. The "no Milanos after 9 PM" dictum has remained in effect, but was occasionally broken by some operators—including the author—who preferred to keep their Peter Witt out all night instead of trading off for a PCC.

Most F-Line operators, nevertheless, prefer the smooth-riding PCC to the noisier, jerkier Milan car, whose controls, especially braking, are trickier to master. Every F-Line operator has to qualify on both fleets. And while the trams are popular with visitors, many regular riders from the Castro don't care for them because of their wooden longitudinal seats and noisier ride. But in many respects, the Milano fleet is more reliable than the PCC fleet. And with their three doors, they are great crowd-swallowers!

The Milanos have their own swing bar couplers to tow or push each other. Beginning in Fall 2007 with rebuilt accident victims 1818 and 1893, Muni made a modification to weld tow bar sockets on the anticlimbers. This gives the trams the capability to push or tow PCCs, making them more versatile.

On February 24, 2011, Car 1 made its first test run from Metro East since its return from rebuilding at Brookville Equipment in December 2010. It's spotted at Embarcadero and Mission, in front of the old Embarcadero YMCA, now one of many boutique hotels which have sprung up in San Francisco in recent years. *Peter Ehrlich*

Unfortunately, the pioneering Witt, 1834, was never equipped with passenger emergency door release switches or otherwise modified to match its sisters. Because of the former issue, the CPUC would not certify it for passenger service, and it has been allowed to languish. Occasionally, it's used as a "yard goat" to move dead Milanos around the yard. It did operate in service to Fisherman's Wharf through August 2000 until the CPUC ban came down. There is hope for this tram, however. In January 2008, the shop slowly began work on returning it to the active fleet by adding electric door controls and passenger emergency release switches and a LVPS battery system. But it still needs extensive body and roof work, and is now in Geneva Shop for this work. As of 2018, it's still there.

Vintage San Francisco Treasures

AMONG ALL AMERICAN transit systems with a desire to preserve the past in transit while moving forward meeting 21st Century public transportation needs, San Francisco Muni stands head and shoulders above every other city still operating surface rail transit. This is because of a number of far-sighted decisions made by officials, managers and supervisors in the 1950s, which preserved several valuable pieces of native rolling stock for future generations to enjoy.

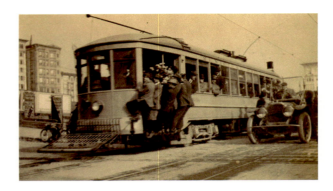 

Car 1 - The People's Car (1912)

(*above left*) The First Day–December 28, 1912. Car 1, the first of the 43 A-Types, carries a crush load of celebrants trying out Muni's brand-new A-Geary Street line. Number One is pictured passing Geary and Jons, with Mayor "Sunny Jim" Ralph acting as motorman. The Municipal Railway of San Francisco, the first publicly-owned street railway in a large American city, was now in operation! *San Francisco History Center, San Francisco Public Library collection* (*above right*) In 1944, Car 1, in a rare period color image, reposes at the California and 32nd Avenue terminal of the C-Geary and California line. *Wilbur Whitaker, Market Street Railway archives*

Fortunately, Old Number One was preserved by Muni. In October 1962, it reappeared on Market Street to celebrate Muni's 50th Anniversary running a 5¢ shuttle between Transbay Terminal and 11th Street. Afterward, Car 1 began a new career of special excursions and appearances. It then entered revenue service on the J-Line in 1982, was a Trolley Festival participant, and ran again when the F-Line opened in 1995, and especially after the Wharf Extension opened in 2000. On April 16, 2004, Old Number One passes a "Roar of the Four" mural at Church and 15th Street on the J-Line. *Peter Ehrlich*

(*left*) To prepare Car 1 for its 100th birthday, Muni sent it to Brookville Equipment Corp. in Pennsylvania for a complete rebuilding. Shortly after the car was returned to Muni in December 2010, Old Number One shines for the camera inside Metro East on January 22, 2011. Its re-inaugural run took place on April 5, 2012. *Michael Strauch*

(*right*) Car 1's interior. At Metro East on February 24, 2011. With its wicker seats and cherry wood finish, and its Eclipse Fenders on the ends, it's no wonder the late columnist Herb Caen called Old Number One "toothsome and inviting!" *Peter Ehrlich*

Car 130 – Reclaimed Wrecker from 1914

(*above left*) Muni's B-Type 130 was saved from the wrecker by Geneva Maintenance Superintendent Charles Smallwood in 1958, and it became a wrecker. Car 130, renumbered 0131, is towing a dead PCC at West Portal in January 1962, before it was painted in yellow work paint. *Jack Smith* (*above right*) In 1983, under orders from Muni GM Harold H. Geissenheimer, Car 130 was reconverted from work service back into a passenger car for the Trolley Festival. In this June 25, 1983, shot inside Metro Center, 130 has received all new windows, new end metalwork and a new canvas roof. Just a month later, 130 made its triumphant debut in 1939 blue and gold "World's Fair" livery as it joined the Muni historic fleet. *Peter Ehrlich*

(*left*) In July 2003, Muni repatriated another preserved B-Type, 162, which it acquired from the *Orange Empire Railway Museum*. On July 14, 2003, four days after 162's arrival at Mint Yard, 130 came in for a minor maintenance problem and posed next to its sister B-Type. In the words of the late Muni motorman Jack Smith, "The two cars exchanged many stories and had much to catch up on." 162, like 130, had also left passenger service in 1958. (*below left*) The interior of B-Type 130 is finished in mahogany. Note the Jewett Car Company builder's decal above the doorway. (*below*) 130 is dedicated to the late, great *San Francisco Chronicle* columnist Herb Caen. For nearly 60 years, he was the pulse of The City. One of the posters commemorating Herb Caen is inside Car 130. *All photos, Peter Ehrlich*

Muni A-Type 1 - The People's Car. The flagship of Muni's rail fleet, Old Number One was the first streetcar built for an American publicly-owned transit system. It was one of 43 constructed by local firms in 1912. Local builder W. L. Holman Car Company outshopped the first 20 cars, and nearby Union Iron Works completed the order after Holman went bankrupt. The A-Type's cost per car: $7,784.

The A-Types were designed by traction consultant Bion J. Arnold, hence were also called "Arnold" cars. They were four motor PAYE (Pay As You Enter) rear-entrance cars, which was the standard streetcar practice on most American systems back in 1912. They featured an improved controller, which operated on a low-voltage power supply instead of the traditional K controller, which had 600 volts under the motorman's hand in a protected cabinet. The A-Types had rattan seats and open California-style ends and a closed center when built, but later the ends were enclosed to protect more passengers from the elements.

After its mates were scrapped in 1951, Car 1 was de-motored but remained on the property until 1959, when it was moved to off-site storage. But in 1962–Muni's 50th Anniversary–it appeared on Market Street restored to its as-built condition, where it ran a 5-cent shuttle between Transbay Terminal and 11th Street. Following the 50th Anniversary festivities, Car 1 began a new career of performing charters, fantrips and special event services. In 1981, the shuttle service was re-enacted on alternate Saturdays during the spring and summer months, albeit free [see Chapters 1 and 2]. Then, in 1982, during the waning months of Market Street streetcar service, Car 1, along with K-Type 178, leased from the Western Railway Museum, initiated weekend revenue service on the J-Church line. It operated during every Trolley Festival, and many of the mini-Festivals between 1988 and 1992.

Car 1 was available for charters or even service on evening trippers when the F-Line began in 1995, but manpower shortages and the lack of training of vintage car operators precluded regular appearances until after the extension to Fisherman's Wharf opened. It had been out of service with electrical problems since 2006, but in early 2009, SFMTA awarded a contract to Brookville Equipment Corp. in Pennsylvania for a complete top-to-bottom restoration for Old Number One. It returned to Muni in December 2010, well in time for Muni's 100th Anniversary in 2012. It was re-inaugurated for its next 100 years of service in a decorous ceremony on Steuart Street on April 5, 2012, with Sen. Dianne Feinstein, Mayor Ed Lee and other dignitaries in attendance [see Chapter 13].

Car 1 is painted in its original gray livery, with red roof and gold leaf trim. The late columnist Herb Caen once described Old Number One as being "toothsome and inviting," with its Eclipse fender, immaculate cherry wood interior and wicker seats. Muni's flagship is truly a crowd-pleaser! With its four motors, Car 1 is also very fast and peppy.

Muni B-Type 130 - Lucky Wrecker. Car 130 was one of 125 B-Types built by Jewett Car Company of Newark, Ohio, in 1914-15, for Muni's expansion wave of the late 1910s and the Panama-Pacific Exposition of 1915. The Bs worked practically every Muni line during their 40-plus year career, and 19 of

On July 10, 2003, Muni B-Type 162, one of 125 B-Types built by Jewett Car Company of Newark, OH in 1914, makes a triumphant return to its native city. It was purchased from the Orange Empire Railway Museum in Southern California. As it nears Duboce (Mint) Yard, where Market Street Railway volunteers will begin its restoration, an F-Line PCC passes by in the other direction. It took over 4½ years to complete 162's restoration. *Peter Ehrlich*

Car 162 – Repatriated "Iron Monster," 1914

(*below*) The interior of 162 was painted in Muni's standard Muni 1950s-era apple green with a cream ceiling. *Peter Ehrlich*

(*above*) B-Type 162 made its first test trip to Church and 30th Street on March 6, 2008. It's taking the Day Street crossover. Behind is St. Paul's Church, where the 1993 movie, *Sister Act*, starring Whoopi Goldberg, was filmed. *Peter Ehrlich*

(*left*) April 19, 2008 was a sterling day in Muni transit history when fully-restored B-Type 162 made its first revenue run on Muni rails in 50 years–a Market Street Railway charter for members who donated $1000 or more toward the car's restoration effort. MSR president Rick Laubscher (in brown jacket), assisted by other MSR members, christens 162 by smashing a bottle of California champagne across its bumper at Geneva Yard. 162 then took a trip on the M, L and K-Lines and part of the J-Line. *Peter Ehrlich*

(*right*) When not in F-Line service, 162 is frequently used for charters. On August 22, 2010, the B-Type sits in the 19th Street stub track off the T-Line. The cranes in the background comprise part of the Union Iron Works Historic District complex from the shipbuilding era. Union Iron Works, and later Bethlehem Steel, constructed streetcars for Muni in 1913 and again in 1923. *Peter Ehrlich*

them were modernized with rear doors in the late 1940s, along with all the K and L-Types. 130 was not modernized, but escaped scrapping after conversion of the B-Geary and C-California lines to motor coach on December 29, 1956, doomed most of its sisters. In 1957, it was again saved by Geneva Maintenance Superintendent Charles Smallwood, who hid it in the back of Geneva Carhouse from top management's prying eyes, then successfully reasoned with them that a sturdy "boxcar" was needed to tow dead PCCs back to the carbarn (in 1957, 66 PCCs from St. Louis were beginning to arrive). So 130 became a wrecker, and was renumbered 0131.

As plans for the 1983 Trolley Festival were developing, orders came from General Manager Harold H. Geissenheimer to rebuild 130 back to a revenue-service car. For three months, Muni craftsmen reworked the old car, and it made its proud re-entry to service on July 25, 1983. [See Chapter 3.]

B-Type 130 has been a stalwart performer ever since—through the Trolley Festivals, during the reconstruction of the Market Street tracks, the first years of the F-Line, and notably on the Wharf Extension. In April 2002, it became the "Herb Caen Car," in honor of the late, beloved *San Francisco Chronicle* columnist Herb Caen, who loved the old "Iron Monsters" and the colorful F-Line trolleys throughout his illustrious career. A display of car cards inside 130 features columns by Caen about Muni's streetcars spanning six decades.

B-Type 130 is painted in its 1939 World's Fair livery of blue and gold. It has been over 25 years since its last rebuilding, and it is in need of a thorough rehab, as was recently done with Car 1. It will get this sometime in 2013 or 2014.

Car 130, however, has the distinction of always being operational throughout its 98-year career. It has never been retired. Not many transit vehicles can make that boast!

Muni B-Type 162 - Iron Monster. 162, a sister to 130, was one of the 19 B-Types partially modernized around 1950. After a successful 44 year career, 162 was sold to the Orange Empire Railway Museum in Perris, CA, where it led a very uneventful life, most of it in a non-operational status, although some restoration work had been performed on the car.

In the early 2000s, Muni began quiet negotiations with OERM on the possibility of reacquiring car 162. OERM already had another restored and fully operational Muni "Iron Monster," K-Type 171, and was on the verge of rationalizing its exhibits and deaccessioning some of them. In early 2003, Muni purchased 162 for $70,000 plus transport costs, along with two "Baby Ten" PCCs. Much of the money was raised by in-kind donations from MSR members, and it made a triumphant return to its home city on July 10, 2003. (Sister B-Type 130 made a visit to Mint Yard four days later, and the two Bs "exchanged many stories and had much to catch up on," in the words of the late Muni motorman Jack Smith.)

MSR immediately began initial exterior and interior restoration of 162. The motors were tested and it was found that three of the four motors were still in good shape. With a controller and brake stand remounted on one end, it assisted sister B-Type 130 on its tow move to Geneva Yard on September 9, 2004.

Muni continued the restoration process. The interior was repainted in the apple green color it last wore in service. A newly-developed low voltage power supply system was installed on the car, and both ends were outfitted with controllers, brake stands and other necessary mechanical and electrical accessories. In September 2007, 162 was moved into Metro Center's Heavy Overhaul for motor placement.

162 is painted in Muni green and cream "Wings" livery, the one remembered by most old-time San Franciscans. Now all eras of the Muni "boxcar" fleet are represented. 162 made its inaugural voyage on April 19, 2008 with a special MSR charter for members who donated $1000 or more toward its restoration.

In 2009, 162 entered revenue service on the Embarcadero Shuttle, and has been a mainstay ever since, until it got was severely wrecked in 2013, when it hit a tractor-trailer that was making an illegal left turn at Embarcadero and Bay. It has since been repaired, and returned to Muni in 2018.

Market Street Railway 798 - California Comfort Car. This car was built from the ground up in 1924 by Muni's competitor, Market Street Railway Company, which outshopped 250 nearly-identical streetcars at its Elkton Shops (now the site of Muni Metro Center yard and shops) from 1923 to 1933. After retirement by Muni after World War II, the carbody was trucked up to Columbia, Calif. in the Gold Rush Country where it was converted to a store. It was rescued from destruction in 1984 with private donations and brought to Muni. Subsequently, a $300,000 partial restoration job was carried out at the Deuel Vocational Institute prison in Tracy.

Later, 798 returned to Muni. MSR took over restoration in 2001 and moved it to Mint Yard, where work continues in 2011. One of the things done, which strengthened the car structurally, was to install a series of carline braces—structural elements that support the sides and roof. Soon, 798 will be moved to Metro Center for completion and placement on its trucks. It will use motors from a Melbourne W2. Muni plans to include this car in a contract to do a complete rebuild of this car, along with other vintage cars, in 2018. (See later in this chapter.)

798 is the last "California Comfort Car," and the sole survivor of the vast Market Street Railway fleet. On November 1, 2011, it was moved to the newly-renamed Cameron Beach Yard (formerly Geneva Yard).

Market Street Railway 578(S) - 19th Century Legacy. Built in 1896 for the first Market Street Railway Company, 4-wheel trolley 578(S) is the quintessential California type streetcar and a cable car lookalike. United Railroads took over MSRy before the 1906 Earthquake and Fire, and afterward, with larger cars coming on line, 578S was converted to a sand car. In this configuration, it survived into the Muni era. To promote a series of 1947 bond issues to modernize Muni, 578S, then numbered as work car 0601, ran up and down Market Street with a plea written on its sides to "Please Vote Yes On One Thru Seven So I Can Go To Streetcar Heaven."

Despite this PR stunt, 578S escaped the scrapper, and in 1956 Muni restored the car to its 1896 passenger-carrying appearance to commemorate the 50th Anniversary of the Great Earthquake and Fire. It then was loaned to the Western Railway Museum in Rio Vista Junction, CA, until recalled in 1984 for use in the Trolley Festivals, specifically the 1985 Festival. It was also a star performer in the late 1987 Trolley Festival experimental Embarcadero service [see *"The 1987 Embarcadero Demonstration"* sidebar in Chapter 3]. In 1986, the "S" suffix was added—on paper only—to distinguish the car from Japanese car 578J.

1896-built "Dinky" 578(S), built for the first Market Street Railway Co., is the oldest electric streetcar still in public transit service in the United States, and perhaps the world. On December 9, 1995, it participated in the last-ever Emporium Christmas parade. (The Emporium was a beloved local department store.) It's passing the old Union Trust Co. bank build-ing at Market and Grant, following the mascot for the short-lived *San Francisco Spiders* hockey team. *Peter Ehrlich*

(top) Market Street Railway 798 was rescued from destruction after it was discovered as part of a cabin in the Mother Lode hamlet of Columbia, Calif. in 1984, and was brought to San Francisco for restoration work. MSR *photo (center)* 798 makes the trek back to The City over Altamont Pass and its wind turbines after partial restoration was completed in May 1992. *Karl Johnson (bottaom)* The "California Comfort Car" has been undergoing slow restoration at David. L. Pharr (Mint) Yard since 2002. This is the last survivor of 250 identical cars built by MSRy in its Elkton Shops between 1923 and 1933. On May 20, 2011, 798 sports a new coat of official "Byllesby Green" on its side. *Peter Ehrlich*

The Blackpool, England "Boat" tram is easily the most popular F-Line vintage car. 228 is right at home with the fishing boats that are moored adjacent to Jefferson Street. This photograph was taken on April 18, 2000, six weeks after the F-Line began running to the Wharf. *Peter Ehrlich*

578S has since operated for special events, on charters, and even in revenue service. It is the oldest operational passenger streetcar still in use for an American transit agency, and probably anywhere in the world. Today it is used only on very special occasions, such as Heritage Weekends.

All of these native treasures have been, or will be (in 798's case), modified for wheelchair access in accordance with ADA regulations.

Gems from Afar

ALTHOUGH SAN FRANCISCO sports a large local vintage car collection, it's the fleet's all-encompassing national and international flavor that really distinguishes the F-Line. The list of cars also includes treasures from other American cities, too.

There are several operational trams and a number of cars awaiting restoration. Here are the ones that operate today.

Blackpool 228 and 233 - The Boat Trams. In 1934, English Electric built 12 open-top, 2-motor trams for the resort city of Blackpool, England, and these became renowned as "Luxury Toastracks," or "Boats." Today, eight survive–five in their native city and country, one at a museum near Washington, DC (formerly at an Ohio museum), Muni's 228, and number 226, which operated in the 1983 and 1984 Trolley Festivals and is now at the Western Railway Museum.

"Boat" 228 came to San Francisco directly from Blackpool in 1984. But this was not its first tour of duty in America. During the Bicentennial period, it went to Philadelphia and ran on a Center City loop serving various Philly historic attractions, including Independence Hall. The trucks were regauged to SEPTA's 5'-2¼. The tram was painted mostly orange and white.

Following the Bicentennial, 228 (then numbered 603) returned to England. It came to San Francisco as a gift in 1984, was again made standard gauge and repainted in Blackpool green and cream. It has been the most popular and exotic tram in Muni's fleet ever since. Its popularity led to an ill-advised ban on its operation by Green Division Manager George Louie in 2005 following rebuilding after an accident. He claimed that the "Boat" was *too* popular, and slowed service on Market Street. (Thankfully, his order was later overturned by his superiors.)

Originally a double-end car, 228 has been modified for wheelchair access, but this, unfortunately, has transformed it to single-end status, at least temporarily. The ultimate goal is to make it a true double-ender again.

Since 2007, the Boat runs on Fridays, Saturdays and Sundays only when the weather is pleasant. Of course, it is always available, and frequently requested, for charters.

A second "Boat," number 233, was purchased from Beamish, United Kingdom, in September 2013. (See Chapters 7 and 13 for pictures.)

New Orleans 952 - Streetcar Named Desire. 952 is one of 73 street-cars built by Perley Thomas Car Works of High Point, NC in 1923-24. In 1964, New Orleans Public Service, Inc. (NOPSI) had two operating lines–Canal and St. Charles. (Canal was the Crescent City's main street, sharing that distinction with San Francisco's Market Street as the last American city sporting a main street with trolleys.) After a tough fight, NOPSI abandoned Canal on May 31, 1964, but 35 of the best 900s were rebuilt and shifted to St. Charles, where they, and the line itself (with continuous operation dating back to 1835) eventually became one of two rolling National Historic Landmarks. (San Francisco's cable cars are the other one.) 952 was not included among the survivors, and went to the Chattanooga, TN Chattanooga Choo-Choo Hotel operation to provide a free shuttle service around the hotel grounds, where the "rooms" were located inside retired railroad Pullman sleeping cars.

When New Orleans announced the creation of a new Riverfront trolley line in 1984, it actively sought the return of Perley Thomas cars from museums and other preservation sites. 952, along with sisters 919, 924 and 957, were repatriated by New Orleans RTA and became the "Ladies in Red" for the new Riverfront Line. This new route opened in August 1988, serving the French Quarter and attractions near the foot of Canal Street, such as RiverWalk shopping mall, the Aquarium and the new Convention Center. The returning New Orleans cars were supplemented with three ex-Melbourne, Australia W2 trams. 952 was renumbered 456.

But because Riverfront's track was standard gauge, owing to it once being part of the New Orleans Public Belt Railroad, the Riverfront fleet was incompatible with St. Charles, which was 5'-2½". RTA, anticipating returning streetcar service to Canal, wanted to broad-gauge Riverfront, which it did in 1997, re-equipping the line with brand new Perley Thomas-lookalike cars built at the New Orleans RTA's Carrollton Shops. Car 957 was also rebuilt as a "new" Riverfront car and renumbered 457. The three Melbourne trams were sold to Memphis, but the Perley Thomas cars became surplus. They couldn't be rebuilt and regauged to run on St. Charles, because that line's historic status covered only the 35 cars assigned there.

In 1998, a deal between Mayors Willie L. Brown, Jr. of San Francisco, and Ernest Morial of New Orleans, brought 952 to San Francisco. Before leaving New Orleans, the respected Carrollton Shops, under the stewardship of legendary Shop Foreman Elmer von Dullen, gave the car a new coat of New Orleans olive green paint, and it arrived on September 6, 1998. Its inaugural twelve days later coincided with the opening of an André Previn opera based on the famous Tennessee Williams play, *A Streetcar Named Desire*, at San Francisco's Opera House, which was attended by Mayors Brown and Morial and other dignitaries.

952's departure from the Crescent City was not without drama of its own, and was akin to a CIA operation. When word of its impending move to San Francisco reached Louisiana preservationists, huge howls of protests and threats of lawsuits ensued. About four days before arriving in the City by the Bay, 952 left Carrollton under cover of darkness. The late Dave Pharr, the Mint Yard boss, told me that he breathed a sigh of relief when the Silk Road Transport truck driver called him to let him know that he was in Texas! MSR provided much of the funding to bring 952 out west.

952 was originally leased from New Orleans RTA, originally for five years. The lease has since been extended yearly. It is a steady performer and popular F-Line car, but it's a two-motor car and somewhat underpowered.

As a hedge against 952 someday returning to the Crescent City, MSR and Muni turned to Orange Empire Railway Museum, and, with the help of the San Francisco Municipal Railway Improvement Corp. (SFMRIC), purchased sister Perley Thomas car 913 in 2005. That car will eventually be restored, but it actually ran on its own power onto the flatbed down in Perris, CA–no mean feat, considering that it had not run regularly since 1964! The car is in excellent condition, but still needs restoration work.

The reality, however, is that 952 really has no place to go. Because it's standard gauge, it can't be used on existing New Orleans trackage, and it's not a member of the landmark St. Charles fleet. So it may just be the right thing to keep it in San Francisco as a goodwill ambassador of the Big Easy.

Melbourne 496 - The Wonder Down Under. The W class of tram has been a Melbourne, Australia icon since 1923. W2 496 was one of over 400 four-motor, drop-center W and W2 class trams constructed between 1923 and 1933. It was imported in 1986 to replace identical W2 648, which starred in the first four Trolley Festivals and was then returned to its owner, the Western Railway Museum. 496 debuted in the 1987 Trolley Festival, appeared in the various holiday mini-Festivals which followed, and on into the F-Line era, when it was occasionally used for trippers. On March 4, 2000, the first day of Fisherman's Wharf service, 496, coming off a charter, was pressed into revenue service to handle the enthusiastic crowds.

Car 496 was the first historic tram to be outfitted with a new low-voltage power supply package. Today, it's in regular service on the Embarcadero portion of the F-Line.

A second W2, 586, awaits restoration.

Melbourne 916 - How The Ws Evolved. In 2009, Muni and the City and County of San Francisco received a gift from State Government of Victoria, Australia in the form of another W class tram—another goodwill ambassador.

916 is a later W version, SW6, built in 1946. It has a wider cab and roomier "saloons" (the ends of the car) than W2 496. Unlike the perimeter seating of the older tram, 916 has transverse seating.

916 arrived on September 15, 2009. The next day it ran on its own power from Metro East via the T-Line, MMX, the F-Line and the J-Line out to Geneva Shop. It was dedicated on October 7, 2009, and work is progressing to make it operational in 2018.

Brussels PCC 737 - European PCC. In 1952, Belgium's La Brugeoise, the European carbuilder which held the PCC license for Europe, built 70 PCCs

New Orleans 952 – Streetcar Named [Muni's] Desire

(*above*) In New Orleans, car 952 was brought back home in 1988 to run as one of the "Ladies in Red" on the new Riverfront Line. Renumbered 456, it's passing Jackson Square on February 28, 1991. Seven years later, this car came to San Francisco. *Peter Ehrlich* (*below*) On Christmas Day 2002, the crew of 952 brought the car down the unopened E-Line tracks to take a peek at the Muni Metro Ferry Portal, and N-Judah trains moving in and out. The Bay Bridge is on the left. *Peter Ehrlich*

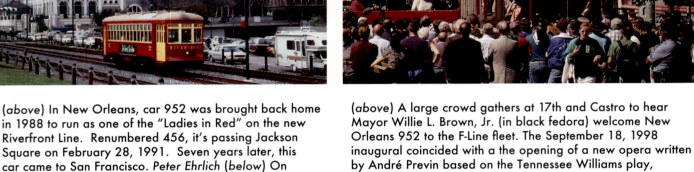

(*above*) A large crowd gathers at 17th and Castro to hear Mayor Willie L. Brown, Jr. (in black fedora) welcome New Orleans 952 to the F-Line fleet. The September 18, 1998 inaugural coincided with a the opening of a new opera written by André Previn based on the Tennessee Williams play, *A Streetcar Named Desire*, which opened at the San Francisco Opera House that day. *Peter Ehrlich*

(*above*) The inside of New Orleans 952, looking toward a PCC behind. The car has been decorated for the Christmas holidays by Market Street Railway volunteers, a time-honored tradition carried out by the F-Line's booster organization. December 25, 2002. *Peter Ehrlich* (*left*) For several months after the devastating New Orleans flooding and destruction caused by Hurricane Katrina in August 2005, 952 carried a banner on its sides with a plea to help victims of the hurricane.
Peter Ehrlich

W2s 496 and 648, and SW6 916 – Wonders from Down Under

Australia has been a good source of trams for American heritage street railway systems, and Muni is no exception.

The first Melbourne W2 to operate on Muni rails actually was obtained for the Western Railway Museum in Rio Vista Junction, CA. 648 served four Trolley Festivals before making its way to the museum. On August 25, 1985, 648 crosses Market Street. Muni's historic Marmon-Herrington trolleybus 776 is visible on the right. *Peter Ehrlich*

In 1987, Muni received its own W2, 496. It's operating on Jefferson Street on March 12, 2000, eight days after the F-Line opened. *Peter Ehrlich*

(*above*) Occasionally, 496 was used as a yard goat, pulling just-delivered PCCs off the flatbeds. PCC 1076 (Washington) is towed across Geneva Avenue by the W2 on January 30, 2007. *Peter Ehrlich*

(*above right*) In 2009, the government of Victoria in Australia presented Muni with car 916, a newer version of the iconic Melbourne W class, with a wider driver's cabin. On October 7, 2009, the newly-delivered SW6 tram rests in Geneva Yard. *Jeremy Whiteman*

(*right*) SW6 916 and W2 496 compare faces at the Ferries on the day of 916's dedication ceremony, October 7, 2009. *Jeremy Whiteman*

for Brussels, among them car 7037. Later, more PCCs were built using parts from ex-Kansas City and Johnstown, Pa. PCCs.

7037 was acquired by Muni with MSR as fiscal agent in 2004, for $25,000. It was modified for ADA and other Muni requirements by Muni shop forces.

In preparation for UN World Environment Day on June 4, 2005–exactly a year after its arrival in San Francisco–and with the mayor of Zürich, one of San Francisco's sister cities, participating in the conference and desiring to have a Zürich tram represented, a deal was struck to paint 7037, and Zürich funded its complete repainting in blue and white, the colors of Zürich's trams. Simultaneously, 7037 was renumbered 737 to avoid a conflict with Muni's 7000-series trolley coaches.

After resolving some operational teething problems, Brussels/Zürich 737 entered regular service as a Wharf shuttle car in 2007, assigned to the vintage fleet. Later, it will be repainted back in Brussels tan livery, again with Zürich footing the bill.

737 is a very fast PCC, and has three doors (as do the Milanos), big picture windows, and a very narrow carbody. There was talk of possibly obtaining more of them, but the day of the four-axle PCC in Brussels ended in 2009.

Now, a list of the streetcars awaiting restoration:

Moscow/Orel 106 - From Russia with Love. 106 is the only Russian tram operating in the Western Hemisphere. It was brought over in 1986,

(*above*) Brussels PCC 7037 has just received new inward folding doors for wheelchair access. Metro Center, January 25, 2005.
(*below*) Now renumbered 737 and painted in Zürich, Switzerland blue and white, the European version of the PCC passes 21st Street on the J-Church private right-of-way on September 18, 2005.
Both photos, Peter Ehrlich

and was dedicated to San Francisco in a decorative ceremony at Transbay Terminal on January 27, 1987, attended by the Soviet Consul-General Valentin Kamenev, Mayor Dianne Feinstein, General Manager Bill Stead, MSR director Maurice Klebolt, and others. Kamenev presented the tram as the "Streetcar Named Desire for Peace."

106 was a single-end, two-axle car with an unusual truck, set up so that the axles could turn independently of each other. This was similar to the Brill "Radiax" truck used under Muni's Union Street "Dinkies" (J-Types) of 1921.

106 was built for Moscow in 1912 during the era of Czarist Russia, and served the Soviet government for over 70 years.

During World War II, 106 was used as a transport vehicle, moving ammo and wounded soldiers. Later, 106 migrated to the small, ancient city of Orel, about 300 kilometers southwest of Moscow, where it eventually entered work service

Shining brightly in its red-and-cream paint scheme, Moscow/Orel 106 stands out in the fog as it passes Grant Avenue enroute to its dedication ceremony at the Transbay Terminal on January 27, 1987. *Peter Ehrlich*

More Vintage Cars Undergoing or Awaiting Restoration

Japanese imports: (*above*) Osaka 151 and Kobe/Hiroshima 578(J) at Mint Yard in 1988. 151 needs a complete restoration. *Karl Johnson collection* (upper *left*) 578(J) has been in and out of service since 1986. On Labor Day 1996, it made a special appearance in service on the J-Line, where it is about to cross Market Street. After having a brake wheel installed in 2006, its re-restoration is nearly complete. *Peter Ehrlich*

(*above*) Hamburg 3557, Maury Klebolt's "Red Baron," rolls in the 1984 Trolley Festival parade. ADA issues have sidelined the car and its restoration is a low priority. *Peter Ehrlich*

Two images of Johnstown 351, which MSR proposes to use as a "teaching trolley" once it's restored. (*upper*) In July 1989, 351 sits in front of Geneva Shop just after arrival in San Francisco. (*lower*) 351's colors match those of Cleveland PCC 1075. It's at Geneva Yard in April 2010, after it was moved out of Mint Yard. Both photos, *Peter Ehrlich*   (*right*) Oporto 189, seen here in 1985, is a victim of conflicting industrial and government regulations. Currently, it's sitting off its truck at Pier 80 while all of the issues, primarily concerning painting, get resolved. *Peter Ehrlich*

before being restored for a museum.

This interesting tram ran throughout the 1987 Trolley Festival and led the 1992 parade on Market Street, celebrating 100 years of electric streetcar service in San Francisco. It also participated in the F-Line Opening Day Parade. But it was subsequently allowed to deteriorate, but not without one last hurrah one day in 1997–May 13, to be exact–when it was used as a rush-hour tripper, delighting railfans but infuriating regular riders. It is not ADA-compliant at this time.

In 2003, MSR had 106 moved to the David L. Pharr (Mint) Yard to start a long, slow and painful restoration process. Muni moved 106 to Geneva Yard in November 2011.

Osaka 151 - Japanese Sister City Tram. 151 was brought to the United States as a result of a request by Mayor Dianne Feinstein, who asked if one could be obtained from Osaka, another of San Francisco's sister cities. 151 arrived in 1988, with MSR's help, but too late for the Trolley Festivals. With four motors and doors at both ends, 151 could be operated by one person. Work began on converting the tram to right-hand operation by activating the "rear" doors, but then restoration stopped and 151 was moved to indoor storage at Pier 80 until funding could be found to complete its restoration. While in storage, the controllers were stolen.

It will be several years before 151 will enter service.

Kobe/Hiroshima 578(J) - Hiroshima, Mon Amour. 578(J) is a 2-motor, double-end car built in 1927 for Kobe. After World War II, it was moved to Hiroshima to help rebuild that war-ravaged city. The car was made available through Japan's Railway Corporate Assembly and entered Trolley Festival service in 1986, leading the parade that year. It ran intermittently through the 1990s, but was sidelined pending installation of brake wheels and roof work, tasks that were completed in 2006 by an outside contractor. In 2010, 578(J) has been repainted, but its return to operational status is slow and indeterminate. With its rear and center doors, 578(J) has to be run with two operators, and having only two motors, it's also a very slow and underpowered car.

Oporto 189 - Portuguese Brill. Little single-truck 189 was one of two such trams that came down from Gales Creek Enterprises in Oregon for the 1983 Trolley Festival. (The other one was 122, which now operates in Dallas.) It was built in 1929 by the Oporto transit agency using J. G. Brill semi-convertible patterns. 189 was purchased outright by Muni at the conclusion of the 1983 Festival, and ran all five years, intriguing passengers with its bouncy ride and noisy gears. Its crowning moment came in 1987, when, along with MSRy "Dinky" 578(S), it ran the experimental Embarcadero service at the end of the 1987 Trolley Festival.

Held out of F-Line service in 1995 because of non-ADA compliance, it was allowed to decay until MSR and then-Muni General Manager Michael Burns came to the rescue. Its deterioration had reached the point where the roof was about to cave in. Burns ordered immediate restoration of the car. It was moved to the Cable Car Shop to begin restoration. The platforms were to be lengthened, using patterns from Memphis, which operates identical cars.

The restoration bogged down, however, over the issue of removing lead paint. It currently is stored under cover, but removed from its truck.

Johnstown 351 - Proposed Teaching Trolley. Johnstown, Pa. abandoned trolley service on June 11, 1960. At the end, it rostered a fleet of PCCs and double-end standard cars, such as 351, built in 1926. Like New Orleans 952 and 913, 351 exhibits the classic American streetcar architecture of the 1920s.

Johnstown 351 came to San Francisco in 1989 following its purchase by MSR from an estate in Sonoma County, whose original owners had planned for its operation as a tourist attraction. This scheme never happened, and after arrival at Muni, the car was moved to David L. Pharr (Mint) Yard for restoration. Very little has been done to 351, but in 2010, it was moved back to Geneva (now Cameron Beach) Yard, where it is now inside the newly-built historic car enclosure. MSR intends to turn the car over to Muni once restoration plans are formulated and carried out.

But MSR has an additional idea for this car. Back in United Railroads and Market Street Railway Company days, there was a special car named *San Francisco,* which carried school kids and their teachers on field trips. The idea is to make 351 a "Teaching Trolley," with learning aids on board the car, to be used for field trips and other functions with schoolchildren when the car is not in regular revenue service. In this way, an early San Francisco tradition would be revived.

Hamburg 3557 - The Red Baron. 3557 was built in 1954 by Linke-Hoffmann-Busch for Hamburg, Germany. Following the end of tram service in 1978 (Hamburg was one of very few German cities to abandon trams), the late Maurice Klebolt, bought the car and had it shipped to San Francisco.

3557 can rightfully lay claim to being the catalyst for the creation of the F-Line. Shortly after its arrival here, Klebolt "presented" the car to Mayor Dianne Feinstein one day in 1979 and had it driven

Newark City Subway PCC 21 loops around to reach Branch Brook Park Station, which supplanted Franklin Avenue as the line's outer terminal, on August 20, 2001, five days before PCCs ended 47 years of distinguished service on this line. Car 21 later became Muni 1077. *Peter Ehrlich*

Former New Jersey Transit 14 makes a test run on April 9, 2002. It's just turned off Don Chee Way onto Steuart Street. 14 was one of the eleven PCCs purchased by Muni starting in 2002 to add to the active fleet. Later, it was mini-rehabbed as 1070 and painted in 1954 Newark colors. *Peter Ehrlich*

around City Hall on a flatbed trailer. Bemused city officials didn't know what to make of this media event, but Muni permitted Klebolt to stash the car at Geneva Carhouse.

Klebolt's audaciousness caught the eye of Rick Laubscher, who, as a member of the San Francisco Chamber of Commerce back in 1982, was working separately from Klebolt on an alternative transit plan for the duration of the cable car system shutdown and rebuilding. This, of course, led to the 1983 Trolley Festival. As cars of international origin began to arrive in San Francisco, Klebolt sprang into action. He persuaded Muni officials to get 3557 ready for service, with a new paint job and minor electrical and mechanical work.

With its speedy ride and on-board taped German music playing inside, the "Red Baron" became quite popular with riders. It ran in all five Trolley Festivals and some of the holiday "Mini-Festivals" which followed, as well as a special posthumous run out to Ocean Beach on the N-Line in 1988 just after Klebolt's untimely passing. Its last hurrah came in the 1992 parade commemorating 100 years of San Francisco electric traction.

The "Red Baron" hasn't turned a wheel since. ADA-access issues, mostly involving changing the door configuration to make the openings wider for wheelchairs, need to be resolved if it is ever to enter F-Line service. It was allowed to languish at Geneva Upper Yard for many years before being moved to Marin Yard and tarped to protect it from further decay. Its restoration is many years away.

The New Jersey PCCs Arrive

IN 2002, THE F-LINE workhorse fleet consisted of 17 PCCs and nine Milan cars (the 10th would enter service in 2004). But planning for future historic streetcar service expansion, such as the E-Embarcadero, the extension into Fort Mason and a possible G-Golden Gate Park route, as well as covering proposed (and much needed) increased service frequencies, dictated the need to acquire more cars, or have more cars from Muni's stockpiled PCC

PCC 1080 (Los Angeles Transit Lines "Fruit Salad") was the first Newark car to arrive at Muni under the first mini-rehab contract with Brookville Equipment Co. It poses with unrehabbed NJ Transit 14 in Geneva Yard on August 21, 2005. But the interiors were shabby, and 1080 went back to Brookville for interior repainting under a contract change. *Peter Ehrlich*

fleet remanufactured. Even more pressing was the ongoing car shortage due to accidents and maintenance issues. At one point, the entire Milano fleet was pulled from service for a month.

An opportunity to procure more PCCs emerged in 2001 when the Newark City Subway replaced its 24 ex-Minneapolis/St. Paul PCCs, which had served the line with distinction for 47 years, with new low-floor light rail vehicles (LRVs). New Jersey Transit mulled over its options for disposition of its PCCs for nearly two years. At least three were intended for preservation in their home state, New Jersey. Muni approached NJ Transit with a proposal to acquire 15 cars, including car 14, which it had purchased in 2002 for evaluation. The price was $15,000 per car. NJT initially accepted the offer, but funding problems on San Francisco's end forced reduction of the order to just 11 cars, and the contract was signed in 2003.

Simultaneously, Muni negotiated with Brookville Equipment Corp. of Brookville, PA to perform a mini-rehab of the 11 cars. This covered items to make the cars compatible with operations on the street, including installing treadle steps at the rear doors, changing the front doors to open inward, installing front and rear trolley poles, exterior painting, and other work. Noticeably absent in the mini-rehab was complete rewiring of the cars and interior repainting, issues which would come to haunt Muni later.

It was estimated that with acquisition, engineering, and specs preparation, the actual rehabilitation costs plus shipping would total about $5.7 million. Ten cars went to Brookville directly from New Jersey; car 14, which was already in San Francisco, was the last car to be sent.

Car 1080 (Los Angeles Transit Lines) was the first "Brookville" PCC, as this class came to be known, to arrive in San Francisco in May 2005. Although 1080 looked stunning in its Los Angeles Transit Lines "Fruit Salad" exterior livery, its interior, which was still as it was when NJ Transit retired the car, was, admittedly, pretty shabby. It became clear that not only would Brookville have to get a contract modification to repaint the interiors of all 11 cars to match the still-pristine interiors of the other PCCs, but that more money would need to be found for this work.

Car 14, the last to go for mini-rehab, became the first to return with fresh paint inside and out, which it did as [New Jersey] Public Service Co-Ordinated Transport 1070. This time, it had the correct gray color below the windows, unlike PCC 1060, received ten years earlier. The car's paint package was complete with its "Ruby Slippers" paint on the trucks and on the headlight trim. The rest of the cars were delivered in 3-6 week intervals, with 1072 (Mexico City) the last to arrive on March 26, 2007.

Here is the list of the Brookville/New Jersey fleet, with their Newark and original Twin City Rapid Transit (Minneapolis/St. Paul) numbers:

1070 - Newark (dark gray/white)
  ex-Newark 14, née Minneapolis 333
1071 - Minneapolis/St. Paul (yellow/black)
  ex-Newark 23, née Minneapolis 362
1072 - Mexico City (cream/dark green/red)
  ex-Newark 20, née Minneapolis 339
1073 - El Paso City Lines (light green/white)
  ex-Newark 22, née Minneapolis 361
1074 - Toronto (maroon/cream)
  ex-Newark 2, née Minneapolis 321
1075 - Cleveland (orange/brown/cream)
  ex-Newark 17, née Minneapolis 336
1076 - Washington (light blue/white)
  ex-Newark 12, née Minneapolis 331
1077 - Birmingham (dark green/red/white)
  ex-Newark 21, née Minneapolis 360
1078 - San Diego (pea green/white/brown)
  ex-Newark 19, née Minneapolis 338
1079 - Detroit (red/cream)
  ex-Newark 11, née Minneapolis 330
1080 - Los Angeles Transit Lines "Fruit Salad" (yellow/green/white)
  ex-Newark 9, née Minneapolis 328

As delivered, the Brookville PCCs were built with General Electric motors and controls. They are 108" wide, dimensionally identical to Muni's "Baby Tens" such as 1040. Like some of the earlier ex-Philly PCCs, cars 1070, 1071, 1072, 1073, 1077, 1078 and 1079 had chrome wings around their headlights, matching their prototypes.

By the end of 2007, four cars had been accepted for revenue service, starting with 1078 (San Diego), followed by 1077 (Birmingham), 1079 (Detroit) and 1075 (Cleveland). In 2010, 1076 (Washington) entered service, but 1079 had been grounded because of a small electrical fire, and 1078 went to Brookville following an in-service failure. Unfortunately, the 50+-year-old wiring inside the cars caused operational headaches such as center doors opening mysteriously while in motion. It was painfully clear that the rehab performed by Brookville should have included a complete rewiring of the cars, something that had never been done during their 47 years of operation on the Newark City Subway.

There were two attempts to move forward with a contract to rewire the Newarks. As part of the contract, the four remaining "Torpedoes" were to be included in the package. The first attempt, in 2007, was bid on, and Brookville was again the best responsive bidder. With regard to the "Torpedoes,"

The Newarks Add More Color to the Fleet

(*below left*) Detroit-hued PCC 1079 stops at San Francisco State University Station on the M-Ocean View line during a test run on October 30, 2006. (*below right*) Caked with road dust, PCC 1073 sports the attractive El Paso City Lines' last livery of light green and white with red trim, as it sits on San Jose Avenue outside Metro Center aboard the low-boy trailer which brought it west from Pennsylvania. The date is December 18, 2006. *Both photos, Peter Ehrlich*

(*left*) The "Brookvilles," as Muni calls them, have been plagued by wiring problems. The first time around, only five of them entered revenue service, and by mid-2011, just three were operational. Brookville got a second contract in 2009 to rewire all eleven cars, which should have been done originally, as the cars were never overhauled during their 47 years of service in Newark. PCC 1071 (Minneapolis/St. Paul-Twin City Rapid Transit) was the pilot car under the rewiring contract. It's pictured inside Metro East on Nov. 20, 2010. Along with the rewiring, a new Westinghouse-based controller replaced the original General Electric control system, as GE was no longer interested in manufacturing PCC controllers. 1071 was conditionally accepted for service in July 2011. *Karl Johnson*

The most reliable of the ex-Newark PCCs, over the course of the first Brookville contract, has been 1077, painted to represent Birmingham, AL. This image was taken on May 5, 2007 at Market, Noe and 16th Streets, looking down from a neighborhood bar and restaurant. The tower of Mission Dolores is off in the distance. Because of its reliability, 1077 was the next-to-last of the "Brookvilles" to be sent back to Pennsylvania for complete rewiring and conversion to Westinghouse-based controllers. 1077 was the formerNewark 21, but it started life as Minneapolis/St. Paul 360. *Peter Ehrlich*

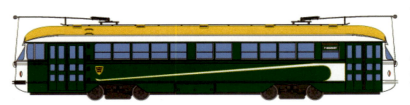

One of the four "Torpedoes" being remanufactured by Brookville Equipment Corp. in 2011/12 will return in this fantasy Market Street Railway Co. "Zip Stripe" livery, which the company proposed in the late 1930s for a group of streamliners. The cash-strapped MSRy, however, was never able to place an order. *MSR drawing*

however, Brookville proposed completely new AC solid-state propulsion packages, similar to those in 18 PCCs remanufactured by Brookville for Philadelphia in 2003. Muni specs covered straight rebuild of the DC motors and controls, and AC propulsion became an alternative. But Brookville threw in the possibility of refurbishing two former Red Arrow lookalike double-end cars, which would have added cars to the fleet, but also would have jacked up the cost. Despite the industry trend toward AC propulsion, Muni decided, in 2008, to let this proposal die because of concerns of adding a new class of equipment to the already overburdened shop force.

Muni engineers then revamped the specs for DC propulsion only. In the meantime a new wrinkle arose to complicate matters. General Electric no longer had any interest in producing PCC controls as the market had basically lain fallow for fifty years. However, Bombardier Transportation had bought out the Westinghouse PCC designs and was eager to continue supplying new PCC controllers. So the decision was made to change out the GE controllers on both the Newarks and the "Torpedoes" to new Westinghouse controllers (but retaining the GE motors). Muni and the San Francisco Municipal Transportation Agency (SFMTA), the Muni's governing body which had replaced the SFPTC in the early 2000s, found enough money–$18 million–in summer 2009 and again awarded the contract to Brookville. The first PCC to head back to Pennsylvania this time was car 1071 (Twin City Rapid Transit). By June 2011, all cars except for 1075, 1076 and 1077, which were still active, had also gone east. By the beginning of 2012, these three had been transported to Brookville. 1071, the pilot car, returned to Muni on November 20, 2010, with its new Westinghouse-based controller, and was tested for several months before being accepted for service in late 2011. Starting in mid-2011, most of the others returned and entered burn-in testing and training. These started to enter service in early 2012. The total price for the entire 16-car contract, including the four "Torpedoes" and car 1040 (see below), was $18.7 million.

The new Westinghouse-based controllers offer extremely smooth acceleration, with no evidence of slugging, which historically has been a bane of PCC operation.

The Last Four Torpedoes Go to Rebuild

REMANUFACTURE OF THE FOUR remaining "Torpedoes" were also included in this contract. These were 1006, which was a Trolley Festival star; 1008, converted to a work motor; and 1009 and 1011, which had been slated for rebuilding back in 1994 but had been damaged in a fire. (All four of these cars have now returned to Muni, with 1011 arriving in September 2013.)

Because these are double-end cars, there had to be some modification to the new Westinghouse controllers in order for them to work as double-enders. But that issue is not perceived as insurmountable.

Both 1006 and 1008 will return in their as-built "Muni Wings" paint scheme. 1009 is slated to receive the livery of the Dallas Railway & Terminal, as delivered on DR&T's 25 Pullman PCCs received in 1945. But the most interesting paint scheme–and one overwhelmingly favored by MSR members and accepted by Muni–is another "fantasy" livery, which was proposed by Muni's competitor, Market Street Railway Co., back in 1938. MSRy wanted to buy new PCC-style street-cars to match Muni's "Magic Carpets," painting them with their patented "White Front" ends and green sides with a white "Zip Stripe' and a yellow roof. Nothing ever came of this proposal, and the cash-strapped MSRy was only able to apply the attractive scheme to a few of its homebuilt cars. So 1011 will pay homage to Market Street Railway Co. in this fashion. (A drawing exists in Charles Smallwood's book *The White Front Cars of San Francisco* for such a car.)

When the four remanufactured "Torpedoes" return to service, there will be sufficient double-enders available to start up the E-Embarcadero line, now slated for 2013, in time for San Francisco's hosting of the America's Cup sailing race competition starting in July 2013.

These are the color schemes for the four "Torpedo" additions to the active fleet:
- **1006** - Muni Wings (green/cream)
- **1008** - Muni Wings (green/cream)
- **1009** - Dallas Railway & Terminal (red/cream)
- **1011** - Market Street Railway 1938 (green, yellow roof, White Front ends, Zip Stripe)

2012: The Newarks return to service

Following their rewiring by Brookville Equipment Co. in Pennsylvania and resolution of door motor problems, ex-Newark, NJ PCCs 1070-1080 gradually were accepted and placed in service by Muni in early 2012. Here is an array of pictures. An image of rebuilt PCC 1040, identical in dimensions to the Newark PCCs, is also included here. [More pictures in Chapter 13.]

(*clockwise from top left*) Toronto's famous "Red Rocket" PCCs are represented by car 1074, here at Ferries on January 15, 2012. The car went in official revenue service a few days later. *Jeremy Whiteman* 1080 (Los Angeles Transit Lines) was the third rewired car accepted for service. It's inbound at Main Street on March 15, 2012. *Elizabeth Krumbach* 1076 (Washington) tows sister 1075 (Cleveland) off the low-boy at Metro East on January 16, 2012. 1076 then became the last car to go to Brookville. *Karl Johnson* PCC 1040, the last of the 25 Muni "Baby Tens" from 1951/52, and the last American PCC built, was spotted at Market and Van Ness during a training/burn-in run on January 26, 2012. Note that 1040 has historically accurate dash lights, which differ from those on the Newark PCCs. The placement of the numerals, and the silver anticlimber, however, are not accurate. *Matt Lee*. El Paso 1073 has a "G-Golden Gate Park" rollsign displayed, as it lays over on The Embarcadero at Mission Street during a burn-in run on January 16, 2012. El Paso's PCCs were the only ones to ever cross an international border (with Mexico) while in revenue service. The G-Line, however, which could carry hundreds of international riders to the Golden Gate Park museums, will probably never get built [see Chapter 7]. *Ethan Tam*

The last PCC in this contract is 1040, the last one of its kind built for United States service in 1952. 1040, too, was a Trolley Festival veteran, and even made a few trips in 1995 on the F-Line. It was rebuilt to as close to its 1952 appearance as possible, with proper "Wings," dash lights in their original locations, and a replica "Golden Glow" headlight that will meet CPUC standards. 1040 returned in late 2011. It re-entered revenue service on March 12, 2012.

Stockpiling PCCs for the Future

IN THE MEANTIME, Muni has been stockpiling PCCs for possible future rebuilding. Most of these have been Muni's own cars. Gradually, through the efforts of MSR, additional ex-Muni PCCs have returned to San Francisco.

As previously mentioned, the push to rebuild more cars was made publicly as early as 1996, and internal Muni memos documenting the need to expand the fleet surfaced even earlier. After the three Morrison Knudsen-rebuilt "Torpedoes" entered service, the author, MSR officials, and others, recognizing their versatility due to being double-enders, urged managers to redouble their efforts to develop plans and specs to get the remaining double-enders, plus "Baby Ten" 1040, the last U. S. PCC built, remanufactured. Frustration set in when every time pots of money were found to carry this out, they would be pulled for some unrelated urgency that cropped up for other capital projects needs, such as overruns in the Automatic Train Control System (ATCS) subway re-signaling project.

But the idea wouldn't go away. MSR kept pressure on to get up to eight more cars rehabbed, and success finally came in 2009 with the combined contract to rewire the "Brookvilles" and rebuild the four "Torpedoes" and "Baby Ten" 1040, as described earlier in this chapter.

Among the other stockpiled "Baby Tens," the closest for a rehab, besides 1040, are 1033 and 1039 (the two PCCs which came from Orange Empire Railway Museum, where at least 1039 was operable), with 1034 being another possibility. The remaining cars–1023, 1026, 1027, 1028, 1031 and 1038–are probably too badly deteriorated for rehab, but stranger things have happened. [See Chapters 11 and 13 for what San Diego did to restore a derelict Muni PCC.]

As for the ex-St. Louis Public Service 1100s, Muni retained 1103, 1115, 1125, 1130, 1139, 1158 and 1168, as well as 1128, which ran in the Trolley Festivals and even in F-Line service as St. Louis Public Service 1704. With MSR's help, cars 1106,

Two of the stockpiled "Elevens," 1139 and 1158, sit at Marin Yard in this image taken April 12, 2008. Both of these cars operated on the last day of PCC service–September 19, 1982. Considering that they have been exposed to the elements for 29 years, they seem to be in remarkably good shape. Other cars sitting in this yard are in much worse condition. *Peter Ehrlich*

1108, 1140 and 1160 were returned to Muni property. All of these cars are stored at Marin Yard..

If there is a call to rehabilitate more PCCs, the likelihood would be for Muni to restore the "Baby Tens", as they're dimensionally identical to the ex-Newarks. Plus, the 1100s have that oddball pedal configuration unique to cars from St. Louis.

Also stored unserviceable at various locations: Ex-Pittsburgh 4008 and 4009, and former Philly cars 2133 and 2147. The two Pittsburgh cars are "new" PCCs with aluminum bodies that were built in Port Authority Transit's shops around 1984, using parts from Pittsburgh's 1700 class. The pair closed out the PCC era in Pittsburgh in 1999 running on the Drake Loop Shuttle. In 2001, they were auctioned off. Then-SFMTA Executive Director Michael Burns successfully bid on them and they were brought out to San Francisco. Corrosion, however, has set in, and the trucks need to be regauged from Pittsburgh's 5'-2½" gauge, so after sitting at Geneva Yard for two years, they were moved to Marin Yard. If money is found to resuscitate these basically sound cars, they would most likely receive Pittsburgh liveries. At last inspection, 4008 is in the better condition.

There is plenty of disappointment, and in some cases, bitterness, surrounding two cars: St. Louis 1704 (ex-Muni 1128) and the aforementioned Philly 2133, which would have become Muni 1064. Both were given extensive cosmetic interior rehabs by MSR at Mint Yard, including installation of tip-up ADA seats from scrapped buses, and, in the case of 1704, conversion of the front blinker doors to inward

1006 and 1040: Two Notable Muni PCCs

1006 was the first of 10 "Torpedoes" built in 1948. 1040 was the last of the 25 "Baby Tens" manufactured in 1951/52, and the last PCC built for U. S. service. Both cars were remanufactured in 2011/12.

(*this column, top*) Although the "Torpedoes" usually were assigned to the N-Judah early in their career, they also ran on the B-Geary. 1006 is outbound at 33rd Avenue and Anza in the Richmond District in March 1952. *Wilbur Whitaker* (*center*) For the 1984 Trolley Festival, 1006 was brought back from storage and was repainted to appear as a double-ender, but still operated as a single-end car. Market and 1st Street, July 20, 1984. *Peter Ehrlich* (*bottom*) The following year, 1006 became a true double-end PCC again, and ran this way through the remaining Trolley Festivals and some mini-Festivals afterward, such as this one on Black Friday (the day after Thanksgiving) in 1990. Here, 1006 is approaching Gough Street. *Peter Ehrlich*

(*this column, top*) PCC 1040 was still in Landor 2-tone orange and white in 1984. It's at Market and Grant working a weekend festival on December 30, 1984. *Peter Ehrlich* (*center*) 1040 made it into F-Line service, but because it wasn't ADA-accessible, it could only be used as a tripper. At. Market and 3rd Street, Sept. 19, 1995. *Peter Ehrlich* (*bottom*) 1040 is getting completely remanufactured at Brookville Equipment Co. in Pennsylvania. This is a progress photo taken in October 2010. *Karl Johnson*

folding doors. Great expense and volunteer labor was poured into rehabilitation of the cars. But when they arrived at Geneva following MSR's restoration work, top Muni maintenance managers deemed that the underframes and lower body panels were too rusted for continued restoration, and the two cars were stripped to bare shells and set aside at Marin Yard. In the case of 1704, this was especially sad, because the car was a star performer in the Trolley Festivals. Even after the F-Line opened, 1704 (and 1040), despite being non-ADA-compliant, would be assigned in tripper service. I would sometimes pull out 1704 as a PM rush-hour tripper in 1995 and 1996 and at the end of the shift, I'd call over to the inspector at Church and Duboce and ask if he needed some help on the N-Judah. If he answered in the affirmative, I would swing the car around to the N-Line, pick up a "swinging load" of long-suffering riders, and speed out to Ocean Beach! Many riders sat back on the PCC's cushioned seats and remembered the days when PCCs ruled the N-Line. Ahhh–those were the days!

In mid-2017, a sense of urgency developed with regard to the stockpiled PCCs. With land space at a premium, caused by the city's building boom along the Central Waterfront, Muni would like to use Marin Yard as a bus training facility. This would mean that the stored fleet would have to be moved elsewhere (perhaps out of The City) and/or the fleet would have to be culled to save those cars that would most likely be rebuild candidates, and scrap or otherwise dispose of the rest. Some other cars, such as unrehabbed Philly PCCs 2133 and 2147; the two Pittsburgh cars; and Hamburg "Red Baron" 3557, are also stored at Marin. One can see the wisdom of retaining the Philly cars, because they could be used to repair other wrecked Philly PCCs (such as just-rehabbed Baltimore 1063, which suffered severe damage to its right front end on New Year's Day 2018 when it plowed into a truck making an illegal left turn on the T-Line as the PCC was pulling in). The others are very low priority for restoration, and the plan is to offer them first to museums, and if unsuccessful, to scrap dealers.

At its May 15, 2018, meeting, the SFMTA Board of Directors authorized the disposal of cars 1023, 1031, 1038, 1054, 1064 (ex-Philly 2133), 1106, 1108, 1125, 1139, 1140, 4008 and 4009. Trucks and certain other parts would be saved, such as the front end of 1054 and the bullseye light fixtures.

1006 and 1040: Two Notable PCCs

TWO OF THE PCCs in the rebuilding pipeline are noteworthy in their own right–1006, the first "Torpedo," and "Baby Ten" 1040, the last PCC built in America. Both were Trolley Festival stars. 1040 returned from remanufacture in late 2011, and 1006 is due back in 2012.

1006 was the first postwar double-end, all-electric PCC and one of just 18 such cars outshopped by St. Louis Car Co. in 1948–ten for Muni and 8 for Illinois Terminal, a St. Louis suburban system. 1006 started its Muni career on lines N-Judah and B-Geary. Built as a two-man car, it was converted to one-man operation in 1954, following repeal of the two-man streetcar ordinance the previous year. Along with its sisters, 1006's #2 end pedal controls were retained for backup movements. 1006, assigned to a charter on the night of September 19, 1982, was the last car to pull into Geneva Yard at the close of streetcar service in 1982. Later that year, it was moved to Pier 70 for storage, along with other PCCs to be retained.

In 1984, 1006 was brought over to Metro Center for cosmetic restoration in its original "Muni Wings" paint scheme and return to service for the 1984 Trolley Festival. The following year, it was reconverted to true double-end status, and ran that way through 1992. It never did run in F-Line service, however, and was allowed to decay in Geneva Upper Yard. In 2002, it was shifted to Marin Yard and tarped to stave off further deterioration.

1006 will retain its double-end "Muni Wings" livery following its remanufacturing at Brookville.

1040 was the last of 25 "Baby Ten" PCCs built by St. Louis Car Co. in 1951-52, the last domestic order for PCCs in the United States. This fact alone makes 1040 one of the two most famous PCCs still in existence, the other one being Brooklyn 1001, the very first production PCC, built in 1936, which is preserved at the Shore Line Trolley Museum in East Haven, Conn.

1040 lived a more or less humdrum life working all Muni lines with loops or wyes, including the B-Geary before its 1956 abandonment, but primarily the K-Ingleside line. From 1957 through 1981, 1040 and its class sisters became mainstays of line J-Church.

In 1978, it was one of just two "Baby Tens" and 30 PCCs overall to receive the Landor "California Poppy Gold," "Sunset Glow" and white livery. In this dress, 1040, along with ex-St. Louis 1704, participated in the 1983 and 1984 Trolley Festivals.

In 1985 Muni repainted 1040 into "Muni Wings" green and cream, but slightly inaccurate. Though non-ADA-compliant, 1040 made a few appearances on F-Line tripper runs in 1995. As proof that patrons do recognize different equipment, one woman boarded 1040, assigned to a morning run, noticed its double seats on both sides of the aisle and more spacious interior overall, and said to the motorman, "Ah! You brought us the Limo today!" But since 1996, 1040, its roof leaking like a sieve, sat corroding away in Geneva Yard until the shop placed a tarp on it. It left for Brookville on December 4, 2009, as part of the "Newark/Torpedo" contract.

1040 returned from Brookville in late 2011 in its original 1952 appearance: accurately-painted "Muni Wings" verdant green and cream, complete with "Golden Glow" headlight and properly-placed dash lights. Except for the addition of front tip-up seats for ADA seating positions, the as-delivered double seating will remain the same. Like the Brookvilles, dimensionally identical to 1040, the front doors were converted to fold inward to allow for wheelchair boarding with the standard folding bridge plate. As mentioned, 1040 returned to service on March 12, 2012.

A Muni "Eleven" Represents St. Louis

ONE OF THE FORMER St. Louis PCCs was reactivated for the Trolley Festivals and ran into the F-Line era: Muni PCC 1128. In early 1983, when plans for the first Trolley Festival were drawn up, one of the cars proposed for the fleet was a representative of the former St. Louis PCCs received by Muni between 1957 and 1962. Originally, car 1170 (née ex-St. Louis 1777) was chosen, but because it was easier to move 1128 out from inside storage, that car was picked instead. It was brought over to Eastshore Lines, a charter bus company whose owner was a trolley fan, for repainting as St. Louis Public Service 1704, and it was sponsored by Anheuser-Busch, the brewing company headquartered in the Gateway City, and the local San Francisco Budweiser distributor. 1704 ran in every Festival, and occasionally as a tripper in F-Line service. In late 1998, it was moved to Mint Yard, where Market Street Railway carried out its conversion to a car which was ADA-accessible. As already noted, Muni ultimately rejected 1704. Nowadays, 1704 sits at Marin Yard with other "Elevens" awaiting restoration. In its place, one of the Brookville-remanufactured PCCs, 1050, will be repainted to represent St. Louis Public Service.

For Trolley Festival Use Only

UP TO NOW, WE'VE been discussing streetcars that were used during the Trolley Festivals and on the F-Line; trolleys which debuted with the F-Line or entered service later; and cars awaiting restoration. But there were some vehicles that ran only during the Trolley Festival years. Among them:

Muni K-Type 178 - Iron Monster. This original 1923-vintage Muni car, built locally by

PCC 1704, formerly Muni 1128, received its original St. Louis livery for the Trolley Festivals. It's at Market and 2nd Street passing the Trolley Festival Boeing LRV 1213 on June 27, 1983. *Peter Ehrlich*

Bethlehem Steel Co. (the old Union Iron Works), was similar to the B-Types, and its class ran all over the system until 1958. (Sister car 181 ended the two-man "Iron Monster" era on May 9, 1958.) 178 is one of two of this class preserved, and is owned by the Western Railway Museum at Rio Vista Junction, CA. The other K-Type is 171, which went to the Orange Empire Railway Museum in Perris, Calif., south of Riverside.

In 1981, the Museum approached Muni with the idea of having it available for charters. Muni leased the car, and then took this idea a step further

Muni K-Type "Iron Monster" 178 was leased from the Western Railway Museum and ran in San Francisco from 1981 through the 1985 Festival. 178 passes the Orpheum Theater at Hyde/8th Streets during the 1983 Festival. This car was built locally in 1923 at the old Union Iron Works shipyard, which had been taken over by Bethlehem Steel. *Peter Ehrlich*

Portland "Council Crest" 503, a 1903 J. G. Brill product, rolls inbound at 17th and Noe Streets during the 1985 Trolley Festival. This elegant car also graced Muni rails during 1983. *Peter Ehrlich*

The Mexican Jumping Bean–aka Veracruz 001–arrives at Transbay Terminal in August 1984. This car operated only between 11th Street and Transbay because it was a rather cantankerous performer. Nevertheless, the public loved its open sides and bouncy gait. *Peter Ehrlich*

in 1982, by placing it in service on the J-Church line, along with A-Type 1. It was still in San Francisco when the Trolley Festival plans took shape, and Muni continued to lease 178 for Festival service for the first three Festivals. After the end of the 1985 Festival, it returned to the Western Railway Museum, where it is in regular service.

Portland 503 - The Council Crest Trolley. Number 503 was a 1903-built Brill double-truck wood streetcar with hand and controller brakes. 503 and others in this class achieved fame because of their assignment to the Rose City's most scenic line, Council Crest. After abandonment in 1950, 503 and sister 506 were preserved locally in Oregon, and went to the Oregon Electric Railway Museum in Glenwood, Ore. With the help of trolley importer Paul Class of Gales Creek Enterprises, Muni leased this elegant car for the 1983 and 1985 Festivals. Meanwhile, the Oregon museum moved to a new site, at Brooks, and four replicas of 503 were built by the Gomaco Trolley Company of Ida Grove, Iowa, and equipped with PCC trucks and electricals–the only wooden-bodied PCC cars anywhere! Originally providing daily service, by the 2000s, these cars eventually only operated on certain holiday weekends on Portland's TriMet MAX light rail route from downtown Portland across the Willamette River to Lloyd Center [see Chapter 12]. Two of them also operated on the separate Portland Streetcar route from 2001 to 2004. However, they're now in St. Louis and on the Willamette Shore Trolley [see Chapter 12 again for their disposition].

Veracruz 001 - The Mexican Jumping Bean. This single-truck open car was brought to San Francisco under the auspices of the Mexican government and the mayor of Veracruz, for the 1984 and 1985 Festivals, where it delighted riders on a shuttle route from 11th Street to Transbay Terminal. With its rollicking gait and noisy gears, it was quickly nicknamed "The Mexican Jumping Bean." Although Muni wanted to buy the car, the mayor of Veracruz, who was running for re-election, wanted it returned with the intention of re-starting that city's extant trolley system. Unfortunately, he was defeated in the election, and today 001 reportedly just sits on a slab of concrete in a downtown plaza, waiting for a call to service that may never come. (A sister car operated at an Ohio museum, but has since been sold to another museum.)

Oporto 122 - Portuguese Brill. 122, along with Muni's 189, came to Muni in 1983 on a lease from Gales Creek Enterprises in Oregon. It was built in 1912 by J. G. Brill and shipped to Oporto, Portugal, in kit form.

When the 1983 Festival ended, Muni purchased 189 outright, but 122 went back to Oregon. Later, it was sold to the McKinney Avenue Transit Authority vintage line in Dallas, where it operates today. (See Chapter 3 for a picture of 122.)

Muni Boeing LRV 1213 - Up from the Mines. The most improbable Trolley Festival specimen was Boeing-Vertol LRV 1213. This was one of a pair of "United States Standard Light Rail Vehicles" built in 1977 and equipped with trolley bases for trolley pole operation. Muni's Boeing fleet, which opened up the Muni Metro subway, eventually numbered 130 cars. All of them were replaced by the end of 2001.

With its poles affixed, 1213 was used as a spare car during the 1983 Trolley Festival, under orders of railfan General Manager Harold H. Geissenheimer. Its appearance on Market Street had people scratching their heads, as the reputation of the

The most improbable, and least popular, car in the 1983 Trolley Festival was Boeing LRV 1213. It was fitted with poles and operated as infrequently as possible–usually when another car was scheduled for preventive maintenance. 1213 waits at Duboce Junction for other Boeings assigned to subway service to clear on July 1, 1983. *Peter Ehrlich*

Boeings in the Muni Metro subway was the butt of jokes due to their unreliability. It was clearly the most unpopular trolley in the Festival as it clanked down Market Street.

1213 also ran during the first week of the 1984 Festival, but quickly shed its poles and returned to subway service. It was retired in September 1998 and presented to the Oregon Electric Railway Historical Society in Brooks, Ore. in 2000, where it still runs.

Milwaukee 978 rests inside Metro Center on July 17, 1983. This was probably a last-ditch effort to determine if it could carry passengers, as it suffered a broken frame while being loaded for its trip to San Francisco. The car didn't pass the test, and never ran in the 1983 Trolley Festival. *Jeffrey Moreau*

Three That Didn't Make It

THERE WERE THREE STREETCARS that were intended for Trolley Festival use that never made it into service, for various reasons.

Milwaukee 978. This car was a representative of the last United States city, besides New Orleans, to run old-fashioned trolleys exclusively (Milwaukee abandoned streetcars in March 1958, just two months before the last "Iron Monster" ran in San Francisco). It was leased from a Wisconsin museum for the 1983 Trolley Festival and was fully operational.

Unfortunately, it was discovered that 978 suffered a broken back (underframe), apparently caused when it was loaded onto the low-boy in Wisconsin for transport to San Francisco. This was a disappointment because 978 could have been operated with just one man, whereas most of the other cars needed 2-man crews. It returned to the Wisconsin museum after the 1983 Festival ended without turning a wheel in revenue service in The City By The Bay.

Milan Interurban 96. This powerful center-entrance tram was brought to Muni in 1985 following the success of Milan "Peter Witt" 1834. Trolley Festival "godfather" Maury Klebolt intended to convert it into a rolling tram restaurant. In its native city, 96 and similar sister trams were powerful enough to pull four trailers. Of course, there were no trailers to pull in San Francisco.

From the beginning, 96 was deemed too powerful, and, in addition had braking problems. Nevertheless, MSR began partial restoration of Car 96 in the late 1980s. The work stopped when it became clear that Muni had no interest in the car, and ultimately, it was sold to a railway museum in Snoqualmie, Wash. In 2016, car 96 passed on to the Oregon Electric Railway Historical Society in Brooks, OR.

Sacramento Northern Birney 62. In 1984, the Western Railway Museum and Muni agreed to a trial of single-truck Birney Safety Car 62 as a possible Trolley Festival participant, intended to replace Muni 178, as it was a one-operator streetcar. [See Chapter 12 for a description of the Birney Safety Car.] Number 62 originally ran in the Yuba City-Marysville, Calif. area, and then in Chico, Calif. as interurban company Sacramento Northern's last passenger operation, becoming the fourth-to-last system still operating Birneys in the United States, quitting in 1948 (followed by Kansas City,

Birmingham and Fort Collins, Colo.). After it was saved by the Bay Area Electric Railway Association, it made a 1951 charter trip on Muni.

On May 19, 1984, car 62 made one trip from Metro Center to Transbay Terminal and back. It became painfully clear that the Birney's railroad-profile wheels couldn't cope with Muni's streetcar girder rail, and it rode on its flanges practically the entire distance. The trial was a failure, and car 62 immediately returned to the Museum. The next day, car 178 came back to Muni.

The Brookville Philly PCC Rehab Contract

IN 1995, THE PCCs FROM PHILADELPHIA ushered in the new F-Market line. Looking pristine in their shiny and multi-hued liveries, they were a delight to see and ride. However, by 2015, they had already accumulated 20 years of very hard, often crush-load service, accumulating more years of service than most PCCs ever did, and some of them were pushing 70 years of age. And, to be frank, the bodies were showing signs of body rot and corrosion, with paint bubbles all over the place. Also, the underframes, which never were completely made rust-free following the original Philly GOH rehab of the early 1980s, and the M-K remanufacture prior to introduction into San Francisco service, were increasingly rusting out. It was time for "another" mid-life rehab! Of course, the

Milan Interurban 96 was a tram which once graced Muni rails but never entered service and has since gone elsewhere. In one of its very few outings, the powerful interurban, which in Milan pulled up to four trailers, heads into the Sunset Tunnel on the N-Judah line on June 19, 1988. Handicapped ramps for LRV use are under construction in this scene. *Don Jewell*

rehab contract would have to include the original three "Torpedoes" as well.

So, in 2014, after evaluating proposals from two bidders, the SFMTA board awarded Brookville Equipment Co., the rebuilders of the ex-Newark PCCs, the four remaining "Torpedoes" PCC 1040, and A-Type Car 1, a $34.5 million contract on the basis of overall bid performance and qualifications, a trend that is becoming more prevalent in the industry, replacing the more prevalent use of low bid awards. Brookville was to completely remanufacture each car from top to bottom to as new condition. The contract was signed on September 17, 2014.

Each of the PCCs would receive an all-new Westinghouse-based controller, a program started with the Newark contract where Brookville replaced the original GE controllers. On this contract, these would replace the original Philadelphia controllers, which tended to be difficult to manage when starting from a stop, and led to jerky operation. In addition, some new "bells and whistles", such as fire-resistant doors and rear windows that open for emergencies, would be added to the ex-Philly cars that weren't on the Newarks. All of them would get the "Golden Glow" replica headlights, a program which started with the rebuilt "Torpedoes" and 1040.

Hard-luck PCC 1056 (Kansas City)

Sacramento Northern Birney made its second visit to San Francisco on May 19, 1984, in a test run to determine its feasibility to operate during the Trolley Festival, which was a failure. At Transbay Terminal with other cars. *Peter Ehrlich*

Muni PCC 1056 (Kansas City) was the pilot car for the Brookville rehab contract for the ex-Philly cars. It's on the turntable outside one of the shop buildings, and will be moved into the paint shop on the right, past the El Paso PCC that will get its rehab for the return of PCCs to that city, which they ran in from 1950 to 1974. 1056 returned to San Francisco in August 2016. This photo is a good opportunity to compare prewar and postwar PCC body styles. Photo, July 30, 2016. *Peter Ehrlich*

was chosen to be the pilot car. This car had been involved in a couple of accidents that put the car out of service for lengthy periods. Muni shops had started to rebuild the car in 2008 when it discovered a cracked bolster, the assembly that the trucks rest on, and work stopped. The contract stipulation was that it would take about two years to finish the work on 1056 and return the car to Muni, after which more cars would head east to Brookville.

In the meantime, in early 2015, PCCs 1060 ("Philadelphia Cream Cheese" blue/silver/cream) and 1051 (Muni Simplified) were involved in a non-revenue backup accident inside the Cameron Beach canopy, and those two were the next to be sent to Pennsylvania. Following the accident victims, cars selected for rehab either had major mechanical or electrical failures or over-extensive corrosion. As this is being written (January 2017), cars 1060, 1055, 1059, 1062 and 1063 are at Brokville. By the beginning of 2018, 1053, 1052 and 1061 are being remanufactured.

The intention, at the beginning, was to send "Torpedo" 1015 (Illinois Terminal) back to Brookville to become the pilot "Torpedo", since 1015 was the most decrepit-looking double-ender. But with only seven of them in the fleet, and five needed for E-Embarcadero service, the decision to rehab the "Torpedoes" toward the end of the contract was made, and instead, 1015 got an in-house cosmetic cleanup, which improved its looks considerably.

Muni, with Market Street Railway's input, is taking advantage of a provision in the contract to permit repainting certain cars into different or more accurate liveries, or, in some cases, having them represent different PCC cities. The cars affected are 1050, 1059, 1061, 1062 and 1063.

The color scheme of 1050 (Muni Wings) is redundant, as that historic Muni livery is now represented by PCC 1040, remanufactured during the Newark contract with Brookville. In addition, there are additional cars sporting "Muni Wings"–"Torpedoes" 1006 and 1008, and B-Type 162. So 1050 was chosen to represent St. Louis Public Service—right down to the Civil Defense logo near the front doors that those cars carried in their Gateway City heyday. As of January 2017, 1050 was still at Muni, waiting its turn to go east.

1059 (Boston Elevated Railway) will be repainted with the more accurate tangerine-and-cream livery, worn by the PCCs there from their beginning in 1941 through the MBTA era.

1061 (Pacific Electric) will get more accurate colors—particularly orange.

1063 (Baltimore) will come back in the striking original 1937 Baltimore colors featuring Alexandria blue below the belt rail, an orange belt rail, and cream around the windows. This scheme is also represented by car 7407 at the Baltimore Streetcar Museum.

The most significant change, however, will come with car 1062 (Louisville). It will return as a Pittsburgh car. In this way, 1062 will swap its status, from representing a city that ordered cars, but never operated them in service, to honor a city that operated 666 PCCs—the city with the second-most new cars of any American city. In this way, Muni will correct a major slight. The Pittsburgh car will have an hourglass front, just like the 1700s that were its newest cars.

The change in liveries and cities has the extra-added benefit of keeping interest in the F-Line constant, a concept which began during the Trolley Festivals.

The pilot car, 1056, returned to Muni on August 26, 2016, a month ahead of schedule. It had to pass 120 days of burn-in before it was acce[ted for service. Initially, it had issues with the reliability of the low-voltage converter, a trait the next car to

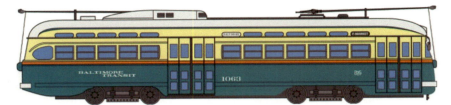

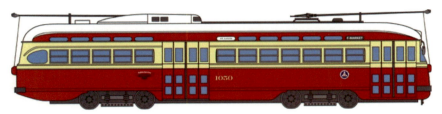

Four PCCs being remanufactued at Brookville will return in different paint. These include (*top to bottom*) 1062, which will swap its current Louisville colors for Pittsburgh; 1063, which will receive an earlier Baltimore livery; and 1050, which will come back as a St. Louis car. (*Not shown*) 1059 (Boston) will get a more accurate tangerine-and-cream color rendition. *MSR drawings*

return, 1051 (Muni Simplified), which came back in late October didn't exhibit. Brookville engineers worked on the problem, and 1056 was cleared for service in January 2017.

By the end of 2017, seven cars had been remanufactured and returned to Muni. All of these passed their burn-in period and are now in service. However, one of them, 1063, in its striking new Baltimore livery of Alexandria Blue and cream, suffered severe right front-end damage on New Years Day 2018, when it plowed into a box truck on its pull-in trip along the T-Line that had made an illegal left turn, a problem that has afflicted the T-Line ever since it opened in 2007.

A New Brookville Contract Wrinkle

IN MIDSUMMER 2017, a new development in the latest Brookville contract occurred when two former Red Arrow double-end cars, similar to the appearance of the "Torpedoes", but which were not PCCs, became available, as they were being deaccessioned by the Shore Line Trolley Museum. The plan is to modify the contract to include these two cars in the remanufacturing program in place of two single-end PCCs, which had been extensively rebuilt in-house by Muni relatively recently, and which were in excellent physical, mechanical, and electrical condition. In the process, the pair of Red Arrows would become true PCCs. Indeed, Muni had purchased two pairs of

These two views of 1063 (Baltimore) show the level of deterioration that most of the Philadelphia PCCs have endured over 20 years of wear and tear in F-Line service, which the contract with Brookville will address and correct. Both photos, June 20, 2015. *Peter Ehrlich*

Red Arrow Cars for Muni!

(*clockwise from top left*) Red Arrow 18, one of the cars to be rebuilt for Muni, leaves the Avon Road stop in Bywood, enroute to 69th Street Terminal, in July 1982, shortly before the end of service of all older stock. *William C. Myers.* Cars 18 and 21 have been loaded onto Silk Road Transport low-boys at the Shore Line Trolley Museum for the trip to Brookville. June 26, 2017. *Lee Carlson.* Car 21 is outside in the yard at Brookville on July 12, 2017. *Peter Ehrlich.* Two pairs of ex-Brussels B3 PCC trucks are at Muni Metro East. These will be placed under the Red Arrows once new bolsters and long kingpins have been fabricated. *Peter Ehrlich*

completely-rehabbed B-3 PCC trucks from Brussels for this purpose. The benefit, of course, would make more double-end cars available for E-Embarcadero service. So, in late June, the Red Arrows were transported from East Haven, Conn. to Brookville. Pending a renegotiation of the contract, these two would enter the program.

In the meantime, PCCs 1007, 1010 and 1015, which were last rebuilt by Morrison-Knudsen in 1994, soldiered on in mixed E-Line service with the Brookville-rebuilt "Torpedoes", although occasionally, one of them would get assigned to an F-line run. However, in November, 1015, working the F-Line, rear-ended a trolley coach on Market Street, and although it received minimal damage, in December, Muni deemed that all three of the cars needed to go to Brookville as soon as possible. This left only four cars for E-Line service, and MSR is trying to get Muni to detail one vintage car every day for full five-car service. The problem, of course, is the same one that has stymied regular operation of the vintage cars for years: They're two-man cars, and Muni is chronically short of qualified operators.

If the change to the contract is negotiated successfully, it would mean that single-end PCCs 1057 (Cincinnati) and 1058 (Chicago) would remain in San Francisco. This way, the number of cars in the contract would not change.

As far as liveries go, both Red Arrows would most likely retain their colors—one in original Philadelphia Suburban 1948 paint, the other in SEPTA's "Gulf Oil" 1970s scheme. This would free up

1007 to be painted differently, perhaps in Muni "Landor" two-tone orange and white, the colors worn by 1008 when it was a non-revenue work car. And the idea of repainting a "Torpedo" as a Pacific Electric car, simply because it's a double-ender, is constantly raised by some railfans—never mind the fact that its door configuration is different from PE's Pullman PCCs—and Muni already has a PE car, 1061, which, although it's a single-end car, has its right side door setup much closer to the appearance of the original Pacific Electric cars. Some people who would like to see 1007 return as a double-end Pacific Electric PCC favor painting it like a "San Berdoo Twelve."

The cars, originally Red Arrow 18 and 21, may possibly be renumbered 1012 and 1013, filling in the "Torpedo" gap when those cars were scrapped in 1979.

If and when work takes place on their remanufacture, Brookville will have to fabricate new bolsters with long kingpins in order to accommodate the PCC trucks; install new Westinghouse controllers, as it has done on the four "Torpedoes" remanufactured in the earlier contract; and considerable other rewiring work. The bodies, however, appear to be sound, though new steel roofs would have to be placed on the cars. Double-width rear doors may be retrofitted.

A little background on the Red Arrows: They were built by St. Louis Car Co. in 1949 for the Philadelphia Suburban Transportation Company as cars 11-24, just one year after Muni's "Torpedoes." They were delivered with high-speed motors and gearing, and St. Louis trucks. They lasted well into the SEPTA era, after that agency took over from the PSTC in 1970. Some, like car 18, got repainted in SEPTA's "Gulf Oil" livery, 21 remained in its maroon and cream its entire service life. They were replaced in 1982 by double-end Kawasaki LRVs. Many cars have gone to museums.

Rebuilding the Milan and Vintage Cars

LIKE THE PCCs, THE MILAN PETER WITT CARS have endured a lot of wear and tear as workhorses of the F-Line fleet. These "Ventotto" cars (so called, because of the year of their birth, 1928) last got rebuilt between 1988 and 1991 in their home city of Milan.

At the time of this writing, only five or six of the 11 cars are in service. One car, 1888, has not picked up passengers in close to 10 years now—even after it got a new coat of historic Milan two-tone green! Several others are languishing because of lack of motors or other critical parts. And the rebuilding of pioneer Milanese tram 1834 is still a work in progress at Geneva Shop.

Then, there's the vintage car fleet. Car 1 got remanufactured by Brookville in 2010 as part of the 2009 umbrella package covering the Newarks, the four remaining "Torpedoes" and 1040. But other cars desperately need remanufacturing. Muni B-Type 130, which last got rebuilt by Muni in 1983 for the Trolley Festivals, with a mini-refurbishing around 1996, is suffering from window rot and other physical deterioration. And the other B-Type, 162, which was restored by Market Street Railway and Muni from 2003 to 2008, got into a devastating wreck in 2013 that crumpled its No. 1 end, when an 18-wheeler made an illegal left turn, against the traffic signal, at Embarcadero and Bay, right into the path of 162! Fortunately, the end was designed to crumple, and there was no underframe damage. But rehab is beyond the capabilities of Muni's maintenance department, so, in late 2017, it went to an outside vendor in Long Beach for rebuilding. It returned in April 2018.

Beyond the "Iron Monsters", there are others that need to get into the program. Among them are Market Street Railway 798, the last Market Street Railway Company home-built "White Front Car". which will become a one-man car; Johnstown 351, already a one-man car and the car the MSR proposes to be a "Teaching Trolley", and New Orleans 913, which Muni got as a hedge back in 2005 just in case sister 952 went back to the Crescent City. Other cars include Osaka 151 (representing San Francisco's sister city), Melbourne 916, and Oporto 189. With the exception of the B-Type and Melbourne 916, all of these are projected for one-man operation. which would make them available at all times to supplement the "Torpedoes" on the E-Line.

The goal is standardization of electrical and mechanical systems, using modern components as needed, while retaining the uniqueness and old-style "feel" and appearance.

As for the Milanos, the best six cars will be retained for remanufacturing. The intention here is to have the six cars in three groups of two cars each representing or retaining the three Milan historic liveries. Much-needed backup controllers would be installed, and the doors would receive sensitive edges. Presumably, the others would be offered to museums, or become parts sources.

Market Street Railway has been in lengthy discussions with SFMTA regarding getting a rehab contract to go out to bid by mid-2018. The contracts could be let separately, or lumped together. At presstime, there has been no further news. But The City, currently enjoying a financial boom, is flush with money, and Muni's engineering staff is almost ready to advertise for a contract (or contracts).

Officially, *MSR*'s desire for cars to be remanufactured are these seven cars:

Muni B-Type 130 (two-man car)
Market Street Ry. Co. 798 (one-man car)
New Orleans 913 (one-man car)
Johnstown 351 (one-man car)
Melbourne 916 (1 or 2-man car)
Osaka 151 (one-man car)
Oporto 189 (one-man car)

CLEARLY, FROM THE MOMENT the F-Line opened in 1995, Market Street would become a more colorful place, as living history passes by every few minutes. The colorful streetcars are a fitting and lasting tribute to one of America's greatest main streets. Market Street Railway has an apt phrase for San Francisco's historic streetcars (and cable cars, too): Museums In Motion.

References:

1. Schneider, F. W., III, and Carlson, Stephen P., *PCC From Coast To Coast* (Interurban Press, Interurbans Special 86, Glendale, CA, 1983), p. 107.

From Louisville to Pittsburgh

Two pics showing how PCC 1062 got magically transformed from representing a city that ordered, but never operated, PCCs, to representing a city that ran 666 of them—the second-biggest new fleet in America. (*below*) 1062, in Louisville Railway Co. dress, is working the N/J free shuttle prior to F-Line opening. It's at San Jose/Pilgrim on the J-Line on April 23, 1995. (*bottom*) Now in Pittsburgh livery, 1062's at Embarcadero/Broadway on December 16, 2017. *Both, Peter Ehrlich*

The State of the Milanos

(*above*) Yellow-and-white 1807 had been out of service for about a year before this photo was taken of it at MME on August 10, 2017. It was waiting for a truck change. In 2018, it's still waiting! (*below*) 1834, the pioneering Milano, was getting its front end rebuilt at Geneva Body Shop on February 21, 2014. It's since gotten its window sash, and has updated electricals, such as door control buttons ad a LVPS power supply, to match the rest of the fleet, but it's really no closer to returning to service. *Both photos, Peter Ehrlich*

Scenes of the Brookville-remanufactured ex-Philly PCCs!

(right) The first of the Brookville-remanufaactured ex-Philly PCCs, 1056 (Kansas City), was brought down to the Ferry Building area by shopman Kevin Sheridan to show the car off to 2016 Heritage Weekend participants. It's returning to Metro East after the demonstration, and is at Embarcadero and Bryant on the Muni Metro Extension. It's lacking its numerals and the Kansas City Public Service logo, because it was still in acceptance testing. September 24, 2016. *Peter Ehrlich*

(*left*) Now accepted and in service, the Kansas City car poses at the Jones/Beach Fisherman's Wharf Terminal on June 9, 2017. (*below left*) 1051 (Muni Simplified), the second car (and first to be accepted), is at Market/Spear outbound, with the Ferry Building behind it, also on June 9. (*below*)1060 ("Philadelphia Cream Cheese" (1938 blue/silver/cream) was the third car to return from Brookville. It's outbound at Embarcadero/Broadway, passing the Pier 9 Restaurant under a beautiful sky, on December 16, 2017. *All photos, Peter Ehrlich*

(left) A picture perfect PCC on a picture perfect day! (But no picture windows on the car.) PCC 1059, the fourth car to be accepted for service, poses on Don Chee Way heading outbound, with the Ferry Building behind it. 1059 simply preens in its new, and accurate Boston Elevated tangerine and cream with a silver roof. September 9, 2017. *Peter Ehrlich* (Boston was the only city to order "Picture Window" PCCs.)

(clockwise from top left) 1062 (Pittsburgh) crosses the J-Line at Market/Church on December 16, 2017. 1062 was the fifth car to be accepted. *Peter Ehrlich*. 1063, in its new Baltimore livery, is at Pier 39. December 14, 2017. It was the 7th car to arrive, but the sixth to go in service. *Peter Ehrlich*. 1055 (Philly green/cream), car number six to return, is on a burn-in run heading toward Fisherman's Wharf in this trailing view at Sansome Street. Dec. 16, 2017. 1055 has since gone into service. *Peter Ehrlich*. 1050, the 8th car, has just arrived at Muni Metro East. 1050 was formerly "Muni Wings". Now it portrays St. Louis Public Service. January 7, 2018. *Allen Chan*

The Night Time is the Right Time

Scenes of Brookville-remanufactured ex-Philly PCCs captured after the sun goes down. (And one daytime pic.)

Two views of 1051 (Muni Simplified) at Ferry Plaza: (*above*) The top of the old SP Building at One Market is outlined in blue. (*right*) Making the turn onto The Embarcadero, with the dancing lights on the Bay Bridge. October 8, 2017.
Both photos, Peter Ehrlich

(*above*) 1056 (Kansas City) has crossed the 4th Street Bridge, on its pull-in trip. Mission Creek, the China Basin Building, and AT&T Park complete the nocturnal scene. October 9, 2017. (*above left*) 1059 (Boston) is at 17th/Castro during a rare lightning/thunderstorm to hit San Francisco. The flash of light above the building is lightning! September 11, 2017. (*left*) The rebuilt Clark B-2 truck under 1055. A new, more powerful magnetic track brake has been retrofitted to the truck.
All photos, Peter Ehrlich

(above) 1062 (Pittsburgh) swings onto Market from the 17th/Castro terminal. The Rainbow flag flies proudly. December 15, 2017. (above right) 1063 (Baltimore) is at MME. It's just been accepted for service. December 13, 2017. (right) 1063 makes a stop inbound at Market and 9th Street. December 15, 2017. *All photos, Peter Ehrlich*

(left) 1055 (Phila. green/cream) crosses The Embarcadero inbound on a burn-in trip, with the illuminated Bay Bridge in the background. Dec. 7, 2017. *Traci Cox* (below left) Now One Market is glowing red, as 1056 and 1080 (Los Angeles) pass on Don Chee Way. October 9, 2017. *Peter Ehrlich* (below) 1062 and 1055, representing both ends of the Commonwealth of Pennsylvania, are at the back of MME. 8 October 2017. *Peter Ehrlich*

(top) Operator Lan Lai stands on the steps of her PCC, Birmingham 1077, at Fisherman's Wharf on December 9, 2010. *Peter Ehrlich* *(bottom)* SFPUC official Bruce Bernhard (left) and Muni General Manager Bill Stead (right) pose with maintainers Romer Manag, Art Michel and Karl Johnson along with a component for Maury Klebolt's car, Hamburg 3557, aka "The Red Baron," outside Geneva Shops, in August 1988. *San Francisco Public Utilities Commission*

Chapter 9 - Behind The Scenes

The men and women who operate, maintain and guide the F-Line

*"I go to bed early, can't wait to come back.
I work at home and come here to rest."*

– F-line operator Danny Miranda,
who retired in December 2010
after an illustrious 32-year career with Muni,
the last 15 working on the F-Line.

THE F-LINE IS A PEOPLE-ORIENTED operation from top to bottom. The operators are the first (and often only) faces that riders see when they board an F-Line streetcar, pay their fare, and settle back to enjoy the ride. But behind the front lines is a very capable crew that supervises the line, maintains the cars, and arranges the way that the cars are scheduled and dispatched.

The operators who run the F-Line streetcars are all assigned to Green Light Rail Division, which is located in the southern part of San Francisco, about a mile north of the border with Daly City. This has always been a rail division, and its roots date back to before United Railroads days, when the San Francisco and San Mateo Railroad established the Geneva Carhouse, located at the southeast corner of Geneva and San Jose Avenues, before the turn of the twentieth century. Despite its brick construction, Geneva Carhouse survived the 1906 Earthquake and Fire, and continued to serve United Railroads, Market Street Railway Company and Muni. After PCC service ended in September 1982, the cars were pulled out of the carhouse, moved to storage or tipped over and carted to the scrapper. The car sheds were demolished to make room for an auxiliary yard for the then-new Boeing-Vertol light rail vehicles (LRVs), but the office functions remained until the Loma Prieta Earthquake of October 17, 1989, when the remaining staff was shifted to Metro Annex diagonally across the street.

In 1984 a new Geneva Shops building was constructed along the east wall of the yard and was used to maintain LRVs and the then very small fleet of historic streetcars used during the Trolley Festivals. But day-to-day dispatching, training and general transportation management functions had Metro Annex was, already been based at the new Metro Annex building. and is, part of Metro Center, a relatively compact yard and heavy maintenance facility constructed beginning in 1977 on the site of the old 1907 "temporary" United Railroads' Elkton Shops. Metro Yard, alongside Metro Center, is the main storage yard for the Muni Metro LRV fleet. The name of the division was known as Geneva Division, even after Muni Metro opened, but was renamed the Curtis E. Green Light Rail Division about 1989, to honor Muni General Manager Curtis Green, who was in charge when the Muni Metro Subway opened in 1980.

The Operators

THE DAY FOR AN F-LINE OPERATOR assigned to a morning run begins with reporting to the division dispatcher's office in Metro Annex. The office is in an enclosure set off from the "gilley room," where operators hang out and relax between shifts, watch TV or play pool. Next to the gilley room are banks of lockers.

The operator picks up his "outfit," which consists of a "paddle," or schedule assigned to his particular "train" (schedule times specific to his streetcar over the course of the day), several books of transfers, operational bulletins and, occasionally, notices addressed to the operator alone, in a sealed envelope, usually disciplinary in nature.

The operator then walks across San Jose and Geneva Avenues over to Geneva Yard to set up his streetcar for service. This includes switching on the battery control to turn the car's auxiliary equipment on, such as interior and exterior lights and on-board radio, checking for outside damage or missing equipment, such as switch iron, wheel block, wheelchair ramp, tow bar, burnt-out lights, broken windows, and checking that the interior is clean. The operator also does a brake test and other safety checks, and sets the roll signs.

It's now pullout time, and the operator swings his car out onto San Jose Avenue, proceeding in service along the J-Church line as far as 17th Street, where the car makes a left turn and heads to 17th and Castro. The car is in service from the moment it pulls out onto the street. Then it's inbound on Market Street and along The Embarcadero to Fisherman's Wharf. If it's a morning rush-hour trip, workers heading to their jobs in the Financial District, the Union Square area or even to the Wharf, will fill the car, and at the Ferry Building, scores of Wharf-bound workers will board. Later in the day, a mix of residents and tourists will ride.

Occasionally, there will be service interruptions and cars will have to switch back short of the terminal to change directions for service. The operators will be given orders along the line by inspectors or Central Control when this is necessary.

In addition, operators have to comply with operational safety rules peculiar to streetcar operation. Muni has painted markings on the pavement at switches, which require a full safety stop, especially at "point-on" switches, where the operator must determine that the switches are set in the proper direction. There is also a 250-foot spacing rule, where operators can get no closer to the car ahead, absent of orders, or at terminals. Usually, this means one block apart. These rules are in place to ensure safe operation of streetcars. Operators can be "written up" for violations if any are observed by supervisors.

There are also large yellow dots at certain locations in the trackway, indicating wire breakers, where a motorman must coast through without power, and markings at handicapped ramps showing where the operator must position his car—be it a PCC or a Milano—for handling wheelchair users.

On The Street

THE F-LINE IS A HIGH-PROFILE, high-visibility line. On Market Street, as we have observed, its colorful cars stand out from the normal trolley coaches and buses which are painted white with orange stripes above the windows (SEPTA-style[1]), or gray with red stripes. On the way down Market, there is constant passenger turnover. The operators call out the stops along the way.

At Ferry Plaza, an on-street inspector, usually in a truck, observes the timely passage of cars and records them on a piece of paper, known as a "rotation sheet," matching scheduled time with the actual time. If there are delays enroute, or missed reliefs, he/she can make adjustments to other cars' schedule times or order switchbacks to get the operator back on schedule. Sometimes, he will be asked to assist to clear a line blockage or investigate an accident, and then he has to drive to the affected location and give out orders there, once the delay has been cleared. He also has to respond to car breakdowns. In this case, frequently, a "Metro

Conductor Bobby Retuta leans out from the back end of B-Type 162 enroute to Fisherman's Wharf on May 21, 2011. The vintage car crew members are the "elite" of the F-Line operators and usually have more seniority. Mr. Retuta has been a Muni operator since 1980. *Peter Ehrlich*

Response Unit" (a glorified name for an on-street troubleshooting shopman) is dispatched to attempt to move the disabled streetcar. Disabled F-Line cars are moved to an off-line location, which can be the Ferries, 11th Street, Mint Yard, or the "straight track" at 17th and Castro (actually, the unused inbound track between Castro and Noe Streets), and maintenance personnel are sent from the Trolley Maintenance Shop on a "road call" to fix the car. Usually, they can get the car running again. But if a car needs to be towed home, it is brought up to Mint

It's operator Danny Miranda's last day on the job and he poses with PCC 1076 at the Ferry Building. Mr. Miranda, a native of Spanish Harlem, came to Muni in 1978, and is wrapping up a distinguished 33-year career with Muni this day, December 9, 2010. He was beloved by his riders, many of whom would pass up other cars to ride with him! *Peter Ehrlich*

Yard (if east of Duboce) or 17th and Church and is towed back to Geneva Shops with a Breda LRV. But PCCs and Milanos can tow or push each other while on the F-Line trackage. Some Milanos have PCC tow bar adapters, which make them more versatile.

The relief point for operators is at Don Chee Way, a stop away from the Ferry Building. Here, operators relieve other operators and continue the trip. The relieved operator now has time off for the rest of the day, or until the next segment of his shift begins, which may be a later relief, or a return to the division to pull out another car. If the second part of the operator's schedule calls for a pullout, paid travel time is built into the run.

At different times since the F-Line began service, this relief point has been at 17th and Castro Streets, Market and Van Ness, or Market and Church. It was moved from Van Ness to Church around 2006 because reliefs missed at Van Ness would affect other bus lines. The move to Don Chee Way was made in 2010 as this spot was off-street and traffic wouldn't be blocked, which made a lot of sense.

Signups and Runs

EACH OPERATOR AT MUNI has a specific assignment each workday. Some have "runs," which are schedules with the same number over five days, and specified days off. The most senior operators usually have Saturday-Sunday off, and some run numbers also do not work on weekends, so those operators also have holidays off. If a run does work weekend schedules, an operator with Saturday-Sunday off will have to work on the holiday. Other runs will have two consecutive weekdays off, or one weekday and one weekend day off.

Operators assigned work on a "block" will work two days on one run, two days on a second run, and one day on a third run.

Finally, there are "extra board" operators. These men and women will be assigned by the Division dispatcher on a day-to-tay basis to work runs which are open due to the regular operators being absent because of vacation, illness or special assignment. Sometimes, extra board operators are put on "report." They report to the Division dispatcher at a specified time and wait until a run opens at the last minute, and then get paid for the entire run plus the time being on report. If no work opens after six hours, the operator is sent home, but is paid for eight hours of work.

The run structures must also comply with legal stipulations from state and federal agencies as well as work rules negotiated between the Transport Workers Union, Local 250-A, and management.

At Green Light Rail Division, to which the F-Line is assigned, extra board operators must be

Two F-Line operators wait to make their reliefs on Don Chee Way, the relief point since mid-2010. *Peter Ehrlich*

qualified on all F-Line streetcars as well as the Breda LRVs (light rail vehicles).

Under the contract with the Transport Workers Union, Local 250-A, Muni is required to hold a General Signup at least once a year. This allows operators to switch to a different Muni division and operate the equipment assigned to that division. Operators can sign into Green Light Rail Division, but must be trained on the type of vehicle–LRVs or F-Line cars–covered by a particular run number or block number. (As mentioned, new extra board operators must qualify on both.) There is an additional restriction, whereby operators who sign on the F-Line must remain on that line for three years before they can change to a Muni Metro run. This way, they become proficient as a surface rail operator, and the training they receive is more cost-effective.

In between General Signups, Muni has to hold Division Signups–also called barn signups–every three months or so. These allow operators to change runs if they can do so. Regardless of the type of signup, runs are bid in seniority order.

At Green Division, most senior operators prefer the Muni Metro side, as there is less contact with the public. There have been many operators, though, such as the just-retired Danny Miranda, a 33-year man who "pulled the pin" on December 9, 2010, and the author, who retired in 2005 after 26 years, who had high seniority and a marked preference for the F-Line. Walt Thomsen and Joe Certain, both Trolley Festival veterans and both now deceased, finished their illustrious careers on the F-Line. Ed Fine, another Trolley Festival man, retired in 1999 after several years as an F-Line operator.

One type of run that an operator works can be a "straight run," where an operator works straight through for up to ten hours from beginning of his shift, whether he pulls out or makes a relief, to the end, whether he is relieved by another operator or pulls the car in. (Some straight runs are both pullout and pull-in.) As mentioned, the length of a run can be anywhere between six and ten hours, but no more than ten hours by law. All work over eight hours is paid at time-and-a-half. If the operator's time on the vehicle is less than eight hours, he or she has "standby time" built into the run, where the operator is "subject to [supervisor's] orders" at either the relief point or at the division, but this rarely happens. Because there is no operator lunch break on a straight run, "lunch pay" of 20 minutes of straight time is added to the run.

Other runs are known as "split runs," where the operator works his run in two parts. The first part of a split run usually pulls out and gets relieved after about four to six hours of work, or pulls in; the second part requires the operator to either pull out again or to relieve another operator, and then pull-in at the end of the day. The time between shifts is known as the "split" and is usually not paid time (exception: see below). However, if an operator has to travel between the relief point and the division, or even between two relief points, for his "second half," travel time between the two points is paid. This amounts to the time it takes to travel between points plus half of the time of a line's headway.

There's more involved with a split run. By law, the "range" of a split run cannot be more than 12 hours. Any time in a split that is greater than two hours must be paid as "standby time," whether it's at the division or at a relief point, where the operator again is "subject to orders." Most split runs have a range of approximately 10 hours. If any time-on-vehicle segment of a split run is over six hours, lunch pay must also be paid.

Regardless of the work performed, by law, an operator must have eight hours' time off between the end of a shift and the beginning of the next day's shift.

When unscheduled overtime occurs, the operator must make out an overtime card, stating the reason for the overtime. Usually, it's because of line delays or orders given. If the total time–run time plus unscheduled overtime–results in the operator getting fewer than eight hours' rest between daily shifts, the dispatcher is required to reassign the operator to a later-starting run.

Operations and Support Staff

BACK AT METRO ANNEX, mention has already been made of the dispatcher's office. In this office, there are two dispatchers in the daytime—one who sets the next day's work– "the detail," and the other handling the current-day assignments. The swing dispatcher takes reports, as does the graveyard dispatcher, who also calls operators to work regular day off (RDO) work and handles extra board operators "on report."

The offices of the Division Manager, the Metro Inspectors, Muni Metro Station Operations and the Light Rail Operations Manager are along the north wall in the corridor behind the Dispatcher's Office. They have views of Metro Yard, where the Bredas are stabled. The Division Manager is the person responsible for managing the day-to-day dispatching and operators, and holds disciplinary hearings when operators get in trouble.

In other parts of the building, there are offices for maintenance heads and the Training Department. The trainers, who hold the same rank and classification as inspectors and dispatchers, are responsible for training Muni Metro and F-Line operators. New operators typically get 25 to 35 days of training depending on mode, but new F-Line operators must be proficient on both PCCs and Milanos before they can go out on their own. Once they have passed preliminary training on each type of car, they are then assigned to veteran operators for a number of days for "line training." Here is where the experience of a seasoned operator helps to fine-tune the rookie. He or she will give the newbie tips not learned in preliminary training, emphasize operating rules, learn unique situations associated with the F-Line, etc. Then the operator will work his signed-on run or the extra board. If the operator doesn't pass muster at any step, or decides that he doesn't want to continue, he is returned to his previous division.

Trolley Maintenance

DIAGONALLY OPPOSITE METRO ANNEX, back in Geneva Yard (now Cameron Beach Yard), is the Geneva Shops Building, built on the east side of the old Geneva Yard in 1984, as previously mentioned. Here, electrical transit mechanics perform running repairs and preventive maintenance on F-Line PCCs, Milanos and vintage cars.

Karl Johnson, who was recently promoted as manager of Geneva Shops, sits in an office on the second floor of the building. He is surrounded by PCC and historic car maintenance manuals, hosts of file cabinets, and bunches of electrical schematics, but still has room to place historical photos and calendars depicting streetcars in various locales all around the room. Johnson, who has been with Muni since 1977, now has personnel in the Paint and Body Shops, as well as electrical transit maintainers reporting to him. Johnson broke in on vintage car maintenance and restoration by doing volunteer work at the Seashore Trolley Museum in Kennebunkport, Maine, and has been a trolley maintainer at Muni for practically his entire career. He is amiable, knowledgeable, and deals well with the everyday

Trolley Maintenance chief Karl Johnson poses with PCC 1055, the first of the 14 ex-Philadelphia cars remanufactured by Morrison-Knudsen delivered to Muni on September 3 1993. Karl retired in 2015. *San Francisco Public Utilities Commission*

reserved for preventive maintenance. The middle track is set up for performing running repairs, that is, fixing cars that have broken down in service, once they have been brought back to the shop. The track alongside the east wall is reserved for keeping open cars such as the Blackpool "Boat" and "Dinky" 578S under protective cover, as well as cars being reassembled for service after enduring accidents or roof rebuilding. Recently, PCC 1061 (Pacific Electric) occupied the most distant spot on this track. Running repairs are sometimes also performed on the preventive maintenance track.

Next to the three repair tracks, there is a paint shop booth in the front of the building and a booth opposite it where major body overhauls are performed. The newest denizen of the body shop booth is Milan 1834, which is now undergoing major body and roof repairs.

The Body Shop uses the westernmost track for mostly minor body work for not only F-Line cars, but also Bredas on occasion. They have performed miracles in returning wrecked cars such as 1056 (Kansas City), 1060 (Philadelphia silver/blue) and 1818 (Milan two-tone green) to the active fleet.

A carpenter is assigned to Trolley Maintenance from the Cable Car Shop. He is overworked, but manages to keep up. In general, short-staffing is a problem, considering The City's chronic budgetary woes and chaotic hiring procedures, but Johnson and his crew does excellent work with the resources that are available.

In the Paint Shop, Supervisor Carole Gilbert and her staff work magic to repaint the streetcars and make them continuously look good on the street. There is not a single shabby-looking PCC or Milano out there, and Gilbert's crew maintains the highest standard of appearance for the multi-hued fleet, making sure that the proper colors are applied for touchups and complete repaints.

Johnson also oversees the shipments of PCCs to and from Brookville for their rewiring or remanufacturing contract and their return and acceptance testing. Because there is more space to perform field testing and work associated with acceptance of returned PCCs, much of this work has been moved over to Metro East, the new facility on the Central Waterfront that opened in 2008. The last PCC in the current Brookville contract–1009–went to Pennsylvania in late June 2011. As of December 2011, most cars–and Car 1, which was rebuilt under a separate contract–have returned.

Besides working on the cars in the shop building, the small cadre of maintainers performs road calls for breakdowns, and tests overhauled cars on the J-Line private right-of-way. As mentioned, the procedure for towing or pushing a disabled PCC or

frustrations of having to balance difficulties concerning manpower shortages with getting such treasures as Car 1 back in service.

One of the tasks Johnson has to do is to set up preventive maintenance (PM) schedules for the F-Line fleet. All PCCs and Milanos receive periodic preventive maintenance inspections, programmed at five different levels of intensity, with level A being the lightest and E the most thorough, where the car's trucks are dropped and sometimes changed out and replaced with a freshly overhauled pair. The vintage cars, not being part of the everyday "workhorse" fleet, usually only get level A or B inspections. The schedules are determined in part by the number of vehicle hours and/or vehicle miles each streetcar travels over the course of a week or a month.

Another one of his tasks is making sure there is an adequate parts supply–no easy feat, considering that the PCCs, Milanos and vintage cars were built for another era, when parts were plentiful. Now they are scarce, and sometimes replacement parts need to be specially machined by Muni's capable machine shop, or sourced by outside vendors.

There are three run-through tracks inside Geneva Shop. The one on the right is usually

(*above*) Trolley maintainer Khalil Ali peers out from under a Milan car inside Geneva Shops on December 14, 2010. (*below*) All types of F-Line cars occupy the maintenance tracks of Geneva Shop in this August 2010 view. There's "Dinky" 578S, "Boat" 228, PCC 1052 and Milan 1811, among others. *Both photos, Peter Ehrlich*

Milan car back to the barn is this: another car will tow the dead car as far as Mint Yard or 17th and Church Streets, and a Breda will take over for the hard trek over Dolores Park grade.

When motors or trucks need to be changed out, that work is done across the street at Metro Center. A sufficient supply of spare motors is on hand here, and motors are rewound by skilled technicians.

At night, car cleaners sweep and disinfect the cars to make them presentable for the next morning. (This is separate from the midday volunteer Market Street Railway car cleaning during the afternoons.) The night maintenance staff works on cars with problems and prepares a list of available cars for the morning yard starter (usually an operator assigned this work either by bidding on it as signable work, or on an overtime basis). If there is a mechanical or electrical problem with the assigned car, the maintenance staff will give the operator a different car.

More complex functions are performed at other buildings. Over at Metro Center, electric motors are replaced and rewound, and machinists make specialized parts for the various F-Line cars. If trucks need to be replaced, that, too, is done at Metro Center.

The Electronics Shop track is right under the Division offices. Here at what is called DTE (Diagnostic Test Electronics), cars such as Milano 1834 are getting their electrical systems checked out, and sometimes overhauls are done here, too.

Other Staff at Muni

There's more to Muni than just operations and maintenance, however. The Schedules and Traffic Department is responsible for creating new schedules for operator signups. This department has a number of traffic checkers who perform schedule and ride checks to help the schedule makers determine whether more service has to be added to certain lines, or if service can be cut from a line. The checkers will often be seen standing at various corners checking scheduled times, or they may be seen riding streetcars and buses recording the number of people boarding and alighting at stops on a particular scheduled trip. This information is fed into a computer program known as "Trapeze," which crunches the numbers and spits out the schedules. Schedules operates under the constraint that there is a limited number of service hours budgeted for weekday and weekend service. What this usually means is that if service needs to be added for the F-Line, for example, it must be taken away from another line or lines.

There are two planning units at Muni: Service Delivery and Long-Range Planning. The Service Delivery unit is in charge of planning to get daily service out on the street. It is required to hold public hearings if funding shortfalls could result in service cuts. Long-Range Planning, however, does planning for major changes in transit service in the future, and publishes both "Short-Range Transit Plans" and "20-year Transit Plans," which are available to the public. It also develops funding plans for future major capital projects.

To distinguish between the two Planning units, for example, planning and future implementation of both the E-Embarcadero and the possible extension of the F-Line to Fort Mason fall under the purview of the Long Range Planning unit, whereas planning to get a sufficient amount of scheduled service for the F-Line is handled by Service Delivery.

There is also engineering staff; Facilities Maintenance (the Overhead Lines Department and Track Maintenance is included here), and staff assigned from other City Departments to handle Muni-related work, and much, much more.

AGAIN, IT'S PULLOUT TIME, and another day of enthusiastic riders are waiting to be picked up by their colorful F-Line cars!

References:
1. SEPTA-Style: Refers to the manner of painting buses in the Landor 2-tone orange and white, with a blended stripe above the windows. This scheme was introduced to Muni's rubber-tired fleet in 1998 by General Manager Michael Burns, who came to Muni from

Jack Smith: The Gentleman Motorman

OF ALL THE OPERATORS who have worked behind the scenes on the Trolley Festivals and on the F-Line, none is as renowned as Jack Smith.

Smith, who was employed by Muni from 1963 to 1994, worked the rail side at Muni for his entire career—as cable car gripman, PCC and LRV operator, and vintage car motorman. On the vintage cars, he was the dean. Smith learned his craft from his father, one of the first black motormen hired by Market Street Railway Company in the 1940s. As mentioned in Chapter 2, he'd "relieve" his father and operate the streetcar while his dad had his lunch.

Smith was also a merchant seaman. He spent many years in Los Angeles around the Pacific Electric interurban, learning from the operators. He perfected his operating technique at Muni, studying with the old-timers. Ultimately, he became the master motorman.

I was honored when Smith selected me as one of his students in 1982. We started on Car 1. He pointed out the vagaries of the braking system, and the need to avoid "stonewall stops" and learn how to brake with finesse. He would have us newbies imagine that there was a tray of champagne glasses, each with "bubbly" in them, and the object was "to not spill a single drop of champagne." Indeed, it's easy enough to make a vintage car go, but it's an art form to make it stop. As we learned operating technique, we would also learn to listen to the sounds the car was making.

In addition to his accomplishments at Muni, in 1976, he and some other Muni operators and shop people were sent to Boston to learn to operate the then-new Boeing LRVs, which were going to be introduced in San Francisco service in 1979. When the new F-Line PCCs arrived, he was principal burn-in motorman.

Smith was ever the tinkerer. On his off days, he would work on restoring the various vintage cars that were at Market Street Railway's Mint Yard, or join the crew at the Western Railway Museum trying to get retired Boeing 1258 running. And the tales he would tell! When he was done with his story, his eyes would twinkle and he'd end with a most mischievous laugh. An example: When there was a call for a blacksmith, he said, "We already have a 'black Smith,' " followed by that infectious laugh.

Smith was the MSR project manager for the initial restoration of Muni B-Type 162, which returned home in July 2003. He was on board the car when it left Mint Yard to be towed to Metro Center once MSR's end of the restoration was completed in September 2004. A week later, on September 18, he died at the age of 72.

Although short in stature, Smith was a giant among Muni men. On the day that he retired—December 28, 1994 (Muni's 82nd anniversary), fellow vintage car motorman John Nevin said in Carl Nolte's column in the *San Francisco Chronicle* the next day, "Muni will fill his position, but they'll never fill his shoes."

Up there in heaven, Jack Smith, the gentleman motorman, is looking down at today's F-Line, and smiling. That mischievous laugh is sure to follow...

Jack Smith (right) is chatting with fellow retired vintage car motorman John Nevin at a function held at Mint Yard on May 22, 2004. Smith was project director for *Market Street Railway* in the restoration of Muni B-Type 162, behind the two men. *Peter Ehrlich*

The ends of the F-Line, America's most popular new historic streetcar service:
(*top*) Fisherman's Wharf and its open-air crab stands, restaurants and chic boutiques.
(*bottom*) Castro Street. The turnaround has been turned into a pedestrian piazza, and a woodwind quintet serenades the waiting passengers and passersby.
Both photos, Peter Ehrlich

Chapter 10 -
So, What's a Ride on the F-Line Like?

"Joy Ride!"

— Slogan on car cards
during the 1985 Trolley Festival

WHEN RIDERS BOARD an F-Line trolley, they are immediately transformed into a world when life was more carefree and easygoing, where the sights, sounds and smells of the city tickle the senses. The riders watch great buildings go by and wonder about their history. They see knots of people walking and enjoying life as it was meant to be. They break into conversation with their seatmates and neighbors, laughing and grinning as the trolley rumbles toward their destination.

One man to another: "It's the fun, relaxing way to get to the Wharf. You see much more of the city when you ride the streetcar."

"Yes, and no worries about parking," replies his friend.

"Everybody seems to have a good time on board the streetcar," adds the first gent.

"And they're so colorful."

Some of the riders learn as they ride, by checking out the informative car cards on the PCCs and Milanos placed there by Market Street Railway. Each PCC has a card describing its history in the city it represents, as well as a brief history of the PCC car itself. On B-Type 130, which is dedicated to the late *San Francisco Chronicle* columnist Herb Caen, one can read his columns extolling the virtues that only a streetcar ride can give, which are placed in the advertising panels above the windows.

The motorman calls out the stops along the way, and some point out landmarks and other places of interest, such as the Filbert Street Steps or where one can catch the connecting bus to reach Twin Peaks. Some passengers tell others to look out for special things. During the first days of the Wharf Extension, one rider said to another, "Don't miss the tulips at Pier 39," as reported in *Inside Track*, the MSR newsletter. Oldsters will exclaim, "I remember riding these cars in Cincinnati," (or Louisville [doubtful, since their PCCs never ran there, even though they were supposed to], or Anyplace, USA). And kids will watch the vintage car operator work the controller and brake handles with eyes wide open. Or they'll watch Coit Tower or the docked boats go by and squeal "Oooh" and "Ahhh!"

In the words of Marina resident Jud Hurley, on the first day of Wharf service, as reported by Rick Laubscher of MSR in *Inside Track*: "I told my wife that Muni finally did something right. I'd like to thank the people who did this."

It's all true. The F-Line cars do add color, charm, and most importantly, living history to San Francisco. That's why MSR terms the line's trolleys, as well as the cable cars, Museums In Motion.

A Ride to the Wharf (inbound)

SO–WE'VE ALREADY PURCHASED our three-day Passports across the street at the cable car turnaround at Powell and Market, and scratched off three consecutive days and the month. Let's catch one of these Museums in Motion streetcars and see where it goes. Ahhh! Here comes a bright orange Milan trolley up to the 5th and Market stop now! The car looks exactly like the picture on the sign at the boarding island. The headsign reads Fisherman's Wharf. So, what are we waiting for? Let's climb on board!

Along the way, we'll point out architectural treasures, fun facts and special things to watch for as the unique street life of Market Street awaits our gazes.

Inside our Milan car, little signs in Italian such as "Vietato Fumare" (No Smoking) are affixed to the wood paneling above the windows. A blinking "Fermata Prenotata" (Stop Requested) sign above the center doorway illuminates when a passenger presses one of the red stop request buttons.

Fifth, Powell Streets

Fifth and Market is the nerve center of San Francisco. On the southeast corner is the San Francisco Shopping Center with its spiral escalators, anchored by a Nordstrom store. It's now part of the

Westfield Shopping Center, which took over the adjoining Emporium Building and reopened as a Bloomingdale's in September 2006. (The Emporium was one of many beloved old-line department stores. Its glass rotunda was retained during remodeling.)

Across the street is Hallidie Plaza, the main entranceway to the Powell Street Muni Metro and BART subway station. The old Bank of America Day and Night Branch building fronts what was originally Eddy Street and the west side of Powell Street. The world-famous cable cars are turned on a turntable here, and have been doing so since 1888. A long line of waiting cable car riders surrounds the turntable. On the northeast corner, the 1904-vintage Flood Building holds court. This Classic Revival landmark, designed by noted architect Albert Pissis (who also designed the Emporium Building across Market Street), was built for silver king James Clair Flood. It survived two earthquakes and an ill-conceived plan by the Woolworth chain to demolish the building in the 1950s. Luckily, the building was literally saved at the last minute by the federal government, which appropriated office space for military functions around the time of the Korean War. Today, its tenants include the offices of Market Street Railway, the F-Line support organization.

The Old U. S. Mint Building, built in 1874 and another example of Classic Revival architecture, is located a block away at 5th and Mission, and is now a museum.

Fourth, Stockton Streets

We reach Fourth Street, and kids are on their knees on the wood perimeter seats peering out the large picture windows of the tram. Looking up Stockton Street, Union Square, one of the pre-eminent retail shopping areas in the United States, is just two blocks away. Until 1951, the original F-Stockton streetcar line called here. The old Art Deco Roos Brothersmen's clothing store building is situated on the

Fifth. Powell and Market is the nerve center of San Francisco. Here, the main shopping district, the cable car turnaround and the F-Line all blend into the streetscape. Milano 1811 is heading outbound in this October 8, 2004 view. *Peter Ehrlich*

northeast corner, currently used by the XXI chain. A silver-and-glass Apple store occupies the northwest corner of Stockton and Ellis. On the south side, the jade-green Pacific Building, now the Hotel Palomar, built in 1915, houses a hotel, offices and an Old Navy store. A walk south on 4th Street leads to the Marriott Hotel (dubbed the "Jukebox Marriott" because of its façade), the Metreon, Moscone Center and the *Zeum* (children's discovery museum). Just east of Fourth Street is another quake survivor, the Humboldt Bank Building, with its ornate dome.

Grant Avenue and O'Farrell Street

After more Wharf-bound riders board the car, usually producing standees, the trolley continues northeastward, passing Grant Avenue, with the Union Trust Company banking temple (now a Wells Fargo branch) on the northeast corner and the 1908 Phelan Building, a wedge building on the corner of Market and O'Farrell. The Chinatown Arch, the gateway to San Francisco's famous Chinatown, is five blocks north on Grant Avenue.

Third, Kearny and Geary Streets

At one time, this was known as "Newspaper Row," with the Call Building on the southeast corner, and the De Young (or Chronicle) Building, recently restored to its 1903 red sandstone appearance, on the northeast corner. Lotta's Fountain, dating to 1875, is situated on a triangular island bounded by Geary, Market and Kearny. Every April 18th, the dwindling number of 1906 Earthquake survivors and their families gather here to commemorate that

The Milanos still have their quaint Italian-language signs, such as "Vietato Fumare" (No Smoking). *Peter Ehrlich*

Market Street scenes from the Union Square area to the Financial District

(*above*) Steam rises from a vent as PCC 1053 (Brooklyn) waits for the signal at Market and 4th Street at night. *Kevin Sheridan*

(*above*) The restored De Young Building, returned to its 1903 appearance in 2007, rises above the Kansas City car at Market and 3rd Streets. (*left*) Yellow-and-white Milan 1811 passes Market and Grant inbound, with an orange Milano following at 4th Street. June 25, 2009. *Both photos, Peter Ehrlich*

Looking down from Crocker Plaza, a PCC passes the Sheraton Palace Hotel, a 1906 quake survivor. *Peter Ehrlich*

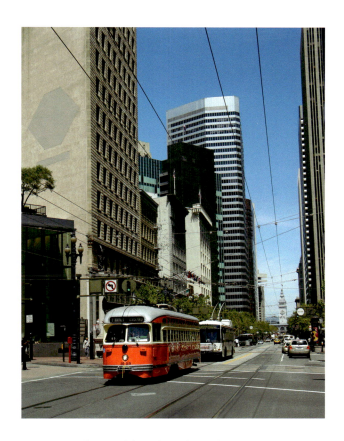

PCC 1059 (Boston) heads outbound at Montgomery Street, the heart of the Financial District. *Peter Ehrlich*

cataclysmic event. We can close our eyes and imagine the ghosts of B-Geary "Iron Monsters" rumbling by, joining or turning off of "The Slot," a colloquial name for Market Street. Central Tower, built in 1898 and renovated to an Art Deco design in 1938, stands on the southwest corner.

Walking south on 3rd Street, one can reach such attractions as the San Francisco Museum of Modern Art, the Jewish Museum, the Yerba Buena Center for the Arts and the Museum Of The African Diaspora (on Mission Street) east of Third. The historic red brick St. Patrick's Catholic Church is on Mission between 3rd and 4th Streets.

Montgomery, New Montgomery and 2nd Streets

We now enter the Financial District. Next stop is New Montgomery/Montgomery Street. (Outbound cars make the stop at 2nd Street.) Montgomery Street is the Wall Street of the West, and is lined with bank headquarters and brokerage houses. On the southwest corner, the Sheraton Palace (locals simply call it the Palace) Hotel, with its world-famous Garden Court, beckons upscale customers. Between New Montgomery and 2nd Street, the façade of the old Hoffman Grill is built into a modern office tower. On the corner of Post and Montgomery, the old Crocker Building has been reduced to a two-story structure with a rooftop park, where on weekdays, one can watch F-Line trolleys and life on Market Street pass by while enjoying a sack lunch. The Willis Polk-designed Hobart Building stands opposite 2nd Street and the lozenge-shaped 595 Market Street modern highrise.

Sutter and Sansome Streets

Continuing inbound, the tram rolls past Sutter and Sansome Streets, with the wedge-shaped Flatiron Building of 1913 fronting Sutter and Market; the white Chevron Towers at 555 and 575 Market opposite, and the glass Crown Zellerbach Building of 1959, the first modern highrise built in San Francisco, which occupies the block bounded by Bush, Market and Sansome streets, as the notable edifices.

First, Bush and Battery Streets; Fremont and Front; Davis, Beale and Pine Streets

Until August 7, 2010, passengers could get off at First Street and walk to the Art Moderne Transbay Terminal at First and Mission to board AC Transit, SamTrans, Golden Gate Transit and Greyhound buses for all points north, east and south of San Francisco. The switches for the original F-Line, which terminated at Transbay, are still in the ground at First Street as well as Fremont, a block further east, but all other traces of the loop were erased in the late summer of 2000. From January 14, 1939 until March 4, 2000, streetcars looped here. Trains to the East Bay arrived and left upstairs until 1958.

Former Brussels, Belgium PCC 737 (in Zürich, Switzerland blue), passes the landmark, 1959-built Crown Zellerbach Building at Market and Battery/Bush Streets. This building was the first modern-era skyscraper in San Francisco. *Peter Ehrlich*

The terminal was razed in late 2010 and the site is now being redeveloped as an office tower and future high-speed rail and Caltrain terminal.

Our Milan car, its gears making sweet music, crosses Fremont/Front and Davis/Beale before stopping again at Main Street. Between Beale and Main are two 1920s structures, the PG&E Building and the Matson Building, dating to 1924 and 1923, respectively. The cylindrical 101 California modern skyscraper looms in the block bounded by Davis, Pine, Front and California.

Main, Drumm and California Streets

Main Street is the last F-Line stop on Market Street, and many riders transferring from BART and Muni Metro, as well as folks coming from the California cable car and the nearby Embarcadero Center, board here. If the streetcar isn't filled up by now, it will be after we leave Main Street.

Lower Market Street

(*this column, top to bottom*) PCC 1050 crosses Main Street en-route to the Wharf in 2008. The shrubbery on the left is part of a planter box built around 2003 to protect the Federal Reserve Bank from terrorism attacks. PCC 1052, representing the Los Angeles Railway, one of the nation's first PCC systems, crosses Spear Street in September 2007. Milano 1859 heads west at Spear Street, alongside the Hyatt Regency Hotel, with the historic Ferry Building completing the sunny scene. September 12, 2004. *All photos, Peter Ehrlich*

(*this column, top to bottom*) Louisville-liveried PCC 1062 passes a mix of old and new office buildings as it crosses 1st and Battery streets in 2008. Sporting a Christmas wreath, PCC 1052 leads Melbourne 496 at Market and Main streets, as 1010 heads outbound. The PG&E Building on the left dates to the 1920s. 1896-built cable car lookalike streetcar 578(S) crosses Main and Drumm streets, with a California Street cable car at its Market Street terminal on the left. May 26, 2005. *All photos, Peter Ehrlich*

More Lower Market, and Steuart Street

(*above*) Seldom-photographed Milano 1888 passes the Federal Reserve Bank in 2003. Work is beginning on making the bank "terrorist-proof." (*top right*) Boston 1059 turns the corner at Market and Steuart, with the arts and crafts tents lining the walkway through Justin Herman Plaza to the left and right of the trolley. May 27, 2009. (*right*) Another scene from 2009 at this intersection shows San Diego 1078 turning onto Market with the Southern Pacific Building providing an impressive backdrop. *All photos, Peter Ehrlich*

F-Line trolleys travel half a block on Steuart Street after they turn off Market Street. (*above*) In May 2010, Melbourne W2 496 passes PCC 1076 (Washington) as it heads for Don Chee Way, The Embarcadero, and Fisherman's Wharf. (*right*) It's Christmastime in 2007, and Embarcadero Center has its traditional building outline lights illuminated for the season as PCC 1055 heads inbound at Steuart and Don Chee Way. *Both photos, Peter Ehrlich*

The California Street cable car line begins here in the small plaza at Market and Drumm, where the entrance to the swank Hyatt Regency Hotel, with its revolving rooftop restaurant, is located.

Spear and Steuart Streets

The new (1983) Federal Reserve Bank covers the block between Main and Spear Streets. Notice the round black planter enclosures and concrete bollards surround this building. They were installed beginning in 2002 to protect this important Federal building from terrorism attacks after the 9/11 catastrophe in 2001. Next up is the old red brick Southern Pacific Building, which was once known as 65 Market Street, but now is part of the One Market Plaza complex, and covers the block between Spear and Steuart Streets. (Until the early 1960s, there was another block of low-rise buildings between Steuart and The Embarcadero, which is how the SP Building got its original address.)

PCC 1076, representing Washington, D.C., turns onto Don Chee Way from The Embarcadero on May 13, 2010, with another San Francisco icon, the Ferry Building, completing the scene. *Peter Ehrlich*

Now we turn south at Steuart, fronting Justin Herman Plaza, which was developed in the 1970s and features the boxy and controversial Vaillancourt Fountain. Justin Herman Plaza is also the gateway promenade to Embarcadero Center, a series of four narrow buildings stretching between Sacramento and Clay streets from the plaza to Battery Street. Each of these office highrises has a number of upscale and basic stores and restaurants at ground level, and it was developed by the same company that built Rockefeller Center in Manhattan.

On most days, arts and crafts vendors line the walkway to the Ferry Building.

Don Chee Way

Halfway between Market and Mission, our trolley will turn left onto a short, trolleys-only street named Don Chee Way, after the late F-Line project engineer. Some cars terminating at the Ferries will continue straight and loop via Mission onto The Embarcadero.

Here at Don Chee Way, we are going to get off to visit the San Francisco Railway Museum, a small but free museum operated by F-Line booster organization Market Street Railway. This delightful museum has pictorial exhibits and artifacts from the heyday of the streetcar in San Francisco, as well as books, DVDs and other collectibles. The ever-cheerful museum manager, John Hogan, always welcomes visitors and is especially friendly with school children. A replica front of one of the ex-Market Street Railway "Haight Street Jewetts" is a special feature at the museum, where kids can play being motorman by actually moving the control handles.

This block, bounded by Don Chee Way, Steuart, Mission and The Embarcadero features the new upscale Hotel Vitale, built on Muni property formerly used as a turnaround for Muni's sizable fleet of electric

1811 passes the *San Francisco Railway Museum*, run by the non-profit group *Market Street Railway*. Burnt-image border rendition, January 23, 2009. *Peter Ehrlich*

Ferry Building

The inside of the Ferry Building was completely renovated in 2003 and the passageway is adorned with upscale food stores. The atrium skylights were also uncovered during the renovation. September 17, 2011. *Peter Ehrlich*

trolley coaches. At the corner of Steuart and Mission is a bas-relief mural commemorating the 1934 General Strike. Catty-corner here is the famous Art Deco Rincon Annex Post Office building, featuring interior murals depicting San Francisco and California history. Although the building is no longer used as a post office (the actual Post Office is further south on Steuart now), the interior has been renovated for retail and restaurant space. On the south side of Mission Street stands the Audiffred Building, which dates to the 1860s and was spared during the 1906 Earthquake and Fire. The trendy Boulevard restaurant occupies the ground floor of this historic building.

For lunch, we can cross Steuart Street to the One Market food court for reasonably priced meals, such as falafel sandwiches from Lena's or gourmet burritos from 360º Burritos. (The One Market food court is closed on weekends.) Or perhaps we could take a stroll across The Embarcadero into the recently renovated Ferry Building for more upscale fare. After lunch, we'll board a different streetcar.

Ferry Building

The Ferry Building, built in 1898, has always been the premier icon of San Francisco, along with the cable cars. It survived the 1906 and 1989 earthquakes virtually intact. In its heyday, hundreds of ferryboats, double-ended in the traditional manner, from all over San Francisco Bay, docked there, and as already mentioned, the Ferry Building was the second-busiest transportation facility in the world, after London's Charing Cross railway station. A three-track loop, with streetcars leaving every few seconds, graced the front of the building until the late 1940s, after Muni's 1944 takeover of Market Street Railway Company and the replacement of former MSRy car lines with trolley coaches.

Today, the Ferry Building still hosts dozens of departures and arrivals each weekday, from Sausalito, Larkspur, Tiburon, Oakland/Alameda, and Vallejo. The newest boats are speedy catamarans, which can make the trip from Vallejo to San Francisco in less than an hour.

The building itself underwent a two-year facelift, which was completed in early 2003. Light again shines from the skylights to the ground level, turning the place into a cheery Galleria with trendy food, wine and cheese shops. On Tuesdays, Thursdays and Saturdays, an open-air Farmers Market with ecologically-grown produce graces the exterior.

The F-Line boarding platforms, with their graceful curved canopy covers, are situated across the northbound Embarcadero Roadway from the Ferry Building. This is the busiest inbound boarding stop on the F-Line, with sometimes a hundred Wharf-bound patrons crowding the stop waiting for transportation. In the other di-rection, crowds pour off the trams and head for the ferries, or across the plaza toward the Embarcadero Muni Metro/BART subway station (even though the cars stop there, too).

A typical inbound F-Line stop marker, with the depiction of a Milan car. *Peter Ehrlich*

Already, a crowd has gathered for service to Fisherman's Wharf. We peer south and note that one of Munis fabulous vintage streetcars, Muni blue and gold 130, has left its layover spot south of Don Chee Way and is moving toward us to pick us up. We'll

Muni B-Type "Iron Monster" 130 picks up passengers at the Ferry Building. This car was built as part of a 125-car order in 1914 by Jewett Car Company of Newark, Ohio. *Peter Ehrlich*

A group of girls are sitting on the front bench of Car 130, watching the motorman and enjoying the ride. *Peter Ehrlich*

board through the open rear platform, just like our grandparents did when they were kids.

Car 130 was built in 1914, arriving in time fore the 1915 Panama-Pacific International Exposition, and survived scrapping by being made into a work car in 1958. Its second passenger-carrying career began in 1983 with the Trolley Festivals. It has beautifully finished mahogany wood seats, windows and ceiling work inside, and is dedicated to the late, great *San Francisco Chronicle* columnist Herb Caen.

Everyone has boarded now, and the conductor gives the time-honored "two bells" signal. We hear the "whoosh" of the air brakes releasing, and the motorman notches up the controller, and the motors begin their musical rise in pitch as the streetcar picks up speed as we head toward Fisherman's Wharf. A gaggle of third-graders sits on the bench in the open end across from the motorman and watch in awe as he maneuvers the power and brake handles.

Washington Street

We're on The Embarcadero now, running on trackage that is lined with Canary Island palms on both sides, separating the median from the three-lane roadways on either side. The first stop is Washington Street. On the left side, the Transamerica Pyramid, a San Francisco landmark since 1972, points skyward. On the right, between Washington and Broadway, are Piers 1, 3 and 5. If we look quickly on the right, we can catch a glimpse of the old ferryboat *Santa Rosa*, now used for offices. Note that at every intermediate stop, there is a graceful arched glass roof shelter with illuminated stop names. "NextMuni" electronic car arrival signs, denoting when the next F-Line tram is due, were added to the shelters in 2007; GPS (Global Positioning System) is used for this purpose. Also, the tracks are set with stones embedded in the concrete to discourage motorists from driving on the tracks.

By now, the adults on the car are engaging in excited chatter about the latest in technological advances, which is so far removed from the simple and carefree aura and technology given off by our "Iron Monster," or about what happened on the latest episode of the TV show Lost, or even about what fun it is to ride the F-line cars. Some of the standees are reading the Herb Caen columns in the car card racks. It's a given: Everybody is really enjoying the ride!

Broadway

The conductor calls out the stops as we head northward. The next stop is Broadway (at one time, officially called Broadway *Street*). Pier 7,

PCC 1050 speeds by Pier 7 at Broadway. The Transamerica Building, a landmark since 1972, rises above the streetcar. *Peter Ehrlich*

Along Tthe Embarcadero

(*left*) PCC 1077 (Birmingham) crosses Broadway. The Ferry Building and part of the Bay Bridge are visible on this beautiful June day in 2007. (*below*) PCC 1062 and two Milanos carry huge loads of passengers on their way to see the *Queen Mary 2*, which stopped in San Francisco on its round-the-world voyage on February 5, 2007. (*Facing page, top left*) Brussels car 737 stops at Greenwich. *Pier 23*, a "waterfront dive," is also a jazz joint. (*top right*) Another view of Pier 23, looking south, with PCC 1062, representing Louisville, Ky., heading to the Wharf. (*middle left*) Reflection of car 1010 in the chrome Fog City Diner. (*middle right*) PCC 1078 (San Diego) passes the old State Belt Railway roundhouse at Sansome Street. The Transamerica Pyramid is off in the distance, and Coit Tower's on the right. April 6, 2012. *All photos, Peter Ehrlich*

which has been rebuilt into a promenade, extends into the Bay, and from its end, one can see Treasure Island, Yerba Buena Island and the Berkeley and Oakland Hills off in the distance. One can fish from the pier or simply watch large container ships and small craft sail by. On the left, a walk along the southerly base of Telegraph Hill brings one to the Broadway entertainment district. There is an upscale restaurant, the Waterfront, which has transformed the façade of the old Pier 7.

Green Street; Greenwich Street

As we leave Broadway, a bright red trolley (1061, the Pacific Electric car) whooshes by us going the other way. In 2013, the world-famous Exploratorium children's museum relocated to Pier 15 at Green Street from the Marina.

At the base of Telegraph Hill, if we look up and to the left, Coit Tower comes into view. The tower was built in 1935 to commemorate firefighters. Next up is Green Street, followed by Greenwich Street.

Greenwich is the stop for the Levi's Plaza office campus, where the famous Levi Strauss jeans are designed; Pier 23 "waterfront dive" restaurant and jazz joint; and the path to the famous Filbert Street Steps, which climb the steep east face of Telegraph Hill, past some charming cottages nestled in a blaze of color, flowers of virtually every hue. The conductor gives the motorman a one-bell signal, an indication that a passenger wants to get off at Greenwich.

After Greenwich, the trackway curves gently to the left at Battery and Lombard Streets. Before the tracks curve, we pass the chrome Fog City Diner.

Sansome and Chestnut Streets

At Sansome and Chestnut Streets, the old State Belt Railroad Roundhouse, converted to offices several decades ago, sits on the corner. Also at

The "Boat" car loops at Pier 39 during the annual Navy Fleet Week on October 7, 2007, as Jefferson Street, deeper in the Fisherman's Wharf area, was closed to traffic. *Peter Ehrlich*

Bay Street, North Point, Pier 39

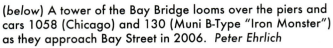

(below) A tower of the Bay Bridge looms over the piers and cars 1058 (Chicago) and 130 (Muni B-Type "Iron Monster") as they approach Bay Street in 2006. *Peter Ehrlich*

(top) "Torpedoes" 1007 and 1010 pass at Bay Street, with Pier 39 in the distance. Taken on February 21, 2005. (center) A seagull flies overhead, and Coit Tower watches over PCC 1010 as it heads past North Point Street. Pier 39 is the next stop, and about half of the passengers on board will get off and begin their Fisherman's Wharf experience. November 25, 2007. (bottom) Cars 1055 and 1063 are short-turning at Pier 39 due to a line blockage further ahead during the annual Navy Fleet Week celebrations in October 2007. *All photos, Peter Ehrlich*

A cruise ship provides the backdrop as PCC 1078 (San Diego), one of the ex-Newark cars, unloads at the inbound Pier 39 stop, one of the busiest on the line. *Peter Ehrlich*

Sansome, one can visit Teatro ZinZanni, a theater-restaurant featuring "Love, Chaos, and Dinner."

Halfway between Sansome and Bay Streets, the line makes another gentle curve, and Houston's Restaurant, which sports an outdoor seating area, perfect for watching F-Line cars as one chomps on burgers, is on the left. We pass another outbound streetcar, this time a two-tone green Milano, as it approaches Sansome.

Bay Street; North Point Street

Bay Street is the stop for visitors going to Alcatraz on Hornblower Yachts, and for passengers connecting to or from cruise ships calling at Pier 35.

At North Point, the inbound tracks leave the right-of-way, cross Embarcadero and run on a narrow single-track right-of-way (the outbound cars share street space with autos).

Pier 39

Now we reach the beginning of the Fisherman's Wharf area. Pier 39 is a collection of shops and restaurants, mostly related to sea life and seafood. There is an aquarium here, and the sea lions that hang out in the water toward the rear of the complex

The incessant chatter of the sea lions that hang out at Pier 39 is a major attraction. The Golden Gate Bridge is off in the background. June 2008. *Peter Ehrlich*

bark incessantly in the hopes that some unsuspecting tourist will throw them a piece of fish. More than half of the people on the trolley will get off here and walk the rest of the way into the Wharf. Being diehards, we choose to stay aboard.

Powell, Mason and Taylor Streets

At Powell, we make a gentle left onto Jefferson Street. Powell is the stop for catching boats of the Blue and Gold Fleet for Bay cruises, trips to Angel Island and Tiburon in Marin County. Boats to Alcatraz used to operate from here, but in 2006, the National Park Service, in a very controversial move, awarded the contract to non-union Hornblower Yachts, and as a result, folks going to Alcatraz are far away from the Wharf. At this point, we are actually running on the street and alongside the curb, but to set the trackway off from the rest of the traffic lanes, the rails are laid in faux Belgian block paving stones.

A fixture from bygone times is the Pier 41 Portal, from which freight car barge ferries to Sausalito once operated. This was discontinued in the 1940s, but the portal was completely

The panorama unfolds in this view from the Pier 39 garage. PCC 1059 (Boston) passes the restored Pier 41 freight car barge portal, where barges heading to Sausalito were floated across the Bay until 1941. The *Jeremiah O'Brien*, one of two remaining Liberty ship's from World War II, is docked at Pier 45. The Golden Gate Bridge is shrouded in fog. *Peter Ehrlich*

Fisherman's Wharf

Fisherman's Wharf has been one of the prime destinations for visitors to San Francisco from all over the world. It's famous for its seafood restaurants and boutique shopping complexes, most of which were converted from canneries and chocolate-making factories. And the views, sights and smells are outstanding!

(*left*) PCC 1057 (Cincinnati) passes the fishing and tour boats moored along Jefferson Street. Coit Tower and the Transamerica Pyramid, built in 1935 and 1972, respectively, provide the background. *Peter Ehrlich*

(*above left*) Looking down from the Anchorage garage in January 2007. (*above right*) A line of streetcars of all types waits to enter the Jones and Beach Terminal in 2005. The Anchorage and Cannery shopping complexes and Aquatic Park are off in the distance. (*right*) A rare nighttime vignette of a Milan "Peter Witt" waiting on Jefferson Street. Some of the fishing boats are lit up for Christmastime in this 2004 picture. *All photos, Peter Ehrlich*

210

Jones and Beach Terminal

Jones and Beach is a good location for the F-Line terminal. It fronts the side of a garage, is located between two streets with heavy pedestrian traffic, and up to four cars can lay over at a time. If either the F-Line or the long-proposed E-Embarcadero is extended to Fort Mason in the future, Jones and Beach will remain as a terminal loop.

(*below*) A serendipitous green-and-cream lineup at Jones and Beach in 2002: The Blackpool, England "Boat" is bracketed by both Muni-liveried PCCs. To paraphrase a Beatles tune, "Sky of Blue, Sea of Green (and Cream)." *Peter Ehrlich*

(*top left*) Two vintage cars – Muni 1 and New Orleans 952 – at Jones and Beach. (*middle left*) Looking south toward Russian Hill, with the New Orleans car and two PCCs laying over. (*bottom left*) The Anchorage garage façade got a facelift in 2007. PCC 1010 (Muni blue/gold, 1939 colors) and two ex-Newark cars, 1075

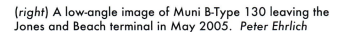

(*right*) A low-angle image of Muni B-Type 130 leaving the Jones and Beach terminal in May 2005. *Peter Ehrlich*

211

Some of the attractions along the Northern Waterfront

(*above left and right*) The wooden Filbert Street Steps are an attractive way to climb steep Telegraph Hill as an alternative to using regular streets. Near the top (*right*), snug Napier Lane, nestled between houses, is a quiet oasis in a bustling city.

The Hyde Street Pier became a unit of the National Park Service in 1989. Some of the exhibits include the 1885 square-rigger *Balclutha*, the 1895 lumber schooner *C A Thayer*, and the ferryboat *Eureka* from 1890.

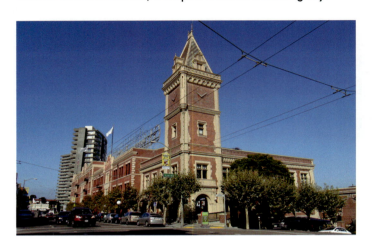

(*above and below*) Ghirardelli Square, the old chocolate manufacturing complex with its distinctive Clock Tower, was renovated in 1964.

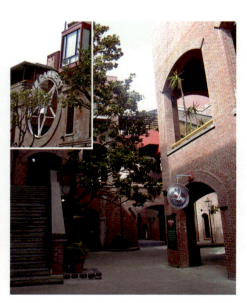

The Cannery, formerly a Del Monte Foods peach canning facility, opened in 1966.

On the facing page, some of the attractions along the Northern Waterfront include the Filbert Street Steps, which climb straight up the east face of Telegraph Hill from Sansome and Filbert streets and are reached from the Embarcadero/Greenwich F-Line stop; the Maritime Museum, now administered by the Golden Gate National Recreation Area, where historic ferries, tugboats and freighters are moored; Ghirardelli Square, created in 1964 as one of the first urban area small-scale shopping places containing clusters of interesting, mostly upscale stores; and the Cannery, a similar development which opened in 1966. *All photos, Peter Ehrlich*

restored in 2003.

After passing Mason Street, the next stop is Taylor Street, the heart of Fisherman's Wharf. Many seafood restaurants compete for lunch and dinner here, and the famous crab stands line the northwest corner of Taylor and Jefferson. Other notable places for food are the new Boudin Bakery, for San Francisco's famous sourdough bread, and the Rainforest Café. For the serious visitor, there is the *USS Pampanito* submarine, and the Liberty Ship *Jeremiah O'Brien*, both of World War II fame, at Pier 45, along with the Musée Méchanique, a collection of antique amusement devices and games, inside Pier 45. Ripley's and the Wax Museum are also here. Another tour boat operator, the Red and White Fleet, is located at Pier 43½. The intersection is dominated by the illuminated "Fisherman's Wharf" sign.

The turntable for the Powell/Mason cable car line is three blocks away at Bay and Taylor.

Crossing Taylor, the tracks make a curious jog to the left, and then return to curbside alongside the myriad of moored fishing boats.

Jones and Beach Streets Terminal

We reach our final destination, and Car 130 pulls onto Jones Street behind another F car. We take our leave from the "Iron Monster" and will walk around to take in the sights, sounds and smells of the Wharf. The Cannery, the Hyde Street Pier and Maritime Museum, the Powell/Hyde cable car line, Aquatic Park and Ghirardelli Square are all within walking distance from the F-Line terminal. Scoma's, a highly-rated seafood restaurant, is just steps away at Pier 47, behind Castagnola's Restaurant. Both of these fine restaurants offer marvelous views of the fishing fleet that gave Fisherman's Wharf its name.

PCC 1057 (Cincinnati) lays over at the Jones and Beach terminal on January 10, 2007. This car matches the PCC image depicted on the car stop sign, indicating the outbound direction. However, the motorman has not yet changed the rollsign to read "Castro." *Peter Ehrlich*

A Ride to Castro Street (outbound)

OKAY. WE'VE FINISHED STROLLING A-ROUND the Wharf, done plenty of shopping, window shopping and just enjoying being some of the millions of visitors (and locals) who come to one of the top destinations in any American city. It's three o'clock and we want to beat the rush home. We could ride the Hyde Street cable car back, but it's not as much fun as riding it toward the Wharf; besides, it's a half hour wait in line. The cable cars will have to wait for another day. So, even if our feet are tired and sore, we decide to walk back to Jones and Beach for an F car ride. But instead of getting off downtown, we're going to ride all the way to Castro Street.

This time, we'll board the first car in line. It happens to be PCC 1057, which is dressed in yellow with green stripes to match cars that ran in Cincinnati until 1951. (The operators call this car the "Bumblebee.") It also matches the picture of the trolley shown on outbound F-Line stop markers. So we join the queue, show our passes to the operator as we board, and head to the back of the car, where

Outbound F-Line stop marker. A new info box was added in 2011. *Peter Ehrlich*

213

A PCC leaves Jones and Beach terminal in this view from Jones and Filbert Streets on Russian Hill. The Liberty ship *Jeremiah O'Brien* is at the top of the picture. *Peter Ehrlich*

comfortable cushioned double seats face forward in the rear half of this 1948-built Art Deco-styled American classic streetcar. The front roll sign already reads "Castro."

Beach Street

The streetcar operator closes the front doors and rings the gong, signaling our departure. The PCC's wheels squeal as we turn onto Beach Street. Using the car's pedal controls like those on an automobile, the operator accelerates her car once we've straightened out. Notice how quiet the car is, compared to the Milan and "Iron Monster" streetcars we rode earlier. That's because of its silent hypoid right-angle gearing and cushioned suspension and trucks.

Again, we're at curbside, in a faux-Belgian Block diamond lane. Beach Street is a rather uninteresting street whose buildings adhere to a strict 40' height limit by city ordinance. There is one interesting building, however. At Beach and Mason, the International Longshoremen's and Warehousemen's Union Hall, a round one-story structure with a bronze roof set in triangular sections, is alongside the stop. Some more people board.

Beach and Stockton Streets

Beach and Stockton, directly opposite Pier 39, is the heaviest outbound stop on the line. In the afternoon, huge crowds jam aboard homeward-bound F cars. Even though it's comparatively early, our car gets a fair number of standees, but not a crush load. That means there will still be room for people to board further down the line. The stop is next to Muni's Kirkland bus yard, which dates back to 1950, when Fisherman's Wharf was not the tourist mecca it is today. Needless to say, its presence is incompatible with its environment, but efforts to

Beach and Mason Streets. On the left is the Longshoremen's Hall. The north side of Beach Street is lined with buildings which were required by city ordinance to be no taller than 40'. Note the ornate decoration on the line pole's bracket arm. *April 18, 2000. Peter Ehrlich*

PCC 1079 (Detroit) crosses Stockton Street in 2007. In the distance are Coit Tower, the Transamerica Pyramid and the Bank of America Building. Muni's Kirkland bus yard lies to the right, and the Pier 39 loop is in the foreground. *Peter Ehrlich*

PCC 1062 (Louisville) leaves the outbound Beach and Stockton stop opposite Pier 39. Muni B-Type "Iron Monster" 162 is waiting in the loop. April 4, 2008. *Peter Ehrlich*

relocate the barn elsewhere have been stymied by lack of money and other issues.

Sometimes, cars will turn back at the Pier 39 loop to get back on schedule, and the operator will swing back onto Beach and beckon waiting patrons to cross the street to board his or her trolley.

A Speedy Ride Along The Embarcadero

After leaving Stockton, our conveyance turns onto The Embarcadero, and picks up a few more passengers at Bay Street. From there, it's a speedy ride back to the Ferry Building, and we can feel how fast and smooth riding the PCC is. The "Bumblebee" is really getting a "buzz on"! A car card on board has a brief history of the PCC car. Another one relates the story of the PCC's time in Cincinnati. Both cards were prepared by Market Street Railway volunteers.

At the Ferry Building, many riders disembark to catch their ferries or even to walk across Justin Herman Plaza to the BART/Muni Metro Station a block west on Market Street. Others will stay on to that stop before they leave the car.

Lower Market Street

From Drumm Street, the ride gets a little slower because of the mix of car and bus traffic. At Third/Kearny Street, the operator spies a man in a wheelchair at the concrete ramp. She'll politely ask patrons in the front tip-up seats to find other seats on the car because she needs those spaces for the wheelchair user. Deftly, she opens the front door (making sure the center doors won't open), sets the portable aluminum platform out for the patron, who boards. She then closes it and inserts it back in its cabinet and proceeds up to the boarding island. This procedure takes less than a minute. (The wheelchair

Muni Metro, but that entails using a cumbersome system of elevators to get into the subway, so he prefers the ease of riding the F car.)

We're on our way again, and at 4th/Stockton, many more riders get off the PCC to go to Union Square. At the same time, riders going out to the Castro District begin boarding the car in greater numbers.

Fifth to Seventh Streets

From Fifth/Powell, the next two blocks give one a slice of the underbelly of San Francisco, with discount clothing shops, seedy theaters and boarded-up storefronts lining both sides of the street. This is the Tenderloin District, one of the roughest areas of San Francisco. The Golden Gate Theater is located at the corner of Taylor and Golden Gate.

At 7th Street, we begin our ride through the Civic Center area. The new Federal Building highrise and the Beaux-Arts U.S. Court Of Appeals

Blackpool "Boat" 228 approaches 7th Street. A Farmer's Market lines U. N. Plaza, setting up on Wednesdays and Sundays. San Francisco's majestic City Hall, built in 1915, is off in the distance. *Peter Ehrlich*

user, who is going to Church Street, could have taken Building, which once upon a time also housed the main Post Office, are visible on the left down 7th Street. After crossing 7th, San Francisco's majestic City Hall, built in 1915 and designed by Bakewell & Brown, is in the distance, reachable by the Civic Center and United Nations Plaza promenades. The plaza hosts a Farmer's Market on Wednesdays and Sundays.

Eighth, Grove and Hyde Streets

Next stop is 8th Street. The Orpheum Theater occupies the northeast corner. The Whitcomb Hotel, dating to the Earthquake era and recently returned to its original name after being part of the Ramada chain, is situated on the south side just up from the southwest corner. The fabulous new (1997) Main

Outbound along The Embarcadero and at the Ferry Building

Once streetcars move onto The Embarcadero, it's a fast ride from the Wharf to the Ferries.

(*left*) 1818 passes Teatro ZinZanni at Embarcadero and Sansome.

(*below left*) PCC 1058 (Chicago) crosses Broadway as another PCC follows a couple of blocks behind. Coit Tower's on the left. This image was taken April 18, 2000.

(*below*) Kansas City 1056 arrives at the unique Ferry Building stop on January 31, 2010. *All photos, Peter Ehrlich.*

(*left*) Milano 1814 is approaching the Ferry Building, leading a procession of outbound cars–a PCC and two more Milanos. The Embarcadero stretches straight for nearly a mile. *Peter Ehrlich*

(*right*) "Torpedo" PCC 1015 (Illinois Terminal) pauses to drop passengers at the outbound Ferry Building stop in this stunning night image. One Market Plaza and one of the Millennium towers light up the night sky. *Kevin Sheridan*

Ferry Building and Vicinity

(*clockwise from top left*) A Milano at the outbound Ferry Building stop, with Embarcadero Center Four looming above. PCC 1007 (Red Arrow) heads inbound from Ferries layover. The Bay Bridge is off in the distance. 1055 (Philadelphia) fronts Justin Herman Park in this view from the Hotel Vitale terrace. San Diego 1078 lays over at Ferries as Milan 1811, in historic yellow/white, heads outbound. "Iron Monster" 162 makes the turn from Embarcadero onto Don Chee Way in this afternoon panorama from the Hotel Vitale. The Ferry Building, another San Francisco icon from 1898, stands tall and majestic. *All photos, Peter Ehrlich*

Civic Center to Franklin Street

The Orpheum Theater is a Civic Center-area landmark. Many Broadway musicals and other plays are presented here. (*above left*) PCC 1061 (Pacific Electric), fresh from a two-year overhaul, and Christmas-decorated Milano 1818, pass the Orpheum at 8th Street on December 16, 2011. *Matt Lee* (*above right*) PCC 1061, again, stops in front of the theater and behind an entrance to the BART/Muni Metro Civic Center Station. April 9, 2007. *Peter Ehrlich*

(*this column, above*) PCC 1053 crosses 9th/Larkin/Hayes. Fox Plaza is above the streetcar, and Bill Graham Civic Auditorium is situated on the right. (*below*) PCC 1051 (Muni Simplified) is about to cross Franklin in this view looking through the center island shrubbery. *Both photos, Peter Ehrlich*

(*this column, top*) Cleveland 1075 pauses at 8th Street. The historic Hotel Whitcomb, which dates to the 1906 Earthquake era, is in the center of the picture. (*bottom*) 496 (Melbourne) heads east near 10th Street. The autos will be diverted off Market Street. *Both photos, Peter Ehrlich*

This image of PCC 1052 (Los Angeles Railway) looks down from the 7th floor of the SFMTA Headquarters at One South Van Ness Avenue. The Honda dealership at one time was the Fillmore Auditorium of late 1960s hippie fame. *Peter Ehrlich*

The Asian Art Museum, in the old Main Library Building, is two blocks up Larkin Street. Civic Center Plaza, fronted by the Library and the museum on the east, the old State Building on the north, City Hall on the west, and Civic Auditorium on the south, is a block away. Again, all of these, except for the new Library, are in Beaux-Arts style, and the Larkin Street side of the Library is an effective modern-style imitation of the other structures.

Van Ness Avenue and 11th Street

After 9th Street comes Van Ness Avenue. Before reaching the stop, a 2-track stub wye, the last remnant of the old H-Potrero crosstown streetcar line (which quit in 1950), is on the left. It is used to turn F-Line cars here from outbound to inbound, or vice versa.

In 2007, the San Francisco Municipal Transportation Agency (SFMTA), the agency that oversees Muni, moved most of its main office management functions to the trapezoid-shaped Bank Of America operations building at 1 South Van Ness. The building is bounded by 11th, Market and South Van Ness.

SFMTA's sales office, which offers passes for sale, is at 11 S. Van Ness.

A walk north on Van Ness brings one to *Davies Symphony Hall*, the War Memorial Opera House, the Veterans Building and the California Public Utilities Commission building. Architecturally, the Opera House and Veterans Building are in the Beaux-Arts style to match City Hall across the street. The newer buildings have matching heights and curved fronts, and are tastefully designed to blend in with the older buildings.

Library is just steps away, on Grove Street.

Ninth, Larkin and Hayes Streets

Next comes 9th Street. The Merchandise Mart occupies the south side between 9th and 10th Streets, while across the street is Fox Plaza, a modern brown slab of a building with offices and apartments. This building replaced the beloved Fox Theater in 1963 and life in this block hasn't been the same ever since. Every summer afternoon, fierce downdrafts caused by the building blow down on Market Street, making this the windiest place in town.

PCC 1010 (Muni blue/gold) crosses 11th Street on April 18, 2005. Another blue-and-gold Muni car, B-Type 130, peeks out from the 11th Street wye. This is the 1939 World's Fair livery, worn by most Muni streetcars until the green-and-cream "Wings" came along in the late 1940s. *Peter Ehrlich*

12th and Franklin Streets; Gough, Haight and Valencia Streets

At 12th Street, the tracks, which are immediately parallel to each other up to this point, diverge to allow a double left turn lane for traffic heading to Franklin Street. The next stop is Gough Street. At this stop, riders can have dinner at the acclaimed Zuni Café, where some diners can sit outside at sidewalk tables.

Octavia Blvd.

Valencia marks the beginning of the median

strip lined with Canary Island palm trees, which have been a feature since 1993, although there was some controversy regarding their planting. At Octavia Blvd., we cross a wide, newly-developed roadway, replacing the hated, neighborhood-dividing double-deck Central Freeway, which was damaged in the 1989 Loma Prieta Earthquake, demolished in stages beginning in 1997 and gone for good in 2003. (Its sister twin-deck structure, the Embarcadero Freeway, was also damaged by the quake and torn down in 1992, and its removal paved the way toward building of the F-Line to Fisherman's Wharf.) As you ride out on Upper Market, note the numerous new apartment and condo developments under construction.

On the right, the San Francisco Lesbian Gay Bisexual and Transgender Community Center,

which opened in 2002 with a brand new building adjoining the historic Fallon Building, a three-story Victorian featuring a curved staircase, stands on the northwest corner.

Laguna, Guerrero and Hermann Streets; Duboce Avenue, Buchanan and Dolores Streets; Mint Yard

Next stop is Laguna, followed by Duboce. (The inbound stops are Guerrero and Dolores.) From Duboce, it's a 3-block walk south on Dolores Street to Mission San Francisco de Asis, locally known as Mission Dolores. This church is one of the 21 Spanish Missions founded by the Spanish between San Diego and Northern California beginning in 1769; Mission Dolores dates to 1776. Also at the Duboce stop is the U. S. Mint, sitting atop a rocky outcropping above Market Street. This Art Deco building was constructed in 1937, replacing the original 1854 building at Fifth and Mission, which still stands. At street level, Market Street Railway

(*above*) There are a few sidewalk cafés along Upper Market, where one can watch F-Line cars go by while having dinner. This one is the Zuni Café, near Gough Street.
(*left*) PCC 1010 passes the historic Fallon Building, now part of the San Francisco Lesbian Gay Bisexual and Transgender Community Center, at Octavia Blvd. on July 17, 2006. *Both photos, Peter Ehrlich*

operates David L. Pharr Yard, where several streetcars were undergoing restoration until quite recently. The yard is still in use by MSR, and available for future restoration projects.

There is also a giant Safeway supermarket sprawled across the block between Duboce and Church Streets.

Church Street

Next we arrive at Church Street, where a transfer can be made to the J-Church Muni Metro streetcar line. This is the only location in San

Milan "Peter Witt" 1811 passes Mint Yard on October 2, 2005. *Market Street Railway* is holding an open house and 1895 "Dinky" 578(S) and Brussels PCC 737 are in the yard. *Peter Ehrlich*

Dolores Street; Church Street; Sanchez and 15th Streets

Church and Market is the only intersection in San Francisco where two streetcar lines cross. (*above*) PCC 1078 crosses the J-Line outbound on June 6, 2009. The U. S. Mint is in the background. (*below*) A night shot of B-Type 162 on a birthday charter in 2009. *Both photos, Peter Ehrlich*

(*above*) PCC 1057 (Cincinnati) is about to pass the Spanish-American War Monument which marks the beginning of Dolores Street. The sign for the giant Safeway store stands above the trolley. July 11, 2009. *Peter Ehrlich*

(*below*) A J-Line Breda LRV is about to bisect two inbound Milanos at Church and Market on May 30, 2005. An outbound PCC is at the top of the grade, and Twin Peaks is in the background. *Peter Ehrlich*

(*left*) Car 1051 (Muni Simplified) rolls to a stop at Sanchez and 15th Street. The multi-gabled building is the Swedish-American Hall. May 28, 2007. (*right*) PCC 1010 heads inbound at Sanchez/15th Street on an overcast day. The string of small shops on the left stretches two blocks westward to Castro Street. November 6, 2003. *Both photos, Peter Ehrlich*

Market, Noe and 16th Streets; and 17th and Noe

(*top left*) It's rare to get two Muni vintage cars in the same picture running in the same direction. But on May 19, 2003, cars 130 (B-Type) and 1 (A-Type) head outbound at Market, Noe and 16th Street. (*above*) Looking east from Noe/16th Street. Milano 1814 is approaching the left turn pocket and stop on November 3, 2007. The lush palm tree is in dire need of a trim!
(*left*) Two modes of transport are in play in this scene from the balcony of the LookOut pub. Milano 1815 has just left the boarding island and will turn left onto Noe Street, while overhead, the supersonic fighter planes of the U. S. Navy–the Blue Angels–fly in perfect formation as part of the annual Fleet Week festivities in San Francisco. October 6, 2007.
All photos, Peter Ehrlich

Milano 1811 (1928 yellow/white) is about to make the turn to reach Castro Street. The other turnout leads east on 17th to Church, used by pull-in cars. Sept. 8, 2004. *Peter Ehrlich*

PCC 1076 peeks around the corner turning from Noe onto 17th Street on its way to Castro. In the distance, another PCC is heading to the carbarn. Aug. 17, 2010. *Peter Ehrlich*

Francisco where two streetcar lines cross each other. The N-Judah streetcar line is a block north at Duboce and Church. Crosstown bus line 22-Fillmore, which travels between the Marina District and Pacific Heights to the Mission and Potrero Hill and "Community Service" bus 37-Corbett, which goes up to Twin Peaks and into the Haight-Ashbury, stop here. There are several good restaurants here, such as Chow, an American food restaurant with excellent salads, and the Aardvark bookstore. Our operator stops twice; first, to let the wheelchair user off at the concrete ramp. In less than a minute, the procedure is completed and she'll pull forward to let others on and off.

Sanchez and 15th Streets; Noe and 16th Streets

After Church Street, our car makes a stop at Sanchez/15th, which marks the beginning of a two-block-long string of small businesses on Upper Market. The multi-gabled Swedish-American Hall is on the north side of Market just before reaching Sanchez. This is followed by Noe and 16th Streets, with restaurants such as the Café Flore on the north side. Evenings and weekends, one can enjoy a beer or mineral water at the LookOut, at the corner of Noe and 16th, and watch the parade of passing F-Line cars and groups of pedestrians from the balcony.

Our outbound streetcar now crosses the inbound tracks and turns south on Noe Street for a block, and will turn right at 17th Street. Cars ending their runs for the day will turn left and follow the J-Church route to the carbarn, about three miles south.

17th Street and Castro: It's now a Piazza!

17th and Castro Streets

We've saved the best stop for last, as we arrive at the 17th and Castro terminal.

This is the heart of the Castro District, the largest and most influential gay/lesbian community in the United States. It is teeming with life as gay and straight couples intermix, share food, drink and laughs.

Castro Street is very lively, anchored by the 1922 Timothy Pflueger-designed Castro Theater, which recently got a facelift. Unlike theaters in many neighborhoods, which have become multiplexes, the Castro remains a one-screen movie palace. Inside, it boasts a mighty Wurlitzer theater organ. The Castro plays revival films and frequently sponsors many special series, and is a host for the annual San Francisco Film Festival.

At the other end of the block, Cliff's Variety is as close to an old-fashioned country general store as

17th and Castro has been transformed into a pedestrian-only piazza, with tables, chairs and decorative plants This group of images were taken in May 2011, after the permanent street furniture was put in place. (*above*) PCC 1077 (Birmingham) loads passengers, with the tables in the foreground. (*left*) This fisheye view encompasses the piazza, a Milano and the Castro Theater. The plants on the left sit on a rollaway platform, which can be moved aside if the tracks leading from the Twin Peaks Tunnel are ever needed for surface running of Muni Metro trains.
All photos, Peter Ehrlich

Descriptive Car Cards

The non-profit streetcar booster organization Market Street Railway has printed up descriptive car cards for insertion in the advertising racks on board all the PCCs and Milan cars, and some of the vintage cars.

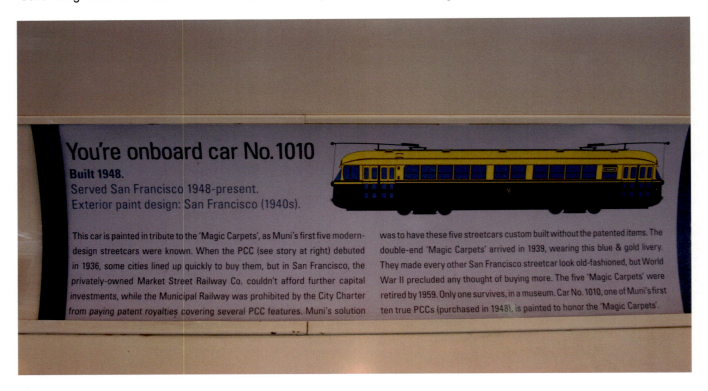

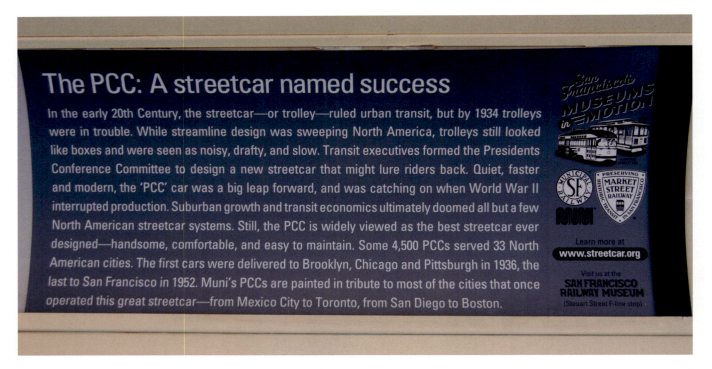

The PCCs also carry these cards describing this unique American invention–a streetcar born out of need, and the most successful ever, as designed from a systems engineering approach. *Peter Ehrlich* [See sidebar in Chapter.1.]

one can get in this modern, vibrant city. Shoppers can get just about anything here, from pots to nails.

On 17th Street, just east of Castro is Orphan Andy's, which is open 24/7, and serves a good basic American breakfast at all hours. The *Castro Coffee Company* and *Rossi's Deli* are excellent places to get cheese and gourmet coffee beans; *Rossi's* also sells sandwiches and 1- and 3-day Visitor Passports. Many other stores on Castro cater specifically to the gay community. But it's well worth a visit, regardless of sexual preference.

In 2009, the city government, acting on a proposal from MSR and other civic groups, made the 17th and Castro an auto-free zone on a trial basis. In 2010, this newly-created "piazza" became permanent. Tables and chairs are set up in this plaza for folks to sit, relax and chow down on their bag lunches or

17th and Castro Streets, before the Piazza

(*above*) 1078 (San Diego) leaves 17th and Castro on May 5, 2007, two years before the "piazza" was created.

More Car Cards

(*left*) Another PCC car card. This one represents PCC 1078 (San Diego). (*below*) Market Street Railway has also printed up car cards describing the Milan, Italy "Peter Witts" purchased in 1998. *All photos, Peter Ehrlich*

pizza slices, and there have even been music groups on hand to entertain the public, passers-by and waiting F-Line patrons.

HERE, AT THE TERMINAL, we'll take our leave of our friendly F-Line car and enjoy the neighborhood. Later, when going back toward downtown, we could take a quick ride on a Muni Metro train to Powell Station instead. But I think we'll go back downtown on another F-Line car, joining the locals who simply enjoy the ride. After all, F Is For Fun!

Two scenes along Muni Metro routes: *(top)* The St. Anne's of the Sunset Church, a Sunset District institution, provides the backdrop for this inbound N-Line train at Judah and 10th Avenue. June 6, 2009. *(bottom)* PCC 1078, liveried as a San Diego car, crosses Ocean Avenue on the M-Ocean View on March 8, 2007 during a test run. Like the J-Church, the M-Line has stretches of backyard, private right-of-way running. *Both photos, Peter Ehrlich*

Chapter 11 - More Tours of Discovery

"California has been a national leader in [light rail] transportation, and accounts for the largest state share of light rail ridership nationwide. California is [also] home to a number of heritage rail transportation systems that are an important part of the state's tourism industry. They also have a special place in the hearts of many long-time Californians."
– from California Streets Blog (http://www.californiastreets.org), accessed September 30, 2011.

ONE OF THE SELLING POINTS that Muni utilized in the 1950s and '60s to urge visitors to use transit to explore San Francisco was a series of pocket maps that bore the title *Tours of Discovery*. It listed attractions such as Golden Gate Park and its museums, Coit Tower, North Beach, Aquatic Park, the Zoo, and other attractions, and showed the ways that the visitor could get there without having to resort to driving. In this way, people could see other neighborhoods of the city, which were just as interesting in many aspects as the usual places that tourists would visit.

Today, many of them can be reached by Muni Metro, the subway-surface streetcar network that began operating in 1980. For other points of interest, one can catch one of the 14 electric trolley bus routes or several bus lines. And if one is really intrepid, he or she can take BART to the East Bay, serving cities like Oakland, Berkeley, Richmond, Walnut Creek, Concord, Pittsburg, Hayward, Dublin/Pleasanton and Fremont, and San Francisco International Airport on the Peninsula.

Farther afield, Caltrain has frequent service between San Francisco and San Jose, where a rider can make a quick connection to Santa Clara County's far-flung light rail system, which has been in existence since 1987. Or a person can take a day trip on Amtrak to explore Sacramento's Old Town, the acclaimed State Railroad Museum and the state capital's RT Metro light rail network. And electric rail systems have been built in Los Angeles and San Diego, too.

But let's start in San Francisco–Everybody's Favorite City–where the cable cars "climb halfway to the stars" and the F-Line carries record crowds to Fisherman's Wharf. Perhaps we've taken a comfortable F-Line PCC or a musical Milan car with large panoramic windows down from the Wharf. We could continue to ride outbound on Market. Instead, let's go into the subway, using the transfers given us by the operator or the Passport we bought earlier, and take a westbound Muni Metro train somewhere.

The Muni Metro Subway

MUNI METRO OPENED in 1980. There are five underground stations in the downtown area, starting with Embarcadero, the station closest to the Ferry Building. All five of the city's remaining streetcar lines that at one time ruled the top of Market Street pass through Embarcadero Station. The J-Church, L-Taraval and M-Ocean View begin their runs here, while the N-Judah and K-Ingleside/T-Third Street arrive there after traveling along the South Embarcadero on the Muni Metro Extension.

As the LRV leaves the station, it will traverse a scissors crossover, which was originally the only way trains could turn back here. Although it's still used at times, most of the switchbacks are made east of the station. The next station is Montgomery, serving the heart of the Financial District, followed by Powell, adjacent to Union Square and one of the finest retail shopping districts in the United States. These stations have broad painted stripes on the trackway walls. Montgomery is blue, Powell, red; but otherwise, they are identical in basic layout.

Next comes Civic Center Station, the gateway to Civic Center Plaza, the Main Library, the Asian Art Museum and City Hall. (This is the last station shared with BART.) Van Ness Avenue Station is the last station shared by all five Muni Metro lines. It has pictures of City Hall's dome on the trackway wall; one depicts the exterior, the other, the inside of the dome.

West of Van Ness Station, there is a crossover and the line climbs under Market Street to Duboce Junction. Here, N-Judah and J-Church trains curve right to reach the surface, splitting again at Church and Duboce. K-Ingleside, L-Taraval and M-Ocean View trains continue straight for two more stations– Church, with its breezy, open mezzanine, and Castro, featuring a curved platform reminiscent of the earliest stations on the New York subway. After Castro, the train ducks into the 11,920' (3.65km)-long Twin Peaks Tunnel, which was opened on February 3, 1918, to speed streetcars from the West Portal area to downtown. Forest Hill Station is reached next after about three minutes of an uphill climb. (One needs to take an elevator to reach the station headhouse, which opens up to an attractive partial plaza with Sherwood Forest and Laguna Honda Hospital across the street and stately homes on either side of the headhouse.)

Next station is West Portal, a modernistic station that leads into the bustling West Portal District shopping street. In anticipation of Muni Metro, the handsome tunnel entrance from 1918 was demolished to make way for this station, but a commemorative plaque and pictures of "Iron Monsters" adorn the platform entrances. When we come back to West Portal, we will explore the vibrant shopping area.

The L-Taraval Line

OUR TRAIN, AN L-TARAVAL, turns right and passes the West Portal Library. It operates on Ulloa Street for about seven blocks, then turns right at 15th Avenue. Just as the train makes the turn, we can catch a glimpse of the Pacific Ocean way off in the distance (if it's not too foggy). Then we reach Taraval Street and the Parkside Shopping District. From here to the ocean, it's all downhill running.

As we turn left at 46th Avenue, it's three blocks to the San Francisco Zoo loop. This loop was built in 1935 as a depression-era Works Progress Administration project. Previously, the tracks continued two blocks to Great Highway, but these stub tracks, still in place, are rarely used. This stub trackage is the oldest in San Francisco, dating to 1923, and is distinguishable by the Belgian block pavers on both sides of each running rail.

The L-Line opened in 1919. Until the 20 K-Types arrived in 1923, the line operated as a shuttle from West Portal, for a time using some of the 1921-vintage E-Union Street single-truckers. Once the K-Types were available, the line continued downtown.

K-Ingleside and M-Ocean View Lines

FOLLOWING A VISIT to the Zoo, we catch a returning L car and ride to West Portal Station. Now we are going to walk outside the station and stroll along West Portal Avenue for two blocks, taking in the ambiance and perhaps grabbing a snack. At 14th Avenue, we'll hop a K-Ingleside car and ride out Ocean Avenue. The K-Line serves City College, and hundreds of students arrive for classes off the K car. From here, it's a short stretch of private right-of way to Balboa Park, where Metro Yard and Balboa Park BART Station are situated. Metro Yard was built in 1977, replacing the ramshackle Elkton Shops, which dated back to post-1906 Earthquake days and was only supposed to be a temporary facility. Cars on the K-line, and the J-Church, end their runs here, right at the entrance to Balboa Park BART. The M-Line stops on San Jose Avenue south of Geneva Avenue. In 2007, the K-Line was through-routed with the T-Third Street route.

The K-Line, which began service in 1918, was originally called the K-Market. The name was changed to K-Ingleside around 1952. At first it operated to Brighton and Grafton, two blocks south of Ocean Avenue. It and URR/MSRy's 12-Line shared trackage on Ocean Avenue. For a brief time after Muni absorbed Market Street Railway Co., alternate K cars ran to Onondaga and Mission. Later, the K-Line used a loop at City College.

Diagonally opposite the station, the old red brick Geneva Carhouse Office Building, which survived– barely–both 1906 and 1989 earthquakes, stands at the entrance to Geneva Yard (now called Cameron Beach Yard), where F-Line cars are stabled. A new Historic Car Enclosure was finally constructed in 2010 after much pressure from MSR. Geneva Shops are in the back. The office building was stabilized for future use as a recreation center, but hasn't opened as such yet.

Going back, we'll take the M-Ocean View. This line was built in 1925 and upgraded to Muni Metro status in 1980. We wind through the Ocean View district, passing a restored Victorian firehouse along the way, and travel up 19th Avenue, passing Parkmerced (one of many Metropolitan Life housing developments built in the late 1940s) and then reach San Francisco State University. The steps on the train rise because this is a high-level station. Next station is Stonestown Galleria, serving one of the first shopping malls built in the United States. Stonestown opened in 1952.

After leaving Stonestown, the steps move down again for low-level boarding, and we enter a stretch of backyard private right-of-way, emerging at St. Francis Circle. This is along the western edge of St. Francis Wood, a very upscale residential district, with large, detached homes. Much of St. Francis Wood was built up with the arrival of Muni streetcar service in 1918.

For the first two decades, the M-Line operated primarily as a shuttle between West Portal and Broad and Plymouth. Regular service to downtown didn't begin until after Muni took over Market Street Railway Co. in 1944, but there was no through night and Sunday streetcar service until late 1982.

The N-Judah Line

RETURNING DOWNTOWN, we'll exit the train at Church Street. Here, the J-Church, which had just left the subway a block north, crosses the F-Market.

West Portal and the K, L and M Lines
The three "tunnel" lines, serving the southwest and southern area of The City, opened in 1918, 1923 and 1925. They form the backbone of Muni Metro.

(*left*) PCC 1075, on a test run in 2007, turns onto the L-Line at West Portal and Ulloa, one of the great streetcar junctions in the United States. (*below*) Breda LRV 1511 drifts down West Portal Avenue near 14th Avenue on July 11, 2006. The Mt. Sutro broadcast tower, erected in the 1980s, dominates the scene. *Both photos, Peter Ehrlich*

(*above*) Two Bredas meet at Ocean and Jules on the K-Ingle-side line. The condo development was built in the 1980s. The tower of the old El Rey Theater, now a Pentecostal church, lies in the background. (*right*) PCC 1015 turns the corner at Taraval and 46th Avenue on an August 24, 2008 charter. The Pacific Ocean is three blocks away. The tracks going down to the ocean were once part of the original L-line. 1015 is turning onto the 1935-era Zoo loop. *Both photos, Peter Ehrlich*

M-Line scenes: (*below left*) The M-Line's 19th Avenue right-of-way unfolds in this view from Crespi Drive. A Breda is leaving San Francisco State University Station heading for town. May 2, 2010. (*below*) Chartered Milan 1818 passes a restored Victorian-era firehouse at Broad and Plymouth in 2009. *Both photos, Peter Ehrlich*

We'll walk one block north to the N-Judah line, the heaviest traveled streetcar line in the city. With a ridership of nearly 45,000 a weekday, the N-line requires two-car trains all day, even on Sundays.

Using our Passports or valid transfers, we climb on board the second car and ride past Duboce Park on the right, and then duck into the 4,232-foot long Sunset Tunnel, which opened in 1928. At the other end of the tunnel is the Cole Valley neighborhood, four blocks south of the Haight-Ashbury of hippie-era fame. We proceed along narrow Carl Street (a portion of which was originally part of the Eddy Street-to-Golden Gate Park line of the Metropolitan Railroad, San Francisco's second electric streetcar company, later becoming URR and MSRy) and swing around an S-curve for the stop at UCSF Medical Center, the heaviest trip generator on the line. The train continues along Irving Street to the Inner Sunset district, whose stores, restaurants and boutiques cater to locals, UCSF employees and patients, and visitors to Golden Gate Park, one block north. The train turns onto 9th Avenue and travels one block to Judah Street, where it will be a straight shot to Ocean Beach. On the way back, we may stop off at 9th and Judah and sample the neighborhood.

From 9th to 19th Avenue, the line runs on a semi-private right-of way, set in concrete and raised above the street. St. Anne's of the Sunset Church stands tall at Judah and Funston (13th Avenue). It had been intended to extend this improvement all the way to Ocean Beach, but residents protested and forced the city to scrap this idea. Nevertheless, it's a relatively fast ride out from bustling 19th Avenue. At the end of the line is Ocean Beach loop, and from here, one can cross Great Highway and walk on the beach. Afterwards, we can grab a latté or other drink at Dick's at the Beach coffee house before we catch an N train for the ride back inbound.

The N-Judah was Muni's last streetcar line to be built (until the F-Line began in 1995). It opened on October 21, 1928, with Mayor James "Sunny Jim" Rolph piloting, as he had done in the past, B-Type 102, the first car through the Sunset Tunnel, to begin service. As mentioned, the two blocks on Carl between Cole and Stanyan were shared with cars of MSRy (and Muni after the 1944 takeover), until 1948, when the 6-Haight and Masonic line was abandoned.

The J-Church Line

WE'VE SAVED THE BEST ride for last. When we reach Duboce and Church, we get off the N train and watch it disappear into the subway. Then we'll walk over to Church and Market to grab a J streetcar. With a Passport, we can board through any door.

Along the N-Judah Line

(*top to bottom*) Car 1 passes a Queen Anne Victorian at Carl and Stanyan on May 22, 2004. A two-car train travels on 9th Avenue in the Inner Sunset small business district, which serves nearby UCSF Medical Center and Golden Gate Park. Ridership on the N-Line is so great that two-car trains are even required on Sundays. June 6, 2009. On September 18, 1983, Trolley Festival cars 189 (Oporto, Portugal) and 130 (Muni B-Type) pose at the N-Line Ocean Beach terminal loop. The line's regular Boeings are in the background. *All photos, Peter Ehrlich*

(above) The streetcar's climb through Dolores Park on the J-Line is the most scenic of Muni's trolley routes. B-Type 162, at the time recently restored, poses at the famous spot at the top of Dolores Park Grade in September 2008. F-Line cars use the J-Church to pull out and pull in. *Peter Ehrlich*

At 16th Street, some folks get off to walk over to Mission Dolores, founded in 1776. The streetcar crosses 17th Street, where we can glimpse F-Line cars up at 17th and Castro if done really quickly, and then dips down to 18th Street.

The line now climbs through Dolores Park via private right-of-way on a steady grade to 20th. Here we get a spectacular view of the San Francisco skyline, with the impressive Mission High School just across from the park. We can get off here to enjoy the park and catch another car a little later. If we're really lucky, we might catch an F-Line car pulling in!

Leaving 20th Street, the J meanders through back yards on a winding trackway. At Liberty, we can see a pipe organ in a mansion window if we look fast. We leave the right-of way at 22nd Street and from here it's a straight shot to 30th Street. At 24th Street, the lively Noe Valley shopping district extends to the right. Later on, we'll pass St. Paul's Church where the movie *Sister Act*, starring Whoopi Goldberg, was filmed. At 30th Street, the J-Line turns left (east); until 1991, this was the terminal. The streetcar then makes a sharp, squealing turn onto San Jose Avenue, once again entering private right-of-way at Randall Street. Now it's a fast ride past Glen Park Station, then the car will duck under Interstate 280 and resume street running out San Jose Avenue, past the park which gave Balboa Park its name. The train will turn right on Ocean Avenue and enter Metro Yard and terminate at its own layover point at Balboa Park Station. (F-Line pull-in cars continue straight on San Jose Avenue to Geneva.)

The J-Church was constructed between 1915 and 1917, and service began on August 11, 1917, via Church, Market, Van Ness, Geary and inner Market to the Ferries. After February 3, 1918, it used Market Street all the way. The extension to Balboa Park opened on July 4, 1991, for pullout and pull-in cars only. Full service followed in 1993.

MMX and the T-Line

NOT DONE WITH EXPLORING San Francisco by streetcar? Ride the T-Third!

(*above right*) Car 1807 makes a stop on the J-Line right-of-way at Liberty Street. This segment passes through back yards. There's a pipe organ in the mansion on the right, visible through the window. (*right*) The J Extension, south of 30th Street, opened in 1991, and returned rail operation to this area for the first time since 1941, when Southern Pacific ceased operations here. A Breda car speeds inbound under the Richland Avenue Bridge in this June 6, 2009 scene taken from the adjacent Highland Avenue Bridge. *Both photos, Peter Ehrlich*

At the Embarcadero end of the subway, the tracks curve right and travel through the Muni Metro Turnback and emerge at Folsom Street. Here, we can see the E-Embarcadero tracks join the line, as we cross onto the Muni Metro Extension (MMX) and Folsom Station, situated between Folsom and Harrison Streets. The old Hills Bros. Coffee Roastery building is on the right. This is a high-level station, as are all the stations on the rest of the line. Low-level platforms for E-Line service are at the Harrison Street end.

The Bay Bridge comes into view and soars above us. Like the Embarcadero portion of the F-Line, Canary Island palm trees line both sides of the trackway. Red's Java House, on the left, is a "waterfront dive" that harkens to an earlier era of San Francisco. Next station is Brannan Street. The building of the MMX, which opened in 1998 [see Chapter 7], has spurred much new development of apartment buildings and condos—one of the side benefits of having a permanent rail line. South Beach Marina is below the station, on the right.

Starting at Townsend Street, the tracks curve gently to the right, and AT&T Park, home of the San Francisco Giants and one of the most delightful new baseball stadiums in the U.S., comes into view. 2nd and King Station serves the stadium. As we cross Third Street, we see a bronze statue of Willie Mays, the "Say Hey Kid". The address of AT&T Park is, natu-rally, 24 Willie Mays Plaza, in honor of perhaps the

Muni Metro Extension opened in 1998. Its stations feature these spectacular curved glass canopies, like this one here at Brannan Street. Much new housing and business development has followed the coming of the MMX. August 31, 2008. *Peter Ehrlich*

greatest Giant ever to play for the team. Mays' career started in New York, and the Giants moved to San Francisco in 1958.

At King and 4th Streets, the lines divide. If we happened to be on an N-Judah train, we would use the station on the far side of King and 4th Street. But instead, our T-Line train will turn left (south) and use the new station on 4th Street. We are now on the T-Third Street Line, which opened in 2007. (The T is through-routed with the K-Ingleside. When inbound K cars reach West Portal station, the operator changes the signs on the car to T. The reverse is done at Ferry Portal, when cars coming from the T-Line change to K signs and head outbound through the subway.)

After leaving 4th and King, we cross Mission Creek on the 4th Street bascule bridge (called the Peter Maloney Bridge). The train then travels one block east to Third Street, where it will curve right (south) and now it's a long, straight shot mostly on private right-of-way past redeveloping Mission Bay. The UCSF Medical Center's Mission Bay campus is a block north of 16th Street, and there is a station here. Next, we pass the Union Iron Works Historic District on the left (some Muni streetcars were built here in 1913 and 1923), with its silent shipyard cranes still standing tall, and enter Dogpatch, an eclectic collection of rundown houses and converted canneries. At 25th Street, the line crosses the first of two junctions where tracks lead to Metro East, which opened in 2008. The other

(*above*) One of the new Siemens LRV-4s that will expand new rail services and replace the existing Breda fleet poses at Folsom Station during a test run. October 9, 2017. *Peter Ehrlich*

An inbound train crosses Newcomb Avenue along the T-Line in 2008. The historic and restored Victorian-era Bayview Opera House, dating to 1888, anchors the Bayview District, a mostly working-class area in southeastern San Francisco. *Peter Ehrlich*

one is at Cesar Chavez Street. South of Marin Street Station, we cross the Islais Creek Bridge, curve gently to the right, and traverse the long Bayview District.

Bayview is home to one of the largest African-American communities in San Francisco, and the coming of the T-Line was seen as a boon by some, and a bane to others. Nevertheless, it's here to stay. Many arts-related businesses are located in the Bayview. There are some architectural gems such as the Bayview Opera House, a wood frame building from the Victorian era used as a cultural center, near the Palou/Oakdale Station, and a number of historic churches. But we can see that this was a large working-class district at one time, and still is.

At Carroll Avenue, we cross one of the two Union Pacific Railroad (originally Southern Pacific) tracks, which serve light industry. (The other one is just south of the Islais Creek Bridge.) Following Gilman/Paul Avenue Station, the line makes a steady climb and the next station, Le Conte Avenue, lies at the beginning of a cut. Then the train crosses the tumultuous US 101 freeway and descends again into Visitacion Valley. There are just two stations here–Arleta Avenue and Sunnydale. Originally, the plan was to connect with Bayshore Caltrain, and this may still happen, pending new development.

A new Central Subway, which will cross Market Street and extend to Chinatown, is under construction, with a planned 2019 opening, which will be operated at the T-Line.

The first use of the MMX tracks for revenue service began on January 10, 1998, with E-Embarcadero shuttle trains [see Chapter 7]. This was replaced by through N-Judah service on August 22, 1998. Limited weekend T-Line service commenced January 13, 2007, with seven-day service following on April 7.

The Cable Cars

OF COURSE, YOU CAME to San Francisco to ride the cable cars. Didn't you? C'mon, admit it!...Anyway, we've sampled the F-Line from end to end, and some of the other streetcar and Muni Metro routes. But the cable cars are what make San Francisco *San Francisco!* Otherwise, there would be no place to leave your heart.

The cable car system, and its means of propulsion, was invented by a Scotsman named Andrew Hallidie in 1873, after he witnessed an accident involving a heavily loaded horse car on a rainy day. One of the horses slipped, sending the car plummeting down the hill, dragging the poor beasts behind.

Hallidie, who was already in the wire rope manufacturing business, set out to invent a system whereby cars were pulled mechanically by a wire cable running under the street, operated by a gripman, who clasped the cable with a mechanical lever system. This cable traveled at a constant speed–usually nine miles per hour–pulling the car along. It didn't matter whether the routes were on grades or flat terrain; the invention caught hold, and soon San Francisco had as many as twelve cable car routes. The invention spread to other American cities, including Chicago, Kansas City, Manhattan, Seattle and many other places. Cable trams also became fixtures in Melbourne, Australia. Wellington and Dunedin, New Zealand, also favored cable cars as they had hilly settings like San Francisco. (Dunedin's cable trams lasted until 1956, making theirs the last such system anywhere outside of San Francisco.)

Most flat systems quickly converted to electric traction as their cities found the electric cars to be speedier and generally safer. Seattle, which had hill-climbing routes, abandoned its last three lines in 1940, the same year that Melbourne's last cable tram line operated.

But enough of history for the moment. Now it's time to ride. If we have Passports, we don't have to pay the seven-buck-a-pop fare. And instead of waiting in line at Powell and Market, we walk two blocks up Powell to O'Farrell Street, where one doesn't have to wait in line to board. It doesn't particularly matter if we catch a Powell/Mason car (yellow dash sign) or Powell/Hyde (maroon sign). As it happens, a Mason car arrives first and we climb on board, hanging on by the outside handholds.

Powell Cable Cars

A fisheye view of the Powell and Market cable car turntable. The waiting line of people will often stretch halfway down the block, and 20-minute waits to ride are common. The crew will rotate the car, push it onto the outbound track, and depart with mostly just a seated load. At the next stop–O'Farrell– the standees will board. May 21, 2008.

(*above*) Powell car 24 crosses Geary Street, Union Square. This plaza is the nerve center of San Francisco and the anchor of the retail shopping district. *Peter Ehrlich*

(*above left*) Car 9, one of the historically-painted cable cars, bumps across the California line. The little octagonal kiosk is the home of the tower-man, who ensures that cars on both lines can climb to this intersection safely. (*below left*) A rare quadruple meet at Powell and California! This phenomenon happened on July 9, 2009. (*right*) Car 15, another car in historic dress, climbs Jackson between Powell and Mason Streets outbound on the Powell/Hyde line. The Bay Bridge lies in the background. *All photos, Peter Ehrlich*

San Francisco's cable cars are part of the historic and everyday fabric of the city. Songs have been written about them. Numerous fiction writers of mysteries and other tomes have featured them prominently. The thrill and enjoyment of being carried along while clinging onto the bars of the open-ended cars has been experienced by thousands of people from all over the world. It is a transportation experience unlike any other.

(*right*) A look at the inside of the Cable Car Barn from one of the balconies. *Peter Ehrlich*

(*below*) A Hyde line car crosses Washington Street. The Cable Car Barn and Museum is here. At bottom right, the Mason line curves and joins the Hyde line. *Peter Ehrlich*

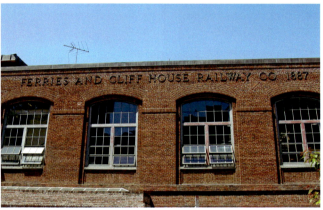

(*above*) The Washington Street façade of the Cable Car Barn. Built by the Ferries & Cliff House Railway in 1887; reconstructed in 1907 and again in 1984. (*below*) The cable winding machinery inside the Cable Car Barn. *Both photos, Peter Ehrlich*

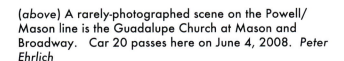

(*above*) A rarely-photographed scene on the Powell/Mason line is the Guadalupe Church at Mason and Broadway. Car 20 passes here on June 4, 2008. *Peter Ehrlich*

(*above*) As car 20, inbound on the Powell/Mason line, crosses Columbus and Lombard, the famous "Crooked Street" is visible at the top. The Powell/Hyde line passes the top of Lombard Street. Not many passengers are riding because it's early in the morning. *Peter Ehrlich*

(*below*) Car 7 crosses Hyde and Union. Outer Hyde Street is lined with trees, and Swensen's Ice Cream is a beloved San Francisco landmark. *Peter Ehrlich*

Outer Mason Line; Outer Hyde Street; California Street

(*above*) Historically-liveried car 25 climbs Hyde Street on June 18, 2009. Wisps of fog still shroud the Golden Gate Bridge. (*below*) Cal car 53 passes Tadich Grill, deep in the Financial District and the oldest seafood restaurant in San Francisco (established 1849). June 12, 2008. *Peter Ehrlich*

(*below*) Car 13, in historic livery, leaves Hyde and Beach. The famous Buena Vista Café's on the left.

(*above*) The California Street cable car line serves Chinatown. Car 56 stops at Grant Avenue on an outbound trip on June 17, 2009. *Richard Panse*

By Post Street, the car is really full. The St. Francis Hotel (locals *never* call it the *Westin* St. Francis!), part of which opened before the 1906 Earthquake and Fire, is on the left, Union Square on the right. Leaving Sutter Street, we climb three blocks of steep grade up Nob Hill. The traffic signal lights are automatically set to green for the cable cars. At Pine, the gripman waits for the all-clear signal given by the California Street towerman, who governs passage of all Powell and California cars. He sits in a little octagonal wooden booth on the southeast corner of California and Powell streets, where he has a clear downhill view of both streets.

At California Street, the gripman "lets go" of the cable and we bump across the tracks and coast to a stop on the farside. The reason he has to do this maneuver is because the California car cable passes over the Powell cable, so the Cal cable is "superior" (California Street Cable Railroad Co. got there first).

Many people get off here to go to the Fairmont and Mark Hopkins hotels. The cable car will now coast downhill to a point between Washington and Jackson Streets, as there is no cable for these three blocks. Since this is a Mason car, the conductor will lift a "gypsy" lever here to allow the car to switch. Some passengers will get off to walk downhill to Chinatown, situated one block to the right.

The gripman "takes rope" and we now share the track with the Hyde Line. For clearance purposes, cars use a "gauntlet" running rail, so the left side wheels of our Mason car run on this rail. We turn left onto Jackson Street for a block to Mason Street, then right. Then we traverse several residential blocks, eventually reaching Columbus Avenue. Here we turn left onto Columbus passing through the northern edge of North Beach. Until 1951, Mason cars and original F-Stockton streetcars shared street space. The tracks leave Columbus at Taylor Street and go northward two more blocks to the terminal at Bay and Taylor. From here it's a three-block walk to Fisherman's Wharf.

The Powell-Mason line has been operating in its original configuration since 1888. From time to time, proposals to extend it the missing three blocks have been broached.

Anyway, we decide to return on the Mason line because we want to visit the Cable Car Barn and Museum before hitting the Powell/Hyde line. So we'll ride back to Mason and Washington. The Cable Car Museum is a must-see, where we can watch the wheels that power the cables spin. There are four cables, one for each section of the Powell lines, and one for California. The cable cars are stored on the level above. Normally, one needs special permission to visit inside the Cable Car Barn, but if we walk up Washington, we can see some of the cars from the street, tucked away inside. In the morning, pullout cars peek out from the barn.

This is the old Ferries and Cliff House Railway carbarn dating to 1887. It was destroyed in the 1906 Earthquake and Fire, but was rebuilt in 1907. The cars used on the Powell lines survive today because they were stationed at another barn well outside the fire zone. As part of the complete reconstruction of the system between 1982 and 1984, the carbarn was made quake-resistant, and its interior was completely rebuilt.

Following the visit to the Museum, we'll board (or try to board) a Powell/Hyde car at Jackson and Mason. The first Hyde car is "full up," so we'll wait for another one. We notice that the gripman has to drop the cable and coast to the farside, since the Mason cable is "superior" to the Hyde cable.

The next car is Car 15, whose yellow livery represents the cable cars from the time of the original Market Street Railway Company of 1893. This is one of several cable cars that represent different eras of the system, and it was built new by the Cable Car Shop (located at the base of Potrero Hill) in 2008, and entered service in 2009. Anyway, there's room, so we climb aboard.

The Hyde Line was cobbled from parts of two original lines—Washington-Jackson, which ran out to Steiner Street in Pacific Heights, and was abandoned west of Hyde Street in 1956; and the Hyde Street portion of the O'Farrell, Jones and Hyde Line, which quit in 1954. The line is considerably more scenic than the Mason line, with trees lining most of the route, which climbs Russian Hill. At Union, Swensen's Ice Cream, a San Francisco original, looks inviting; maybe a visit on the way back. But don't try to bring a cone on a cable car–that's a no-no! (Around 1972, one of President Lyndon Johnson's daughters was refused passage by a gripman for trying to bring an ice cream cone on board!)

Now we come to the most spectacular part of the line, the steep grade between Lombard–the "Crooked Street"–and Bay Street. We can see the Golden Gate Bridge from the left side, while beautiful houses line the right side of Hyde Street, with the Hyde Street Pier and the San Francisco Maritime Museum straight ahead.

We arrive at Hyde and Beach. The Buena Vista Café, where the Irish Coffee was invented, is on the southwest corner. The Hyde and Beach cable car turntable and Aquatic Park are across the street on the northwest side. The Hyde Street turnaround is named for Mrs. Friedel Klussmann, who is considered to be the savior of the cable car system back in the 1940s.

As it turns out, it's not a bad wait for the climb up Russian Hill back to California Street and the transfer to the Cal line. In the late afternoon, waits of a half hour or more are common.

The California Street line is different from the Powell lines, as it has no turntables, so it requires double-end cars. These came to Muni from the California Street Cable Railroad Company when The City took over its operations in 1952. The Cal line, which started operations in 1878, originally ran out to Presidio Avenue in north central San Francisco, but was truncated to Van Ness in 1954. We'll ride first out to Van Ness, climbing Nob Hill and passing by the Fairmont, Mark Hopkins and Huntington hotels; the Pacific Union Club, Grace Cathedral, and Masonic Auditorium. The supermarket at Cal and Hyde Streets was the site of Cal Cable's carbarn.

There's only enough time at Van Ness for the gripman and conductor to change ends and set the grips for the return journey, so we stay on board. East of Powell, we pass Grant Avenue, the gateway to Chinatown. (Grant Avenue is the tourists' Chinatown; the *real* Chinatown is Stockton Street, a block west, and the cross streets such as Washington and Jackson Streets.) Then we head into the Financial District and its skyscrapers, finally reaching Drumm Street and Market Street.

We've noticed that the Powell cars have two roof styles. Most cars have an ordinary deck roof. But some Powell cars have what are called "Bombay" roofs, with little "eyelids."

The reason can be traced to the car's original builder. The Bombay-roof cars were built by either Mahoney Bros. or Ferries & Cliff House Railway, while Carter Bros. built the deck roof Powell cars. Hammond and Holman were the builders of the California cars, all of which have deck roofs. Muni has built many new cars to replace worn-out originals, most often using parts taken from the old cars.

Muni, with the encouragement of Market Street Railway, has painted certain cars in historical liveries. Car 15, which we rode, was one of them. Here's the list, and the years of their paint scheme's use.

1 - Original Powell Street Railway, 1883-1888
3 - Muni green and cream, 1960s-1982
9 - Market Street Railway Company green with "White Front," 1927-1944
11 - First Market Street Railway Co. Tuscan Red livery, for Sacramento/Clay Line, 1893-1902
12 - Market Street Railway 1936-1944
13 - United Railroads green/red trim, 1907-1921
15 - First Market Street Railway Co. yellow, for Powell/Mason Line,1893-1902
16 - Muni blue/gold, 1944-1947
25 - United Railroads red, 1905-1908
26 - Muni green/cream with white letterboard at bottom of carbody, 1946-early '60s. The letterboard inscription reads simply "Municipal Railway."

In addition, car **24** commemorates San Francisco Giants baseball legend Willie Mays, who wore number 24 on his uniform.

San Francisco's cable cars are a wonderful anachronism–19th Century technology working in a 21st century environment. And it works well!

Muni's Trolley Coach System

NOT FINISHED WITH San Francisco public transportation? Try the electric trolley coaches!

Trolley coaches (in other cities, they're called trolleybuses, trolley buses, ETBs or trackless trolleys) arrived in San Francisco in 1935, when Market Street Railway Co. converted its streetcar switchback 33-18th and Park route. Major expansion of the

Two images of the famous switchback on the 33-Stanyan trolley coach line. *(left)* 2007: A modern Skoda coach begins to negotiate the hairpin turn onto Clayton Street. *(right)* A first-generation Marmon-Herrington trolley bus makes the turn. The coach actually has to swing out into the eastbound traffic lanes! This is what the scene looked like in 1970. *Both photos, Peter Ehrlich*

Trolley Coaches, New and Preserved

(above *left*) Since 2013, Muni has been rapidly replacing its rubber-tire fleet with new Xcelsior diesel-hybrid motor coaches and trolley coaches from New Flyer Industries of Winnipeg, Canada. Brand-new NFI Xcelsior XT60 articulated trolleybus 7279 is working line 14-Mission at 11th Street. The Art Moderne Coca-Cola Bottling Co. building is undergoing a facelift, and will be incorporated into a new apartment complex to be built on this block. February 3, 2018. A new fleet of 185 40' trolleys is now being delivered by New Flyer. (*above right*) 1950 Marmon-Herrington TC48 776 was the basis for the creation of historic streetcar booster group Market Street Railway, which was formed in 1976 to save this coach from being scrapped. It's at Jackson and Pierce in Pacific Heights, previewing the soon-to-open conversion of the 24-Divisadero line from diesel to trolley coach. August 21, 1983. (*below right*) Another trolleybus in Muni's historic rubber-tired fleet is 1976 Flyer E800 5300, seen at Washington Square on September 10, 2017, working a portion of Muni's second trolley coach route, the 41-Union, in Heritage Weekend service. In 1947, the 41 line replaced the E-Union Street "Dinky" streetcars, and was through-routed with Muni's first ETB line, the R-Howard. Coit Tower, on Telegraph Hill, is visible in the distance. *All photos, Peter Ehrlich*

trolley coach network occurred from 1948 to 1952, as Muni replaced the worn-out Market Street Railway Co.'s streetcars it inherited in 1944. Power was cheap; Muni used hydroelectric power from San Francisco's own Hetch Hetchy Water and Power system. And they are wonderful hill-climbers—clean and quiet. The 55-Sacramento (now the 1-California), one such hill-climbing route, was added in 1981, much to the relief of commuters who had to rely on breakdown-prone diesel buses until then; and the 24-Divisadero in 1983, which brought trolley coach service to Bernal Heights and the Bayview Districts. (Hydro power is still used to power Muni electric vehicles today.)

Getting back to the 33-18th and Park (now the 33-Stanyan): The line's signature was the hairpin turn from Market onto Clayton Street just south of the Haight-Ashbury, and this version of the "switchback" remains today. The 33 itself was extended in 1988 northward from its original Golden Gate Park terminal to Children's Hospital in the Richmond District. It is perhaps the most interesting line, but there are others, such as the 5/5R-Fulton, which runs along the north edge of Golden Gate Park for its entire length from Stanyan Street to Ocean Beach. It's a fast ride, especially on one of the new articulated New Flyer trolley coaches! (The 5-Fulton was one of the former Market Street Railway Co.'s

routes converted to trolley coach operation in the late 1940s.) The 5 also serves the museum area in Golden Gate Park; get off at 8th Avenue and Fulton and it's a short stroll to the De Young Museum and the California Academy of Sciences.

Then there's the 30-Stockton, which traverses the main shopping street of Chinatown, and which also skirts the edge of Fisherman's Wharf, and continues to the Marina District, terminating near the Palace of Fine Arts, the last survivor of the 1915 Panama-Pacific International Exposition. (Oddly enough, surplus trolley coaches were stored in this building in the '60s!) The coaches get extremely crowded as they pass through Chinatown.

The newest trolley coach line in San Francisco is the 31-Balboa. This route, electrified in 1992 (although trolley buses didn't actually begin running on the 31 until 1994), serves the Tenderloin, Western Addition and Richmond Districts and Lone Mountain College (now part of the University of San Francisco). In 1932, the 31 was Market Street Railway Company's last streetcar line to be built, extending only to 30th Avenue. It was also one of the last ex-MSRy streetcar lines to be converted to motor coach, in 1949. This line's most unique feature is the famous "Balboa Dip" between 22nd and 24th Avenues in the Richmond District, where a sharp grade takes buses down to 23rd Avenue and an identical climb back up to 24th. In streetcar days, cars would have to get a running start to make it to the other side! Nowadays, electric trolley buses handle the grades with ease.

Golden Gate Bridge; Twin Peaks by Muni Bus

THERE ARE SEVERAL PLACES that visitors love to visit that are reachable only by diesel bus routes. But at least they connect with rail or electric trolley bus lines in most cases.

The 28-19th Avenue line will take us to the Golden Gate Bridge. It begins at Aquatic Park, passes along Fort Mason (where, some day, the F-cars will call), and it connects with the 30-Stockton trolley coach at Van Ness and North Point. Board there, or along Lombard Street (which is a block south of Chestnut), and get off at the Toll Plaza. Coming from the other direction, it runs along busy 19th Avenue in the southwestern half of the city, which crosses the N-Judah and L-Taraval streetcar lines and parallels the M-Ocean View for a few blocks. The 28's southern terminal is the Daly City BART Station.

The 37-Corbett bus takes people from the 17th and Castro area (diagonally opposite the F-Line terminal) to Parkridge and Burnett. It's a short walk to Twin Peaks.

The Cliff House is reached by riding the 38R-Geary Rapid from downtown (Union Square area) to the end of the line and walking downhill. Here, too, are Land's End, the Seal Rocks and the ruins of the old Sutro Baths, which burned down in 1966. One can continue walking down the hill to Cabrillo and La Playa and catch a 5-Fulton (or 5R-Fulton Rapid) trolley coach back toward town. The condos in this area replaced Playland-at-the-Beach in the 1970s.

BART

BART (Bay Area Rapid Transit) is the first of the new breed of subway systems to be built in the United States. It was built as a result of a 1962 regional bond issue, approved by voters in San Francisco, Alameda and Contra Costa Counties. The original 72-mile system consisted of two trunk routes: Concord/Daly City, through downtown San Francisco, and Richmond/Fremont. It opened in stages in the East Bay beginning September 11, 1972. Service within San Francisco began in late 1973, and systemwide service commenced in 1974. Gradually, it has expanded service into San Mateo County, opening to San Francisco International Airport and Millbrae on June 22, 2003. The Concord Line has been extended deeper into East Contra Costa County to Pittsburg/Bay Point, and on May 10, 1997, the Dublin/Pleasanton line started up. Total mileage is now up to 104. Extensions to Warm Springs (Fremont) and San Jose are under construction or in the planning stage.

Construction of BART began in 1964 with building of the Concord Test Track and in earnest in 1966. Construction was fascinating. In building the Transbay Tube, 57 identical prefabricated concrete-and-steel sections, containing two bores each, were constructed at a nearby shipyard and floated and sunk into place. In 1967, BART began construction of the double-bore Market Street Subway, requiring intricate shifting of streetcar traffic around station sites. The Market Street Subway was finished in 1971.

The initial rolling stock, built by Rohr Corp., an aerospace company, became an instant icon, with slant-nose "A" cars and cabless "B"-cars. While this provided a sleek, futuristic look, the decision restrict-

BART opened in stages beginning in 1972. A train arrives at Walnut Creek on the Concord/Pittsburg line on July 21, 2006. Today, BART carries 446,000 riders each weekday–small, compared to New York or Chicago or Washington, but essential to the transportation needs of the far-flung Bay Area. *Peter Ehrlich* (A picture of one of the iconic shovel-nose A cars can be found in Chapter 1.)

ed train lengths and the ability to adjust service during the day. Two orders of cars built in 1985 and 1994 introduced flat-front cab ends, where such cars can be used in mid-train to break up trains during non-rush hours. Nevertheless, the shovel-nose fleet maintains its iconic status and will continue to do so until total fleet replacement occurs sometime in the late 2010s.

The fleet was odd, too, with respect to track gauge: 5'-6". While this resulted in the smoothest-riding subway car fleet in the United States, it set BART off from other systems which used standard gauge (4'-8½") for more flexibility. The cars were built of brushed aluminum. There were three builders: Rohr (for the A an B cars in 1972), Alstom/Soferval (C1) and Morrison-Knudsen (C2). A new "Fleet Of The Future", being built by Bombardier, started service in January 2018.

Riding BART is fun. In the Transbay Tube and at many other locations, particularly along or in the middle of freeways, trains reach speeds of nearly 80 mph. There are many elevated stretches, and one can see wonderful panoramas of San Francisco and the rest of the East Bay at many spots. Except for the SFO Airport/Pittsburg-Bay Point line, where rush-hour trains operate every five minutes, headways on each line are set at 15-minute intervals all day. At night and on weekends, trains run every 20 minutes. Fares are distance-based, using a mag-netic-stripe ticket for both entry and exit. Recently, a contactless "Smart Card"–called "Clipper," which is also usable on other Bay Area transit systems, including Muni–was added.

Compared to cities such as Atlanta and Chicago, whose airport fares are the same as other points on their systems, the BART fare from SFO to downtown San Francisco is extraordinarily expensive. But it's a very fast ride. Seats are cushy and comfortable.

Riding BART is like a cross between a regular subway and, say, Metro-North Railroad in the New York City area. It's well used, with over 446,000 riders a weekday.[1] During the period following the 1989 Loma Prieta Earthquake, when the Bay Bridge was damaged and closed, BART operated 24/7, but normally, service ends just after midnight.

Light Rail and Vintage Cars in San Jose

IF WE TAKE CALTRAIN from San Francisco to San Jose, we can then ride Santa Clara [County] Valley Transportation Authority (VTA) light rail, a 42.2-mile light rail system, whose hub is in downtown San Jose. Service extends from Mountain View through Sunnyvale and Santa Clara to north San Jose and over to Alum Rock. Trains also operate to Santa Teresa and Almadén in south San Jose and to Campbell. Headways are every 15-30 minutes.

Streetcars in San Jose

(*above*) A train of LRVs arrives at San Jose Diridon Station enroute to Campbell on October 1, 2005. Connections to Caltrain, the Peninsula commuter train, are made here. (*below*) San Jose Railroads Birney 143 operates in Kelley Park in 1998. The car was restored by the non-profit San Jose Rail and Trolley Corp., which also restored all of the cars occasionally operated on the Valley Transportation Agency (VTA). *Both photos, Peter Ehrlich*

Purchasing a Day Pass from a ticket machine allows one to ride the bus system as well.

The San Jose fleet consists of 100 low-floor cars built by Kinkisharyo in 2003. One or two car consists are most frequent, but three-car trains are occasionally operated. Similar cars operate on New Jersey Transit's Newark City Subway and Hudson-Bergen lines.

San Jose also operates a fleet of vintage cars, usually at Christmastime. Two of these were completely restored from chicken coops, but were at one time original San Jose trolleys, by the non-profit San Jose Rail and Trolley Corp. at Kelley Park. Another is a W2 from Melbourne, Australia. Finally, there is a Peter Witt from Milan, Italy, converted to a double-ender.

Over in Kelley Park in east San Jose is a delightful re-creation of what San Jose was like at the turn of the [20th] century. There is a restored hotel, firehouse, houses and shops, and a model of the giant pyramid-shaped structure that illuminated downtown San Jose until it blew over in a windstorm. A trolley runs around the grounds, and recently was extended into the park itself. Three cars—San Jose Railroads 124, an ex-Fresno Birney, and a former Oporto, Portugal, single-trucker provide service. Take VTA bus #73 from downtown. The park and the Trolley Barn are open Thursday through Monday.

Western Railway Museum

THE WESTERN RAILWAY MUSEUM, located at Rio Vista Junction on State Highway 12, and roughly midway between the Bay Area and Sacramento, is well worth a visit, and a ride along a restored stretch of the old Sacramento Northern interurban line is a must!

The Western Railway Museum's origins date to 1946, when a group of trolley enthusiasts saved an Oakland streetcar from the cutting torch. Over the next 20 years, the collection got larger and in 1966 the site at Rio Vista Junction opened.

Gradually, the line, which was once part of the Sacramento Northern interurban, was extended both north and south, and electrified some four miles south to Gum Grove. Ultimately, electrification will reach all the way to Montezuma, at the north bank of Carquinez Strait.

WRM has an extensive fleet of cars from San Francisco, Oakland's Key System (including two 1887-vintage wooden Manhattan elevated cars that ran in the East Bay during World War II), Sacramento Northern and other locales. The Museum recently restored two important exhibits: Muni PCC 1016, the first of the 25 PCCs of 1951/52,

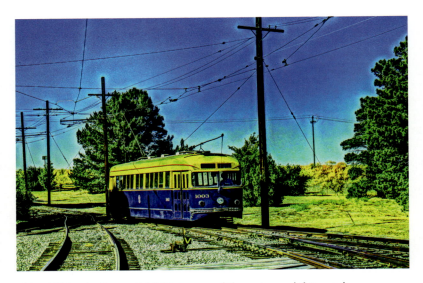

Muni "Magic Carpet" 1003 is one of the prize exhibits at the Western Railway Museum. It was built in 1939 and has the PCC body style, but isn't a true PCC. This phzoto was taken in September 2007. HDR image. *Peter Ehrlich*

and a sister to Muni's own 1040; and Sacramento Northern interurban motor 1005, built in 1912 by Holman Car Co. in San Francisco. Other Muni cars include K-Type 178, which ran in San Francisco between 1981 and 1986; "Magic Carpet" 1003, built in 1939 and a PCC-lookalike; and Boeing LRV 1258. There are also two trams which operated in Muni's Trolley Festivals in the 1980s: Blackpool "Boat" 226, a sister to Muni's "Boat" 228, which operated during the 1983 and 1984 Trolley Festivals, and Melbourne W2 648, sister to Muni's 496, which ran from 1983 to 1986 in San Francisco.

The Museum also has one of the best-stocked bookstores of any trolley museum, with numerous DVDs and other memorabilia for sale.

The Western Railway Museum is now accessible by public transportation (weekdays only). We can take Amtrak's Capitol Corridor from the Bay Area to Suisun City-Fairfield, then a Delta Breeze bus to the Museum. Both agencies have web sites; check for schedules.

SMART

SONOMA-MARIN AREA RAIL TRANSIT, or SMART, began operations on August 25, 2017, along much of the lower segment of the old Northwestern Pacific line. NWP was a subsidiary of the Southern Pacific Railroad, and was notable in the early part of the 20th Century for operating an extensive third-rail electric commuter train system in Marin County, serving various North Bay suburbs of San Francisco such as Sausalito, Mill Valley, San Rafael, San Anselmo, and others.

In its heyday, NWP ran all the way to Eureka on the north coast of California, some 270 miles north of San Francisco. Most of the line south of Willits was allowed to deteriorate and become impassable, but sporadic freight operations continued for several more years, until the SMART district was created by the state legislature in 2002 to bring in a new passenger rail service. In 2008, voters of Marin and Sonoma counties approved a ¼-sent sales tax to fund construction of SMART. This tax increase, plus other funding sources, raised approximately $428 million to construct the first segment of the line, from downtown San Rafael to Sonoma County Airport, a 43-mile run. The full

SMART

SMART (Sonoma-Marin Area Rail Transit) opened on August 25, 2017 on a 43-mile stretch from San Rafael to Santa Rosa. (*top right*) Nippon Sharyo DMU 111 lays over at San Rafael. (*right*) Some of the wetlands and waterfowl around Novato that can only be seen from the train. Both photos, September 11, 2017. *Peter Ehrlich*

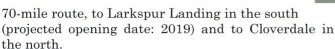

70-mile route, to Larkspur Landing in the south (projected opening date: 2019) and to Cloverdale in the north.

SMART uses Nippon Sharyo-built diesel multiple-unit (DMU) trains, two cars long. These are virtually identical to the ones used in Toronto's Airport service. The even-numbered car (facing north) has a snack bar; the odd-numbered one, a lavatory. At the moment, the schedule is erratic, with a big gap in service during the late morning. But the ride is quite comfortable, and reaches speeds up to 79 mph.

Freight service is maintained by the Northwestern Pacific, under the aegis of North Coast Railroad Authority. At stations along the route, gauntlet tracks are in place for freight operations past the stations.

The line is very scenic, especially when traveling through the wetlands areas of Novato. This is scenery one cannot see while driving on paralleling US 101.

Sacramento

THE SACRAMENTO LIGHT RAIL SYSTEM, called RT Metro, opened its first line from downtown to Watt/I-80 in northeast Sacramento, on March 12, 1987. It expanded to the east side later that year. A new South line began service in 2003, and the East line was extended out to Folsom in 2005. A spur to Amtrak in downtown opened the same year. We can take Amtrak's Capitol Corridor trains from the Bay Area to Sacramento. The routes, except for the in-town portions, were largely built along existing or former railroad rights-of-way.

RT Metro rosters 36 cars built by Siemens, 40 cars from CAF USA, and 21 former San Jose UTDC LRVs. These run in trains of two to four cars in length. Headways are every 15 minutes throughout the day. The two light rail routes carried about 51,000 riders each weekday in 2012[2]–another instance where instituting light rail has produces large ridership gains. However, recently, ridership has plummeted to 41,300 weekday riders[3], probably caused by a number of factors, including fare increases, service cuts, and a perception that the region's homeless population makes the system unsafe.

(above) A train crosses Capitol Mall in 2002, with the handsome California State Capitol providing the backdrop. Sacramento's two light rail routes carried nearly 51,000 riders each weekday, but that number has dropped considerably in just four years, despite some expansion. *Peter Ehrlich*

A new northward extension, which will eventually reach Sacramento Airport, is under construction or undergoing preliminary engineering, and the South Line was extended to Cosumnes River College in 2015.

RT Metro also has a vintage car in its fleet, PG&E 35 (ex-San Jose Railroads 129), which it uses for special occasions.

Any visit to Sacramento should also include a visit to the fabulous California State Railroad Museum, which has, among other artifacts, the last Southern Pacific cab-forward steam locomotive in the United States, and a sleeping car exhibit that really makes one feel like you're riding in an old-time sleeper from the 1920s! Old Town Sacramento abuts the museum, and is a wonderful area to walk around.

Los Angeles

BUT WAIT! THERE'S MORE IN THE GOLDEN STATE! Visit Los Angeles and San Diego for more urban rail experiences.

Los Angeles County Metropolitan Transportation Authority (LACMTA) operates three light rail lines and two subway routes. The heaviest is the Blue Line, from downtown L. A. to Long Beach, much of it over the old Pacific Electric right-of-way. The Blue Line, which opened in 1990, has the highest single-line ridership of any California streetcar/light rail-based line–about 90,000 weekday riders.[4] There is also the Green Line, which runs east and west across the Century Freeway (I-105) corridor in south Los Angeles, between Norwalk and El Segundo/Redondo Beach. It comes close to, but does not enter, Los Angeles International Airport–a big mistake, which may get rectified in the future. Because of two recent major extensions of the Gold Line and the Expo Line, weekday ridership of the Los Angeles light rail system has catapulted to second place in the United States, with 211,700 riders, behind only Boston.[5] Not bad for car-crazy Los Angeles, which hadn't seen electric rail transit since 1963.

The Gold Line was built in stages: First, the line from Union Station to Pasadena was opened in 2003, followed by the route to East Los Angeles, which began service in November 2009, and the extension from Pasadena to Azusa, which opened in March 2016. Extensions are planned from Azusa to Montclair, and later for the East Los Angeles leg. Much of the line on the Pasadena/Azusa end was formerly used by Santa Fe Railway's Super Chief and other name trains.

The 8.5-mile Expo Line (also known as the Aqua Line), which opened on April 28, 2012, joins with the Blue Line at Washington/Flower in downtown, then heads

(below) Sacramento runs an ex-San Jose vintage car for special occasions. PG&E 35, similar to cars that ran here until the late 1940s, operates on K Street in 1991. This car was formerly San Jose Railroads 129, and was acquired by the Sacramento transit agency, RT Metro, in the mid-1990s *Peter Ehrlich*

San Jose and Sacramento Scenes

(*this column, top*) San Jose's Valley Transportation Authority (VTA) operates its fleet of vintage cars during the Christmas season only. Here is San Jose & Santa Clara Interurban 1, running on the San Jose Transit Mall, on December 10, 2005. VTA rosters three other cars, including trams from Milan and Melbourne. (*lower*) San Jose began its vintage car operations with high hopes and two restored trolleys on November 18, 1988, just a year after its light rail system began operation. San Jose Railroads 129 is about to be passed by a train of original UTDC LRVs on Vintage Car Opening Day. 129, and some of the LRVs, are now in Sacramento, and the rest of the UTDCs were sold to Salt Lake City. (*top right*) Peninsular Railway 73 crosses S. 1st and San Fernando on its first day of service, May 12, 1989. St. Joseph's Cathedral is receiving a new copper dome. Alas, budget woes have restricted vintage car operations in San Jose. *All photos, Peter Ehrlich*

(*right column, upper middle*) The Gold Line terminates at the Amtrak Station. CAF car 222's in the lead here. (*lower middle*) A train of ex-San Jose UTDCs passes a sidewalk café on the K Street Mall. These cars are the only "boomer" LRVs, and 21 were acquired by RT Metro in 2003, but not put in service until 2015. (*rightl*) A two-car Siemens train is at the Cosumnes River College Station. Car 112's shrinkwrapped to hide its original (and now decrepit) paint scheme from 1987. This part of the Blue Line opened in 2015. These Sacramento photos were taken on December 15, 2017.
All photos, Peter Ehrlich

Los Angeles: Light Rail since 1990

For car-crazy Los Angeles, which ripped up its passenger rail systems by 1963, the turnabout to re-embrace rail transit since the early 1990s has been quite remarkable.

(left) Los Angeles painted two of its Blue Line Nippon Sharyo LRVs in commemorative Pacific Electric colors to celebrate its own 10th Anniversary in 2000. One of them is shown in Long Beach in 2003. *(below left)* A Siemens Gold Line train heads toward East Los Angeles on the 1st Street Bridge, which PCCs had crossed over 45 years earlier. The East L.A. extension had just opened, and the date is November 16, 2009. *(below)* The original Gold Line opened in 2003 and runs through Pasadena. A brand-new Breda train stops at the spectacular Memorial Park Station in downtown Pasadena on June 16, 2008. *All photos, Peter Ehrlich*

west along Exposition Blvd. (south of the Santa Monica Freeway) out to Culver City, principally along the right-of-way of the old Pacific Electric Santa Monica Air Line. On May 20, 2016, the Expo Line was extended into Santa Monica. It's then a short walk to the Pacific Ocean and such attractions as the Santa Monica Pier.

More extensions to the light rail system are planned. A new north-south Crenshaw Blvd. line, to connect with the Expo Line, is now under construction, and extension of both this line and the Green Line into Los Angeles International Airport (LAX) is in the planning stages. Finally, construction has begun on a plan to continue building the light rail subway from 7th and Flower to Union Station. This would allow for through-routing of the Blue Line with the Pasadena end of the Gold Line, and the Expo Line with the East Los Angeles leg.

Nippon Sharyo, Siemens and AnsaldoBreda built the rolling stock for L.A.'s light rail lines. Kinkisharyo is now building the next batch of cars for the existing lines and many extensions that are proposed or under construction.

The Red and Purple Line subways run from Union Station through downtown L. A., then out Wilshire to Vermont Avenue, where the Purple Line continues westward to Western Avenue, while the Red Line curves north under Vermont and west under Hollywood Blvd., and then makes a fast run through the Santa Monica Mountains to Universal City and North Hollywood. The Purple Line will be extended westward to Westwood, and possibly the Pacific Ocean, in the future.

There is also an extensive commuter rail system, called Metrolink, serving Los Angeles, Ventura, Orange, San Bernardino, and Riverside Counties.

(this column, top to bottom) An inbound Blue Line train and a Union Pacific freight train approach Florence Station on what was once the Pacific Electric's four-track main line to Long Beach and other south Los Angeles Basin points. August 26, 2011. *Peter Ehrlich*. A train approaches Grand Avenue on the Blue Line. *August 26, 2011. Peter Ehrlich*. At the west (El Segundo) end of the Green Line, the route leaves the freeway median. Siemens 218 approaches the El Segundo/Nash Station. The sculpture marks the presence of the aviation industry in El Segundo. August 2, 2005. *Salaam Allah*

(*this column, top to bottom*) Siemens 246 breaks through a banner during a VIP run on April 27, 2012, a day before service began on the new Expo Line. *Mark Clifford/ Research Library & Archives, LACMTA.* A new Kinkisharyo train leaves Downtown Santa Monica on May 26. 2016, just six days after the Expo Line "reached the sea". Santa Monica Pier and other attractions are a short walk away. *Peter Ehrlich.* A train of AnsaldoBreda cars leaves Azusa Downton Station on the Gold Line Extension. The old Santa Fe Azusa Depot is in the center of the picture, above the train. May 26, 2016. This extension opened on March 5, 2016. *Peter Ehrlich*

Both of these 2016 extensions resulted in a tremendous spike in Los Angeles light rail ridership.

And don't forget Angel's Flight, a funicular in the downtown area.

San Diego

To get to San Diego, we take Amtrak's frequent Pacific Surfliner trains, for more riding aboard the nation's first new light rail service: The San Diego Trolley! The Trolley meets us at the beautifully-restored Spanish-style Santa Fe Depot in downtown San Diego. It's one of the most convenient transfer arrangements in any U. S. city.

San Diego Trolley was the first new-generation streetcar system in the United States. Its first line was built entirely with state, county and local funds—another first for recent mass transportation projects in the U. S. The system's total length is now 53½ miles. It's part of the San Diego Metropolitan Transit System.

The line from downtown to the Mexican Border at Tijuana (actually, San Ysidro) opened on July 16, 1981. After leaving "Center City", it runs along the rail alignment of the old San Diego & Arizona Eastern, an SP subsidiary. This line is now known as the Blue Line. Freight service is done at night by the San Diego & Imperial Valley.

Extensions included a new East Line, opened in 1986, occurred in 1989, 1990 and 1995. This route is now called the Orange Line. Bayside opened in 1990. originally as part of the Orange Line. It's now served by the Green Line.

Service to Mission Valley began in 1997, and the rest of Mission Valley, including to San Diego State University, opened in 2006. This route is named the Green Line.

Ridership on the three San Diego Trolley lines average 98,000 a weekday in 2011[6], but the bulk of the riders are carried on the original line from Center City (as downtown San Diego is called) to San Ysidro/Tijuana. In 2016, system ridership increased to 114,500.[7] This makes the Trolley the fifth-busiest LRT system in the United States.

San Diego has 52 SD100s, from 1993-1998; 11 S70 low-floor cars from Siemens, vintage 2004; and 65 somewhat shorter Siemens S70s, built between 2011 and 2014. The original Siemens-Duewag U2s, 71 of which were built in four orders between 1981 and 1990, were retired in 2015. The 11 3000-series can only run on the Green Line, because of their length. The SD100s are usually found in the middle of trains, sandwiched in between low-floor cars. Four of the U2s have gone to trolley museums.

Current service patterns have both the Blue and Orange Lines terminating in downtown San Diego, with the Green Line running along the Bayside Line from 12th and Imperial, out to Old Town, then into Mission Valley to Santee. Daytime service is every 15 minutes on all routes, with only the Blue Line seeing a ramped-up rush-hour service.

Expansion is in the works. The 11-mile Mid-Coast Extension to UC San Diego, in La Jolla, is under construction, and is slated for a 2021 opening. It will become an extension of the Blue Line when finished.

A new historic streetcar service started in August 2011, using PCC cars, one of which once ran on Muni. The first car, San Diego 529, the former Muni 1122, is now in service, which runs Tuesdays, Thursdays and weekends on a clockwise loop [see Chapter 13]. Additional PCCs for the "Silver Line" loop came from Philadelphia and Newark, and are undergoing restoration by the non-profit San Diego Vintage Trolley organization, which has space for its restorations in the San Diego Trolley Shops at 12th and Imperial. United Transportation Systems in Pennsylvania restored ex-Newark 10, a sister to Muni's "Brookville" PCC 1078, for the San Diego group. That car, is now San Diego 530, and is now in service. The third car will be 531, formerly SEPTA 2186.

WITH ELECTRIC RAIL TRANSIT SYSTEMS operation in every major city, and with three of them within the top five nationally in terms of ridership, California is indeed the Golden State for electric traction!

References:

1. BART Ridership data, (2016, 4th Quarter figures). Source: Wikipedia, "List of United States Rapid Transit Systems by Ridership," <https://en.wikipedia.org/wiki/List_of_United_States_rapid_transit_systems_by_ridership>,, accessed February 20, 2018.
2. Sacramento Regional Transit Facts and Figures Report, May 2012. <http://www.sacrt.com/rtfactsheets.stm#N_1_>, accessed May 11, 2012.
3. Sacramento RT Metro ridership data. (2016, 4th Quarter figures). Source: Wikipedia, "List of United States Light Rail Systems by Ridership," <https://en.wikipedia.org/wiki/List_of_United_States_light_rail_systems_by_ridership>, accessed February 20, 2018.
4. LACMTA ridership data, Service Performance Analysis Unit, July 2011. <http://thesource.metro.net/2011/08/15/metro-ridership-update-systemwide-up-over-a-year-ago-and-new-record-month-for-gold-line-but-bus-numbers-remain-flat/>, accessed August 22, 2011.
5. LACMTA ridership data. (2016, 4th Quarter figures). Source: Wikipedia, "List of United States Light Rail Systems by Ridership," <https://en.wikipedia.org/wiki/List_of_United_States_light_rail_systems_by_ridership>, accessed February 20, 2018.
6. American Public Transit Association (APTA) report, January-March, 2011. <http://www.apta.com/resources/statistics/Documents/Ridership/2011_q1_ridership_APTA.pdf>, accessed July 13, 2011.
7. San Diego Trolley ridership data. (2016, 4th Quarter figures). Source: Wikipedia, "List of United States Light Rail Systems by Ridership," <https://en.wikipedia.org/wiki/List_of_United_States_light_rail_systems_by_ridership>, accessed February 20, 2018.

San Diego: First "New Wave" Surface Electric Rail System!

The San Diego Trolley was the first new light rail system in the U. S., opening in 1981.

(*this column, top to bottom*) Easy transfers are made at the Santa Fe Depot between the Trolley and Coaster and Amtrak trains, such as in this 2009 scene. Siemens-Duewag SD-100 2022 loads passengers at the replica San Diego & Imperial Valley depot in Lemon Grove on the East (Orange) Line on February 4, 1997 High-tension wires run along much of the South (Blue) line. A train of original Duewag U2s stops at National City 24th Street on November 17, 2009, headed for Center City These pioneering, iconic LRVs were retired by 2015. *All photos, Peter Ehrlich*

(*this column, top to bottom*) New low-floor car 3010 stops at the subterranean San Diego State University Station on the Mission Valley (Green) Line, April 10, 2008. S70 4057 arrives the San Ysidro/Tijuana terminal of the Blue Line on September 28, 2016. The second PCC to go in service on the Silver Line loop service was 530, formerly Newark 10 (and identical to Muni 1078). It's at Fifth Avenue Station in Center City on September 27, 2016. *All photos, Peter Ehrlich*

Little Rock, Arkansas, is one small city whose elected officials and transportation planners studied San Francisco's F-Line and decided to introduce a historic trolley service in their city. River Rail double-truck Birney replica 410 turns from 2nd Street onto Spring. The old U. S. Bankruptcy Court is behind the streetcar. Behind it is the Metropolitan Bank tower. This car was built by Gomaco using parts from Milan, Italy, and is air-conditioned. Taken November 13, 2004, 12 days after River Rail opened. The system is now called Rock Region Metro Streetcar. *Peter Ehrlich*

Chapter 12 - Vintage Cars (and Modern Ones) in Other U. S. Cities

"A girl can be gay
In a classy coupé,
In a taxi all can be jolly,
But the girl worth your while
Is the one who can smile
As you're taking her home on the trolley."

– Old early 20th century rhyme

SAN FRANCISCO'S F-LINE may be the most successful historic streetcar line in the United States in terms of fun, ridership and general appeal. But it is by no means the first. There are many other cities that operate, or have done so, or are planning new vintage and modern streetcar systems.

New Orleans

NEW ORLEANS' ST. CHARLES STREETCAR is to the Big Easy as the cable cars are to the City by the Bay. It has been in generally continuous operation along its original route since 1835, when the St. Charles and Carrollton Railway introduced horsecar service, later converting to steam-powered trams. Today, the fleet consists of 35 oft-rebuilt Perley Thomas streetcars from 1923/24.

The St. Charles Streetcar is world-renowned. It passes through some of the most wonderful neighborhoods in the Crescent City–the Garden District, Uptown, Riverbend and South Carrollton, running primarily on grassy "neutral ground" private rights-of-way lined throughout with stately oak trees, and serving Audubon Park, the Zoo and two universities along the way. Its dark green trolleys, with their mellow gear and motor sounds, blend in magnificently with their environment. Akin to the cable cars, the St. Charles Streetcar is designated a National Historic Landmark, and its cars are grandfathered by the Americans with Disabilities Act (ADA), which means that, because they are historic vehicles operating on their original lines, they don't have to be modified for wheelchair usage.

Things were not always that peaceful in New Orleans. In 1964, New Orleans Public Service, Inc. (NOPSI) was operating Canal and St. Charles, the last two streetcar lines in New Orleans. NOPSI wanted to abandon Canal, but its closure was hard-fought by the citizenry. Ultimately, NOPSI agreed to rebuild its 35 best Perley Thomas cars (originally, there were 73) and move them to St. Charles. Time passed; eventually, conductors were dropped (1972), and ownership passed to the new Regional Transit Authority (RTA) in 1983. In 1988, with the Federal government's help, the entire line was completely rebuilt from cars to track structure, giving the line a continued presence.

In the meantime, in August 1988, RTA opened a new standard-gauge Riverfront Line, using three former 900-series Perley Thomas cars brought back from museums, and three ex-Melbourne, Australia, W2s. Four of these opened the line, and the other two–a Perley and a W2–were added in 1990, when the line was double-tracked. This new line served the French Quarter and the new Riverwalk shopping complex, but was detached from St. Charles because of track gauge differences (St. Charles is 5'-2½"). The W2s provided ADA access. They were also the only non-native streetcars ever to run in service in the Crescent City.

In 1997, RTA decided to broad-gauge Riverfront and the six standard-gauge cars became surplus. The three W2s went to Memphis, and one of the Perleys joined Muni's F-Line fleet in 1998 on a long-term lease [see Chapters 5 and 8]. The other two Perleys are still in New Orleans, but have no place to go. They can't be added to the St. Charles fleet, because the 35 cars there have "protected" landmark status, and they can't run on Riverfront any more, because they're not ADA-accessible, nor are they broad-gauge. So they are stored.

In their place, Carrollton Shops built six new Perley Thomas lookalikes and rebuilt an original 1923 car with a special setup for wheelchair users on the Riverfront Line. Although they may look like the 1923 cars overall, these have brand-new trucks and chopper controls, motors and other electronics. Tracks were laid on Lower Canal Street to allow Riverfront cars to reach Carrollton Shops via the St. Charles Line.

On April 18, 2004, streetcars returned to Canal Street with a vengeance. 24 new Perley Thomas look-

New Orleans and Portland—

Streetcars in the Big Easy

All photos on four pages by Peter Ehrlich.

The St. Charles Line has been in near-continuous operation since 1835. It is one of two rolling National Historic Landmarks in the U. S. (San Francisco's cable cars are the other.)

(*right*) Perley Thomas 923 is at Riverbend, where St. Charles ends and meets S. Carrollton. This scene was taken in the NOPSI era on September 15, 1972, and NOPSI had just converted the cars to one-man operation.

The classic American trolley line. New Orleans' Perley Thomas streetcars were built in 1923, and the line's 35 cars have been rebuilt several times over the years.
(left) In 2004, iconic car 972 passes stately homes along an oak-lined, grassy "neutral ground." (*below left*) 945 nears St. Charles/Foucher during a horrendous rainstorm. April 11, 2013. (*below*) 972, the highest-numbered Perley, switches back at S. Carrollton and Plum. This is a Sepia-tone image, but the car is in full color! March 8, 2017.

Scenes of Riverfront, Canal, Loyola and Rampart/St. Claude and more St. Charles are on the next three pages.

(facing page, right) Loyola opened in 2013. When the line opened, it operated to Riverfront. It features these massive shelters like the one at Union Passenger Terminal, where 2011 is taking its layover. April 9, 2013. (*far right*) The line out Rampart Street started up on October 3, 2016, and was through-routed with Loyola. Von Dullen 2023 is headed out to St. Claude/Elysian Fields in this March 6, 2017 view at Rampart/St. Philip.

Two Cities Where Streetcars Work Well

(above) Two of the original Riverfront cars, a repatriated Perley and a Melbourne W2, pass at Conti Siding on February 22, 1989. Jax Brewery is in the background. (top right) Homebuilt Perley lookalike 458 passes Jackson Square and St. Louis Cathedral on April 9, 2017. (right) Streetcars returned to Canal on April 18, 2004. HDR image from 2017. (below right) After Hurricane Katrina's devastation, New Orleans got Canal and Riverfront going in December 2005 with borrowed Perleys. 947 turns onto Canal from Riverfront on January 11, 2006. (below) A branch from Canal out to City Park opened on the same day streetcars returned to Canal. 2013 lays over in City Park on April 10, 2013. That's the General Beauregard statue behind the streetcar.

New Orleans and Portland—

New Orleans and Portland are two American cities which operate successful full-time streetcar systems – one with traditional old cars from America's great trolley era (and modern replica heritage cars), and one with modern, low-floor versions. plus light rail. Both get the job done – moving large masses of passengers in comfort and safety.

Streetcars in the Crescent City!

More Canal Street scenes!

(*above*) New Orleans residents and streetcar fans celebrate as Von Dullen car 2004, the first car, leaves Canal Station in the wee hours of the morning of April 18, 2004. After 40 years, streetcar service has returned to the Crescent City's main street! (*top left*) The meet between new and old takes place at Canal and Carondelet. Perley 900 passes outbound Von Dullen 2003 here on April 9, 2013. HDR image. (*left*) Night scene with Canal car 2017, headed out to City Park, at Canal/Bourbon. April 10, 2013. (*below left*) For three years, while the Von Dullens were in rehab following Katrina, Perleys ran all service on Canal, Canal/City Park and Riverfront. Here's car 900 passing a sidewalk café on N. Carrollton. August 10, 2008. The red cars would return by the end of the year. (*below*) Between 2013 and 2017, Canal Station stabled both types of cars, This was because of the rebuilding of the outer part of the St. Charles tracks, and then the refurbishment. of Carrollton Station. 954 and a slew of Von Dullens are inside Canal Station on November 17, 2013.

Two Cities Where Streetcars Work Well

Two scenes on Rampart/St. Claude, and one on Loyola.

(*above left*) Loyola/Rampart car 2020 is turning onto Rampart, heading out to Elysian Fields. The Saenger Theater, built in 1925, recently was completely refurbished. 2020 is passing Louis Armstrong Park, heading westbound on Rampart. The *faux* clerestory roof on the Von Dullens hides air-conditioning units. The doors in the middle are used by wheelchair-bound riders. The Riverfront Perley lookalikes have similar doors, but are not air-conditioned. (*below left*) Loyola has a rather wide "neutral ground", but, unlike St Charles and Canal, tracks run beside it, as 2017 is doing at Tulane Street on November 17, 2013. (*below right*) Grinder 29 was built in 1895, and converted to work service in the late 1910s. It's inside Carrollton Station on July 5, 2017. It's the last Ford, Bacon & Davis-designed trolley in existence, and was recently rebuilt by RTA.

More St. Charles

(far left) 971 is on an Electric Railroaders Association charter at Riverbend on July 5, 2017. The author's automobile is on the left. (left) 910 had just returned from remanufacturing. It's passing the landmark Loyola University tower on February 8, 1992.

New Orleans and Portland—

Streetcars in the Rose City

All photos, two pages, by Peter Ehrlich.

Portland Streetcar, the first modern streetcar system in America opened in 2001, and has been credited with making the city a more environmentally-friendly place to live, work and play. The reason: Spurring transit-oriented development. There are two lines, and plans for more. Also in Portland: MAX Light Rail, whose successful system began in 1986 and now has the fourth-highest ridership for a light rail system in the United States.

(*above*) The sign on the building in the center of the picture implores residents to "Go by Streetcar." Indeed, the Portland Streetcar has aided the transformation of a once-gritty warehouse district into a modern mecca where residents live and take the streetcar to work or play. Photo of Skoda/Inekon 005 at NW 11th Avenue/Lovejoy taken on October 8, 2012. Portland Streetcar opened in 2001. (*left*) New housing developments have followed Portland Streetcar wherever it goes. These new condo buildings were under construction in 2009, along the Willamette River, just after the line opened its second extension south of downtown. Car 010, one of the newer Inekon trolleys, makes the turn at SW Moody and Lowell. (*below left*) For a time, Portland Streetcar operated two of the Council Crest replica trolleys on its line on weekends. 514 lays over at the Portland State University terminal in 2004. (*below*) Portland Vintage Trolley had four Council Crest replica cars built by Gomaco in 1991. They had PCC trucks, motors and controls. Car 514 crosses the Steel Bridge on the MAX route on February 15, 1992. HDR image. Unfortunately, budget cuts forced reduced service and eventual elimination. Two cars now run on the Willamette Shore Trolley, and two went to St. Louis.

Council Crest Replica Trolleys

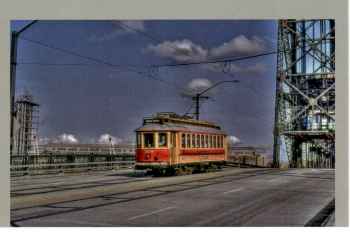

Two Cities Where Streetcars Work Well

Portland Streetcar Expansion

In 2012, Portland Streetcar opened its first major new line across the Willamette River. The Central Loop line was ultimately completed in 2015, when the fabulous new Tilikum Crossing Bridge opened.

(*right*) Inekon 010 crosses the Broadway Bridge on October 8, 2012. (*below*) With the opening of the Tilikum Bridge on September 12, 2015, the Central Loop line was now complete, and cars ran as A-Loop (clockwise) and B-Loop (counter-clockwise). United Streetcar 024 leaves the stop at SW Moody/Meade as a B-Loop car, headed for the bridge.

(*above*) A night scene on the Tilikum Bridge, Opening Day, September 12, 2015.

Portland's pioneering MAX Light Rail system opened in 1986, and now comprises five lines and 60 miles.

(*left*) Two Siemens trains cross the Steel Bridge, which dates to 1912. June 19, 2006. (*below*) A Bombardier Type 1 car leads an outbound Blue Line train at Skidmore Fountain. June 18, 2006.

TriMet MAX Light Rail

alike streetcars, manufactured by Carrollton Shops and painted candy apple red, were rolled out from a new carbarn on Canal (actually, the site of the old barn) and a new era on Canal Street began. Streetcars had returned to New Orleans' main drag! Along with the traditional Cemeteries Route, a new branch to City Park and the museum there was built along North Carrollton Avenue, a street that never had trolley service. The new cars have *faux* clerestory roofs, are air-conditioned and are fully ADA accessible. They were dubbed "Von Dullens" after their designer, legendary Carrollton Shops Director of Maintenance Elmer von Dullen.

Then came the devastation wreaked by Hurricane Katrina on August 29, 2005. Canal, its carbarn and all of its new cars, plus six of the seven 1998 Riverfront cars, were completely inundated by water and rendered useless. The St. Charles fleet, however, was untouched by flooding, but their home line was badly damaged in the hurricane. What to do?

RTA received a special dispensation from the ADA under an emergency provision and transported eight non-ADA-compliant Perleys to Riverfront, and began limited Riverfront and lower Canal operations in late 2005. The return of the streetcar, regardless of form, was a symbol that the city was slowly recovering from Katrina's devastation. Full service to Canal, using the St. Charles Perleys, was restored in 2006.

Gradually, Canal dried out, St. Charles was rebuilt, and by June 2008, cars were up and running on all three lines—all of them using original 1923/24 cars. Meanwhile, Carrollton Shops, with the help of Brookville Equipment Co., started the slow process of returning the new Canal fleet back to operating condition, a task which was largely complete by late 2008. Service levels on St. Charles are robust, but the new lines have relatively infrequent service—which has recently improved, especially on Canal.

Despite having to rebuild from Katrina's damage, expansion was always in RTA's mind. A new line, Loyola, began service in January 2013. Cars operated from Union Passenger Terminal via Loyola to Canal, where they turned river bound and ended up on the eastern portion of Riverfront. Because Loyola cars had to mix with two Canal services and the Riverfront cars, service tended to be quite erratic—similar to the scheduling problems Muni's E-Embarcadero cars face.

A second new line, Rampart/St. Claude, began service on October 3, 2016. It was through-routed with Canal, providing a cross-Canal service. Immediately, schedules on Loyola improved, with both branches of Canal seeing improved headways.

Rampart/St. Claude runs east from Canal through Bywater, and past Louis Armstrong Park. At Esplanade, the street curves rightward and becomes St. Claude, and the line terminates at Elysian Fields Avenue.

Further expansion may route cars south on Elysian Fields to connect with Riverfront. In early 2018 Canal/Cemeteries cars terminated at a new outer terminal. In addition, there are dreams of linking up the St. Charles Line via South Carrollton to Canal, but it's unlikely to happen. Another idea is to build a short inbound track from Howard and Canrondelet on the St. Charles line to connect with Loyola, to be used as an emergency diversion for St. Charles cars as necessary.

There is also a proposal to build a real light rail line from downtown to the Airport.

Still, New Orleans is home to one of the finest historic streetcar lines in the world.

For pictures of New Orleans cars, see the "New Orleans and Portland—Two Cities Where Streetcars Work Well" sidebar.

Detroit

IN 1976, THE CITY OF DETROIT, in an attempt to bolster its sagging image, instituted a historic streetcar line, originally just three-fourths of a mile, along Washington Blvd. near the Renaissance Center. This was the first purpose-built vintage trolley system in the U. S. It used a number of narrow gauge, single-truck trolleys from Lisbon, Portugal, and a British double-deck car. The Detroit Citizens Railway, later known as the Detroit Downtown Trolley, endured a rather leisurely existence over the next two decades, but the city failed to really keep up interest and maintenance and the line fell into disrepair, with cars running sporadically and erratically. Ridership, which totaled 75,000 in 1979, plummeted to 3300 nearly 20 years later. The line was finally pulled up in 2003, and the cars are stored somewhere in the Detroit area.

In 2017, Detroit opened a new modern streetcar line along Woodward Avenue, dubbed the "Q-Line." See later in this chapter.

Seattle

SEATTLE's WATERFRONT STREETCAR was the brainchild of the late City Councilman George Benson. It was launched on May 29, 1982, using a number of former Melbourne, Australia W2 trams still painted in M&MTB livery and logos. It linked a number of attractions along the Waterfront and was extended into the International District in 1990. The Waterfront Streetcar was designed throughout for wheelchair access, with high level platforms meeting the flush platforms of the W2 trams. It was fully integrated into the King County Metro route and fare

Seattle, then and now

(*left*) The Waterfront Streetcar used a number of former Melbourne, Australia W2 trams (similar to San Francisco's 496) an a route skirting Seattle's very vibrant waterfront and alongside the doomed Alaskan Way freeway structure. Controversy over the need to move the terminal caused the line to cease operations in 2005. In this shot, car 482 heads north. The new Seattle Seahawks football stadium lies in the distance. (*below left*) The South Lake Union Streetcar, which opened in late 2007, serves many University of Washington research facilities and supporting businesses all along its route, which connects to the downtown retail shopping area. This scene is at the downtown terminal, with the iconic Monorail from 1962. November 13, 2008. (below) The First Hill Streetcar line opened in February 2016. Its Inekon Trio low-floor cars operate under wire upgrade, but use battery power heading toward Pioneer Square, as 402 is doing in this March 24, 2016, photo at Broadway/Pike. An outbound car is in the distance. *All photos, Peter Ehrlich*

structure system. The carbarn was located at the north end of the line.

In 2005, a bureaucratic tussle broke out between the Seattle Art Museum, the city and King County Metro. The Art Museum wanted the carbarn area land to create a new sculpture garden, which forced the line to search for new space for a carbarn in the Pioneer Square District. Ultimately, negotiations with the prospective landowner fell through, and the Waterfront Streetcar suspended operations indefinitely on November 18, 2005, angering hundreds of transit boosters in the Seattle area. The cars are stored near the Seattle King County Metro operating base in the SoDo (SOuth of DOwntown) District. Prospects for the return of the Waterfront Streetcar are uncertain and are contingent on replacement of the Alaskan Way viaduct freeway, which is a seismic liability. In 2016, three W2s were sold to St. Louis for the Delmar Loop Trolley organization there.

In the meantime, in 2007, Seattle Streetcar created a new modern streetcar line using Czech-built Skoda/Inekon Astra low-floor cars similar to those in Portland (see below). This line runs from Seattle's downtown shopping district in Westlake to South Lake Union, and serves a burgeoning medical tech and research area. A second 2.3-mile modern trolley line, the First Hill Streetcar, was constructed and opened in 2016. It operates from the Pioneer Square/International District up First Hill, then northward along the Broadway corridor. Six Inekon Trio low-floor trams operate on this line. Cars use normal overhead current collection uphill to Broadway, but downhill to Pioneer Square, they run on battery power.

Although its route lies generally east of the South Lake Union Streetcar, the two routes are not yet connected. That will change by about 2021, when a new First Avenue route, the "Center City Connector", will link up both routes.

Seattle finally joined the ranks of U. S. light rail cities in 2009 with the opening of Sound Transit's Link LRT line, running from downtown Seattle via the Downtown Seattle Transit Tunnel, which was originally constructed for bus use, to a station near Sea-Tac International Airport. In December 2009, Link was extended into the airport. Its first expansion north of downtown, to the U-District, opened in tunnel in 2016.

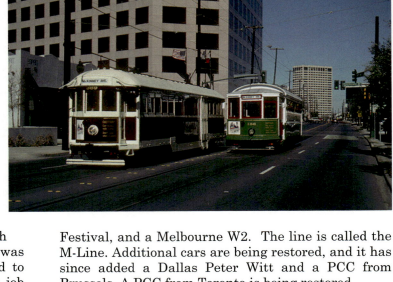

(right) Dallas's McKinney Avenue Transit Authority began operations in 1989. Two of its cars, ex-Melbourne W2 tram 369 and Dallas original Stone & Webster trolley 186, pass on McKinney Avenue in January 1990, a year after opening. The tram line has helped to redevelop and revitalize this area northeast of downtown. *Peter Ehrlich*

Seattle also operates an extensive network of trolley coaches.

Dallas

THE McKINNEY AVENUE TRANSIT AUTHORITY began operations in the summer of 1989 using four restored streetcars, two of which are Dallas natives. In the early 1980s, it was discovered that when the city of Dallas planned to repave McKinney Avenue, the previous paving job had simply covered the tracks of the original trolley line. A non-profit group with a trolley collection wondered whether a historic trolley line could be built for relatively low cost, using the original rails. It could, and was built, and opened for service in 1989.

McKinney Avenue Transit Authority (MATA) is a classic operation with cars running every day and connecting with downtown Dallas and a high-use Dallas Area Rapid Transit (DART) light rail station. It operates through a charming mixed-use district with upscale boutiques and restaurants and loops around a brand-new condo development on its east end. The rolling stock features a Dallas Stone & Webster trolley from 1913, a Birney, a car from Oporto, Portugal, which ran in the Muni 1983 Trolley Festival, and a Melbourne W2. The line is called the M-Line. Additional cars are being restored, and it has since added a Dallas Peter Witt and a PCC from Brussels. A PCC from Toronto is being restored.

Despite its name, MATA is a private, non-profit organization. It is an example of what can go right when such a group works together with a city and DART, the regional transit operator. Fares, passes and transfers are integrated with DART, and as mentioned, MATA's M-Line connects with DART at CityPlace.

Expansion of MATA further into downtown was completed in 2015 with a loop line that brings service closer to DART in downtown. With the planned introduction of single-end cars to the fleet, a turntable was installed at CityPlace, at the east end of the line, in 2011.

A word about DART: DART light rail began service on June 14, 1996, and has become one of the most successful operations in the United States. A new route opened in 2009 and was extended in December 2010. A line to Dallas/Fort Worth Airport reached the airport in 2014, and more expansions are under construction or in the planning stages. Weekday ridership is now above 100,000, making DART the sixth-busiest in the nation. The systems's total length is

(left) With the Dallas skyline in the background, a Brookville "Liberty" streetcar on the city-owned Dallas Streetcar line crosses the historic Houston Street Trinity River Bridge, using battery power. This modern streetcar line opened on April 13, 2015. High-Dynamic-Range (HDR) photo, June 29, 2015. *Peter Ehrlich*

about 93 miles.

In April 2015, the city of Dallas instituted its new Dallas Streetcar, a route from Union Station to the Dallas Methodist Hospital Center, across the Trinity River on the Houston Street Bridge. A further extension into the Bishop Arts District in Oak Cliff opened in August 2016.

The line uses four Brookville Liberty low-floor streetcars. These trams use battery power across the historic Houston Street Bridge, which is wire-free. Once the streetcar has crossed the bridge, the pantographs are raised. The cars are also recharged at the Union Station layover. DART provides operating crews and maintains them at their Central Maintenance bse.

The line is 2.45 miles long and, overall, cost a little over $100 million to construct. Service is every 20 minutes, and the fare is free. Expansion further into downtown Dallas, and a possible tie-in to the McKinney Avenue line, is planned.

Oporto, Portugal single-truck cars and a Melbourne W2 on a 2½-mile route on its Main Street pedestrian mall. The transit agency, Memphis Area Transit Authority (MATA), acted on a recommendation of consultant Paul Class of Oregon, who had accumulated a number of Melbourne and Oporto trolleys, which he later sold to Memphis. This returned trolley service to another American city's main street (San Francisco had been the last), and cars ran the whole length of Main Street from the Pinch District in the north to Beale Street and beyond in the south. It also makes Memphis the only city (other than Seattle) to build a brand-new system, using antique cars in daily service on a full day's schedule, from scratch.

In 1997, a 2-mile Riverfront Loop line was added, with cars running southbound at 10-minute intervals either via Main Street or the new line along the

(*top* right) Memphis is the only city in the United States to build a brand-new heritage streetcar system with regular full-day service, using old trolleys, from scratch (not counting suspended systems in Detroit and Seattle). The system opened in 1993 and has expanded twice. Cars 204, a former Oporto, Portugal single-trucker, and ex-Melbourne W2 234 meet on Main Street at Peabody Place in 2004, after conversion to pantograph operation. The system's "Main Street Trolley" moniker is a registered trademark of the transit agency, MATA. (*lower right*) Gomaco replica Birney 453 and four Melbourne W2s will be among the first of six Main Street Trolley® cars to return to operation in Memphis in April 2018. W2 540, one of the selected rebuilds, is behind 453, and work on renovating that tram was done in-house. The W2 on the right is not one of the cars to go through the program. Scene inside the MATA "garage" on July 7, 2017. *Both photos, Peter Ehrlich*

Memphis

MEMPHIS BEGAN ITS Main Street Trolley® line on April 26, 1993, using six restored former

Mississippi River, and five-minute headways north. An inland route, two miles long, on Madison Avenue was added in 2004. Main Street Trolley's ex-Melbourne fleet has expanded considerably, with nine more W2s added over the years, most rebuilt by Gomaco Trolley Company of Ida Grove, Iowa. A hodgepodge of one-of-a-kind cars, including a brand-new car from Gomaco (identical to Tampa, Little Rock and Charlotte), rounds out the fleet. Like the F-Line cars, Memphis trolleys come in many colors.

Memphis is unusual in that its service is handled entirely with vintage trolleys. All are wheelchair-accessible, and fares are tied in with the bus system. There is talk of building a new light rail line to the Airport, which would use the Madison Avenue line in part, but at presstime, no action has been taken.

Then, disaster struck. Two of the ex-Melbourne W2s caught fire in December 2013 and April 2014. After the second fire, MATA shut the entire system down. It was clear that the system, including the trolleys, would have to be completely renovated. But the debate on how—or how much—to do, raged for several years. Finally, in 2017, six cars, including the Gomaco replica Birney and a new car added to the fleet, Melbourne W5 799, were selected to be rebuilt by Gomaco (one car was done in-house). The Main Street line reopened on April 30, using the replica Birney, four W2s and the W5.

At this time, there is no word on whether any of the Oporto single-truckers will be rehabilitated. But operationally, they exhibited none of the problems that have plagued the W2 fleet.

Portland

PORTLAND HAS BECOME one of the leaders in both light rail and small streetcar technologies in the United States. Its Metropolitan Area eXpress (MAX) light rail system, started in 1986 by TriMet, has grown to become one of the most heavily used systems in the U. S.

MAX light rail began service from Portland to Gresham in 1986. The first major extension, to the west, penetrated the hills west of Portland to Hillsboro in 1998 and was renamed the Blue Line. A line to the Airport–the Red line–opened in 2001, the Yellow Line in the Interstate corridor started in 2004, and both the Green Line via the south I-205 corridor and the SW 5th and 6th Avenue Mall lines began in 2009. Portland now has the second-highest ridership for a new LRT system at over 124,000 riders every weekday (and the fourth overall in the United States). Total track length is 60 miles.

The newest line, the 7-mile Orange Line, serving Southeast Portland and Milwaukie, opened on September 12, 2015, using the brand-new stayed-cable Tilikum Crossing Bridge. Operationally, it's through-routed with the Yellow Line, along the SW 5th/6th Avenue Mall, to North Portland.

MAX was also the first system in the United States to introduce low-floor LRVs, a great boon for wheelchair users and other mobility-impaired individuals. These cars, built by Siemens, went into service in 1998.

Further expansion into southwest Portland to the suburb of Tualatin is in the planning stages.

In 1991, Portland Vintage Trolley began service during non-rush hours from Lloyd Center to downtown Portland using MAX tracks across the Steel Bridge and through downtown. The cars, built by Gomaco, are replicas of those that served the famous scenic Council Crest streetcar line, which was one of the last to fold up in 1950. These cars are unusual in that they have bow collectors and sit on PCC trucks and use PCC-type controllers from scrapped Chicago "L" cars. Thus, they are the only wooden-bodied PCC cars anywhere. (Actually, they have steel frames and wood sheathing.) After the first few years of near-daily service, Portland Vintage Trolley operations have since cut back to only seven operating dates a year due to budget cuts, but, with good planning, one was able to ride a replica Council Crest car with rattan seats and bare bulbs, just like the original cars which operated until 1950. Until 2009, the vintage cars operated across the downtown Portland mall on the original MAX line, but were shifted to the new tracks along the Mall on SW 5th and 6th Avenue which opened in 2009. Unfortunately, further budget cuts restricted their use to holiday weekends, and then, complete discontinuance. Two cars went to the Willamette Shore Trolley, and two have gone to St. Louis for the Delmar Loop Trolley operation there. (An original 1903 Council Crest trolley, part of the Oregon Electric Railway Historical Society museum collection at Brooks, Ore., ran in the 1983 and 1985 Muni Trolley Festivals.)

The OERHS also operates the Willamette Shore Trolley from the South Waterfront District (connecting to Portland Streetcar) to Lake Oswego over the old Southern Pacific Jefferson Branch, which at one time ran electric interurban trains between Portland and Willamette Valley towns. In 2011, this service was suspended temporarily, but reopened in 2013 using two of the Council Crest cars. In the future, the line could become part of either TriMet MAX or Portland Streetcar (see next paragraph).

Even as MAX has expanded, the City of Portland, starting in 1990, became interested in a small-scale, low-budget, quick-to-implement modern streetcar line. Called the Portland Streetcar, the first line, serving the developing Pearl District in northwest Portland, connecting with the west side of downtown and terminating at Portland State University, opened in July 2001. It has since been extended to the South Waterfront District, and wherever Portland Streetcar tracks are laid, new apartments, condos and offices follow in a complementary partnership, which has improved Portland's tax base and made the city's economy grow.

Portland Streetcar's multi-colored Czech-built low-floor cars, seven of which were built by Skoda-Inekon from 2001 to 2002, operate about every 13 minutes during the day, and fares are the same as those on TriMet MAX and buses. For the first four years, Portland Streetcar also operated two Portland Vintage Trolley Council Crest replica vintage streetcars on weekends, borrowed by the city from TriMet, their official owner, but they have since returned to TriMet. Several Inekon cars of a slightly different style were added to the fleet in 2007, and in 2012, the fleet, and the line, expanded some more when a new route crossing the Willamette River and running east of it, opened. This line was called the Central Loop Line. New American-built streetcars, based on the Skoda models, were manufactured at the local plant of United Streetcar LLC (a unit of Oregon Iron Works) for this expansion. In 2015, the loop was completed with the opening of the Tilikum Crossing Bridge, shared with TriMet Orange Line LRV trains, buses, pedestrians, and bicyclists—but no autos! When Tilikum opened, the Central Loop Line became the A-Loop (clockwise) and B-Loop (counterclockwise). At this time, there are further expansion plans, but nothing concrete.

For pictures of Portland streetcars and light rail, see the "New Orleans and Portland—Two Cities "Where Streetcars Work Well" sidebar.

Kenosha

IN 2001, KENOSHA OPENED A LOOP trolley line serving the redeveloped Lake Michigan waterfront, the central business district, and Metra commuter rail. This extremely low-budget loop was built for less than $20 million and uses five former Toronto PCCs. Subsequently, two more PCCs were put into service. Like the F-Line's PCCs, Kenosha's cars represent other PCC cities–Chicago, Pittsburgh, Toronto, Johnstown, Pa. and Cincinnati. In 2015, a car representing "Muni Wings" was added. On most days, usually only one car operates, but up to three cars run on holidays As of and special occasions. 2011, the streetcars operate weekends only but in January and February; seven days a week other months of the year.

A proposed north-south route, approved by the City Council in 2014, was shot down by the mayor in 2015. But when he was defeated for re-election, hopes to build this new line rose again.

(top to bottom) Kenosha restored six former Toronto PCCs, and, like San Francisco, adorned them in colors worn by other PCC cities. 4606, in Chicago livery, passes the Kenosha Public Museum during a Flag Day celebration in June 2003. This small loop line was put in service in 2001 for only $20 million. The newest PCC in Kenosha's fleet is 4617, which is painted "Muni Wings", and went into service in 2015. *Both photos, Peter Ehrlich*

Tampa

IN 2002, TAMPA's TECO LINE STREETCAR opened its 2.7-mile line between downtown Tampa and historic Ybor City (once famous for Havana-style cigars). Tampa was the first city to institute double-truck Birney replica trolleys built by Gomaco. There are nine of them in the fleet, plus an open-bench car obtained from Charlotte, and original Tampa single-truck Birney 163, a survivor from the original Tampa system, which closed in 1946.

The line passes new development along the waterfront, where cruise ships dock, and is so popular that service on Friday and Saturday nights operates until 2:00 a.m. Most recently, TECO Line has been extended further into downtown Tampa.

The nine replica double-truck Birneys are noteworthy in that they include motors, controllers

(above) Tampa's TECOLine was the first system to feature Gomaco's replica double-truck Birneys, which use parts from scrapped trams from Milan. They also feature air conditioning. Car 428 heads into downtown past the Channelside shopping center along the waterfront. The Tampa Aquarium is situated on the left. *Peter Ehrlich*

and other parts from scrapped Milan, Italy "Peter Witts"—even the holders supporting the interior handlebars!

Tacoma

IN 2003, SOUND TRANSIT instituted its Tacoma Link modern streetcar. This L-shaped line serves downtown Tacoma, the arts area surrounding the old Union Station, and the rebuilt Milwaukee Road freight house, where Sounder commuter rail trains terminate, as well as buses, and a nearby Amtrak station. Service is free, and the Czech-built Skoda-Inekon cars operate every 10-15 minutes.

A 2.4-mile extension from the Theater District to the Hilltop neighborhood, serving Tacoma General Hospital and the Stadium District along the way. Five new Brookville "Liberty" trams have been ordered for the extension. Construction is set to begin in 2018, and the line will open in 2022.

Little Rock

LITTLE ROCK'S METRO STREETCAR (formerly River Rail) is a historic streetcar line that opened in November 2004. It is unique in that it serves historic districts of two cities: Little Rock and North Little Rock, across the river. The line features two loops on both sides of the river, and a spur off the Little Rock loop to the Clinton Presidential Library. There are five cars—replica double-truck Birneys, patterned after the ones in Tampa, built by Gomaco of Ida Grove, Iowa. Although they have the Milan car features, they are equipped with magnetic track brakes for better control when descending either side of the Arkansas River Bridge. Ridership is about 100,000 a year—small, compared to the F-Line, which has over 100,000 riders a *week*—but nevertheless important to the economy of the cities it serves.

Metro Streetcar has two routes. One is a Little Rock loop, running clockwise, called the Green Line; the other serves the loop, the Clinton Library and North Little Rock and is known as the Blue Line. Service operates from about 8:30 a.m. to 10:00 p.m. daily. On Sundays, only the Blue Line operates.

There are plans for extending the line further into downtown Little Rock.

Although Metro Streetcar is operated by the local transit agency, Rock Region Metro, its fares are separate from its other transit services. In 2007, the name of the agency changed from Central Arkansas Transit (CAT) to Rock Region Metro.

Charlotte

THE CHARLOTTE TROLLEY, Inc., began life with the mission of restoring original Charlotte car 85, which was built in 1927 and was the last car to run in the Queen City in 1938. In 1997, Charlotte Trolley opened a line from the Atherton Mill district

(*below*) Little Rock's Metro Streetcar 410, a 2004 Gomaco product, passes the Argenta Drug Store in North Little Rock. The store, which features a soda fountain, is the oldest drug store in the State of Arkansas. It takes its name from N. Little Rock's original name, Argenta. HDR "Painterly" image. *Peter Ehrlich*

south of downtown, as far as Stonewall Street, along an old Norfolk Southern branch. Once a new bridge was built over Stonewall Street, the trolley ran into downtown Charlotte, dubbed "Uptown" by natives. Originally, car 85 used a towed diesel generator, but the line was electrified in 2004.

Since relying on car 85 was insufficient, three double-truck replica Birneys built by Gomaco were added in 2004, with some features making them compatible with the new LYNX light rail line, which opened in 2007. In 2006, the line was shut down for conversion to Charlotte's first light rail line. The goal was to operate one of the Gomaco cars during non-rush hours along with the new Siemens S70 LRVs, but this was cut back to weekends only and suspended for good in 2010 due to budgetary cuts by the light rail operator, Charlotte Area Transit System (CATS). The Gomacos were stored, and Car 85 ultimately went to Historic Spencer Shops (the old Southern Railway shops) in Spencer, NC.

Instead, CATS built a separate route in the downtown area, the 1.5-mile CityLynx Gold Line between CTA/Arena and Presbyterian Hospital in the Elizabeth Avenue District. This stretch, Phase 1, opened in July 2015, is currently served by the three Gomaco trolleys and is free. The Gomacos pull out of the LYNX New Bern shops as early as six in the morning, and it is fun to listen to the sound of their Milan, Italy, motors getting up to speed! However, both ends of the route will be extended under Phase 2, and the length will total 10 miles when completed. New Siemens S70 trolleys will replace the Gomaco cars.

Even when just the vintage cars operated, the building of the original line caused new housing and condo developments to be built—a win-win for both the trolley and the city.

Tucson

TUCSON STARTED WITH A VINTAGE CAR operation, Old Pueblo Trolley, and now runs a modern streetcar line. Sun Link Streetcar. The original Old Pueblo Trolley operated an L-shaped line on original Tucson trackage from a lively neighborhood just north of downtown Tucson on 4th Avenue to the University of Arizona retail shopping precinct just west of campus. It opened its line on April 13, 1993, using a Birney leased from Orange Empire Railway Museum. Old Pueblo Trolley now rosters an ex-Osaka, Japan trolley and single-truck cars from Brussels and Lisbon.

In 2009, the line was extended into downtown Tucson using new track that crosses under a railroad. All of this trackage eventually became part of the Sun Link Streetcar, and OPT operations were suspended at the end of 2011 to reconstruct the trackage.

The new Sun Link Streetcar, or Tucson Streetcar, reconstructed and double-tracked the OPT route, extended it into downtown Tucson and into the Mercado District. On the east end, service was extended along the north edge of the University of Arizona to the Arizona Health Sciences Center. Eight United Streetcar trams, similar to those in Portland and built in 2012, operate on the line. A new shop facility was built, close to the OPT carbarn. Overall, the project cost was close to $175 million.

The line runs mostly in mixed traffic and is 3.9 miles long. Operations began on July 25, 2014. Ridership totals about 2,500 a day, with 10-15 minute service at most times. Fares are $1.50.

Although 5th Avenue is used for carbarn access and passes the OPT carbarn, currently rails into the OPT site have been severed. This is unfortunate, because OPT had hoped to run a vintage car on weekends and holidays.

Atlanta

THE ATLANTA STREETCAR is a 2.7-mile loop line that began operating on December 30, 2014, returning surface rail transit to the Georgia capital for the first time since 1949. Four Siemens S70 streetcars are used. It runs from the Martin Luther King, Jr., Historic District through Woodruff Park, past Peachtree Center and over to Centennial Olympic Park just north of the Central Business District.

Cars operate every 15 minutes. Initially, fares were free; starting in 2016, the fare became $1.00. There are no transfers between the Atlanta Streetcar and MARTA. The line is owned by the City of Atlanta. Actually operation is by MARTA employees.

There is talk of expansion, particularly to the Bulkhead MARTA station north of downtown, and creating a Belt Line.

Salt Lake City

THE SALT LAKE CITY SUGAR HOUSE STREETCAR, or S-Line, is a two-mile long east/west line that began service on December 8, 2013. It connects the Sugar House district of Salt Lake City with the city of South Salt Lake City and the Utah Transit Authority's TRAX light rail lines. The name "S-Line" was chosen because the names of all three cities and neighborhoods begin with the letter "S".

Connecting at TRAX Central Pointe Station, the route runs eastward along a linear park created as part of the S-Line to Fairmont, in the neighborhood of Sugar House. Service is provided by Siemens S70 streetcars, almost identical to those used on TRAX, but geared lower for the generally lower-speed

Streetcar Scenes in Charlotte (*above*) and Tucson (*right*)

(*facing page*) Tucson's Old Pueblo Trolley operated on 4th and University Avenues from 1993 to 2011, when the city rebuilt the route and extended it into downtown Tucson for the Sun Link modern streetcar, which opened in 2014. (*top left*) Old Pueblo Trolley's ex-Osaka, Japan car 869 lays over at the University/Tyndall terminal on January 18, 2009. (*top right*) A twilight scene at the same intersection, University and Tyndall, with a Sun Link streetcar. This modern line started up on July 25, 2014. Photo, November 18, 2014. (*bottom left*) Tram 102 passes an Easter Island figure at 4th Avenue and 8th Street. The tracks in the foreground lead to the carbarn, and Old Pueblo Trolley's facility is a block away. November 18, 2014. (*bottom right*) Car 103 is inbound, passing Viento de Agosto Park in downtown Tucson, enroute to the Mercado District on November 18, 2014. *All photos, Peter Ehrlich*

(facing page) Charlotte instituted a vintage trolley service in 1997.
By 2004, service had been extended into downtown Charlotte (called "Uptown"). All photo, Peter Ehrlich.
(top left) Car 85, built by Perley Thomas in 1927, loads at 6th Street in "Uptown" Charlotte for the trip south to Atherton Mill. Car 85 was the last car to run on Charlotte's first trolley system in 1938. Photo, October 23, 2005. (top right) Gomaco 91 stops at Carson Street on October 23, 2005. Much new housing and other development followed the opening of the line, which is now part of LYNX light rail. (middle left) After a few years of storage following cessation of vintage car service on LYNX, a new line—the CityLynx Gold Line—began service from Trade Street at the CTC Arena to the Elizabeth neighborhood east of town. This fisheye view, taken on August 19, 2015, shows both a LYNX light rail train and one of the Gomaco cars in front of the CATS bus terminal. (middle right) One has to get up very early to catch the Gold Line pullout cars! Here's car 92 passing through the CTC Arena Station at six in the morning. August 21, 2015. (bottom left) Car 92 passes through the Charlotte Piedmont Community College (CPCC), the line's biggest trip generator, on August 20, 2015. (bottom right) Occasionally, it snows in Charlotte, but the snow doesn't usually stick. Here's car 91 turning at Presbyterian Hospital near the east end of the line on a snowy January 17, 2016.

operation.

Extension eastward along Highland Drive and to Westminster College is planned; however, funding and final alignment is not in place yet.

Fares are tied in with TRAX and other transit services in the Salt Lake City region.

TRAX light rail began service in 1999 and consists of three lines. It serves the southern and southwest suburbs, the University of Utah, and the airport It has become the the ninth-busiest LRT system in the United States.

Washington

THE DC STREETCAR opened its first of several-planned modern streetcar routes. the H Street/Benning Road line, between Union Station and Oklahoma Avenue, on February 27, 2016, after several years of delays caused by cost overruns, late infrastructure peripheral projects (such as substations), accidents during the testing period, and a fire aboard one tram. Although the line had been completed and testing was underway, at one point it was threatened with complete cancellation.

The line is 2.4 miles long and runs in mixed traffic. Six low-floor cars are deployed: three built by Inekon of the Czech Republic, and three by United Streetcar LLC of Clackamas, Ore. (nearly identical to the units in Portland and Tucson). The Inekons are their Trio model.

Fares are free for the time being. The operator is the District of Columbia Department of Transportation.

As mentioned, there are plans for more DC streetcar lines. One of these has actually been built: a route to Anacostia, but it remains idle to this day. An extension of the H Street/Benning Road line to either Minnesota Avenue or Benning Road Metrorail stations is being actively pursued, which would make the route more useful on its east end. Also under consideration: a north/south route, and a line from Union Station to Georgetown.

Kansas City

ON MAY 6, 2016, KANSAS CITY reintroduced streetcar service with its KCStreetcar line. This marked the first passenger electric rail service in the Fountain City since Kansas City Public Service abandoned the Country Club Line in 1957. KCStreetcar was also the first of two consecutive new streetcar cities in America to introduce the CAF (Spain) Urbos-3 low-floor tram, a design that is in use extensively in Europe. Currently, there are four cars, but two more are on order.

This 2.2-mile route, which cost approximately $102 million to build, operates entirely in city streets. It runs from Union Station, along Main Street in the Central Business District, and over to the RiverMarket district. Daily ridership exceeds 5,700 passengers. Service is free, as a city assessment district provides the bulk of the line's operations funding.

Currently, there are two extension plans being hammered out. The first would extend the line north from RiverMarket to Berkley Park along the Missouri River. The second would extend the line southward from Union Station to University of Missouri-Kansas City.

It helps that the line's success has the enthusiastic backing of Mayor Sly James and most of the City Council.

Also, original Kansas City PCC 551 is on display at RiverMarket. It was formerly Muni 1190.

Cincinnati

THE CINCINNATI BELL CONNECTOR Over-the-Rhine streetcar loop line opened for service on September 9, 2016. Originally just called the Cincinnati Streetcar, its brand name changed when telecommunications company Cincinnati Bell assumed a 10-year agreement for naming rights of the line and its rolling stock. It operates five CAF Urbos-3 low-floor streetcars, the second city to roster these Spanish trams. The car numbers begin at 1175, which continues the numbering system of the PCCs that operated in the Queen City 65 years earlier.

The 3.6-mile route serves the Riverfront and its park (called Banks), and the two sports stadiums along the Ohio River; downtown Cincinnati; and the gentrifying Over-the-Rhine district. Findlay Market, near the north end of the line, is a big patronage draw. The cost to build the line was about the same as in Kansas City—$102 million.

To build the line, its backers had to overcome several hurdles, among them two failed ballot measures, opposition from the governor of Ohio, and election of an anti-streetcar mayor, John Cranley, in 2013. He tried to cancel the entire project, but discovered that if he were to proceed to do so, the City would have to pay back to the Federal Government its share of the costs. In the meantime, a decidedly pro-streetcar City Council was subsequently elected.

Initially, service was free. But in 2017, fares were instituted, and as a result, Cincinnati Bell Connector's ridership is considerably less than that of the similar Kansas City line.

Nevertheless, there are expansion plans, principally extending the route up the steep grade to the University of Cincinnati.

Detroit (again)

THE Q-LINE IN DETROIT WAS THE PRODUCT of a public-private consortium created to re-introduce a rail line to Woodward Avenue, whose PCCs operated the last streetcar line in the Motor City, ending in 1956. The intention was to replace a state-canceled light rail route.

The proposed 3.3-mile line was originally known as M-1 Rail (as Woodward is State Highway 1). But Quicken Loans purchased the naming rights in March 2016.

Construction began July 2014. The total cost for the M-1 Rail totaled $137 million, with both public and private funds. Six Brookville "Liberty" low-floor streetcars were ordered. These were nearly identical to the ones in Dallas. As in both Cincinnati and Kansas City, the numbers of the cars picked up where the previous system left off, thus, the first car was number 287. As in Dallas, the cars operate over wire-free stretches, and there are strategically-located charging stations at the Grand Boulevard. outer terminal and other locations along the route.

More Scenes of Modern Trolleys in the U. S.

(*top left*) Tacoma started a free low-floor streetcar service in 2003, using Skoda Inekon trams like those in Portland. ar 1003 has passed the old Union Station, now an exhibition hall and gallery, in this 2004 image and is heading east toward TacomaDome. (*top right*) Atlanta opened in December 2014 and uses Siemens S70 cars. 1002 is at Auburn and Piedmont in this sepia-tone image, but the tram is in full color! February 26, 2015. (*middle left*) The Sugar House streetcar. or S-Line, in Salt Lake City also deploys the Siemens S70. 1176 stops at Sugarmont on the 2-mile line. Note the linear park. June 14, 2015. (*middle right*) United Streetcar 203 passes H and 9th Streets on Washington, DC's DC Streetcar on March 4, 2016. Service began a week earlier. (*bottom left*) Kansas City runs CAF Urbos-3s, such as 804, pictured at Union Station on May 10, 2016, four days after KCStreeetcar opened. (*bottom right*) Cincinnati Bell Connector also has CAF streetcars. On the second day of service—Sept. 10, 2016—1177 passes the landmark Findlay Market inbound. *All photos, Peter Ehrlich*

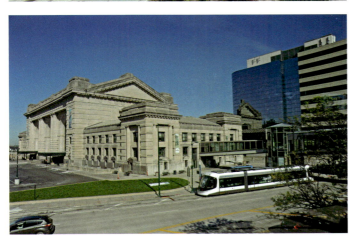

(*left*) Detroit's Q-Line (M-1 Rail) returned electric streetcars to the Motor City for the first time since 2003, when the Detroit Citizens Railway quit. Brookville "Liberty" low-floor streetcar 287 is passing new condos at Woodward and Adelaide. Here, the tram is running under wire, but there are extensive stretches of wire-free operation, and the cars use battery power. Downtown Detroit is in the background. Taken April 30, 2017, twelve days before the start of service. HDR image. (*below left*) Car 290, in "winter dress" shrink-wrap, stops at Grand Circus outbound. The Detroit People Mover, which opened in 1987, is in the background. *Both photos, Peter Ehrlich*

The first day of service was May 12, 2017. Fares were free up to Labor Day, when the base fare of $1.50 was instituted (a $3 Day Pass is also available). Fares are not tied in with those of the local transit system.

The route runs from Congress Street in downtown Detroit and connects with the Downtown People Mover. The route also passes near the Detroit Tigers baseball stadium (Comerica Park), serves both the Main Library and the Detroit Institute of Arts, and the Amtrak station near the outer end of the line. It operates entirely in mixed traffic.

St. Louis

COMING IN 2018: THE DELMAR LOOP TROLLEY. This is a 2.2-mile heritage streetcar line that will run on Delmar Blvd. and DeBaliviere Avenue, from the Missouri History Museum in Forest Park to University City, terminating near Washington University. The actual line's name comes from old streetcar days, when PCC streetcars from several lines terminated at "Delmar Loop." Two stations of the St. Louis Metro will be served.

The line cost $51 million, and used a combination of Federal, city and county money, and private donations. However, there have been recent requests for more money to get the line into operation.

Originally, the plan was to use two single-ended Milan Peter Witts. But when the line was constructed, it built stub-end terminals at both ends, so using those trams was no longer possible. In addition, these trams had deteriorated owing to years of outdoor display. Instead, Delmar Loop Trolley purchased two Portland Vintage Trolley Council Crest lookalike cars built in 1991 by Gomaco, and three former Seattle Waterfront Streetcar Melbourne W2s. Along with the Council Crest cars, one of these is being rebuilt by Gomaco.

Construction began in March 2015, and was completed by the end of 2016. After lengthly delays due to budgetary and managerial problems, the line finally opened in November 2018.

Oklahoma City

COMING IN 2018: THE OKC STREETCAR. The Oklahoma City Streetcar—also called the MAPS 3 Streetcar—saw its beginnings in 2005 as part of the City's MAPS 3 $777 million initiative, and it was approved by the city's voters in 2009. It consisted of a 1-cent sales tax increase. This initiative funded other Oklahoma City improvement projects as well as the streetcar.

(left) Brookville Liberty low-floor car 201802, in "Redbud" livery, pokes its nose out of the OKC Streetcar carbarn. Testing on the Downtown/Bricktown Loop portion of the line will begin in June. The skyscraper is the Devon Energy Center, tallest building in the state of Oklahoma. May 8, 2018. *Peter Ehrlich*

The overall cost for building the current 6.9-mile loop route (which also consists of a downtown loop) was approximately $131 million. Groundbreaking took place on February 7, 2017, and work is to be completed by December 2018—the projected month for opening of the line.

Originally, five Inekon Trio trams, built in the Czech Republic, were to be purchased. But when Inekon failed to come up with required financial-guarantee information, the City Council rescinded the contract and awarded it to Brookville Equipment Corp. instead. Brookville is now building the Oklahoma City fleet, which has been increased to seven cars, with an option for more. There will be sections where the streetcars will operate wire-free, on battery power. Three different color schemes were chosen for the cars—two in "Clear Sky Blue", two in "Bermuda Green", and three in "Redbud" (alternating shades of maroon, red and magenta). The first car to arrive was one of the red cars.

The line serves Bricktown in the south (where the downtown loop is located), the business district, and the Automobile Alley and Midtown neighborhoods. The cars will run in mixed traffic. Although the routes are owned by the city, EMBARK, the area transit agency, will be the designated operator.

OKC Streetcar opened on December 14, 2018.

El Paso

COMING IN 2018: EL PASO STREETCAR. El Paso operated the only international PCC line in the world, using 20 ex-San Diego air-electric PCCs on a route that crossed the Rio Grande into Ciudad Juarez, Mexico. This line quit in 1974. Now, six of the long-stored PCCs have been remanufactured for service on two new El Paso lines, slated to begin operation in late 2018. Neither, however, will cross the Mexican border.

The 4.8-mile, $97 million El Paso Streetcar is being built under the auspices of the Camino Real Regional Mobility Authority. It was first conceived in 2012, and approved by the El Paso City Council in July 2014, and construction began in December 2015, and has been completed.

The choice of rolling stock for the new line was interesting. Nearly all of the remaining PCCs from the original operation were still stored, and the best six were selected to be remanufactured by Brookville Equipment Corp. The first of these, car 1506 (original numbers were retained) was rolled out at the

(right) Of all the new streetcar lines that plan to open in 2018 and beyond, El Paso is unusual in that, instead of buying new streetcars, it chose to rebuild some of its stored fleet of 1937-vintage PCC cars. The first two of them, 1512 and 1506, reside in the Sun Metro carbarn on May 11, 2018. There will be six cars in total; two other historic El Paso paint schemes will grace the others. Operator hiring, testing and training will begin in June 2018, and full service is planned for a late 2018 opening. *Peter Ehrlich*

Pennsylvania facility in January 2018, and was delivered to El Paso in March. Although the overall pre-war PCC body style was retained, the cars will have rebuilt Clark B-2 trucks, all-new motors and controls, and are being outfitted with air-conditioning, wheelchair lifts, and other modern appurtenances. They will operate with pantographs. Inside, the original bulls-eye light fixtures will be retained. They will be repainted in three historic El Paso liveries. 1506's light mint green and white with red trim paint scheme is also represented by Muni's 1073 as an El Paso tribute livery (see pages 169 and 171 in Chapter 8).

The two loops, the Downtown Loop and the Uptown Loop, are laid out in basically a southeast-to-northwest alignment, with both connecting at the downtown transit center. The Uptown Line also serves several historical El Paso neighborhoods, the UTEP campus, and the Las Palmas Medical Center, plus other attractions. Like most new streetcar installations, the PCCs will operate in mixed traffic.

El Paso Streetcar opened for service November 9, 2018; SunMetro, the city's overall transit agency, will assume operations.

Milwaukee

COMING IN 2018: THE MILWAUKEE STREETCAR, aka "THE HOP". Milwaukee was the last non-PCC system to abandon streetcars, which it did in 1958. It is in the process of building a new downtown-oriented line, with the expectation that the route will open in late 2018—some 60 years after the closure of the original system.

The Hop line will be 2½ miles long, and substantial portions of it will be wire-free. It will run from the north lakefront neighborhood on a two-way alignment, then separate into southbound and northbound one-way trackage through downtown, and end up at the Milwaukee Intermodal Station (Amtrak). Along the way, it will serve attractions such as the Milwaukee Public Market. There will be a separate route running to the "Couture" highrise development at the lakefront. Total cost for The Hop construction is estimated at about $124 million. The Potawatomi Hotel and Casino is the line's sponsor.

Brookville Equipment Corp. is building five "Liberty" streetcars for Milwaukee, nearly identical to those supplied for Dallas, Detroit and Oklahoma City. The first car was delivered in March 2018, and all five cars are now "At the Hop" as of September. Service began "Hopping" on November 2, 2018. They will run on battery power on stretches of wire-free trackage.

Further extensions southward to the new Wisconsin Sports and Entertainment Center and the Bronzeville neighborhood are planned.

Tempe

COMING IN 2020; THE TEMPE STREETCAR. This line, which will be tied into the Phoenix Valley Metro light rail line, will be a separate line, basically an "L" shape, running in the City of Tempe. It will be nearly 3½ miles long, and connect with the Valley Metro LRT in two places. It will also serve neighborhoods in Tempe and the Arizona State University campus. Construction of the line is set to begin in March 2018 and be completed by 2020. The project is estimated to cost $186 million, and is funded with a combination of sales taxes and federal grants.

Once again, Brookville got the contract to build five "Liberty" streetcars with battery power to operate across the Valley Metro LRT at Mill and 3rd Street without having to use wires.

As an aside, Phoenix Valley Metro's light rail line opened in December 2008, and has been extended eastward within Mesa and northward in Phoenix. A new South Line is now under construction. Valley Metro is the 13th-busiest LRT

(left) On June 8, 2018, the Milwaukee streetcar held an open house for the public to inspect the first of the new Brookville Liberty streetcars at its carbarn at 4th and Clybourn. Here, eager residents line up to inspect Car 01. The carbarn was also open, and car 02 was inside. A November 2, 2018 opening has been set.
Peter Ehrlich

Other Possibilities

THERE ARE NUMEROUS OTHER CITIES across the United States that are studying and proposing modern streetcar lines as a way of revitalizing their cities and/or acting at development tools, as Portland has done. Among them are Omaha, Neb.; both Minneapolis and St. Paul, Minn. (separate systems); Sacramento/West Sacramento, Calif; Miami Beach, Fla.; Boise, Idaho; downtown Los Angeles; and a slew of others. The one that has come closest to actually proceeding to the construction phase, at this time, is Orange County, Calif. OC Streetcar will be a 4.3-mile route between downtown Santa Ana and Garden Grove. Part of the route will trace the old Pacific Electric's route into Santa Ana. Eight Siemens S70 cars, similar to those in Atlanta and Salt Lake City, have been ordered. Groundbreaking is slated to begin in late Summer 2018, and be completed by 2021. Estimated cost: $300 million.

One city that had advanced far enough to actually order streetcars, and had started some construction–Fort Lauderdale, Fla.–was cancelled when a new anti-streetcar mayor was elected in March 2018.

Fort Collins

FORT COLLINS was the last small-town, all-Birney system in the United States, and quit in 1951. In 1985, a section of the original system along Mountain Avenue to City Park was unearthed, reconstructed and, in 1987, placed in service, using a single original Fort Collins Birney, car 21. The line runs weekends only. Its goal of reaching downtown Fort Collins remains elusive because of the need to cross an active railroad line just west of downtown.

Recently the Fort Collins Municipal Railway Society obtained a second ex-Ft. Collins Birney from Charlotte, car 25. It is in the process of being restored—ironically, at the original Fort Collins Municipal Railway carbarn on Howes Street!

Vintage Cars In Three Cities

(*above*) Original Fort Collins Birney 21 rolls down Mountain Avenue, one of that city's original routes, in 1996. (*left*) One of the Gomaco-built "Narragansett" 15-bench replica open cars trundles along the Merrimack Canal at the Lowell National Historic Park on June 5, 2011. The National Park Service began trolley operationsat this site, replicating old textile mills, in 1984. (*below* Los Angeles' Big Red Cars roll gain! Replicas of the Pacific Electric's semi-interurban 500-class cars run on a remnant of PE's San Pedro Line. Big Red Car 501 crosses 6th Street, San Pedro's main drag, in June 2008. Unfortunately, service was suspended in September 2015. *All photos, Peter Ehrlich*

It was announced, prior to the opening of the 2018 operating season, that a pavilion in City Park, with a visitors center and space for Society exhibits and–possibly–covered storage for the second Birney, may soon be built. In the interim, the Society's present barn on Mountain Avenue is being expanded.

Lowell

THIS LINE IS RUN by the National Park Service and runs around the Lowell National Historic Park grounds in Lowell, Mass.. It uses one closed and two open replica New England cars built by Gomaco, and New Orleans 966 on loan from the Seashore Trolley Museum. Service began in 1984.

Yakima

THE YAKIMA INTERURBAN LINES ASSOCIATION was formed with the purpose of saving one of the electric freight operations in Apple Country–the line to Selah. It uses two ex-Oporto, Portugal single truck trolleys and two original Yakima Brill Master Unit cars built in 1928. Cars run on weekends from Memorial Day to the end of September. Service to Selah was suspended in 2005 after copper thieves stole hundreds of feet of the overhead wire, but service has since been restored.

Los Angeles (San Pedro)

IN 2003, THE PORT OF LOS ANGELES opened a 1½-mile-long line at San Pedro that was a remnant of the vast Pacific Electric interurban system that blanketed the Los Angeles area during the first fifty years of the twentieth century. Replica "Big Red" cars operated over this railway, which also is a freight railroad, on Fridays, Saturdays and Sundays, and other days as needed to serve the cruise ships. Unfortunately, the Port of Los Angeles in September 2015, has chosen to redevelop the port, and this forced a suspension of the San Pedro Red Cars.

Los Angeles is also considering building a downtown circulator streetcar line, using either modern or replica historic streetcars.

There is also the Angel's Flight funicular, which operates up Bunker Hill in downtown Los Angeles.

Philadelphia and Boston

BOTH PHILADELPHIA AND BOSTON still operate PCCs, and these systems, while using modern LRVs on other lines, each have single routes featuring PCCs.

In Philadelphia, ride line 15-Girard, which uses 18 original Philly cars (the same models as those on the F-Line) which have been completely rebuilt by Brookville, and equipped with modern AC controls, new trucks, and air-conditioning. They have been dubbed "PCC-IIs."

Boston has the isolated Mattapan-Ashmont PCC-operated route running out of Ashmont in southeast Boston. It uses a high-speed right-of-way dating to 1928, and seven air-electric PCCs built in 1944/45, heavily rebuilt in 1984 and again in 1998/99, are in daily service. Starting with car 3230 in 2008, all of them were retrofitted with air-conditioning.

Philadelphia and Boston
Two Eastern cities that have retained PCCs are Philadelphia and Boston. (*above*) PCC-II 2323, rebuilt with solid state electronics and air-conditioning, moves westward through a Girard Avenue small business district in September 2010. (*right*) Car 3268 travels along a bikeway approaching Milton on the Mattapan-Ashmont line in July 2008. *Both photos, Peter Ehrlich*

Self-Propelled Streetcars In The U. S.

THERE ARE A NUMBER OF PLACES across the United States where rail cars, usually powered by on-board diesel engines, operate, without resorting to drawing current from the traditional overhead wire. Galveston, Texas, operates four old-style trolleys built by Miner Railcar. Astoria, Ore. uses a former San Antonio trolley, which pulls a diesel generator along a five-mile freight railroad along its historic waterfront. Denver runs a replica 15-bench "Narragansett" open car built by Gomaco, similar to those in Lowell and Tampa, but with power from a diesel generator mounted at one end, along the South Platte River serving a number of riverside attractions. Battery-powered trolleys run at two retail developments in Los Angeles and the San Fernando Valley. The newest city to join this group is Savannah, Ga., which started running a former Melbourne W5 tram using an on-board diesel generator. (The Galveston operation has been closed since 2008 because of flooding caused by a hurricane.)

Most of these are seasonal or part-time operations, and none are tied into the transit systems operated within their cities.

(above) Georgia Power Co. (Atlanta) 948 makes its debut on Members Day at the Shore Line Trolley Museum on April 30, 2011, after a multi-year restoration. This car was considered for Muni's 1983 Trolley Festival when plans were being developed, but ultimately rejected. *Peter Ehrlich*

Trolley Museums across the U. S.

NO DISCUSSION OF vintage car operations would be complete without mention of the various trolley museums in the U. S., some of which originated as far back as 1939. We've already mentioned the *Western Railway Museum* in Rio Vista Junction, CA [Chapter 11, website www.wrm.org]. Here are more:

Seashore Trolley Museum, Kennebunkport, Maine. Considered the granddaddy of the trolley preservation movement; began in 1939. Also operates the cars in Lowell, Mass. Collection is primarily New England-specific, but also has cars from Dallas, Cleveland, Sydney and other cities, including Muni PCC 1155. Has one of the best bookstores devoted to the trolley era. Website: www.trolleymuseum.org.

Shore Line Trolley Museum, East Haven, Conn. Specializes in Connecticut and New York trolleys. The collection includes Brooklyn & Queens Transit PCC 1001, the first production-order PCC built in the United States. Another PCC in Shore Line's collection is a sister to Muni's ex-Newark cars. Website: www.bera.org.

Connecticut Trolley Museum, East Windsor, Conn. Specialty: New England. Website: www.ct-trolley.org.

Electric City Trolley Museum, Scranton, Pa. Specializes in eastern Pennsylvania cars. Operates over a portion of the old Laurel Line interurban that ran between Scranton and Wilkes-Barre, Pa. until 1952. Its cars operate to certain home games of the Scranton/Wilkes-Barre RailRiders, a minor league farm team for the New York Yankees. Website: http://www.ectma.org/ .

Rockhill Trolley Museum, Orbisonia, Pa. (across the road from the *East Broad Top Railroad*). Also known as *Railways To Yesterday*. Mostly Pennsylvania cars, but first museum to preserve a San Diego Trolley I2. Website: www.rockhilltrolley.org.

Pennsylvania Trolley Museum, Washington, Pa. Has an extensive Pennsylvania trolley collection. 5'-2½" gauge. Website: www.pa-trolley.org.

Baltimore Streetcar Museum, Baltimore, Md. Originally created specifically for Baltimore streetcars, but recently, cars from Philadelphia and Newark have been added and are being restored. Website: www.baltimorestreetcar.org.

National Capital Trolley Museum, Wheaton, Md. Eclectic fleet from the Washington, DC area and elsewhere. A sister car to Muni's Blackpool, England "Boat" trams was recently added to the collection. Website: www.dctrolley.org.

Illinois Railway Museum, Union, Ill. Features mostly cars from the Midwest and Chicago area; extensive, operational interurban line. Also operates railroad equipment. One of the largest and most varied museums in the United States. Website: www.irm.org.

(above) Pullman "Red Rocket" 144 is the quintessential Chicago streetcar and one of three preserved. It's operating at the Illinois Railway Museum in 2006. Muni and some MSR officials explored the possibility of acquiring sister car 460 from the CTA collection in 1984, but that car ultimately joined the museum's collection. *Peter Ehrlich*

Fox River Railroad Museum, South Elgin, Ill. Mostly cars from Illinois, but the exhibits include Muni PCC 1030. Website: www.foxtrolley.org.

East Troy Trolley Museum, East Troy, Wis. Mostly cars from the Midwest. Website: www.easttroyrr.org.

Midwest Electric Railway, Mt. Pleasant, Iowa. Although it's open most of the year, its specialty is providing streetcar transportation, operating at Muni-like frequencies, around the site of the Old Threshers Reunion, held for five days each year around Labor Day. The fleet includes the only operating Milan "Peter Witt" situated between California and Italy, but other cities, including Waterloo, IA, and Rio de Janeiro, are also represented. No working website, but the Old Threshers Reunion website is www.oldthreshers.com.

Minnesota Streetcar Museum, Minneapolis, Minn. Minnesota-specific collection. Two operations; one on an original Twin City Rapid Transit streetcar route, the other in suburban Excelsior. Its collection includes the oldest existing American streetcar in service–Duluth 78, built in 1893, and a sister PCC car to Muni's 1071. Website: www.trolleyride.org. (*Note*: Even though Duluth 78 is the oldest operating streetcar in the U. S, beating Muni's 578(S) by three years, it's a *museum* car, whereas 578(S) is the oldest car in active *public transit* service.)

Fort Smith Trolley Museum, Fort Smith, Ark. Uses original Fort Smith Birney 224, and the restoration of a former Hot Springs, Ark. car has been completed. The line was recently extended to the Fort Smith Convention Center. Website: www.fstm.org.

Orange Empire Railway Museum, Perris, Calif. Mostly exhibits from Southern California. Former Muni K-Type 171, a sister to 178 at *Western Railway Museum*, has been restored to 1939 blue/gold livery. Muni has repatriated B-Type 162 and PCCs 1033 and 1039 from OERM, and has purchased New Orleans 913. (See Chapter 8.) OERM operates on both standard gauge and 3'-6" track. Website: www.oerm.org.

Oregon Electric Railway Museum, Brooks, Ore. Has cars from Muni, Sydney and elsewhere. Ex-Muni PCCs 1118 and 1159 are preserved here, as is Boeing 1213, which starred in Muni's 1983 Trolley Festival and is in operating condition, and Milan, Italy interurban 96, which graced Muni rails for a time. Also operates the Willamette Shore Trolley between southeast Portland and Lake Oswego, using two of the former Portland Vintage Trolley Council Crest replicas. Website: www.trainweb.org/oerhs/.

Northwest Railway Museum, Snoqualmie, Wash. Located about 27 miles east of Seattle; features mostly old mainline trains. Website: www.trainmuseum.org.

Three museums in Canada are worth mentioning:

Halton County Radial Railway Museum, Milton, ON (near Toronto). Large collection of Toronto cars and cars from elsewhere in Canada, and Chicago. Website: www.hcry.org.

Fort Edmonton Park, Edmonton, AL. The *Edmonton Radial Railway Society* operates restored Edmonton and Toronto streetcars in the park, and ex-Melbourne and Osaka trams across the High Level Bridge crossing the North Saskatchewan River. Website: www.ftedmontonpark.com/index-streetcars.html.

The *Fraser Valley Historical Railway Society* operates three restored British Columbia Electric Railway (BCERy) interurbans on a line out of Surrey, BC. It operates over a portion of the famous BCERy interurban line to Chiliwack. Website: www.fvrhs.org.

And then there is the last electric freight operation in the United States. Up in Mason City, Iowa, Iowa Traction runs 1920-vintage Baldwin-Westinghouse box cab electric locomotives. Mostly, they switch hopper cars for a local grain mill, but it's a fascinating operation. The locos use trolley poles! Iowa Traction also has a restored Chicago, North Shore and Milwaukee interurban available for charter.

(*above*) Iowa Traction, in Mason City, Iowa, is the last electric freight operation in the U. S. 1920-vintage Baldwin-Westinghouse loco 54 switches grain cars as former North Shore interurban 727, on a charter, looks on. September 1, 2006. *Peter Ehrlich*

There are many heritage tramways and tramway museums overseas, too. Most German systems, and a few in other countries as well, have sizable fleets of vintage trams available for charter. The system in Prague, Czech Republic, rosters an extensive fleet of pre-World War II stock and operates them for charters, special occasions, and on weekends from late March through the first week of November on a special historic route, Line 41. The Prague system's website: http://www.dpp.cz/en/.

Special mention should also go to Torino, Italy, which in March 2011 instituted its Line 7–the first dedicated historic streetcar route in Europe. Trams from Torino and other Italian cities ply the elegant downtown streets. The creation of Line 7 was inspired by the F-Line! Website: http://www.atts.to.it/linea/index_e.php.

Another vintage tram service operates in Barcelona, Spain, where the Tibidabo Blue Tram runs original single-truck cars from the 1900s into the hilly Tibidabo district. It's quite a charming ride. The Tibidabo line is separate from the new light rail tramways installed in the late 2000s..

Blackpool, United Kingdom is another system that has preserved its quite colorful heritage, while running an everyday fleet of new trams along a rebuilt Promenade line. Every year, from April through November (and at Christmastime), double-deck and single-deck trams from its heritage fleet operate in short-turn service, or even all the way to Fleetwood. Among them are several "Boat" trams, sisters to Muni's 228 and 233; a number of "Balloon" double deckers; an open-top "Balloon", and other single-deck cars. Every year, from September through the first week of November, Blackpool Transport runs its "Tour of Illuminations", and the Promenade line is aglow with colorful exhibits. Special illuminated trams run interspersed with the modern trams and other vintage cars, so passengers can get a close-up view of the exhibits.

England is also home to some of the finest tramway museums in the world. The *Crich Tramway Village* is one of them. Located between Sheffield and Leeds, in Derbyshire, Crich features mostly trams from the U. K, but cars from New York, Den Haag (Netherlands), Oporto, and even Johannesburg, are some of the exhibits, as is Blackpool "Boat" 236, a sister to the two now running at Muni. The site is laid out as a village street, with apothecaries, vegetable and fruit stands, snack shops, and more businesses. Website: www.tramway.co.uk.

Another British tramway museum is the one at Beamish. This museum, located about 100 kilometers north of Leeds, also is laid out as a small town street with shops. Beamish was the source for Muni's second Blackpool "Boat" tram. Website: www.beamish.org.uk.

Christchurch and Auckland, New Zealand also have vintage car operations in their cities, though the operation in Christchurch is being rebuilt after that city's two devastating earthquakes in 2010 and 2011.

Bendigo, in Victoria, Australia, also operates a vintage car line. And Melbourne still runs its iconic W class trams on two lines.

And Muni "Torpedo" PCC 1014 is at the *Sydney Tramway Museum* in Loftus, NSW, Australia, getting lots of oving care. It's one of the most popular exhibits.. The Sydney Museum's website: www.sydneytramwaymuseum.com.au/.

And then, of course, is the Milan, Italy tram system, where over 150 of their iconic 1928-vintage Peter Witts still operate—the oldest regularly-active fleet in Europe! Muni has 11 of the "Ventotto" in regular service. (See "**Milan's Icons: The Peter Witt Trams**" sidebar in Chapter 6.) *Azienda Trasporti Milanesi* rosters a number of historic Peter Witts and other trams for charter. Website: www.atm-mi.it/.

WITHOUT GOING INTO MUCH DETAIL on the individual museums, the general reason for their existence is that all of them have nurtured historic streetcar collections, saving valuable artifacts from the scrapper's torch. Each one features rides, carbarn visits and general visitor amenities. Some have "themes" built into their infrastructure. All have extremely interesting collections that harken back to the era when streetcars ruled our cities. The smallest, in Oregon, has (as mentioned) an active Muni Boeing LRV, for example. One of the largest, the Illinois Railway Museum, has a five-mile-long interurban line where ex-Chicago area interurban trains can work the old magic and get up to nearly mile-a-minute speeds, just like in the old days. All are delightful places for the "average Joe" to visit and bring the grandkids and one hopes make them streetcar fans.

Yet these are museums for *retired* streetcars. To see living antique streetcars in daily revenue passenger service, you have to visit Memphis, New Orleans, Dallas or San Francisco. And San Francisco, of course, is "Everyone's Favorite City!"

SUMMARY

TO SUMMARIZE OVERALL SERVICE LEVELS in each city, I have divided them into categories. Most systems provide year-round service; others are seasonal. Those with self-propelled cars are not included in this list.

There is also a list of cities where modern streetcar systems (but not light rail) are actually—in 2018—under construction. Numerous other cities are proposing or planning modern trolley lines, but they are not listed here.

With reference to the system's fare structure: "Linked" means that riders can also use the same fare media—transfers, day passes, etc., on other trains and buses operated by that agency, or another city agency, or that the streetcar service is free. "Unlinked" means that a separate fare must be paid on other city transit services.

Systems providing daily service, up to 24 hours a day, seven days a week, AND Linked to their city's fare structure: San Francisco, New Orleans, Portland (Portland Streetcar), Tacoma, Seattle, Memphis, Dallas, Tucson, Salt Lake City (Sugar House streetcar), Kansas City, Philadelphia and Boston.

Systems providing daily service, up to 16 hours a day, seven days a week, BUT Unlinked to their city's fare structure: Atlanta, Detroit, Tampa, Little Rock, Cincinnati, Lowell and Kenosha (weekends only in January and February).

Systems providing non-daily or seasonal service: Fort Collins, Fort Smith, Yakima, San Jose, Portland (Willamette Shore Trolley).

Systems that have suspended their historic streetcar service, but may re-institute the service in the future: Seattle (Waterfront Streetcar), Los Angeles (San Pedro).

Abandoned systems, and systems that have suspended service, but are unlikely to resume service: Detroit (Detroit Citizens Railway, abandoned 2003), Portland (Portland Vintage Trolley, (suspended c. 2010). Two cars are now in St. Louis, two more on the Willamette Shore Trolley.

Modern Streetcar systems under construction: Tempe, Ariz. Construction of a new third route in Seattle, and in Orange County, CA, is about to begin.

Two Scenes from Overseas

(*left*) Blackpool, England open-top "Balloon" 706 makes a stop at Cabin, during the annual Fall "Tour of Illuminations". Although base service is maintained by a new fleet of Bombardier Flexity Swift LRVs, an extensive fleet of historic trams is operated from spring to fall. 706 was built in 1935. October 14, 2015. *Peter Ehrlich*

(*right*) Prague, the capital of the Czech Republic, rosters an extensive collection of pre-World War II trams, which it uses for charters, special events and on Line 41, which operates between the end of March and the beginning of November on weekends only. Car 349, built 1915, is outside the Tramway Museum at Vozovna Stresovice on April 7, 2018. *Peter Ehrlich*

Scenes from the Trolley Museums across the United States

(*top left*) Connecticut Company Narragansett 15-bench open car 303 awaits riders at Seashore Trolley Museum's Visitor Center on June 4, 2011. Seashore is the oldest trolley museum in the U. S., and traces its beginnings to 1939. (*top right*) Philadelphia "Nearside" car 6618 gets restoration work inside Seashore's shop, also June 4, 2011. (*center left*) San Diego Trolley U2 LRV 1019 and Johnstown, Pa. double-truck Birney 311 meet on the Rockhill Trolley Museum's line on August 22, 2015. This was 1019's debut day; 311, Rockhill's first trolley, rejoined the active fleet after an extensive re-restoration. (*center right*) Baltimore PCC 7407 and Philadelphia PCC 2168, at the Baltimore Streetcar Museum, have interesting histories. 7407 was the last car to run in Baltimore in 1963, while 2168 was one of the very last unrebuilt PCCs in Philly. July 5, 2015. (*bottom left*) 1893-vintage Duluth 78, at the Minnesota Streetcar Museum's Excelsior, MN site, is the oldest active museum trolley in the United States. High-Dynamic Range (HDR) image. September 1, 2014. (*bottom right*) San Francisco Muni "Baby Ten" PCC 1016, a sister to Muni's own 1040, and the first of that group of 25 arriving 1951/52 (1040 was the last), is on the Western Railway Museum's ex-Sacramento Northern right-of-way at Bird's Landing on March 16, 2013.
All photos, Peter Ehrlich

Nostalgia Rides the Subway Too

UP TO NOW, I've written about vintage street railways in the United States, especially San Francisco. But there is one city whose subway system stands alone in the preservation movement and operates vintage subway trains, delighting historians, transit fans and regular straphangers: the New York Subway.

Two somewhat related groups provide historic subway trains for special events: Railway Preservation Corp., and the New York Transit Museum. A 1970s slogan for these nostalgia subway trains was "Catch All the Trains You Missed."

Most frequently, a set of IRT Lo-Vs, built around 1920, operates for New York Yankees home openers and special games, and a large group of IND R1/9s provide Christmastime runs on the 6th Avenue line, and other fantrips.

There are also some vintage BMT subway and elevated cars in various stages of restoration, and a number of colorful 1948-1964-vintage IRT "SMEE" R-Types, which operate occasionally.

Historic rapid transit cars are also rostered on the Chicago Transit Authority's "L" system, but operate infrequently.

(*left*) A four-car train of IRT Lo-Vs from 1917-1922 passes the new Yankee Stadium on October 20, 2010. The train had just let off a load of fans who enjoyed the ride on the uptown Lexington Avenue Express. Note the blimp flying overhead. (*below left*) One of the enduring characteristics of all prewar New York subway stock was the ceiling paddle fan. One of these rotates on an IRT car from 1922, keeping the passengers nice and cool! (*below*) These young Yankee fans are really digging the ambience while they ride the Lo-Vs. These IRT workhorses were fun, noisy and fast! October 9, 2009. All *photos, Peter Ehrlich*

Nostalgia Rides the Subway Too (More IRT)

The Lo-Vs have operated other special trains, such as this 2014 "Ghosts & Ghouls" train, seen (*above*) laying over at Bedford Park Blvd. on the Lexington/Jerome Line, while the participants "get scared" at nearby Woodlawn Cemetery. (*right*) The same train passes 125th Street, with a commemorative 50th Anniversary sign of the Lo-Vs' last run in 1964. Note the Jack o'Lantern marker lights. October 25, 2014. *Peter Ehrlich*

The other IRT Division Nostalgia Train is the "Train of Many Colors", which were the so-called "SMEE" type cars built between 1948 and 1964. Ironically, these were the cars that replaced the Lo-Vs. They have usually operated on the Flushing Line, for Mets home games and other events.
(*above*) R33WF 9306 arrives at the new 34th Street-Hudson Yards station, which opened in 2015 and extended the Flushing Line to the Hudson River. The Mets were in the World Series that year. October 31, 2015. On June 8, 2014, the Subway celebrated the 50th Anniversary of the 1964 World's Fair with a special "Train of Many Colors" run. (*above left*) 9306, in original blue-and-white livery from that era, passes 103rd Street/Corona Plaza on an outbound express run. (*below left*) R36WF "Redbird" 9587 "blows past" 52nd Street/Lincoln Avenue inbound. The station's a blur, but the train is in perfect focus! 9587/86 is a historically significant pair of "Redbirds", as not only were they the first ones to re-enter service following rebuilding in the early 1990s, but also were the last ones to leave service in 2003.
Also June 8, 2014. *All photos, Peter Ehrlich*

Nostalgia Rides the Subway Too
(BMT/IND trains)

BMT (Brooklyn-Manhattan Transit) and IND (the city-owned system) subway cars were wider and longer than those of the Interborough Rapid Transit, or IRT, which built the first subway.

(left) As this restored train of wooden el cars is about to leave Astoria Blvd. in Queens, an Amtrak Acela passes in the background. The 1900s-vintage BU (Brooklyn Union) set is celebrating the Subway's 100th anniversary in October 2004. (below) The three-car train of BUs passes Neck Road inbound on the Brighton Line during Parade of Trains Weekend, June 26, 2016.
Both photos, Peter Ehrlich

(*left*) The conductor stands between the first and the last of the famous IND R1/9s. 1,703 of these sturdy vehicles were built between 1932 and 1940, and the lost ones ran in 1977, but their 60-foot design is still influencing New York subway car construction. December 10, 2011. (*below*) The R1/9s run the annual Holiday Train. This one's at 86th Street on the new Second Avenue Subway, which opened January 2017. Photo, November 26, 2017. *Both photos, Peter Ehrlich*

(*above*) A gaggle of San Francisco Giants fans celebrates that team's 2010 World Series championship on board a vintage IND subway car. December 26, 2010. *Peter Ehrlich*

Nostalgia Rides the Subway Too
(more BMT/IND trains)

The BMT/IND Division of the New York Subway has a more extensive variety of vintage subway equipment than the IRT. (*above*) The lineup at Ocean Parkway for the Parade of Trains consisted of (l to r) R40 4280; BU 1404; R1 381; and BMT D-Type 6112. High-Dynamic Range (HDR) photo. June 25, 2016. (*top left*) BMT AB Standard 2390 approaches Kings Highway on the Brighton Line on a Parade Of Trains run. June 25, 2016. (*center left*) Since the Second Avenue Subway opened in 2017, it has become the starting point for nearly every special BMT/IND train. R11 8013 leads the "Train of Many Metals" on a trip to Coney Island on July 30, 2017. The R11s were an experimental series of futuristic cars built in 1949. Only ten were built. (*lower left*). R10 3184 is part of the same "Train of Many Metals." The train is leaving Stilwell Avenue for Coney Island Yard layover. It's coupled to two R42s. July 30, 2017. (*bottom left*) This train of 1925-built BMT "Triplex" articulated units has just come off the Williamsburg Bridge and is approaching Marcy Avenue on the Broadway Brooklyn line during an August 2001 fantrip. The Williamsburg Bridge and the Williamsburg Savings Bank dome provide the backdrop. All *photos, Peter Ehrlich*

Chicago

The other legacy rapid transit system to field a collection of historic trains is Chicago.

(*right*) Cars 4272/4271, which operated from 1924 to 1973, sit at Skokie Shops in August 2006. They are used sparingly. (*left*) Interior view of 4271, with historical displays in the windows. *Both photos, Peter Ehrlich*

Modern Streetcars

United Streetcar LLC, unveiled the first of an entirely American-built line of low-floor streetcars in Portland on July 1, 2009. It is based on the successful Inekon cars already operating in Portland and other Pacific Northwest cities. Portland ordered five more cars for a new 2013 extension, and Tucson and Washington also placed orders before the plant shut down. *Steve Morgan*

BETWEEN 1981 AND 2001, the trend in the United States, which, after a 30+-year-long dormancy in streetcar manufacture and usage, began to reverse, was to build light rail transit (LRT) systems. Starting with San Diego in 1981, some 17 American cities had embraced light rail, and, for the most part, these installations had provided speedy alternatives to driving or riding the bus, while generally improving the quality of life and spurring development.

But "light rail," in reality, was another form of large-scale transport. Its trains consisted of long and wide cars coupled into up to four-car trains, and they ran long distances between stations outside of the downtown cores. What was needed was a smaller scale modern service that fit into neighborhood sensibilities and attitudes, just like the old-time trolley car did in its day. And it would not take large amounts of money to construct. In 2001, the city of Portland, Oregon, pioneered a new concept of rail service: the small-scale modern streetcar.

Portland did this by building its Portland Streetcar line. This line is operated in mixed-use traffic, on city streets, running on quiet residential streets and urban thoroughfares with ease, serving major trip generators such as a hospital and a university, and generally blending in with its environment. It introduced the small-scale, low-floor trolley, which stopped at simple platform stations along its route. Finally, and of significant importance, it was extendable at relatively low cost.

Portland Streetcar started out with just five Czech-built Skoda-Inekon trolleys—three-section low-floor trams that were easy for mobility-impaired persons to board and alight, and featured large, panoramic views. Each one was painted in different colors on each side and end, making for a cheery sight on the streets of Portland. They had a nominal top speed of 18mph, but could keep up with auto traffic nevertheless.

More than that, the coming of the Portland Streetcar spurred changes in land use favoring building of condos and apartment buildings and transit-oriented villages. The Pearl District, just northwest of Union Station is such an example. New condos and reconstructed town houses, which were once gritty warehouses and factories, were transformed into wonderful places to work, play and live. And as new condos have grown along the banks of the Willamette River south of downtown Portland, so has the Portland Streetcar been extended to reach these new developments. It all fits in nicely.

Portland Streetcar has now extended across the Willamette River to the M. L. King/Grand Avenue north-south corridor near Lloyd Center.

Tampa, Fla. was one of three southern cities which embraced the replica old-time streetcar look. Gomaco-built 430 is inside the city's downtown Transportation Center building in this night scene on April 26, 2003. The line has since penetrated further into downtown Tampa. *Peter Ehrlich*

And Portland Streetcar has spurred a new growth industry: that of manufacturing of new streetcars! In 2005, Oregon Iron Works of Clackamas, Ore., announced that it would begin fabrication of new low-floor streetcars through its United Streetcar LLC subsidiary under license from Skoda of the Czech Republic. It has built cars for Portland, Tucson and Washington; but alas, has had to close up shop when no further orders came through.

So far, the "modern streetcar" concept has taken hold in the Pacific Northwest. Sound Transit in Washington State opened its Tacoma Link in 2004 using three cars identical to Portland's. They run on Tacoma's main commercial street, past its Convention Center, past the redeveloped museum area surrounding Union Station, and up to a transportation center adjacent to a redeveloped Milwaukee Road freight station.

Seattle began its South Lake Union Streetcar in 2007. It serves a burgeoning medical and biological research district and the southeast corner of Lake Union, and it, too, has helped spur development. Three cars are rostered. The First Hill streetcar line opened in 2015, with five cars.

Tucson was next, opening in 2014 with eight United Streetcar vehicles.

Washington, DC began its H Street/Benning Road line in 2016. It has three cars from United Streetcar and three from Inekon.

Other manufacturers have jumped in after United Streetcar folded. Siemens has produced cars for Atlanta and Salt Lake City; CAF sold its "Urbos-3" model to Cincinnati and Kansas City; and Brookville Equipment Corp., long a rebuilder of PCCs (including those for San Francisco), has won orders from Dallas, Detroit, Oklahoma City, Milwaukee, Tempe, and, most recently, Seattle/Tacoma. for its low-floor Liberty model.

NOW A WORD ABOUT the "other" modern streetcar: the replica double-truck Birneys produced by Gomaco Trolley Company of Ida Grove, Iowa.

The double-truck Birney was a one-man car built as an alternative to the single-truck Birney Safety Car of 1919, designed by a Stone & Webster Engineering Co. engineer as a way streetcar companies could cut platform costs. However, the single-truck Birney was considered too bouncy and too small for heavy urban operations, as cities such as Brooklyn, Boston and Detroit soon found out. (In Detroit, where the citizens of the 1920s preferred the roomy Peter Witts to Birneys, they received the derisive moniker "Half-Witts.") Soon, most big cities offed their Birneys to small operations that wanted to modernize their own fleets on the cheap, and the last operators of Birneys were Yuba City/Marysville, Calif.; Kansas City; Birmingham; and finally Fort Collins, Colo., in 1951. The Birney was also introduced to Australia and New Zealand, and many Birneys still operate in Bendigo, Victoria, Australia.

The double-truck Birney was a means of offering the safety features and one-man operation of the smaller version, but one that could carry more passengers. Cities such as Tampa and Phoenix operated double-truck Birneys.

Gomaco, whose principal business was manufacturing large road-building equipment, began its Gomaco Trolley Co. subsidiary in the 1970s, and built and refurbished cars to order for Lowell, Denver, Portland, Memphis, and other locales. The company also embraced the double-truck Birney replica concept. It built cars using parts from scrapped Milan, Italy Peter Witts and incorporated them in brand-new carbodies. It has received orders for cars from Tampa, Little Rock, Memphis and Charlotte. They are fully accessible (but high-floor), and make those wonderful musical gear sounds that make one think they're in Milan! (Or San Francisco, for that matter.)

Although the market has been allowed to go somewhat dormant of late, Gomaco can still fabricate new double-truck Birneys for any city that chooses to buy.

Whether a city chooses the modern streetcar or an old-timey replica, the small-scale streetcar line is here to stay!

Brookville Equipment Corp. of Brookville, Pa. has become a leader in the new streetcar building industry. This is a generic Brookville Liberty low-floor car for either Milwaukee or Oklahoma City. The nose of Muni PCC 1053 (Brooklyn) peeks out from one of the rollup doors, and that car will be delivered to San Francisco in a day or so. March 29, 2018. *Peter Ehrlich*

San Francisco Muni kicked off its 100th Anniversary celebration on April 5, 2012, with a ceremony at Justin Herman Plaza, fronting Don Chee Way ant the *Market Street Railway*'s San Francisco Railway Museum. (*top*) SFMTA graphic artist Chimmy Lee designed the 100th Anniversary logo. *SFMTA* (*bottom*) (left to right) Mayor Ed Lee, former Mayor Willie L. Brown, Jr., unknown woman, Operator Angel Carvajal, Senator (and former Mayor) Dianne Feinstein, and MSR president Rick Laubscher celebrate the re-inaugural first run of 1912-built Car 1, Muni's flagship. The car ran to 11th Street and back to Don Chee Way. *Pierre Maris*

Chapter 13 - Muni's 100th Anniversary, and Photo Addendum

"I've developed a tremendous fondness for these metal giants."

California Senator Dianne Feinstein,
who, as a child, rode the "Iron Monsters" such as Car 1 before she could even read.
As Mayor in the 1980s, she was an enthusiastic backer of the Historic Trolley Festivals,
and worked hard to get a permanent historic streetcar line up and running.
(Quoted in the San Francisco Chronicle, *April 6, 2012.*)

Car 1's Re-inaugural

ON APRIL 5, 2012, MUNI KICKED OFF a year-long celebration of its centennial with a decorous ceremony at Don Chee Way, opposite Market Street Railway's San Francisco Railway Museum and close by the Ferry Building.

The event was led by California Senator Dianne Feinstein, who, as Mayor from 1978 to 1988, worked tirelessly to advocate for and promote the Trolley Festivals and secure funding and direction to build the most successful new historic streetcar line in the United States, the F-Line. [See Chapters 2 and 3.] Sen. Feinstein has agreed to be the honorary chair of Muni's Centennial Committee.

Mayor Ed Lee, another Muni Centennial Committee co-chair, ran the car up to Market and 8th Street, under the watchful eyes of Motorman Angel Carvajal and former "motorman" Sen. Feinstein, who demurred when Mayor Lee offered her the controls. (Madame Feinstein had piloted the first car in each Trolley Festival parade, emulating *her* predecessor, Mayor James "Sunny Jim" Rolph, who ran Car 1 on Muni's Opening Day on December 28, 1912, and the first N-Judah car in 1928, when that line opened.)

The ceremonial run of beautifully-restored Old Number One, will usher in a year of celebration for Muni, the first publicly-owned transportation system in a major US city.

Since Muni opened in 1912, it has grown to carry well over 700,000 riders each weekday, and its route coverage–with every resident of The City a quarter-mile or less from a transit line– a most admirable feat, considering that most cities have routes that don't cover nearly the territory that Muni does. And with streetcars, electric trolley buses, cable cars and regular buses, and a subway, too!–the variety of transit offered by Muni is unique in this country.

The Promise of Good Things to Come

BUT THE RETURN OF OLD NUMBER ONE wasn't the only bright light in the firmament. In 2011, construction started on the new crosstown Central Subway, which, when it opens in 2019, will speed riders from Chinatown, the most congested district in San Francisco, and connect with the previously-opened T-Third Street line. At Market Street, riders will be able to transfer to the already-existing Muni Metro and BART, as well as surface buses and the F-Line.

Muni's long-beleaguered surface bus system won't be ignored, either. Plans call for both the Van Ness Avenue corridor and Geary Corridor to become Bus Rapid Transit later in the decade of the 2010s, with new, high-capacity buses. (In the case of Geary, however, there are many who feel that Geary should return as a rail line, as it was until 1956.) And with the largest electric trolley coach (ETB) fleet in the United States, and its diesels–including diesel-electric hybrids–run on the cleanest possible diesel fuel, making Muni's rubber-tired fleet perhaps the greenest in America.

Over the next few years, lines J-Church and N-Judah will see speeded-up service by eliminating stop signs and most conflicts with other vehicles.

On the historic streetcar side, already, the newly-rebuilt "Brookville" PCCs have returned to service following replacement of their original General Electric controllers with new Westinghouse-based electrical propulsion systems, making their operation more dependable. And on the F-Line itself, a record 22 cars are now scheduled every day, allowing for 5-6 minute headways during most times of the day. There will be enough double-end PCCs and vintage cars to begin a regular E-Embarcadero service in 2013. Operation into Fort Mason, linking the under-served western portion of the Fisherman's Wharf area with the east part, and the rest of the line, is likely to happen by mid-decade, with a favorable Final Environmental Impact Report issued by the Golden Gate National Recreation Area in February 2012. GGNRA and the San Francisco Municipal Transportation Agency (SFMTA) are working closely to bring this extension to fruition. [See Chapter 7.]

This chapter closes with a slew of images that have been added to the book since writing the first twelve chapters, and this forms the addendum part. Many of these are images of the new Brookville PCCs, but there are some historic shots as well.

But the tale of the F-Line continues to be told...

(*left*) Another serendipitous lineup occurred on August 15, 2011, when all three active Milanos in historical liveries showed up at Jones and Beach Terminal–in numerical order, yet! Yellow-and-white 1807 leads the parade, followed by sister 1811. Two-tone green 1818 is rounding the corner. *Matt Lee* (*below*) A group of F-Line operators ham it up during a layover at the Ferries in 2002. *Peter Ehrlich*

Milano Mix

(*above left*) Milano 1856 leads both Muni-liveried ex-Philadelphia PCCs at Market and Church, in this telephoto view from Sanchez. October 2, 2011. *Jeremy Whiteman* (*left*) Milano 1811 is on its pull-in trip on the night of April 5, 2012. The Milan cars are usually off the streets by nine o'clock. *Peter Ehrlich* (*above*) San Francisco is famous for its foggy mornings, when nearly the entire city is blanketed in fog. But it usually doesn't get *this* foggy! Thick tule fog has descended on the area around the Ferry Building on the morning of January 29, 2003, as two shapes disguised as streetcars pass. The fog was so thick that the Ferry Building tower was completely invisible, even though it was less than 100 yards away. *Peter Ehrlich*

Opening Day, September 1, 1995

(*left*) Looking down at the parade of cars which stretched all the way to First Street on F-Line Opening Day. *Joseph Saitta* (*above*) "Tsar Nicholas II" is talking to motorman Jack Smith (right) and another man standing in front of Russian car 106 during the F-Line Opening Day Parade lineup on Market Street. *Don Jewell*

Restoration pix

(*above*) Muni painter Leon Bernal is painting the windows of Muni B-Type 162 during the car's final restoration process in Geneva Shop. October 5, 2004. *Peter Ehrlich* (*above right*) Muni shop workers pose alongside newly rebuilt and repainted PCC 1057 (Cincinnati) in front of the Historic Car enclosure in Cameron Beach Yard on August 10, 2011, after a year's worth of body and roof repairs. The shop force, which included body workers and painters, did a superb job of returning "The Bumblebee" to service. *Jeremy Whiteman*

(*above*) Brand-new cable car 26 shines in its 1950s-era Municipal Railway livery at the Cable Car Barn before going out for its first test run on January 18, 2012. *Matt Lee*

Now You See It, Now You Don't!

In Chapters 3 and 5, there are pictures showing the hated, view-blocking double-deck Central Skyway. Damaged by the 1989 Loma Prieta earthquake, the top deck was lopped off in 1997. Here are two images showing the single remaining deck in 2002 (*left*), and in 2004 (*right*), a year after the freeway was removed for good. Now one can see Market Street in its full glory! *Both photos, Peter Ehrlich*

Car 1 Re-Inaugural Pix – April 5, 2012

(*facing page, center left*) At 5:30 a.m. on the morning of April 5, 2012, Old Number One is a cheery sight as it stops at 4th Street enroute to its starring role at the Ferries. But its eclipse fender isn't down! *Peter Ehrlich* (*center right*) As dawn breaks, Car 1 reposes on The Embarcadero. The lights on the Bay Bridge cables are still illuminated. *Peter Ehrlich* (*bottom left*) A crowd gathers around Muni's first streetcar on Don Chee Way before the ceremony. *Karl Johnson* (*bottom right*) Sen. Dianne Feinstein and Mayor Ed Lee inside the tent erected for the celebration, with Car 1 behind them. *Peter Ehrlich* (*this page, top left*) Mayor Ed Lee at the controls of Car 1 before it leaves for its VIP trip to 11th Street. He actually got to operate the car on Market Street, emulating his predecessors Dianne Feinstein and James "Sunny Jim" Rolph. (*top right*) As the crowd cheers, Motorman Angel Carvajal pilots Old Number One out of Don Chee Way with the invited VIPs. (*middle left*) The VIP run ended at 11th Street. *Karl Johnson* (*middle right*) After the first run, Car 1 made a public trip to Pier 39 and back. It's leaving Embarcadero and Bay returning to the Ferry Building. (*bottom left*) Part of the interior car card depicting Car 1's (and Muni's) history Motorman Angel Carvajal poses alongside Car 1's 100th Anniversary banner inside the Geneva Historic Car enclosure the next day. *All photos on this page, Peter Ehrlich except as noted*

A Bevy Of Brookvilles

In early 2012, the rewired ex-Newark PCCs began entering revenue service.

Facing page: (*left column, top to bottom*) 1070 is clad in the original Newark City Subway colors of 1954, right down to its "ruby slippers." It's looping via Mission and The Embarcadero as it heads to the Wharf because of the ceremony involving Car 1 which occupied the inbound track on Don Chee Way. April 5, 2012. *Peter Ehrlich* Detroit 1079 was the second rewired Brookville to enter service. This night shot at 8th Street was taken on April 4, 2012. *Peter Ehrlich* Car 1074 (Toronto) leaves 17th and Castro in the pouring rain on March 16, 2012. *Adolfo Echeverry* PCC 1080 (Los Angeles Transit Lines) scoots among the palms, both real and in shadow, as it approaches Broadway on April 7, 2012. *Peter Ehrlich* (*right column, top to bottom*) Car 1072 represents Mexico City. It's passing U. N. Plaza on April 5, 2012, shortly after the car had passed its burn-in testing phase. 1071 (Minneapolis/St. Paul was the pilot car for this contract. It's shown turning at Market/Noe/16th Street, April 7, 2012. In this view of the Historic Car enclosure in Cameron Beach Yard (formerly Geneva Yard), cars 1075 (Cleveland) and 1073 (El Paso) are still undergoing burn-in testing. Also shown: Car 1 (A-Type), both yellow Milanos and PCC 1055 (Philadelphia green/cream). April 6, 2012. *All photos in this column, Peter Ehrlich*

(*above*) Maroon Belles: Brookville PCC 1074 (Toronto) and "Torpedo" 1007 (Red Arrow) bracket another Brookville, 1071 (Twin Cities) at Jones/Beach Terminal. The Anchorage Garage has just received a new, more subdued paint scheme. April 7, 2012. (*below*) Another PCC rehabbed by Brookville, and dimensionally identical to the New Jersey cars, was car 1040, the last PCC built for U. S. service in 1952. 1040 passes one of Muni's new-fangled bus stop shelters at Market and Grant on April 7, 2012. *Both photos, Peter Ehrlich*

(*below*) Angelenos: Two PCCs representing the City Of Angels—1948-liveried 1080 (LATL "Fruit Salad") and 1937-hued 1052 (Los Angeles Railway)—pass each other at Market, Noe and 16th Streets on April 7, 2012. *Peter Ehrlich*

(*above right and right*) Two Los Angeles cars were recently rebuilt and repainted in-house—1052 (Los Angeles Railway), at Embarcadero and Broadway, and 1061 (Pacific Electric), seen passing the Hotel Vitale at Embarcadero and Mission. 1052 now has real black Railroad Roman numerals. April 7 and 5, 2012. *Both photos, Peter Ehrlich*

Night Shot at Castro

(*above*) Chicago 1058, in its new "Green Hornet" colors, makes a stunning departure from 17th and Castro on the night of April 6, 2012. The rainbow flag flies in full glory. *Peter Ehrlich*

(*above*) Milano 1814 is being rebuilt inside the Geneva Body Shop following a devastating rear-ender accident on the J-Line private right-of-way in the Bernal cut, when a Breda slammed into it. The tram was painted two-tone green when finished.
(*below*) Yellow 1807 and green 1818 meet at Market and 5th Street. Both photos were taken on April 6, 2012. *Peter Ehrlich*

Car Interiors

(*right column, top to bottom*) Inside a double-end "Torpedo" PCC. Half of the seats face back-ward. The tall box houses the folding wheelchair ramp, the radio electronics and other supplies, and is common to all PCCs. 1040's interior. This car has its original apple green around the windows. The Philadelphia cars have left side single seats. The single seats in the Newarks are on the right side. The window bars were retained from the Newark City Subway days. Note the crank windows. The spartan, yet functional, interior of a Milano. *All photos, Peter Ehrlich*

Fort Mason, 1947

Until 1950, Muni cars on the H-Potrero operated into Fort Mason. B-Type car 88 leaves the "U. S. Docks" terminal sometime in 1947. The H-Line was abandoned in 1950. Plans call for the F-Line to reach Fort Mason, but via the old State Belt Railroad tunnel under the fort.
Robert T. McVay, Walt Vielbaum collection

San Diego, 2011

A former Muni PCC returns to service!

On August 27, 2011, San Diego Vintage Trolley introduced revenue service with the first of three ex-Muni PCCs to be restored. (*left*) PCC 529, formerly Muni 1122, makes its first revenue trip, approaching America Plaza. Car 529 last carried passengers on September 19, 1982–nearly 30 years earlier. (*below left*) The next day, car 529 passes Petco Park, the new home of the *San Diego Padres* baseball team. The southern part of San Diego's downtown has been completely transformed over the last 30 years with new hotels, condos, apartments and other attractions, making San Diego one of the most livable and vibrant cities in the United States. *Both photos, Peter Ehrlich* (*below*) Muni's version of the San Diego Electric Railway is car 1078. Originally from Minneapolis/St. Paul, 1078 served the Newark City Subway, where it was car 19, for 47 years. Muni acquired it and ten sisters in 2002, and some, including 1078, were placed in service in 2007 following a mini-rehab by Brookville Equipment Co. All 11 cars were rewired by Brookville under a second contract, and 1078 returned to service with a new Westinghouse controller in 2012. At Market and 8th Street before dawn, April 5, 2012. *Peter Ehrlich*

Bibliography, Discography and Internet

Selected Bibliography:

The People's Railway, by Anthony Perles, with John McKane, Tom Matoff and Peter Straus. Interurban Special 69, Interurban Press, Glendale, California, 1981.
Inside Muni, by John McKane and Anthony Perles. Interurban Special 79, Interurban Press, Glendale, California, 1982.
Tours of Discovery, by Anthony Perles. Interurbans Special 89, Interurban Press, Glendale, California, 1984.
The White Front Cars of San Francisco, by Charles Smallwood. Interurban Special 44, Interurban Press, Glendale, California, 1978.
San Francisco's Municipal Railway–MUNI, by Grant Ute, Philip Hoffman, Cameron Beach, Robert Townley and Walter Vielbaum. Arcadia Press, Charleston, SC, 2011.
PCC: The Car That Fought Back, by Stephan P. Carlson and Fred W. Schneider, III. Interurban Special 64, Interurban Press, Glendale, California, 1980.
PCC From Coast to Coast, by Fred W. Schneider, III and Stephen P. Carlson. Interurban Special 86, Interurban Press, PO Box 6444, Glendale, California, 1983.
An American Original: The PCC Car, by Seymour Kashin and Herre W. Demoro. Interurban Special 104, Interurban Press, Glendale, California, 1986.
Un tram che si chiama Milano, by Guido Boreani. (In Italian.) Calosci–Cortona, Italy, 1995.
Street Smart: Streetcars and Cities in the 21st Century, edited by Gloria Ohland and Shelley Poticha. Reconnecting America, Oakland, California, 2011.

Selected magazine articles:

PCCs by the Bay, by Peter Ehrlich, *Passenger Train Journal,* Issue 222, June 1996, *Pentrex.*
Market Street Returns–Blending Preservation and Economics in San Francisco, by Walter Rice, Emiliano Echeverria and Robert Callwell, *Locomotive & Railway Preservation,* Issue 86, November-December 1996, *Pentrex.*
Streetcars to the Wharf, by Peter Ehrlich, *Passenger Train Journal,* Issue 245, Winter 2010, *White River Productions.*
På nygamla spår (Historic Streetcars of San Francisco), by Peter Ehrlich (In Swedish.), *Bussar & Spårvagnar,* Winter 2011, *Bussar & Spårvagnar.* English translation available on request. Contact the author at milantram1859@gmail.com.

Selected Discography (DVDs):

1906 Trip Down Market Street, *Market Street Railway, San Francisco,* 2011. A remake of an early movie made just a few days before the 1906 Great Earthquake and Fire, which devastated the city.
San Francisco Trolleys, Volume 1, *Valhalla Video,* Tustin, CA, 2001. Video of a charter of Car 1 in 2001; also shows various F-Line PCCs and other cars.. 2-disc set.
San Francisco Trolleys, Volume 2, *Valhalla Video,* Tustin, CA, 2001. More F-Line PCCs and other cars.. 2

Selected Internet sites:

San Francisco Muni web site (SFMTA): http://www.sfmta.com/
Market Street Railway (San Francisco F-Line support organization): http://www.streetcar.org/
The Cable Car Home Page (All about Cable Cars in San Francisco and elsewhere in the United States and around the world): http://www.cable-car-guy.com/
NextMuni Tracking Map (Shows which F-Line streetcars are on the street, and on the J-Line, for pullouts and pull-ins, at any given moment):
http://www.nextmuni.com/googleMap/googleMap.jsp?a=sf-muni&r=F#
SFMuniHistory (Yahoo! Groups discussion group about San Francisco transit history):
http://finance.groups.yahoo.com/group/SFMuniHistory/

U. S. Streetcar Systems (an overview of streetcar and light rail systems in the United States):
http://www.railwaypreservation.com/vintagetrolley/vintagetrolley.htm
APTA Home Page (American Public Transit Association): http://www.apta.com/Pages/default.aspx
APTA Streetcar and Heritage Trolley Site (APTA's Streetcar and Heritage Trolley Subcommittes's page. An overview of small modern streetcars and historic trolley operations in the U.S.):
http://www.heritagetrolley.org/
BART web site (subway in San Francisco, Alameda and Contra Costa counties): http://www.bart.gov/
VTA web site (Santa Clara Valley Transportation Authority, covers San Jose, Mountain View, Sunnyvale, Campbell and other locales in Santa Clara County)**:** http://www.vta.org/

Trolley Museums: See Chapter 12, pages 275-276.

Other cities with vintage or modern trolleys:
- **New Orleans: Regional Transit Authority (NORTA):** http://www.norta.com/
- **Dallas: McKinney Avenue Transit Authority (MATA):** http://www.mata.org/
- **Memphis: Memphis Area Transit Authority (MATA):** http://www.matatransit.com/
- **Kenosha: Kenosha Transit:** http://www.kenosha.org/departments/transportation/
- **Philadelphia: Southeastern Pennsylvania Transportation Authority (SEPTA):** http://www.septa.org/
- **Boston: Massachusetts Bay Transportation Authority (MBTA):** http://www.mbta.com/
- **San Diego Vintage Trolley:** http://www.sdvintagetrolley.com
- **Portland: Tri-Met/Portland Streetcar:** http://trimet.org/streetcar/index.htm
- **Tacoma: Sound Transit Tacoma Link:** http://www.soundtransit.org/Schedules/Tacoma-Light-Link-Rail.xml
- **Seattle: South Lake Union Streetcar:** http://www.seattlestreetcar.org/
- **Little Rock: Rock Region Metro Streetcar:** https://rrmetro.org/
- **Tampa: TecoLine Streetcar:** http://www.tecolinestreetcar.org/
- **Charlotte: CATS LYNX and Gold Line:** http://charlottenc.gov/cats/Pages/default.aspx
- **Detroit: Q-Line (M-1 Rail) Streetcar:** https://qlinedetroit.com/
- **Cincinnati: Cincinnati Streetcar:** http://www.cincinnatibellconnector.com/
- **Kansas City: KCStreetcar:** http://kcstreetcar.org/
- **Oklahoma City: OKC Streetcar:** https://embarkok.com/learn/services/okcstreetcar
- **El Paso: El Paso Streetcar:** http://www.sunmetro.net/streetcar
- **Milwaukee: Milwaukee Streetcar, the HOP:** https://www.themilwaukeestreetcar.com/

Picture sites:
- **www.nycsubway.org:** Extensive Muni image collection; also streetcar and subway photographs from around the world. http://www.nycsubway.org/
- **Milantram's Flickr site:** The author's photo collection of Muni and other cities' transportation. http://www.flickr.com/photos/milantram/
- **Market Street Railway's Flickr site:** *Market Street Railway's* F-Line streetcar photo collection. http://www.flickr.com/groups/marketstreetrailway/
- **Jeremy Whiteman's photo site:** Contributor Jeremy Whiteman's Muni photo site. http://whiteman.zenfolio.com/sfmuni/
- **Michael Strauch's photo site**: Contributor Michael Strauch's Muni photo site. http://www.streetcarmike.com/index_muni_streetcar.html
- **Kevin Sheridan's photo site:** Contributor Kevin Sheridan's Muni photo site. http://www.phase.com/bythebay/under_the_wires/
- **Richard Panse's photo site:** Contributor Richard Panse's Muni photo site. http://RPansePCC.rrpicturearchives.net/

Glossary

A list of terms and acronyms used in the book, mostly specific to the transit industry, or to Muni.

ADA – Americans With Disabilities Act, passed in 1990 to allow wheelchair and other handicapped individuals to ride public transit vehicles, as well as eliminating barriers and other encumbrances in daily life facing such individuals.

APTA – American Public Transit Association, an industry-wide organization promoting public transit use in the United States.

ATCS – Automatic Train Control System, the new signaling system installed in the Muni Metro subway in 1998.

ATM – *Azienda Trasporti Milanesi*, the Milan, Italy transportation provider. It ordered 502 Peter Witts in 1928-30; car 1834 came to Muni in 1984, and ten more arrived in 1998 for the Fisherman's Wharf Extension. About 150 Witts still operate in Milan.

Baby Tens – Refers to the 25 PCCs purchased by Muni in 1951-52. These were the last production PCCs built for an American transit system. Car 1040, the last PCC built, is in this group and, in 2011, was restored by Brookville Equipment Corp. in Brookville, Pa.

BART – San Francisco Bay Area Rapid Transit District, the rapid transit system opened in 1972 serving San Francisco, Alameda, Contra Costa and (later) San Mateo counties. BART built the Market Street Subway in San Francisco.

Bell Signals – Usually given by the conductor to the motorman on two-man cars or cable cars. "Two Bells" means proceed from a stop; "One Bell," stop at the next passenger stop if moving, or stop moving if backing. "Four Bells" (in groups of two): Back up from a stop; "Three Bells," emergency stop.

Block – Refers to an operator's work assignment where an operator works one run two days a week, a second run two days a week, and a third run one day a week.

Brookville "Liberty" Streetcar – Refers to the line of modern low-floor streetcars built by Brookville Equipment Corp. in Brookville, Pa. for Dallas, Detroit, Oklahoma City, Milwaukee and others.

Brookvilles – Refers to the 1070-1080-series ex-Newark PCCs acquired in 2002 and rebuilt by Brookville Equipment Corp. Also called "Newarks."

Bull Gear – The main gear which winds the under-street cables in and out of the Cable Car Powerhouse.

Cable Car – A rail car propelled by mechanical means by being attached to an under-street moving cable. Invented in San Francisco in 1873 by Andrew Hallidie.

CAF Urbos-3 – Refers to the line of modern low-floor streetcars built by Spanish company Construcciones y Auxiliar de Ferrocarriles for Cincinnati and Kansas City.

Caltrain – The commuter rail service between San Francisco and San Jose. Was originally established by the Southern Pacific Railroad.

CalTrans – California Department of Transportation.

CAPTrans – The city's Citizens Advisory Panel on Transportation, (1970s/1980s), which reported to the city's Board of Supervisors.

Carbarn – The building where streetcars are stored when not needed for service. Derived from horse car days, when both horses and the cars they pulled were kept in "barns." In later years, often referred to as a Car House. F-Line cars have a "Car House" sign.

CAT – Central Arkansas Transit, the Little Rock operator of River Rail streetcars, and Little Rock's transportation provider. Now called Rock Region Transit.

CATS – Charlotte Area Transit System, the Charlotte area transportation provider. Operates LYNX Light Rail and the CityLYNX Gold Line Streetcar, which uses Gomaco replica double-truck Birneys.

Chopper [control] – Refers to the entirely electronic method for current drawn by a streetcar to feed the power to the motors and move the streetcar. Previously, streetcars' current passed through a series of resistances before reaching the motors. Technically, the current is "chopped" before it reaches the motors. Chopper control is considered to be a smoother way of applying power to move streetcars. Also known as **Solid-State** control. Nearly all streetcars, subway cars and electric rapid transit and commuter trains built after 1976 use chopper control.

Conductor – The employee who stands on the back platform of a two-man streetcar or cable car, collects the fares (or ensures that the passengers have paid their fare), and signals the motorman (or operator) that it is safe to proceed from a passenger stop, or when someone wishes to alight at a subsequent stop. A conductor has other duties, too–many safety-related–but these are too complex or secondary to list here.

CPUC – California Public Utilities Commission. The state agency which regulates railroad and rail transit in California.

CTA – Chicago Transit Authority, the transportation provider of Chicago's "L" and surface transit system.

DART – Dallas Area Rapid Transit, the transportation provider of Dallas' light rail, the modern Dallas Streetcar, and buses.

DC Streetcar – The name of the H Street/Benning Road streetcar line operated by the Washington, DC Department of Transportation, which opened in 2016.

Detail – The next day's assignment of an extra board operator, or work assigned to an operator working his day off (RDO), or special assignments.

Division – Muni operator work assignment location. F-Line operators are assigned to Green Light Rail Division, but there are six other Divisions at Muni–two for trolley coaches, three for motor coaches, and one for cable cars. (Other transit agencies may call these Depots or Stations.)

Elevens – Refers to the 70 ex-St. Louis PCCs purchased by Muni between 1957 and 1962 to replace the "Iron Monsters." Also called "1100s."

EMBARK – The Oklahoma City transportation provider, which will operate the new OKC Streetcar beginning in late 2018.

ERPCC – The Electric Railway Presidents' Conference Committee, an organization formed by street railway company executives to develop a new, modern streetcar to compete with automobiles and buses for riders. After production began, the ERPCC's name was changed to Transit Research Corporation (TRC).

ETB – Electric Trolley Bus. On Muni, these were known as trolley coaches. (See **Trolley Coaches**.)

Extra Board – Operators assigned to the Extra Board work as "detailed" by the dispatcher to open runs.

Farside – A passenger stop located across an intersection. Opposite of **Nearside**.

FTA – Federal Transportation Agency, an agency under the aegis of the US Department of Transportation, which acts on cities' transportation projects and administers funds for their construction. (Replaced UMTA.)

GGNRA – Golden Gate National Recreation Area. A unit of the National Park Service (NPS), under the aegis of the United States Department of The Interior. GGNRA encompasses the former Presidio Army Base, Fort Mason, Fort Point, Land's End and Fort Funston in San Francisco, and several beaches, seashores and historic sites in Marin County, on the other side of the Golden Gate Bridge. The proposed F-Line extension to Fort Mason is under GGNRA's purview.

Gilley Room – A large room in a transportation division building where operators assemble. (From the Gaelic, meaning for "lad or servant" which gives it some relevance for describing a room for conductors and motormen when platform staff were predominately Irish in the late 1800s and early in the 20th Century. Also spelled "gilly room."

Grip – The device which grips a cable car to an under street moving cable.

Gripman – The operator of a cable car.

Headway – The scheduled time interval between vehicles in service on the line. Headways decrease or increase depending on the passenger service requirements during different periods of the day.

I-280 Transfer Fund – The means by which the City and County of San Francisco was able to move money, originally designated to build freeways, for area-related transportation projects. This eventually permitted The City to build segments of the E-Embarcadero and F-Market and Wharves streetcar lines.

Inekon Trio – Refers to the line of modern low-floor streetcars built by Czech Republic builder Inekon for Seattle, Portland and Washington.

Inspector – Short for Transit Service Inspector, the first-line, blue-uniformed, on-street supervisors who deal directly with the operators in issuing transit line management orders, making minor repairs, investigating accidents, and addressing other service-related issues.

Iron Monsters – Refers to Muni's fleet of 2-man cars built between 1912 and 1928. The term was allegedly coined by the late *San Francisco Examiner* columnist Dick Nolan during their final years of service. Also called "Boxcars" or "Battleships," the latter due to their somber gray livery. There were four series: A-Types (1912), B-Types (1914), K-Types (1923) and L-Types (1927).

IRT, BMT, IND – Refers to the three components of the New York Subway. IRT was short for Interborough Rapid Transit, the operator of the first subway in 1904; BMT, an acronym for the Brooklyn-Manhattan Transit, whose subways mostly opened in the 1910s; and IND, for the City-built Independent system, which began service in 1932. All three merged in 1940. Both the IRT and BMT also operated extensive elevated systems.

LACMTA – Los Angeles County Metropolitan Transportation Authority, Los Angeles' transportation provider from 1993.

LAMTA – Los Angeles Metropolitan Transit Authority, Los Angeles' transportation provider from 1958 to 1964. Los Angeles city streetcars, and the Pacific Electric Long Beach line, were abandoned under LAMTA's aegis.

LARy – Los Angeles Railway, Los Angeles' transportation provider until 1946, when LATL took over.

LATL – Los Angeles Transit Lines, Los Angeles' transportation provider from 1946 to 1958. Under LATL, much of the city streetcar system was ripped up.

Let Go – The term marked on the pavement along the cable car lines where a gripman must release the cable car grip and coast, to avoid striking the "superior" cable at California Street or outbound at Jackson and Mason, or where the cable is otherwise not in use.

Line Training – Operators who are new to streetcars are assigned to senior operators after receiving preliminary training from the Training Department in order to perfect their skills.

LRT – Acronym for Light Rail Transit.

LRV Pay – An extra 32 minutes of pay added to a streetcar run, paid at time-and-a-half. Originally, this was considered extra pay for the hazard of running a train in the Muni Metro subway, as operators had to know and respond to emergencies such as subway fires and other hazardous situations. But when F-Line operators finally received this benefit, this was then simply called "Rail Pay." This extra pay is also given to cable car gripmen and conductors.

LRVs – Light Rail Vehicles. A modern euphemism for streetcar, but many systems, including Muni, operate LRVs in trains up to four cars in length. Also refers to the 130 Boeing-Vertol LRVs acquired by Muni between 1977 and 1983, the 151 Breda LRVs purchased starting in 1996, which replaced the Boeings, and the new Siemens LRV4s now being delivered.

Lunch Pay – An extra 20 minutes of pay built into an operator's run on all straight work over six hours.

Magic Carpets – Refers to Muni's first streamlined streetcars built in 1939, which had many features found on contemporary PCC cars. Also called "One-Arm Bandits" because of their single controller/brake handle. Officially called C-Types.

Market Street Railway – The non-profit organization which has lobbied for historic streetcar operation in San Francisco, and supports Muni in its efforts to provide the service. In this book, abbreviated to **MSR**.

Market Street Railway Company – The private company which operated, in competition with Muni, streetcars and buses from 1921 until 1944. It succeeded United Railroads, and was taken over by Muni on September 29, 1944. Also refers to the first company by this name in the 1890s. In this book, abbreviated to **MSRy**.

MATA – The acronym for either Memphis Area Transit Authority, the transportation provider in Memphis, or the McKinney Avenue Transit Authority vintage car operation in Dallas.

M&MTB – Melbourne and Metropolitan Tramways Board, Melbourne, Australia's transportation provider from the 1920s to the early 1990s. The W2s and W6s in use by Muni were built by the M&MTB.

MBTA – Massachusetts Bay Transportation Authority, Boston's transportation provider since 1964, which also includes the Mattapan-Ashmont PCC-operated line. Successor to MTA, of "Charlie And The M. T. A." of song fame.

Metro Response Unit – A glorified term for a maintenance worker whose assignment is to fix mechanical and electrical problems with a streetcar or LRV while on the street.

Milanos – Refers to Muni's ex-Milan, Italy, trams purchased in 1998 for the Fisherman's Wharf Extension. Also called "Peter Witts." (In Milan, they are also known as "Ventotto," named for the year of their birth–1928.)

Motorman – The operator of a streetcar. Nowadays, such an employee is simply referred to as an "operator."

Motor Coach – Muni's "official" term for a bus.

MSR – See **Market Street Railway.**

MSRy - See **Market Street Railway Company**.

MTA – The New York State-administered agency in charge of all of the New York City subways, buses, commuter railroads, and intrastate bridges. Also refers to the acronym used by the Boston transportation provider from 1947 to 1964, of "Charlie And The M. T. A." song fame.

MTC – Metropolitan Transportation Commission. An umbrella agency which recommends Bay Area transit projects and distributes federal and state funds for these projects.

Multiple-Unit (MU) – Refers mostly to subway trains and electric trains composed of several cars, all of which can be controlled by a single employee. Developed in the 1890s by Frank J. Sprague.

Muni – San Francisco Municipal Railway.

Muni Metro – The replacement for Muni's surface streetcar system in the 1980s. Operates on the upper track level of the Market Street Subway built by BART, continuing out to Castro Street and then through the 1918-built Twin Peaks Tunnel to West Portal.

Muni Metro East – The streetcar storage and maintenance facility located at 25th and Illinois (a block away from Third Street). Opened in 2008.

Muni Metro Extension (MMX) – The extension of Muni Metro from Embarcadero Station along The Embarcadero and King Street south of downtown. Opened in 1998.

Nearside – A passenger stop located at the intersection of two streets. Opposite of **Farside**.

NIMBY – "Not in My Back Yard!" A phrase uttered by a person, or groups of people, opposed to a certain project. It's fine, anywhere else, but not where *they* live.

NOPSI – New Orleans Public Service, Inc., the company operating streetcars in New Orleans until public takeover in 1983.

NPS – National Park Service, a function of the United States Department of the Interior. Includes and operates the Golden Gate National Recreation Area.

OERM – Orange Empire Railway Museum, Perris, California. Muni has purchased B-Type 162, PCCs 1033 and 1039, and New Orleans 913 from *OERM*.

OKC Streetcar – The name of the new Oklahoma City Streetcar, which will begin service in December 2018. Also see **EMBARK**.

Outfit – The materials given to the operator for use on his vehicle over the course of the day. This includes a printed schedule, or "paddle," covering the times the streetcar is in service; books of transfers; operations bulletins; and notices personal to the operator.

Paddle – The printed schedule covering the times that the vehicle is in service. It shows when the car pulls out, when operators get relieved on the line, and when the car pulls in.

PAYE – Pay As You Enter. Refers to the design and method of passengers paying their fare when boarding a streetcar, which was developed in the 1900s. Passengers boarded the rear platform of a streetcar and paid the conductor standing on the platform, and then went inside to ride. This method of collecting fares became almost universal in the street railway industry.

PCC – The modern, Art Deco-styled, standardized streetcars produced under license from the Electric Railway Presidents, Conference Committee (ERPCC) between 1936 and 1952 for American transit systems. Designed from the ground up, using a systems engineering approach.

Peter Witts - Refers to the front-entrance, center exit design of a streetcar, invented by Cleveland, Ohio traction commissioner Peter Wit in 1912. The Milanos operated by Muni are of this original design, and most PCCs were derived from the Peter Witt.

Philly Cars – Refers to the 1050-1063 series of ex-Philadelphia PCCs acquired by Muni in 1992 and rebuilt by the Morrison-Knudsen Corporation in Hornell, N.Y.

Platform Employee – An old term referring to the motorman or conductor of an early two-man streetcar, who stood on the lowered platforms of the car while performing their duties. When these streetcars were replaced by newer streetcars or buses, which didn't have platforms, the term to describe an operator was retained.

PM – Preventive Maintenance. Each F-Line car is subject to periodic preventive maintenance inspection at varying levels of intensity.

Point-On Switch – A switch where the switch points face toward the operator and can be set for straight ahead movements or diverging movements.

Private Right-of-Way – A reserved stretch of streetcar trackage separated from automobile traffic, often built through parks and in between houses.

Property [the] – Refers to the real estate owned by a transportation agency, specifically yards, divisions, carbarns, maintenance facilities, etc.

PSTC – Philadelphia Suburban Transportation Company (Red Arrow), the company that operated trolleys, buses and the Norristown High-Speed Line until takeover by SEPTA in 1970. Two former Red Arrow trolleys will soon be remanufactured by Brookville Equipment Corp. for Muni.

PTC – Philadelphia Transportation Company, Philadelphia's transportation provider up to 1967.

Pull-In – The time a streetcar pulls into the yard at the end of the day or schedule.

Pulling the Pin – Retiring from a operator's job at Muni. (Also a term used by American railroads.)

Pullout – The time a streetcar pulls out of the yard at the beginning of the day or schedule for service.

Range - The number of hours and minutes covering a split run or shift.

RDO – Regular Day Off. Operators assigned to such work do so on a voluntary basis, and are paid time-and-a-half for this premium work.

Roar of the Four – Refers to the constant growl of traction motors, gears and wheels of the four-track operation of streetcars on Market Street between the 1910s and 1940s.

Rotation Sheet – A printed schedule of all timepoints for a line, used by inspectors or other Muni personnel.

RTA – New Orleans Regional Transit Authority, which succeeded NOPSI as New Orleans' transportation provider in 1983

Run – The specific schedule assigned an operator. The run can be a "straight" run, where the operator works between eight and ten hours on a vehicle without a break, or a "split" run, where the operator gets relieved on the first part of the run or pulls in, and comes back later to relieve another operator on a different "train," or pulls out a new car. By law, an operator cannot work more than ten hours straight, or twelve hours with a split.

SEPTA – Southeastern Pennsylvania Transportation Authority, the transportation provider for the Philadelphia-area trolleys, trackless trolleys, subways, buses, regional commuter rail, and the Norristown high-speed line. Successor to PTC since 1967.

SFMRIC – San Francisco Municipal Railway Improvement Corporation, a non-profit corporation set up in 1968 by San Francisco to acquire new rolling stock for Muni. In this manner, new buses, trolley coaches and streetcars have been purchased. In essence, SFMRIC purchases the vehicles and leases them to Muni. This method was used to partially fund the purchase of New Orleans 913 from Orange Empire Railway Museum in 2005.

SFMTA – San Francisco Municipal Transportation Agency. This agency currently oversees Muni's operations, and has done so since 2000.

SFPTC – San Francisco Public Transportation Commission. This agency oversaw Muni's operations from 1994 to 1999.

SFPUC – San Francisco Public Utilities Commission. This agency oversaw Muni's operations from 1912 to 1994.

Siemens S70 – Refers to the line of modern low-floor streetcars built by Siemens for Atlanta and Salt Lake City. Siemens is also building the new SF200 LRV-4s for Muni.

Signup – The means by which operators decide which runs to work, or to work the extra board. These can be General Signups, where operators can switch divisions, or Division Signup, where operators can pick runs at their assigned division only.

Skoda 10T – Refers to the line of modern low-floor streetcars built by Czech Republic builder Skoda (when it was merged with Inekon) for Portland and Tacoma. The line of streetcars built by **United Streetcar LLC**, based in Clackamas, Ore., for Portland, Tucson and Washington was based on this design.

SLPS – St. Louis Public Service, the transportation provider in St. Louis into the early 1960s. Muni leased or acquired 70 PCCs from SLPS in 1957.and 1962

SLRV – United States Standard Light Rail Vehicle. The term for the streetcars produced under the auspices of the US Department of Transportation, and sold to Boston and San Francisco by Boeing-Vertol Company between 1976 and 1985. Only 275 were built.

Solid State [control] – See **Chopper [Control]**

Standard Gauge – The distance between running rails on most streetcar systems and main line railways around the world. It's 4'-8½", or 1435 mm. Other systems (such as New Orleans) use a 5'-2½" (1588mm) gauge; Milan, 4'-9" (1445 mm).

Streetcar – A rail car operated by electricity, usually by drawing power from an overhead wire; also called a trolley car. (In modern days, also refers to a Light Rail Vehicle, or LRV.)

SunMetro – El Paso's transportation provider. Will begin operating the El Paso Streetcar, using remanufactured PCCs which were originally built in 1937, on the new El Paso Streetcar line in late 2018.

Swinging Load – Refers to a streetcar carrying a full load of standees hanging on to the stanchions and bars, in addition to seated passengers.

Take Rope – The term marked on the pavement along cable car lines indicating that the cable car's gripman can resume gripping the cable, after a period of coasting.

TECOLine – The operator of Tampa's heritage streetcar line.

The Hop – The name of the new Milwaukee Streetcar, which began service in November 2018.

Torontos – Refers to the 11 ex-Toronto PCCs purchased by Muni in 1973 for the 17th Street Detour.

Torpedoes – Refers to the 10 double-ended PCCs purchased by Muni in 1948. Also called D-Types or "Big Tens."

Traction – The term given to electrically-powered transit.

Trailing Switch – A switch where the switch points are away from the operator, such as at crossovers.

Train – The number of the specific schedule of a streetcar in service, from pullout time to pull-in time.

TRC – Transit Research Corp., successor to the Electric Railway Presidents' Conference Committee. See ERPCC.

TriMet – The Portland, Ore. transportation provider.

Tripper – A short-duration "train" which pulls out and pulls in, usually during the morning or evening rush hour, when more cars are needed for scheduled service.

Trolley Coach – A rubber-tired bus powered by electricity, using two trolley poles to draw power and return current. Also know as a Trackless Trolley, Trolley Bus, or ETB (electric trolley bus). Many systems, including Muni, instituted trolley coaches as streetcar replacements. One advantage was that they could be operated by one person, cutting labor costs.

Truck – The four-wheel mechanism at each end of (or underneath the frame of, in the case of a four-wheel car) a streetcar. Most streetcars have front and rear trucks. These contain the wheels, motors and gearsets.

UMTA – Urban Mass Transportation Administration, a Federal agency in the US Department of Transportation. Replaced by FTA.

United Railroads (URR) – The company which consolidated nearly all privately-run street railway transportation in San Francisco between 1902 and 1921.

USDOT – United States Department of Transportation.

VETAG – Vehicle Tagging System, an electronic push-button control system used by streetcars to throw switches, pre-empt traffic signals and perform other functions while in operation.

VTA – Valley Transportation Agency, Santa Clara [CA] County's transportation provider.

WRM – Western Railway Museum, Rio Vista Junction, California. Muni has leased K-Type 178, Blackpool "Boat" 226 and Melbourne W2 648 from WRM for the Trolley Festivals.

White Front Cars – Refers to the patented paint scheme created by Market Street Railway Co. in 1927 for its cars, promoted as a safety feature.

WPA – Works Progress Administration, one of the agencies created by the Roosevelt Administration to help pull America out of the depths of the Depression. The L-Taraval line's Zoo loop was a WPA project.

Index

A

AC Transit (Alameda-Contra Costra Transit District)	95,96
Adams, Phil	83,145
Agnos, Art	45,67,69,71
Alameda County, CA	18,240
Alcatel Corporation	91
Ali, Khalil	194
Alstom/Soferval	241
Altamont Pass, CA	144
America's Cup Finals, 34th	113,125,156,324
American Car Company	8,10
Americans With Disabilities Act (ADA, 1990–Federal Law)	85,121, 126,164,166,251,258
Amtrak	203,242,219,221,235
Angel's Flight	247
Anheuser-Busch	48,159
Aquatic Park	123,124,203,213
Arnold, Bion J.	10,139
Astoria, OR	275
AT&T Park	119,137,208,280
Ateliers de La Brugeoise (Belgian PCC builder)	27,161
Atlanta, GA	241,265
Atlanta Streetcar	265,269
MARTA	265
Auckland, New Zealand	277
Austin, TX	236
Australia	61,123,129,237
Australia, Government of	50
Automatic Train Control System (ATCS)	86,87,91,119,156
Azienda Trasporti Milanesi (Milan, Italy transit agency)	106,114,135,136

B

Baccari, Al	124
Balboa Park	228,209
Baltimore, MD	25,134,275
Baltimore Streetcar Museum	275
"Barbary Coast"	7
Barcelona, Spain	277
BART	10,17-19,22,30,35,36,38,71,97,112,176,180,181,240,241
Concord/Daly City Line	25,240
Concord Test Track	240
Dublin/Pleasanton Line	240
Market Street Subway (includes Muni Metro level)	240
Pittsburg-Bay Poinr/ADo/Millbrae Line	240,241
Richmond/Fremont Line	240
Transbay Tube	17,240,252
Warm Springs, San Jose Extensions	240
BART Balboa Park Station	228,207
BART Daly City Station	240
BART Walnut Creek Station	240
Barton, Carl	49
"Battleships"	12
Bay Area Electric Railroad Association	161
Bay Meadows (race track)	65
Bayview District	233
Bayview Opera House	233
Beach, Cameron	127
Beamish Tramway Museum (England)	328
Bechtel Corporation	44,48,66
Belgium	25
Bendigo, Victoria, Australia	277
Benicia, CA	136
Benson, George	226
Bernal Heights	214
Bernal, Leon	21
Bernard, Larry	32
Bernhard, Bruce	188
Berkeley, CA	40,203
Bethlehem Steel Co.	125,145,159
Biagi, Tom	90,133
Bini, Rino	49
Birmingham, AL	161,237
Birney Safety Car	177,178 263
Blackpool, England	145,277
Boeing-Vertol Company	18,22,162,189
Boise, ID	273
Bombardier Transportation	123,155,241
"Bombay Roofs"	238
Boston, MA	18,22,27,40,41,129,130,232,234,237
Boeing-Vertol Burn-In Program (1976)	195
Mattapan-Ashmont Line	232
Opening of Riverside Line, 1959	134
"Boxcars"	16,158
Breda Costruzione Ferroviarie	106,136,246
Bridge Railway [SF-Oakland Bay Bridge]	17
Brill, J. G. Co.	25,47,53,150,159,160,231
Brill "Radiax" Truck	63,150
British Columbia Electric Ry.	234
Brooklyn & Queens Transit Co.	24,233
Brooklyn, NY	24,25,100,131,135,237
Brooklyn, NY PCC 1001	24,25,158,233
Brooks, OR	159,160,262,276
Brookville Equipment Corp.	14,22,29,32,109,112,121,123,136,139,142,144, 154,156,157,158,193,184-187,220,258,260,261,264,268,270-272,288,285, 287,324
Liberty Streetcars	261,268, 270-272
Brown, A. Page	11
Brown, Gov. Jerry	41
Brown, Willie L., Jr.	90,92,94,146,148,286
Brugge, Belgium	27
Brussels, Belgium	149,150
Buffalo, NY	114
Burns, Michael	106,121,150,158
Butler, Lee E., Jr.	46, 94
Byllesby Engineering and Management Co.	10

C

Cable Car Museum	237
Cable Cars	7,107,109,174,203,233-238,239
Caen, Herb	42,48,83,140,142,173,181
CAF USA	243,268
California Academy of Sciences	126,239
"California Comfort Car"	11,13,144,145
California Department of Highways	40
California Public Utilities Commission (CPUC)	106,113,136,138,139,156
California, Southern	74
California, State Of	38,64,220
California State Railroad Museum	227,244
California Street Cable Railroad	8,14,237
Callahan, John	136
Caltrain (Peninsula Commute Service)	97,176,227,233,241
Caltrain Depot (formerly SP Depot)	38-41,67,91,101,105,119
CalTrans (California Dept. of Transportation)	39,42
Cameron, Don	43
Campbell, CA	216
Canada	37
Canary Island Palm Trees	68,74,103,119,208
Cannery, The	188,189
Capitol Corridor (Amtrak)	242,243
CAPTrans [Citizens Advisory Panel (to the Board of Supervisors)]	37,42
Carter Bros. (cable car builder)	238
Carter, President Jimmy	41
Carvajal, Angel	287
Castro District	43,48,50,84,89,90,107,138,139,199
Castro District Merchants Association	90
Castro Street Fair	99
Castro Theater	89,199
"Cathedral Of Traction" (MessinaDepot, Milan, Italy)	116
Cauthen, Gerald R.	37-39
Centennial of Electric Streetcar Service in S. F.	71-74,150,152
Central Freeway	36,58,85,87,88,196,242
Central Subway	287
Central Waterfront	112,129,169
Certain, Joe	94,167
Charing Cross Station (London)	11,180
Charlotte, NC	263-265
Charlotte Area Transit System (CATS)	265-267
Charlotte Trolley, Inc.	264,266,267

CityLYNX Streetcar	265-267	East Troy, WI	276
LYNX Light Rail	265-267	East Windsor, CT	275
Chattanooga Choo-Choo Hilton	148	Eastshore Lines	159
Chattanooga, TN	148	Edmonton, AL	276
Chee, Don	101,103	*Edmonton Radial Railway Society*	276
Chicago, Aurora & Elgin Railroad	42	"Eighty-Hundreds" (Philadelphia's name for Peter Witts)	25,114
Chicago City Railway	8	*Electric City Trolley Museum*	275
Chicago, IL	18,25,26,28,68,114,133,233,240.2411,228	Electreic Railway Presidents' Conference Committee (ERPCC)	24,28,129
Chicago, North Shore & Milwaukee Railroad	42,234	*Electric Railroaders Association*	120
Chicago Transit Authority	44,235	11th Street Wye	42,54,76,77
Chico, CA	162,237	Elkton Shops	11,36,38,144,165,228
China Basin	38	El Paso, TX	25,28,27
Chinatown	17,174,236-240	SunMetro-El Paso Streetcar	271
Christchurch, New Zealand	277	El Segundo/Redondo Beach, CA	220,221
Cincinnati, OH	152,268	Embarcadero Center	48,179
Cincinnati Bell Connector Streetcar	268,269	Embarcadero Demonstration (1987 Trolley Festival)	61,64,65,119
Civic Center (San Francisco)	40,191,195	Embarcadero Freeway	38,40,45,64,196
Clackamah, OR	268	Embarcadero Roadway	37,40,101,103,180
Clark B-2 Trucks	25	Dedication Ceremony, June 16, 2000	107
Clark Equipment Co.	25	Embarcadero, The	6,38,40,41,43,44,63-65,83,93,103,107,112,119,190,
Clark, Steven	107		181,192
Class, Paul	47,159,228	Emporium, the–Last Christmas Parade (1995)	159
Clay Street Hill Railway	7	England	145
Cleveland, OH	18,27,114,147	English Electric	145
Cleveland Transit System	133	ETI/Skoda 14Tr-SF (trolley coach)	238
Cliff House	240	Eureka Portal	44
Clipper Cards (SmartCard fare system)	112,241	European Union	115
Coaster (San Diego County commuter rail)	219		F
Coit Tower	65,183,203	Fast Passes	112
Cole Valley	206	Feinstein, Dianne	27,29,37,38,39,41,43,49,53,56,57,60,62,66,67,69,133,
"Collingwood Elevated"	18,31		142,150,152,286,287,242
Columbia, CA	144	*Ferries & Cliff House Railway*	47,48,237,238
"Committee To Acquire Trams From Melbourne"	37-39	Ferries Loop	6,11,13
Communist Bloc [Countries]	25	Ferry Building	6,11,13,38,40,41,45,64,65,88,103,107,112,113,17,119,121,
Concord, CA	203,214		122,125,128,163,190,240
Connecticut Trolley Museum	275	Ferry Portal	114,120,146,208
Contra Costa County, CA	17,240	Financial District	190,227
Cranley, John	268	Finck, Nicolas	131,133
*Crich Tramway Village (*England)	277	Fine, Edward	53,65,94,191
Crissy Field	38,39	First Street (between Market and Mission, Transbay Terminal loop)	92,96
"Crooked Street"	237	Fisherman's Wharf	38-40,45,64,65,71,83,100,101,105-107,109,112,119,
Culver City, CA	220		121,127,136,139,145,150,190,204,205,209,210,213,214,229,237,239
Curtis, Art	106	Fisherman's Wharf Citizens Advisory Committee	45
Czech Republic	227,228,230,231,233	Fisherman's Wharf Extension	3,11,69,71,74,90,97,101-103,105,106,108,111,
	D		114,119,121,124,135,142,149,211
Dahms, Lawrence	41	Fisherman's Wharf Extension Track Construction	104-107
Dallas/Fort Worth International Airport	259	Fremont to Steuart	103
Dallas Railway & Terminal	155	Phase 1 (Broadway to North Point)	102,103
Dallas, TX	36,37,53,123,150,161,260,268	Phase 2 (Fisherman's Wharf Loop)	102-105
Dallas Area Rapid Transit (DART)	260	Pier 39 Loop Contract	101,102,105
Dallas Streetcar	260	Phase 3 (Mid-Embarcadero)	102,105,106,120
McKinney Avenue Transit Authority	54,162,260	Mission to Folsom (E-Line construction)	120
Daly City, CA	8,18,165,209	Fisherman's Wharf Merchants Association	45,121,124
De Young Museum	126,239	Fisherman's Wharf Port Tenants Association	45
Delmar Loop Trolley (St. Louis)	259,262	"Five Year Engagement, The" (comedy movie)	117
Democratic National Convention (1984)	46,53,54,56	Flieger, Albert	16
Denver, CO	275	Flyer E800 (trolley coach)	230
Department of Transportation (U.S.)	42	"Flying Scotsman" (train)	39
Deposito Messina (Milan, Italy–the "Cathedral of Traction")	116	Folsom, CA	220
Detroit, MI	30,50,114,135,258	Ford. Nathaniel Sr.	121,126
Detroit Citizens Railway/Detroit Downtown Trolley	258	Fort Collins, CO	161,230,231,234,237
Detroit PeopleMover	270	Fort Collins Municipal Railway Society	231
QLineStreetcar (M-1 Rail)	268,270	Fort Edmonton Park	276
Detroit Edison	24	Fort Mason	38,39,64,111,120,123-125,127,171,240,287,247
Detroit Peter Witt 3865	93,94	Fort Mason Center	124
Deuel Vocational Institute	144	Fort Mason Extension	124-126,152,170
"Dogpatch"District	125,232	Fort Mason Tunnel	38,39,64,120,125
Dolores Park	57,170,231	Fort Smith, AR	276
Dublin/Pleasanton, CA	227,240	*Fort Smith Trolley Museum*	276
Duboce Portal	18	Fort Worth, TX	236
Dunedin, New Zealand	233	Fox, Gerald D.	36
Duomo, the	114	*Fox River Trolley Museum*	276
	E	Fox Theater	16
East Bay	17,18,112,240	France	27
East Haven, CT	158,275	Frank, Phil ("Farley" cartoonist)	113
East Portal (Twin Peaks Tunnel)	14,43	*Fraser Valley Historical Railway Society*	276
East Troy Trolley Museum	276	Fremont, CA	203,214

G

Gales Creek Enterprises	47,150,159,160
Galveston, TX	275
Garcia, Sam	83,89,90
Gay Pride Day	52
Geary Street, Park and Ocean Railroad	8,10
Geissenheimer, Harold H.	26,43,47,49,53,66,67,142,144,160
General Electric	31,87,123,153,155,287
Genoa, Italy	136
Ghirardelli Square	113,188,189
Gilbert, Carole	131,169
Glenwood, OR	47,159
Golden Gate Bridge	11,40,118,185,237,240
Golden Gate National Recreation Area (GGNRA)	118,124,288
Golden Gate Park	10,40,125,230,239
Golden Gate Transit	95,96,215
Gold Rush (1849)	7
Goldberg, Whoopi	157,231
Goldschmidt, Neil	41
Gomaco Trolley Company	115,159,256,261,263,265
Great Earthquake and Fire (1906)	7-9,28,47,57,59,127,145,165,237
Great Freeway Revolt (1959)	40
Green, Curtis E.	44,67,189
Greyhound	95,96
Groner, Powell	133

H

Haight-Ashbury District	40,206
Hallidie, Andrew	7,233
Halton County Radial Railway Museum	276
Hamburg, Germany	37,50,52,152
Hammond Car Company (cable car builder)	238
Hayward, CA	203
Henry Ford Museum	94
Hetch Hetchy Water & Power	14,239
High Point, NC	160
Hiroshima, Japan	60,150
Hirshfeld, Dr. Clarence	24
"Hiss Of The Four (takeoff on "Roar Of The Four")	69
Hogan, John	98,182
Holman, W. L. Company	9,125,139,179,238,242
Hongisto, Richard	45
Hornell, NY	77,130,131
Horse Cars	7,10
Hudson-Bergen Line (Jersey City, NJ)	216
Hurley, Jud	109,173
Hurricane Katrina (August 29, 2005)	148,258
"Hyde Street Grip"	14
Hyde Street Pier	237

I

I-280 Concept Staff Recommendation	44
I-280 Transfer Fund	40,41
Ida Grove, IA	159,160,228,230,237
Illini Railroad Club	42
Illinois Railway Museum	30,94,275,276
Illinois Terminal Railroad	25,42,89,158
ILWU Longshormen's Hall	113
Inekon (Czech Republic streetcar builder)	259,263,268
Inner Sunset District	93,128
"Inside Track" (tracks on Market Street)	12,
"Inside Track" (tracks on 1st Street)	93,94
Inside Track (*MSR* Newsletter)	99,101,173
Interurban Electric Railway (Southern Pacific)	94
Iowa Traction	2764
"Iron Monsters"	6,14-16,28,30,52,54,58,90,100,142,144,146,169,176,180, 204,239
Islais Creek	233
"Italian Standard Transport Vehicle Orange"	115,137,138
Italy	27,116

J

Jacobs, John	44
James, Sly	268
Japan	66
Japan Railway Corporate Assembly	60,150
Jeremiah O'Brien (Liberty Ship)	185,189,190
Jewett Car Company	142
Johnson, Karl	50,129,133,164,168,169,183,324
Johnson, Ken	32
Johnson, President Lyndon (daughter of)	237
Johnstown, PA	25,149,152
Jordan, Frank	79,83,90
Jurmann, Walter	7
Justin Herman Plaza	103,105,179,191,238

K

Kahn, Gus	7
Kamenev, Valentin	60,61,150
Kansas City, MO	30,149,161,233,268
KCPS PCC 551 (ex-Muni 1190)	268
KCStreetcar	268,269
Kansas City Public Service	133,268
Kawasaki	182
Kaper, Bronislaw	7
Kelley Park (San Jose)	242
Kennebunkport, ME	169,275
Kenosha, WI	27,147,263
"Key Stops"	86,126
Key System	17,94,125,217
King County Metro (Seattle area)	259
Kinkisharyo	216
Klauder, Louis Associates	18
Klebolt, Maurice H.	37,42-44,47,48,51,53,60,61,64-67,69,71,98,101,133, 150,152,161,164
Klussmann, Friedel	14,237
Kobe, Japan	60,150
Korean War	123,174

L

"Ladies In Red"	148,150
Lai, Lan	164
Lake Oswego, OR	228,233
Lancastrian Transport Trust (England)	328
Landor, Walter & Associates	31
La Scala Opera House	115
Land's End	215
Laubscher, Rick	35,44,45,50,53,66,90,98,101,133,143,152,173,286
Lee, Chimmy	238
Lee, Ed	125,142,287
Lemon Grove, CA	219
Levi Strauss & Co.	48,183
Levin, Jaimie	131,133
Linke-Hoffmann-Busch AG	152,228
Little Rock, AR	250,264
Central Arkansas Transit (CAT) (now Rock Region Metro)	250
River Rail (now Metro Streetcar)	250,264
Loftus, NSW, Australia	234
Loma Prieta Earthquake (1989)	40,64,89,101,165,241
Lombard Street ("The Crooked Street")	214,215
Long Beach, CA	218,220
Los Angeles, CA	25,27,28,43,103,203,244,273
Los Angeles County, CA	220
Los Angeles, Port of	231
Los Angeles County Metropolitan Transportation Authority (LACMTA)	244,246,247
Los Angeles International Airport	235
Los Angeles Union Passenger Terminal	246
Lotta's Fountain	9
Louie, George	126,145
Louisville, KY	147,173,183
Louisville Railway Co.	133
Low-Voltage Power Supply (LVPS)	121
Lowell, MA	231,234,237
Lowell National Historic Park	231

M

MacDonald, Jeanette	7
Mack Truck Co.	30
Macris, Dean	44
Mahoney Bros. (cable car builder)	238
Manag, Romer	164
Manhattan, NY	179,233
Marelich, Tony	16
Marin County, CA	17,112,242
Marin Yard	32
Marina District	38,40,120,239

Market Street Beautification Act	35,37,42
Market Street Design Planning Study	42
Market Street Railway (F-Line booster organization)	9,11,35,44,48,52,61,66, 69,71,74,83,89,90,93,94,98-100,103,105-107,112,120,121,123-127,130,131 138,145,152,158,161,164,166,170,172,174,175,177,179,182,173, 181-183,191,197,198.203,215,220.224,225,238,239
Market Street Railway Company (1893)	8,10,57,145,209,213
Market Street Railway Company (1921)	10,13,14,17,32,37,43,49.74,84,93, 96,98,99,106,144,145,152,155,156,165,171,228,230,240
Market Street Track Reconstruction	70-83
Phase 1 (Rail Replacement, Lower Market)	69,70
Phase 2 (First and Fremont Streets)	70,71
Phase 3 (Upper Market)	74,75,77,105
Phase 4 (11th Street to Duboce)	77-81,105
Market Street Streetcar Plan, The (San Francisco Tomorrow)	36
Market Street Transit Thoroughfare	69,78
Marmon-Herrington (TC44 trolley coach)	238
Marmot-Herrington (TC48 trolley coach 776, preserved)	44,96,239
Mason City, IA	276
Matoff, Tom	36,37,39
Mays, Willie (the *Say Hey Kid*)	232
McKinney Avenue Transit Authority	52,160,227
McLaren, John	125
Melbourne & Metropolitan Tramways Board	39,258
Melbourne, Australia	53,129,276,277
Melbourne W2s,W5s, SW6s	51,129,145,148.149.217,251,258,259,261,262,277
Memphis, TN	36,37,51,148,152,261
Main Street Trolley®	261
Memphis Area Transit Authority (MATA)	261,262
Metrolink (Los Angeles commuter rail)	246
Metro-North Railroad	241
Metropolitan Railroad	8,230
Metropolitan Transportation Commission	41,42
"Mexican Jumping Bean" (Veracruz 001)	53,160
Mexico	53,160
Mexico City, Mexico	30
Miami Beach, FL	273
Michel, Art	90,164,324
Midewst Electric Railway	276
Midwest Threshers Reunion	117,276
Milan, Italy	114-117,129,135,138,161,217,220,230,233,265
Milano, Comune di	53
Millbrae, CA	216
Milton, ON	276
Milwaukee, WI	48,272
Milwaukee "HOP" Streetcar	272
Miner Railcar	232
Minneapolis-St. Paul, MN	28,152,273,276
Minnesota (Ironworld, Chisholm, MN)	53
Minnesota Streetcar Museum	276
Miranda, Danny	165-167
Mission Bay	38,123,125,208
Mission Creek	232
Mission Dolores	88,153,196,231
Molinari, John	37,69
Montréal, PQ	25
Morial, Ernest	96,148
Morrison Knudsen Corporation	77,87,130,131,134,135,156,241
Moscone, George	37,66
Moscow, Russia	150
Mountain View, CA	216
Mt. Hoold Freeway (Portland, OR)	44
Mt. Pleasant, IA	276
Muni Metro Meltdown (August 24, 1998)	91,94
Museums In Motion (MSR Calendar)	101
Music Concourse (Golden Gate Park)	125
Mussolini, Generalissimo Benito	114,115,152

N

Napoleon	92
National Capital Trolley Museum	275
National Park Service (U. S. Department of The Interior)	125,126,185,231
National Trust For Historic Preservation	74
Netherlands, The	27
Nevin, John	43,49,171
Newark, NJ	25
Newark City Subway	152,154,155,216
Newark, OH	142
New Flyer Industries XT60 Xcelsior (articulated trolley coach	239
New Jersey Transit (NJT)	152
New Orleans, LA	10,51,93,101,161,251-255,258
Canal Line	148,224,251,253,254,258
Canal Line-City Park Branch	254,258
Canal Station	54
Carrollton Shops	148,251,252,258
Carrollton Station	255
Loyola Line	253,255,258
Rampart/St. Claude Line	253,255,258
Riverfront Line	94-96,146,148,251,253,258
St. Charles Line	94,101,148,251,252,255.259
New Orleans Public Belt Railroad	148
New Orleans Public Service, Inc. (NOPSI)	148,251
New Orleans Regional Transit Authority (RTA)	148,149,251
Newsom, Gavin	109,125
New York City, NY	18,27,96,250
New York City Transit Authority	133
New York Subway	103,227,280-283
New York Transit Museum	280
New Zealand	237
Niewiarowski, Ron	40,41,45
NIMBYism	90,208
9/11 (September 11, 2001 tragedy)	109,179
1934 General Strike	180
1981-1986 Short Range Transit Plan	49-51,56
1979-1984 Short Range Transit Plan	39
Nippon Sharyo	243,246
"No-Wires-On-Market-Street" (ordinance)	8
Nob Hill	237.238
Noe Valley	231
Nolte, Carl	195
North Bay	242
North Beach	203
North Coast Railroad Authority	243
North Hollywood, CA	220
North Little Rock, AR	264
Northeast Sewage Treatment Plant	65
Northern California Railroad Club	32,96,103
Northern Waterfront	71,107
Northern Waterfront Survey (Dept. of City Planning)	39
Northwest Railroad Museum	276
Northwestern Pacific	242
Norwalk, CA	220,221
Nothenberg, Rudy	44,69

O

Oakland, Antioch & Eastern	9
Oakland, Army Base	124
Oakland, CA	40,203
Oakland, Port of	66
Ocean Beach	7,10,52,75,152,230,214
Oklahoma City	271
EMBARK—OKC Streetcar	271
"One-Armed Bandits"	28
Oporto, Portugal	36,47,150,160,216,261
Orange County, CA	273
Orange Empire Railway Museum	142-144,146,149,156,159,231,276
Orbisonia, PA	275
Oregon Electric Railway Historical Society	47,159,161,262,276
Oregon Iron Works	263
Orel, Russia	150
Osaka, Japan	152,231,234
Over-The-Rhine (Cincinnati)	268

P

Pacific Electric Railway (interurban)	25,26,43,133,171,244,246
Pacific Heights	213
Pacific Ocean	204,205,220
Pacific Surfliner (Amtrak)	247
Palmer, William "Chip"	60
Panama-Pacific International Exposition (1915)	155,181,239
Panhandle Freeway	40
Parkmerced	228
Parkside District	204
Pasadena, CA	218,220
"Path Of Gold" street lights	35-37
PCC Car, general information	24-27,129,135,160,228
PCC Car, Muni-specific	28-33

Pegler, Alan	39
Peninsula Commute Service	38
Pennsylvania Trolley Museum	275
Perley Thomas Car Works	148,251
Perris, CA	144,149,160,276
Peter Witts	55,116-119,129,135,136,138,217,237
Pharr, David L.	90,91,148
Philadelphia, PA	19,25,27,57,114,123,129,130,132,145,155,156,232,234
Retirement of Nearside Cars, 1955	133
Philadelphia Suburban Transit Company (Red Arrow)	182
Phlueger, Timothy	199
Phoenix, AZ	237
Pier 39	64,105,107,112,119,183,190
Pistoia, Italy	136
Pittsburg, CA	203,214
Pittsburgh, PA	24-26,43,66,172,183
Playland-At-The-Beach	125,240
Poetry Plaques (at F-Line boarding islands)	107
Port Authority Transit (Pittsburgh)	158
Port Of Los Angeles	220,231
Port of Oakland	64
Port of San Francisco	44,106,126
Portland, OR	37,41,42,48,125,159,160,224,225,227,228,234,236,237
Portland Streetcar	160,256,257,262,263
Portland Vintage Trolley	37,87,256,262
TriMet-MAX Light Rail	160,256,257,262
Willamette Shore Trolley	256,262
Post of Point San Jose (old name for Fort Mason)	123
Potrero Hill	213
Presidio Army Base (see Presidio, the)	
Presidio & Ferries Railroad	8,11
Presidio, The	38,39,64,124,126
Previn, André	146,148
"Proof-Of-Payment"	91,112
Pullman-Standard	25

Q

Queen Mary 2	137

R

Railway Preservation Corp.	280
Reagan, President Ronald	41
Red Arrow (Philadelphia Suburban Trans. Co.)	135
Red Garter Band, the	55
Regular Day Off [work] (RDO)	91,109
Reitzes, Robin	136
Renne, Louise	44
Retuta, Bobby	166
"*Revisione Generale*" (Milan Peter Witt Overhaul)	117,138
Richmond, CA	203,214
Richmond District	125,214
Richmond-San Rafael Bridge	40
Richmond, VA	7,11
Rio Vista Junction, CA	39,45,145,159,242
"Roar Of The Four"	10-12,17,69,74,93,105,140
Rockhill Trolley Museum / Railways To Yesterday	275
Rodriguez, Kenny	65,69,106,107,135,136
Rogers, Rich	62
Rohr Corporation	240
Rolph, James L "Sunny Jim"	10,49,140,230,287
Russia; Soviet Union	66,150
Russian Hill	213

S

Sacramento, CA	9,17,227,243,244
Sacramento Northern Railroad	9,96,163,242
Sacramento Regional Transit District	127,217,244
PG&E 35 (vintage car)	244
RT Metro Light Rail	203,243-245
Sacramento Streetcar (proposed)	273
Salt Lake City, UT	265,267
Sugar House Streetcar (S-Line)	265,267,269
TRAX Light Rail	265,267
SamTrans (San Mateo County Transit District)	96
San Antonio, TX	275
San Bernardino County, CA	220
San Diego, CA	25,30,219,220,247
San Diego & Arizona Eastern Railway	248
San Diego & Imperial Valley Railroad	248
San Diego Metropolitan Transit System	248
San Diego Trolley	248,249
San Diego Vintage Trolley	248,249,295
San Francisco & San Mateo Railroad	7,28,165
San Francisco Bay	180
San Francisco Board of Supervisors	37,40,42,45,50,66,90,105
San Francisco Chamber of Commerce	44,48,50,56,152
San Francisco Chronicle	43,113,158,171,173,181,239
San Francisco City Attorney	77,136
San Francisco City Charter	16,28-30,47
San Francisco City Hall	52,66,152,191,195,206
San Francisco City Purchaser	136
San Francisco Convention and Visitors Bureau	44
San Francisco County, CA	240
San Francisco Department of City Planning	44,45
San Francisco Department of Public Works	38,101
San Francisco Giants	119,137,232,235
San Francisco International Airport	18.227,240
San Francisco Maritime Museum	188,189,237
San Francisco Municipal Railway (Muni) **entire book**	
(see separate section)	
San Francisco Municipal Transportation Agency (SFMTA)	13,17,39,41, 93,95,108,121,125-127,144,155,158,240
San Francisco-Oakland Bay Bridge	11,17,40,41,93,95,108,122,146,208, 210,216,281
San Francisco Opera House	148
San Francisco Planning Commission	45
San Francisco Planning and Urban Research (SPUR)	68
San Francisco Public Transportation Commission (SFPTC)	85,121,136,155
San Francisco Public Utilities Commission (SFPUC)	39,41,42,44,136
San Francisco Railway Museum	98,103,179,238,239
San Francisco Redevelopment Agency	44
San Francisco State University	228
San Francisco Tomorrow	36-38
San Francisco Zoo	52,74,228
San Jose, CA	53,117,227,241,242,278
San Jose Rail and Trolley Corp.	241
San Mateo County, CA	18,214
San Ysidro, CA/Tijuana, Mexico	248
Santa Clara, CA	216
Santa Clara County, CA	109,203
Santa Clara Valley Transportation Authority (VTA) Light Rail	109,117, 205,241,245
Santa Monica, CA	246
Santa Monica Mountains	218,220
Santa Rosa (ferryboat)	31
St. Anne's Of The Sunset Church	21,226,230
St. Charles & Carrollton Railway (New Orleans)	251
St. Francis Circle	52,76,228
St. Francis Wood	204
St. Louis B-3 Trucks	87
St. Louis Car Company	8-10,25,27-29,130,133,182,158
St. Louis, MO	25,270
Delmar Loop Trolley	270
St. Louis Public Service Co.	16,30,49,159
St. Paul's Church	145,231
Savannah, GA	157,275
Schnitzer Steel (scrapper)	32
Seal Rocks	240
Seashore Trolley Museum	169,275
SEA-TAC International Airport	259
Seattle, WA	39,50,51,258-260
Link LRT	259
Downtown Seattle Transit Tunnel	259
First Hill Streetcar	259
Monorail	259
Seattle Streetcar	259
South Lake Union Streetcar	50,259
Waterfront Streetcar	39,258,259
Selah, WA	274
"Seven Hills"	7
17th Street Detour	18,24,28,48,159,233
Shore Line Trolley Museum	24,48,158,275
Siemens	243,244,246,248,265
Sierra Nevada (Calif. mountain range)	129
Silk Road Transport	132,134,161
Sister Act (movie, starring Whoopi Goldberg)	157,231
Sklar, Richard	43,44

Skoda-Inekon	259,,263,264
Smallwood, Charles	32,50,142,155
Smith, Jack	42-44,48,49,54,59,60,65,133,141,144,171
Snell, F. D.	39
Snoqualmie, WA	161,276
Sonoma County, CA	152,243
Sonoma-Marin Area Rail Transit (SMART)	242,243
Sound Transit (Seattle, Tacoma)	259,264
Sounder (Seattle-area commuter rail)	230
South Elgin, IL	276
South Lake Tahoe, CA	179
Southeastern Pennsylvania Transportation Authority (SEPTA)	122,130,145,182
Southern Pacific Depot	10.38,39
Southern Pacific Railroad	8,38,94,231,242
Bayshore Shops	38
Jefferson Branch, Portland, OR	261
Spain	27
Sprague, Frank J.	7
Stacy & Witbeck	77,78
Standard Power & Light Corp.	10
State Belt Railroad	13,35,38,39,45,64,120,123-125,185
State Division of Bay Toll Crossings	38
Stead, William	62,150,164
Stone & Webster	237
Stonestown Galleria	228
Straus, Peter	36,37,39,43,44,51,131,133
"Streetcar Named Desire" (New Orleans 952)	93,94,114,146,148
Streetcar Named Desire, A (Tennessee Williams play)	94,146,148
"Streetcar Named Desire For Peace" (Moscow/Orel 106)	60,150
Suisun City-Fairfield, CA	217
Sunday Streets	121-123
Sunnyvale, CA	216
Sunset District	93
Sunset Tunnel	126,230
Surface Rail System for the San Francisco Waterfront, A (Cauthen)	37,38,43
Sutter Street Railroad	8,10
"Swinging Load"	101
Sydney Tramway Museum	122,277
San Francisco Municipal Railway (Muni)	
Body Shop	168,169
Bond issues	13,14
Bus Rapid Transit (Van Ness, Geary Corridors-future)	239
Cable Cars in Historic Paint Schemes	214
Capital Projects	106,112
Cable Cars in Historical Livery:	
1 (Original Powell Street Railway, 1883,1888)	238
3 (Muni green and cream, 1960s-1982)	238
9 (Market Street Railway Co. "White Front")	234,238
11 (1893 Market Street Railway Sacramento/Clay Line Red)	
12 (Market Street Railway 1935-1944))	
13 (United Railroads green/red trim, 1907-1921)	236,238
15 (1893 Market Street Railway yellow/red)	234,238
16 (Muni blue/gold, 1939)	238
25 (United Railroads red, 1905-1908)	236,214
26 (Muni green/cream, white letterboard, 1946)	214,241
Car Types:	
A-Types, "Arnolds"	9,10,125,139
B-Typse	10,14,30,125,144,146,161
C-Types, "Magic Carpets"	16,17,28,29,32,135,136,155
D-Types, PCC "Torpedoes"	13,14,16,17,22,28-30,79,87,89,109,121,123,126,127,129,130,134,135,155-158
"Haight Street Jewetts" (ex-MSRy)	13,98,124
J-Types, "Union Street Dinkies"	61,150,204
K-Types	14,17,125,142,171,204
L-Types	14,142
LRV, Boeing-Vertol	19,22,84,91,92,121,136,165,171
LRV, Breda	90,91,119,120,127,128,136,146,167,160,172
LRV, Siemens LRV-4	232
Milan "Peter Witts," Milanos	106,109,114-117,128,137,146,154,169-171,182,246
Misc. Vintage Cars	182
PCCs [general term]	14,16-19,22,28,167-170,173
PCC "Baby Tens"	14,16,17,22,28,31,32,49,109,129,144,154,154,158,159
PCC, ex-St. Louis "Elevens"	17,30-32,49,129,142,156,158.159
PCC "Torontos"	13,18,30,31,134
PCC, ex-Philadelphia cars	77-79,123,134,155,246
PCC, ex-Newark cars, "Brookvilles"	29,109,112,123,152-155,158.159,163,239,244-246
Centennial Committee	239
Central Control	109,166
Central Subway	233
Community Affairs	131
Consolidation [with MSRy], Sept. 29,1944	11,13,124,131,204
Consolidation Vote, May 16, 1944	13
Department of Community Affairs	131
Department of Finance	108
Divisions, Yards, and MaintenanceFacilities	
Cable Car Barn	235,237,241
Cable Car Shop	136,150,171,213
Cameron Beach Historic Streetcar Yard (Geneva Yard, renamed 2010)	127,145,152,168,228,241,244
Geary Carhouse	9,28
Geneva Carhouse	21,22,28,126,129,142,152,165
Geneva Carhouse Office Building	228
Geneva Division	167
Geneva Paint Shop	133,168,169,241
Geneva Shop	149,158,164,165,167-170,228
Geneva Upper Yard	21,22,152,158
Geneva Yard	49,62,77,90,126,127,131,143,144,145,147.151,152,158,159,165,168,228
Geneva Yard Reconstruction (forF-Line cars)	77
Green Light Rail Division	107,113,165,167
Historic Streetcar Enclosure (Geneva Yard)	127,138,228,241,244
Islais Creek Division (future bus yard)	112
Kirkland Division (buses)	112
Marin Yard	152,155,156,158,159,169,206
Metro Annex	165,168
Metro Center	31,36,48,50,61,63,141,144,145,149,153,58,161,162,165,170,209
Metro East	9,126,127,140,142,144,149,153,155,157,163,169,232
Metro Yard	106,137,165,168,228,207
Mint Yard (David L. Pharr Yard)	48,49,52,55,56,71,90,91,142,144,145,148,150-152,158,159,166,168,169,171
Potrero Division (trolley coaches)	28
Washington-Mason Cable Car Barn and Powerhouse	47,49,211,213
DTE (Diagnostic Test Electronics Shop)	170
Facilities Maintenance	170
Fleet Engineering	123,170
F-Line Milan Cars (Milanos, Peter Witts, "Ventotto" listed in text (except 1834):	
Milano 1507 (later 1807, orange)	136
Milano 1807 (orig. 1507, orange)	106,136,138
Milano 1807 (orig. 1507, yellow/white)	138
Milano 1811 (orig. 1911, orange)	138
Milano 1811 (orig. 1911, yellow/white)	117,138
Milano 1911 (later 1811, orange)	136
Milano 1814 (orange)	111,138
Milano 1515 (later 1815, orange)	106,136
Milano 1818 (orange)	136
Milano 1818 (2-tone green)	99,138,139,169
Milano 1556 (later 1856, orange)	106,136
Milano 1859 (orange)	106,136,140
Milano 1588 (later1888, orange)	136
Milano 1888 (orig. 1588, orange)	111,136
Milano 1888 (orig. 1588, 2-tone green)	138,182
Milano 1793 (later 1893, orange)	106,136
Milano 1893 (orig. 1793, orange)	103,139
Milano 1795 (later 1895, orange)	136
Milano 1895 (orig. 1795, orange)	136,138
Milano 1979 (parts car)	136,138
F-Line PCC Cars listed in text:	
PCC 14 (Newark-NJ Transit, was to become 1070)	154
PCC 1006 (Muni Wings)	14,123,155-158
PCC 1007 ("Stealth" livery, gray/silver/red)	87,134,135

PCC 1007 (Red Arrow)	120,123,135
PCC 1008 (Muni Wings)	13,123,155,156
PCC 1009 (Dallas)	123,134,155,156,171
PCC 1010 (Muni 1939 blue/gold)	89,96,120,134,135
PCC 1011 (MSRy Zip Stripe)	123,134,155,156
PCC 1014, at Sydney Tramway Museum	123,129
PCC 1015 (Illinois Terminal)	89,106,134,135
PCC 1040 (Muni Wings)	14,83,86,125,155-158
PCC 1050 (Muni Wings)	14,83,131,133
PCC 1051 (Muni Simplified)	77,83,96,131,133
PCC 1052 (Los Angeles Railway 2-tone yellow)	131,133
PCC 1053 (Brooklyn)	32,101,131,133
PCC 1054 (Philadelphia 1938 silver/blue)	109,131,133
PCC 1055 (Philadelphia green/cream)	77,131,133
PCC 1056 (Kansas City)	109,131,133,169
PCC 1057 (Cincinnati)	131,133,135,169,189,241
PCC 1058 (Chicago green/cream)	109,131,133
PCC 1058 (Chicago "Green Hornet" livery, Mercury green/Croydon cream)	109,131,133,172
PCC 1059 (Boston)	83,131,134
PCC 1060 (Newark-PSCT)	77,109,131,133,154
PCC 1060 (Philadelphia 1938 silver/blue)	111,131,133,169
PCC 1061 (Pacific Electric)	109,131,133,160
PCC 1062 (Louisville)	77,131,133
PCC 1063 (Baltimore)	131,133,134
PCC 1070 (Newark-PSCT)	133,154,155
PCC 1071 (Minneapolis/St. Paul)	109,153-155,233
PCC 1072 (Mexico City)	154,155
PCC 1073 (El Paso)	153-155
PCC 1074 (Toronto)	154
PCC 1075 (Cleveland)	154
PCC 1076 (Washington)	154
PCC 1077 (Birmingham)	154
PCC 1078 (San Diego)	154,48
PCC 1079 (Detroit)	154
PCC 1080 (Los Angeles Transit Lines) "Friot Sa;ad")	154
PCC 2133 (was to have been 1064)	130,156,158
F-Line Vintage Cars, specific: (Trolley Festivals and beyond)	
Blackpool "Boat" 226,228,233	49,50,52,53,56,57, 83,89,9098,112,113,120,121,135,145,148,169
Brussels/"Zurich" PCC 7037/737	27,149,150
Hamburg "Red Baron" 3557	37,48,50,152,164
Johnstown, PA 351	98,149,152,182,183
Kobe/Hiroshima 578J	57,60,152
Market Street Ry. "Dinky" 578S	8,57,60,65,99,120,145
Market Street Ry. 798	11,98,144,145,182,183
Marmon-Herrington trolley coach 776	49,52,100,149
Melbourne W2 648,496,586	39,48,52,53,57,60,61,89, 101,107,112,113,121,147,149
Melbourne SW6 916	147,149,182,183
Milan Interurban 96	162,234
Milano 1834	53,86,89,90,106,135,138,139,162,170,182
Milwaukee 978	48,50,53,161
Moscow/Orel 106	60,69,150,241
Muni A-Type 1	9,43,47,49,51,53,60,89,106,112,113, 120,121,126,139,142,159,171,238,239,242,243
Muni B-Type 130	10,49,50,52,53,69,89,90,96, 106,112,113,126,155,156,158,182,183
Muni B-Type 162	10,14,98,112,113,121,123,125, 126,157,158,182,241
Muni Boeing LRV 1213	49,53,160,233
Muni Boeing 2-Car Train on Market Street	57
Muni K-Type 178	16,43,44,48-50,52,53,142,159,161,162
Muni PCC "Torpedo" 1006	32,53,57,69
Muni PCC "Baby Ten" 1040	28,47,52,53,83,86,129,155
New Orleans 952,913	93,94,98,99,112,113, 120,121,123,146,149,152,182,183,251
New Orleans 952 (as Riverfront 456 in N.O.)	146
Oporto 122,189	47,52,53,57,65,150,151,160,182,183
Osaka 151	150,151,182,183
Portland "Council Crest" 503	47,52,54,59,159
Sacramento Northern Birney 62	162
St. Louis PCC 1704 (ex-Muni 1128)	47,52,53,86,156, 158,159
Veracruz 001	53,57,160
White "Baby White" 062 (motor coach)	62
Finance Department	106

Last Day Of PCC Operation (Sept. 19, 1982)	19,29,32,158
Lines:	
A-Geary and Park	10,140
B-Geary and Ocean	10,14,17,28,30,142,157,158,176
C-Geary and California	13,14,30,140,142
California Street Cable Car Line	179,236,238
Central Subway (under construction)	209,239
E-Embarcadero	39,45,49,65,69,103-105,112,118-120, 121,123,125,127,128,148,152,156,170,232,233,287
E-Embarcadero Demonstration (1987)	34.61,64,65,150
E-Union	13,16,49,61
F-Market, F-Market Street & Wharves	entire book
Opening of F-Line, Sept. 1, 1995	77,82-87,89,98, 119,133,135,150,241
Opening of Wharf Extension, March 4, 2000	103,106, 149
F-Stockton	10,49,106,213
G-Golden Gate Park (proposed line)	125,152,163
H-Potrero	13,123,247
J-Church	10,22,28,30-32,43,44,48,57,71,74,76,77,87,112, 121,125,131,142,143,149,151,158,160,165,169,170, 188,227,228,230,231,232,287
K-Market Street (later K-Ingleside)	11,13,15,16,18,28,30, 31,52,74,143,158,227-229,232
K-Ingleside/L-Taraval Shuttle	31
L-Taraval	15,16,18,28,30,31,33,50,52,74,130,143,227, 229,240,278
L-Taraval/M-Ocean View Shuttle	31
M-Ocean View	15-18,28,30,54,57,58,143,153,226-228,240
Muni Metro [general term]	10,18,19,22,30-32,35,36,40, 42,49,51,71,77,84-87,89-92,112,113,119,138,148,165,167, 168,176,180,181,201,227,204,208,209
Muni Metro Extension (MMX)	69,74,91,101,103,119-123, 148,149,227,232,233
Muni Metro Subway	18,31,48,74,86,91,107,111,121,160, 161,165,239
Muni Metro Turnback (MMT)	40,93,208
N-Judah	16,18,22,28,30-33,52,56,57,71,76,77,91,93,101, 119,122,125,126,129,131,147-149,152,158,161,196, 228,229
O'Farrell, Jones & Hyde Cable Car Line	237
Powell/Hyde Cable Car Line	233,237,213
Powell/Mason Cable Car Line	233,237,212,213
R-Howard (trolley coach line)	49
T-Third Street	8,38,103,119,124,125,127,137,143, 149,227,231-233,239,280
Washington-Jackson Cable Car Line	237
Z-Excursion	72,74,76
1-California	239
5/5R-Fulton	69,96,239,215
6-Haight & Mssonic (ex-MSRy streetcar)	208
6-Parnassus	96
8-Market	54,74,83,87
21-Hayes	69
24-Divisadero	52,239
28-19th Avenue	30
30-Stockton	239,215
31-Balboa	240
32-Embarcadero	102,107
33-Stanyan (18th & Park, in MSRy days)	238,239
37-Corbett	240
38-Geary	96
38L-Geary Limited	96,215
55-Sacramento	239
Richmond Expresses	112
Muni Metro Stations:	
Arleta Avenue Station (T-Line)	233
Brannan Street Station (MMX)	119,232
Carroll Avenue Station (T-Line)	233
Castro Street Station	18,30,31,48,84,85,89,92,227
Church Street Station	18,30,48,227
Civic Center Station	17,69,79,227
Embarcadero Station	17,38,41,85,91,93,94,12,119,121, 123,188,191,227
Eureka Station (Twin Peaks Tunnel)	43
Folsom Street Station (MMX)	94,119,121,232

Forest Hill Station	228
Fourth Street and King Station (T-Line)	232
Glen Park Station (J-Line)	231
Gilman/Paul Avenue Station (T-Line)	233
King & 2nd Street Station (MMX)	119,232
King & 4th Street/Caltrain Station (MMX)	119,121,232
LeConte Avenue Station (T-Line)	233
Marin Street Station (T-Line)	233
Montgomery Street Station	17,69,91,227
Palou/Oakdale Station (T-Line)	233
Powell Street Station	17,69,91,201,227
San Francisco State Station (M-Line)	153,228
Stonestown Station (M-Line)	228
Sunnydale Avenue Station (T-Line)	233
UCSF/Mission Bay Station (T-Line)	126,137
Van Ness Avenue Station	17,227
West Portal Station	15,132,204
Muni Opening Day, December 28,1912	9,154,239
Muni 50th Anniversary (1962)	34,139,140,156
Muni 75th Anniversary (1987)	34,60
Muni 100th Anniversary (2012)	154,238,239,242,243
Overhead Lines Department	170
Paint Schemss, specific reference to:	
1912 gray and maroon	52
1939 World's Fair blue and gold	28,50.142
1946 Muni "Wings" green and cream	13,28,30,32,53,131, 144,155,156,158,159,209
1963 Muni "Simplified" green and cream	131
1968 red, gold and white (on buses and "Torontos")	30
1975 Landor 2-tone orange and white	18,19,22,31,32,50, 129,157,158
1995 "Stealth" livery (silver, gray and red)	87,135,166
1998 SEPTA-Style, Landor colors	166,170
PCCs in storage at Marin Yard (18)	158
Planning Division	19,22,36,37,39,51,71,131,170
Rail Change Control Board	126
Schedules and Traffic Department	107,170
Station Operations	168
Track Department	57,171
Training Department	168
Trolley Maintenance Department	50,86,135,167
Work Cars:	
0131 (Muni B-Type 130 as wrecker)	142
0304 (Line Car)	77
0601 (MSRy "Dinky" 578S as sand car)	145
C-1 (Muni utility car, 1923)	96,106
T	
Tacoma, WA	264,269
Tampa, FL	263
TECOLine	263
Telegraph Hill	64,183
Telegraph Hill Dwellers Association	45
Tempe, AZ	272
Tenderloin District	214
Texas	136
The Hague, Netherlands	27
Thomsen, Walter	83,98,113,131,167,220
Tibidabo Blue Tram (Barcelona)	277
Tijuana, Mexico	220
Tilikum Crossing Bridge (Portland)	262,263
Torino, Italyy	277
Toronto, ON	25,30,129.229.234
"Tour Of Illuminations" (Blackpool, England)	277
"Tours Of Discovery" (Muni Map)	227
Transbay Terminal (Transbay Transit Terminal)	6,11,13,16,38,46,51,53, 56,57,61,69,77,87,90,92,94-98,125,126,136,139,142,150, 160,161,167,176
Last Day of Regular Service (March 3, 2000)	92,96,97
Transbay Tube (BART)	17,240,241
Transit Museum Society (Vancouver, BC)	234
Transit Research Corp. (TRC, successor to ERPCC)	25,27,28
Transport Workers Union, Local 250-A	65,91,126,167
TriMet (Portland, OR)	160,228
MAX Light Rail	160,225,228
Trolley Coaches	11,14,35,37,50,205,238,239
Tucson, AZ	230,231,234,236
Old Pueblo Trolley	265-267
Sun Link Streetcar	267,265
Twin City Rapid Transit (Minneapolis/St. Paul)	155
Twin Peaks	89,240
Twin Peaks Tunnel	10,14,15,18,43,44,48,74,89,227
2008-2027 Short Range Transit Plan	113,121,123
U	
UCSF Medical Center	21,126,230
UCSF Mission Bay Campus	232
Union, IL	275
Union Iron Works	10,125,139,143,159
Union Iron Works Historic District	38,123,125,126,143,232
Union Pacific Railroad	233
Union Square	166,175,234,235,237
United Nations World Environment Day	149
United Railrods (URR)	8-13,15,38,74,145,152,165,228
United States Army	123
United States Department Of Transportation	18,22,41
United States Navy Fleet Week	106,136,198
United States Standard Light Rail Vehicle	18,22,160
United Streetcar LLC	263,265,268
United Transportatioon Systems	220
University of Arizona	265
University of San Francisco (USF)	240
Urban Mass Transportation Administration	41
Universal City, CA	220
URR, MSRy Cars:	
San Francisco (school trolley	152
URR, MSRy Lines and Routes:	
6-Haight & Masonic	206
7-Haignt	125
12-Mission & Ocean	74,204
15-Third & Kearny (to Fisherman's Wharf)	106
16-Third & Broadway	11,125
20-Ellis	10
31-Balboa	11,12,216
33-18th & Park (first trolley coach line)	238
40-San Mateo Interurban	11
Castro Street Cable Car Line	13
Fillmore Street Counterbalance	13
Land's End Line	11
Sacramento/Clay Cable Car Line	8,11,13
UTDC (ex-San Jose LRVs in Sacramento)	243
V	
Valencia Grade (Market, between Laguna/Guerrero and Valencia)	92
Vallejo, CA	112
Vancouver, BC	30,234
Ventura County, CA	220
Veracruz, Mexico	53,160
Verne, Jules	17
VETAG (Vehicle Tagging System)	113,120,121
Victoria, Australia, Government of	149,151
Visitacion Valley District	209
Visitacion Valley 1918 URR Wreck	10,13
Visitor Passports	112,173,203,206,209
Vitale, the (Hotel)	98,180
von Dullen, Elmer	148,258
W	
Walnut Creek, CA	227.250
Warm Springs (Fremont), CA	240
Washington, DC	25,26,240,267
DC Streetcar	267-269
District of Columbia Dept. of Transportation	268
Washington, PA	275
Watry, Duncan	131,133
Wellington, New Zealand	209
West Portal	15,52,143,227
Western Addition	214
Western Railway Museum	16,30,39,43,48,51,52,54-57,60,61,127,144, 145,147-149,160,162,171,2242,233
WRM cars which ran on Muni during Trolley Festivals:	
Blackpool, England "Boat" 226	48,242
Melbourne, Australia W2 648	48,149,242
Muni K-Type 178	48,160,242
Sacramento Northern "Birney" 62	162
WRM cars, others:	
Muni "Magic Carpet" 1003	29,242
Muni "Baby Ten" 1016	242

Sacramento Northern Interurban 1005	242	World War II	17,96,114,123,125,144,150,191
Westinghouse	31,123,130,153,155,182,287	World's Fair (1939)	144
Wheaton, MD	275	Works Progress Administration	204
"White Front Cars"	6,101,12-14,95,155	Wright, Douglas L.	41,42,44,45
White Front Cars Of San Francisco, Smallwood, Chas. L. (book)	32,155	**XYZ**	
Wiley "Birdcage" traffic signal	98	*Yakima Interurban Lines Association*	231
Willamette Shore Trolley	229,234	Yakima, WA	36,37,231,234
Williams, Tennessee	94,146	Zürich, Switzerland	149
Witt, Peter (Cleveland traction commissioner)	114,135		

(*left*) Remanufactured ex-Philly PCC 1061 ()Pacific Electric), resplendent in its new, accurate livery, has arrived back in San Francisco aboard a Silk Road Transport low-boy. It's at MME on October 2, 2018. *Allen Chan*

(*above*) It's an historic day as original O'Farrell, Jones & Hyde double-end cable car 42 climbs the famous Hyde Street Hill, carrying revenue passengers on the Hyde Street portion of its home line for the first time since 1954! The original line was abandoned May 15, 1954, but its Hyde Street portion became part of a new Powell/Hyde route in 1957. Alcatraz, Hyde Street Pier, Angel Island and Marin County are in the background. This was part of Muni Heritage Weekend in 2018. September 8, 2018. *Peter Ehrlich*

Picture Index

Ali, Khalil (in Geneva Shop)	194
Atlanta 948 at *Shore Line Trolley Museum*	275
Aquatic Park (GGNRA rendition)	124
Aquatic Park Conceptual E-Line Terminal	130
Atlanta Streetcar 1002	269
Balclutha (Squarerigger, Hyde Street Pier)	**212**
Baltimore Streetcar Museum PCCs 7407, 2168	279
BART, Civic Center Station	17
BART, Walnut Creek Station	240
Bay Bridge Illumination	281
Bayview Opera House	208
Bernhard, Bruce	188
Blackpool, UK Balloon 706, Tour of Illuminations	278
Boston PCC 3268	274
Brooklyn PCC 1001 (in Brooklyn)	24
Brooklyn PCC 1001 (at *Shore Line Trolley Museum*)	25
Brookville Equipment Corp., Brookville, PA	285
Brown, Willie L. Jr.	146,286
Brussels PCC trucks at Muni Metro east (for Red Arrow cars)	181
Cable Cars	
7	236
9 (Market Street Railway "White Front")	234
12	235
13 (United Railroads 1907-1921)	236
15 (1893 Market Street Railway Co.)	234
18	234
20	235,236
24	234-235
25 (United Railroads 1905-1908)	236
26 (Muni 1940s-1950s)	289
42 (O'Farrell, Jones & Hyde)	131,136,137,315,329
53	236
56	236
Cable Car Barn Façade	235
Cable Car Barn Interior	235
Cable Winding Machinery, Cable Car Barn	235
Quadruple Meet at Powell/California	234
California Cable Car Line Reconstruction at California & Hyde	48
C A Thayer (Lumber schooner, Maritime Museum)	212
Cannery, The	212
Carvajal, Angel	286,291
Charlotte 85 (original car)	266
Charlotte 91	266
Charlotte 92	266
Charlotte Lynx 104	266
Chicago PCC 4309	26
Chicago Transit Authority "Plushies" 4271/72	283
Chicago Pullman 144 at *Illinois Railway Museum*	276
Cincinnati Bell Connector Streetcar 1177	269
Cohen, Dan	134
Dallas McKinney Avenue 369, 186	260
Dallas Streetcar 302	260
Deposito Messina, the "Cathedral Of Traction" (Milan)	116
Detroit People Mover	270
Detroit QLine Streetcar 287	270
Detroit QLine Streetcar 290	270
Don Chee Way Construction	104
Ehrlich, Peter	235
11th Street Wye Reconstruction	78
El Paso PCC 1504 at Brookville	179
El Paso PCCs 1512, 1506 at SunMetro carbon	271
"Emperor Norton"	135
Eureka (Ferruboat, Maritime Museum)	212
Feinstein, Dianne	61,67,286,290
Ferry Building, 1889	8
Ferry Building Area Special Work Construction	104
Ferry Building interior	204
Ferry Building Loop, 1939	6
Filbert Street Steps	212
Fisherman's Wharf Extension Construction	102
Fisherman's Wharf Extension Construction at Ferry Building	104
F-Line Milan Cars (Milanos, Peter Witts, "Ventotto")	
Milano Car Card	225
Milano Car Interior	294
Milano 1793 (later 1893, orange)	111,150
Milano 1807 (orig. 1507, orange)	107,231
Milano 1807 (orig. 1507, yellow/white)	152,183,288,294,325,327
Milano 1811 (orig. 1911, yellow/white)	ix,xi,117,124,141,151,194,198, 199,203,206,210,217,218,220,222,288,244
Milano1811 Interior	246
Milano 1814 (orange)	151,216,222,294
Milano 1814 (2-tone green)	141
Milano 1815 (orig. 1515, orange)	3,141,221-223
Milano 1818 (2-tone green)	ix,xi,99,111,117,127,151,216,218,229,288, 294,325
Milano 1834 (orange)	54,59,71,86,88,95,149,183
Milano 1856 (orange)	220,288
Milano 1859 (orange)	140,149,201,325
Milano 1888 (orig. 1588, orange)	202,240
Milano 1893 (orig. 1793, orange)	151,217,221
Milano 1895 (orange)	110,288,278
F-Line PCC Cars:	
PCC Car Card	224
PCC 14 (Newark, was to become 1070)	154
PCC 1006 (Muni Wings)	13,33,59,63,70,126,139,173,324,326
PCC 1007 (Muni Wings, before remanufacturing)	148
PCC 1007 (Stealth Livery, gray/silver)	87,148
PCC 1007 (transitional painting)	148
PCC 1007 (Red Arrow)	98,118,122,134,148,208,210,217,293,324.326
PCC 1008 (Muni Wings)	324
PCC 1009 (Dallas)	131,133,324-327
PCC 1010 (Muni 1939 blue/gold)	96,148,201,207,208,211, 214,219-221,326
PCC 1010 Car Card	224
PCC 1010 Interior	204,294
PCC 1011 (MSRy Zip Stripe)[drawing]	170
PCC 1011 (MSRy Zip Stripe)	132,135,324,327
PCC 1015 (Illinois Terminal)	87,91,122,148,216,229,290
PCC 1040 (Muni Wings)	29,59,63,171,173,293
PCC 1040 (Landor)	173
PCC 1040 at Broookvillle	173
PCC 1040 Interior	246
PCC 1050 (Muni Wings)	3,76,86,201,205,211,216,240,325
PCC 1050 (St. Louis) [drawing]	180
PCC 1050 (St. Louis)	185,319
PCC 1051 (Muni Simplified)	76,77,96,140.149,184,186,210,211,218, 221,240
PCC 1052 (Los Angeles Railway 2-tone yellow)	79,88,111,113,146, 156,170,201,219,288,293,327
PCC 1052 Interior	246
PCC 1053 (Brooklyn)	24,76,79,95,146,196,199,211,218,222,285
PCC 1053 (Brooklyn) at Brockville	285
PCC 1054 (Philadelphia 1938 silver/blue)	85,88,95,146
PCC 1055 (Philadelphia green/cream)	24,76,89,118,144,185-187, 193,202,208,217,292
PCC 1056 (Kansas City)	i,88,97,199,184,186,187,199,216
PCC 1056 (Kansas City) at Brookville	179
PCC 1057 (Cincinnati)	6,45,76,86,87,88,110,124,141,62,210,213, 214.221,289
PCC 1058 (Chicago green/cream)	76,84,94,208,210,216
PCC 1058 (Chicago "Green Hornet" livery, Mercury green/ Croydon cream/Swamp Holly orange)	105,142,294
PCC 1059 (Boston)	xi,111,146,140.199,202,209,211
PCC 1059 (Boston, corrected livery)	140,185,186
PCC 1060 (Newark-PSCT)	97,111,146,241
PCC 1060 (Philadelphia 1938 silver/blue)	3,89,140,132,184
PCC 1061 (Pacific Electric)	76,85,108,110,132,218,293
PCC 1061 (Pacific Electric, corrected livery)	315
PCC 1062 (Louisville)	76,88,92,183,206,201,206,207,215
PCC 1062 (Pittsburgh)[drawing]	180
PCC 1062 (Pittsburgh)	183,185,187,319
PCC 1063 (Baltimore Yellow)	103,118,180,178,199,208
PCC 1063 (Baltimore-Alexandria Blue livery)[drawing]	180
PCC 1063 (Baltimore-Alexandria Blue livery)	185,187
PCC 1070 (Newark-PSCT)	292
PCC 1070 Interior	294

PCC 1071 (Minneapolis/St. Paul)	129,134,141,169,291,293
PCC 1072 (Mexico City)	141,292
PCC 1073 (El Paso)	169,171,292
PCC 1074 (Toronto)	171,292,245,324
PCC 1075 (Cleveland)	103,110,124,165,171,211,218,229,292
PCC 1076 (Washington)	2,110,124,134,147,171,190,202,203,222
PCC 1077 (Birmingham)	136,169,164,169,188,206,211,223
PCC 1078 (San Diego)	x,45,202,207,208,217,221,225,226,295
PCC 1078 (Car Card)	225
PCC 1079 (Detroit)	134,169,214,292
PCC 1080 (Los Angeles Transit Lines "Fruit Salad")	37,136,138,167,171,187,292,293
PCC 2133 (Philadelphia, was to become 1064)	144
F-Line and Trolley Festival Vintage Cars, buses and Trolley Coaches::	
Blackpool "Boat" 226	54,62,73
Blackpool "Boat" 228	55,59,73,84,131,135,137,160,194,195,207,211,215,328
Blackpool "Boat" 233	126,131,134,135,328
Brussels (Zürich) PCC 7037/737	110,164,200,207,220
Flyer E800 trolley coach 5300	139,239
GMC 3287 (motor coach)	139,329
Hamburg "Red Baron" 3557	55,58,165,188
Johnstown, PA 351	165
Kobe/Hiroshima 578J	58-60,165
Mack 2230 (motor coach)	138
Marmon-Herrington trolley coach 776	59,131,126,137,138,147,239,329
Market Street Ry. "Dinky" 578(S)	9,56,64,65,108,122,131,134,137,159,194,201,220,268,319,329
Market Street Ry. 798	159
Melbourne W2 496	61,71,136,108,110,136,163,201,202,218,326
Melbourne W2 648	51,52,54,58,163
Melbourne SW6 916	163
Milan Interurban 96	178
Milano 1834	54,59,71,86,88,95,135
Milwaukee 978	177
Moscow/Orel 106	59,60,70,71,73,164.289
Muni A-Type 1	20,34,42,43,46.51,52,54,55,62,73,108,110,120,122,125,134-136,140,153,154,165,211,222,230,238,290-292,325,329
Muni A-Tyoe 1 Car Card	249
Muni A-Type 1 Interior	154
Muni A-Type 1 passengers	134
Muni B-Type 130	14,49,51,52,56,57,59,63,71-73,96,108,133,135,146.155,178,196,205,208,210,211,219,222,230,329
Muni B-Type 130 "Herb Caen" Car Card	155
Muni B-Type 130 Interior	155
Muni B-Type 162	vi,100,122,155-157,190,195,215,217,221,231,289
Muni B-Type 162 Interior	143
Muni Boeing LRV 1213	51,175,177
Muni Boeing 2-Car Train on Market Street	57
Muni K-Type 178	20,43.52,54-56,62,175
Muni PCC "Torpedo" 1006	13,33,59,63,70,157
Muni PCC "Baby Ten" 1040	29,59,63,157,173
New Orleans 952	93,94,108,110,111,121,122,162,211
New Orleans 952 (as Riverfront 456 in N.O.)	162
Oporto 122	50-52,62
Oporto 189	34,51,52,55,58,64,65,77,93,141,165,230
Orion 9010 (motor coach)	139
Osaka 151	165
Portland 503	51,55,176
Sacramento Northern Birney 62	178
St. Louis PCC 1704 (ex-Muni 1128)	55,58,165,175
St. Louis trolley coach 506	136,329
Veracruz 001	53-55,176
White "Baby White" 062 (motor coach)	63,132,139,140,329
F-Line Opening Day Parade	84,289
F-Line Opening Day Poster	82
F-Line Operators at Don Chee Way	191
F-Line Operators at Ferries	288
F-Line Stop Marker, inbound	204
F-Line Stop Marker, outbound	213
F-Line Stop Marker and Billboard	79
Flieger, Albert	16
Fog City Diner	207
Fort Collins 21	273
Fort Mason (on H-Potrero Line)	247
Fort Mason Extension Conceptual Images	118,124
Geissenheimer, Harold	67

Geneva Carhouse Demolition	22
Geneva Historic Car Enclosure	291
Geneva Historic Car Enclosure Dedication (Dec. 2, 2010)	129
Geneva Yard Reconstruction	77
Ghirardelli Square	212
Green, Curitis	67
"Haight Street Jewett" (mockup at *S. F. Railway Museum*)	99
Hyde Street Pier (GGNRA)	212
Iowa Traction steeplecab loco 54 & ex-North Shore 727, Mason City, IA	277
Jeremiah O'Brien (Liberty Ship, Pier 45)	214
Johnson, Karl	188,193
Kamenev, Valentin	61
Kansas City KCStreetcar 805	269
Kelley Park, San Jose Railroads Birney 143	241
Kenosha 4606	263
Kenosha 4617 (in "Muni Wings" livery)	263
Key System GMC 2103 (motor coach)	138
Klebolt, Maurice H.	61,67
Lai, Lan	134,188
Laubscher, Rick	67,286
Lee, Ed	286,290
Little Rock 410	250,264
Los Angeles PCC 3146, etc.	27
Los Angeles PCC 3163	27
Los Angeles Breda LRV 708	246
Los Angeles Breda LRV 749	247
Los Angeles Kinkisharyo LRV 1018	247
Los Angeles Nippon Sharyo LRV 120	247
Los Angeles Nippon Sharyo LRV 126 and Union Pacific train	247
Los Angeles Nippon Sharyo LRV 148	246
Los Angeles–San Pedro "Pacific Electric" replica 501	273
Los Angeles Siemens LRV 216	246
Los Angeles Siemens LRV 218	247
Los Angeles Siemens LRV 246	247
Lowell 1601	273
Manag, Romer	188
Marelich, Tony	16
Market and 1st Street, Jan. 17, 1939	12
Market and 6th Street, 1904	9
Market and 6th Street, Nov. 11, 1918 (Armistice Day)	11
Market and Church Reconstruction	75
Market and Duboce Reconstruction	78
Market and Eddy, 1937	12
Market and Grant, March 31, 1905	9
Market and Grant, 1909	9
Market and Valencia Reconstruction	78
Market Street Railway cars:	
435,471(ex-135,171)	13
827	13
Memphis 180	37
Memphis 204, 234	261
Memphis Gomaco 453, Melbourne W2 540 in Carbarn	261
Michel, Art	91,188
Milan 1673	115
Milan 1723	114
Milan 1847	117
Milan 1970	115
Milan Sirio	117
Milano 1818 in Milan	116
Milano 1859 in Milan	115
Milwaukee "HOP" Streetcar	272
Minnesota Streetcar Museum Duluth 78	279
Mint Yard	196
Miranda, Danny	190
Mission Dolores	196
Moreison-Knudsen, Hornell, NY with Muni PCCs being rebuilt)	145
Motor Coach, New Flyer XE40 8853	138
Mt. Pleasant, Iowa Milan 1945	117
Muni Centennial Logo	286
Muni Cars (other than F-Line cars):	
A-Type 36	10
Boeing LRV 1215	19
Boeing LRV 1227	19
Boeing LRV 1250	177
Boeing LRV 1269	50
Boeing LRV 1290	144
Boeing LRV 1328	86

Boeing 2-car train, Duboce Junction	19
Breda 1402	148
Breda 1407	221
Breda 1428	120
Breda 1442	233
Breda 1456	110
Breda 1457	137
Breda 1463	232
Breda 1467	226
Breda 1472	230
Breda 1474	229
Breda 1491	229
Breda 1506	231
Breda 1511	229
Breda at Ferry Portal, with Blackpool 228	137
Breda at Ferry Portal, with Blackpool 233	328
Bredas at Ferry Portal, with New Orleans 952	162
Bredas at San Francisco State University Station	229
B-Type 88 (1947)	295
B-Type 130 (as wrecker 0131)	141
B-Type 153	15
B-Type 154	16
B-Type 159	15
C-Type "Magic Carpet" 1002	29
D-Type PCC 1011	16
D-Type PCC 1012	29
D-Type PCC 1013 (at St. Louis Car Co.)	29
K-Type 170	15
K-Type 181 (Last Run)	16
K-Type 187	16
Line Car 0304	77
"Magic Carpet" 1003 at *Western Railway Museum*	242
PCC at Market/Valencia, Nov. 1971	18
PCC 1017	33
PCC 1018 (at St. Louis Car Co.)	29
PCC 1019	33
PCC 1023	18
PCC 1034	15
PCC 1038	21
PCC 1103 in St. Louis	30
PCC 1105	14
PCC 1108	31
PCC 1125	21
PCC 1139	172
PCC 1146	33
PCC 1158	20,172
PCC 1160	31
PCC 1162 (to be scrapped)	32
PCC 1163	32
PCC 1167 (to be scrapped)	22
PCC 1170	33
PCC 1188	31
Siemens LRV-4 2005	232
Siemens LRV-4 2009	319
Muni ex-Philly PCCs at Morrison-Knudsen	145
Nevin, John (with Jack Smith at Mint Yard with 162)	195
Newark PCC 14 in San Francisco	156
Newark PCC 21, Branch Brook Park, Newark, NJ	167
New Flyer Xcelsor XDE40 8853 (motor coach)	138
New Orleans Canal 2004 (1st Day of new Canal Line)	254
New Orleans Canal 2010	236
New Orleans Canal 2017	254
New Orleans Canal 2019	253
New Orleans Canal 2022	253
New Orleans Grinder 29	255
New Orleans Loyola 2011	253
New Orleans Loyola 2017	455
New Orleans Loyola/Rampart 2020	255
New Orleans Rampart 2020	255
New Orleans Rampart 2023	253
New Orleans Riverfront 450	253
New Orleans Riverfront 454 (Melbourne W2)	253
New Orleans Riverfront 456 (future Muni 952)	162
New Orleans Riverfront 458	253
New Orleans St. Charles 900, Canal 2003	254
New Orleans St. Charles 900 on Canal/City Park Line	254
New Orleans St. Charles 819	255
New Orleans St. Charles 923 (NOPSI Era)	252
New Orleans St. Charles 945	252
New Orleans St. Charles 947 on Canal	253
New Orleans St. Charles 954 at Canal Station	254
New Orleans St. Charles 971 with my car	255
New Orleans St. Charles 972	252
New York Subway BMT AB Standards	284
New York Subway BMT BUs	282
New York Subway BMT BUs with Amtrak *Acela*	282
New York Subway BMT D Triplexes	283
New York Subway BMT/IND Lineup @ Ocean Parkway	283
New York Subway BMT/IND R10 3184	283
New York Subway BMT/IND R11 8013	283
New York Subway IRT Lo-Vs	280,281
New York Subway IRT Train Of Many Colors	281
New York Subway IND R1/9s	282
Novato, CA Wetlands (seen from SMART)	243
"*Nuestros Silencios*", Spanish Sculpture Set	135
Oklahoma City OKCStreetcar 201802	281
100th Anniversary of Electric Traction Celebration	73
Oporto 205 in Oporto, Portugal	36
Pacific Electric PCC 5019	27
Palm Tree Placement, Market/Noe/16th Street	68
Pier 39 Sea Lions	209
Philadelphia PCC 2122	144
Philadelphia PCC 2124 at Morrison-Knudsen (future Muni 1058)	145
Philadelphia PCC-II 2323	274
Pittsburgh PCC 1614	26
Pittsburgh PCC 1713	26
Pittsburgh PCCs 1735,1744	26
Poetry Plaques	105
Portland Streetcar 005	256
Portland Streetcar 010	256,257
Portland Streetcar 024	257
Portland Streetcar 025 on Tilikum Bridge	257
Portland TriMet MAX 119	257
Portland TriMet MAX trains on Steel Bridge	257
Portland Streetcar–United Streetcar LLC 015	284
Portland Vintage Trolley 511	37,256
Portland Vintage Trolley 514	256
Portland Vintage Trolley 514 on Portland Streetcar	256
Prague, CZ Vintage tram 349	278
Queen Mary 2	137,206
Retuta, Bobby	190
Rockhill Trly Museum San Diego 1019, Johnstown 311	279
Sacramento PG&E 35	244
Sacramento RT Metro 112 at Cosumnes River College	245
Sacramento RT Metro 218 at State Capitol	244
Sacramento RT Metro 222 at Sacramento Valley Station	245
Sacramento RT Metro UTDC 308 on K Street Mall	245
Salt Lake City Sugar House Streetcar 1176	269
San Diego Trolley Siemens-Duewag U2 1030	249
San Diego Trolley Siemens-Duewag U2 1054	249
San Diego Trolley Siemens-Duewag SD100 2022	249
San Diego Trolley Siemens S70 3010	249
San Diego Trolley Siemens S70 4057	249
San Diego Vintage Trolley PCC 529 (ex-Muni1122)	295
San Diego Vintage Trolley PCC 530 (ex-Muni 1123)	219
San Diego Vintage Trolley PCC 530 (ex-Newark 10)	249
San Francisco Railway Museum	98,99
Heritage Weekend Car Departure board	134
Santa Clara SCCTA LRVs and Vintage Car 129	245
Santa Clara VTA 947, Diridon Station, San Jose	241
Santa Clara VTA Vintage Car 1	245
Santa Clara VTA Vintage Car 73	245
Santa Clara VTA Vintage Car Milan 2001	117
Seashore Trolley Museum Connecticut Co. open 303	279
Seashore Trolley Museum Phila Nearside 6618	279
Seattle First Hill Streetcar 402	259
Seattle South Lake Union Streetcar 303+Monorail	259
Seattle Waterfront Streetcar 482	259
SEPTA Red Arrow 18 in Philadelphia	181
SEPTA Rad Arrow 21, 18 at *Shore Line Trolley Museum*	181
SEPTA Red Arrow 21 at Brookville	181
17th and Castro Reconstruction	75
17th and Noe Reconstruction	75
Shopmen and Officials with Hamburg 3557	164

SMART DMU 111 at San Rafael	243	Tucson Sun Tran United Streetcar 102	267
Smith, Jack (with John Nevin at Mint Yard with 162)	195	Tucson Sun Tran United Streetcar103	267
Stead, William	61,188	Tucson Sun Tran United Streetcar, University & Tyndall	267
Sunday Streets	122	United Railroads 1376	38
Tacoma Link Streetcar 1003	269	U. S. Navy "Blue Angels"	198
Tampa TecoLine 428	284	"Vietato Fumare" (sign on Milan car)	198
32-Embarcadero (bus)	102	Washington DC Streecar 203	269
Transbay Terminal Demolition	96	Washington PCC 1495	26
Trolley coach, Marmon-Herrington TC44 687	238	Washington pre-PCC 1053	26
Trolley coach, ETI/Skoda 14Tr-SF 5457	238	Western Railway Museum Muni PCC 1016	279
Trolley coach, New Flyer Xcelsior XT60 7279	239	Whiteman, Jeremy	134
Tucson Old Pueblo Trolley ex-Osaka 869	267	Wiley "Birdcage" signal	98

(left) The Reds Have It Now: Two formerly green F-Line PCCs have shed their old colors and representations for new red paint: In the foreground, 1050 (now representing St. Louis, previously Muni Wings) follows 1062, which had been transformed from green-hued Louisville, a city that ordered but never operated PCCs, to red-and-cream Pittsburgh, which amassed 666 of them. Both cars are sitting at the 17th/Castro terminal on August 9, 2018.
Peter Ehrlich

122 years of traction history meet in Dolores Park. 1893 Market Street Railway Co. 578S, inbound, meets brand-new Siemens LRV4 2009 outbound on the J-Line, under the park pedestrian bridge at 19th Street. September 6, 2018. *Peter Ehrlich*

Points Of Interest in San Francisco

A list of buildings, stores and other attractions, primarily from Chapter 10.
Listed in order as one rides an F-Line streetcar.

Inbound trip, 5th Street to Fisherman's Wharf

Hallidie Plaza, Market, Powell and 5th Street North. Subterranean plaza and entrance to BART and Muni Metro Powell Street Station.
Flood Building, Market and Powell. Designed by architect Albert Pissis, built 1904.
Bank Of America Day And Night Branch Building, Hallidie Plaza.
Westfield Shopping Center, Market opposite Powell; also fronts 5th Street. Includes Nordstrom, opened 1988, and Bloomingdale's, in the old Emporium store space. The original Emporium store was also designed by Albert Pissis. The glass rotunda has been preserved.
Union Square. A park located din the center of one of the premier downtown shopping districts in the United States. Fronted by Stockton, Geary, Powell and Post Streets. Many stores such as Macy's, Neiman-Marcus (which preserved the old City of Paris glass rotunda) and Saks Fifth Avenue are here, as is the **St. Francis Hotel**.
Old U. S. Mint, 5th and Mission Streets. Built in 1874. One of the last examples of Classical Revival architecture in the Western United States. Houses the San Francisco Historical Society and Museum.
Hotel Palomar, Market and 4th Street. Jade-green façade, built 1915.
Marriott Hotel, 4th and Mission Streets.
Moscone Center, 4th and Howard Streets. This is the space used for conventions; also features the **Zeum** (children's Museum) and a carousel.
Phelan Building, Market and O'Farrell. A flatiron-design building, constructed 1908, designed by architect William Curlett.
Union Trust Company, Market and Grant. A banking temple that's now a Wells Fargo branch.
Yerba Buena Center For the Arts, Mission and 3rd Streets. An urban park with a small performing hall. Adjacent to Moscone Center.
Museum Of Modern Art, 3rd Street between Mission and Howard.
Jewish Museum, Jessie Street west of 3rd Street. Located in an old Pacific Gas & Electric substation.
St. Patrick's Church, Mission between 3rd and 4th Streets.
Museum of the African Diaspora, Mission east of 3rd Street.
Chinatown Arch, Grant Avenue and Bush Street (five blocks north or Market). Gateway to Chinatown
Central Tower, Market and 3rd Street. Built in 1898, renovated to an Art Deco appearance in 1938.

Logo of Detroit PCC 1079.
Peter Ehrlich

De Young (Chronicle) Building, Geary, Kearny and Market Streets. Restored to its 1903 appearance in 2007.
Lotta's Fountain, Market, Kearny and Geary. Created in 1875, it flows every April 18th to commemorate the great Earthquake and Fire of 1906.
Sheraton Palace Hotel, Market and New Montgomery.
Crocker Building, Montgomery and Post Streets (at Market).
Hobart Building, Market and 2nd Streets. Built 1914; designed by architect Willis Polk.
595 Market Street, Market and 2nd Streets.
Flatiron Building, Market and Sutter.
Chevron Towers, 555 and 575 Market Street.
Crown Zellerbach Building, Market ant Bush. First modern highrise in San Francisco, built 1959, designed by Skidmore, Owings & Merrill
PG&E Building, Market and Beale.
Matson Building, Market and Main.
101 California, California, Davis and Market.
Embarcadero Center. Four buildings on Sacramento Street from **Justin Herman Plaza** to Battery Street. The ground and second floors of each building house mostly upscale stores.
Federal Reserve Bank, Market and Main.
Hyatt Regency Hotel, Market and Drumm.
Southern Pacific Building, also called **One Market Plaza**. Market and Steuart Streets. Two newer towers rise behind the building.
Justin Herman Plaza, foot of Market Street. Park created in the 1970s as the gateway to the **Ferry Building** and **Embarcadero Center**.
San Francisco Railway Museum. Run by the non-profit *Market Street Railway*.
Hotel Vitale, Mission, The Embarcadero and Steuart. Built on the former Muni bus turnaround.

Rincon Annex Post Office Building. Mission and Steuart Streets. Art-Deco former Post Office.

Audiffred Building, Mission, The Embar-cadero and Steuart. Mansard-roof building from the 1860s which survived the 1906 Earthquake and Fire.

Ferry Building. Fronts the east side of The Embarcadero. Built in 1898, designed by architect A. Page Brown. Once the second-busiest trans-portation terminal in the world;, now a vibrant marketplace and one of the premier icons of San Francisco.

Transamerica Pyramid, Washington and Montgomery Streets. A landmark since 1972. Visible from the F-Line.

Levi's Plaza. Battery between Union and Greenwich Streets. Corporate headquarters campus for the Levi's jeans maker.

Pier 23. The Embarcadero opposite Greenwich Street. "Waterfront Dive" (eatery) and jazz joint.

Filbert Street Steps. Wooden and concrete staircase up the steep east face of Telegraph Hill.

Telegraph Hill. Steep hill along the north-eastern waterfront.

Coit Tower. 1935 Art Deco tower built on Telegraph Hill, built to commemorate Lillie Hitchcock Coit, who was a major supporter of firefighters in San Francisco.

State Belt Railroad Roundhouse. Sansome and Chestnut. Former roundhouse for the State Belt Railroad, now housing offices.

Alcatraz. Former Federal penitentiary, now part of the Golden Gate National Recreation Area. Accessible by boat from Pier 31, on The Embarcadero just south of Bay Street.

Pier 35 Cruise Ship Terminal. The Embarcadero opposite Bay Street.

Pier 39. Tourist complex built in 1978. Specialty shops and restaurants and the *Aquarium Of The Bay*. The Pier 39 is also famous for its sea lions, which have been hanging out here since 1989.

Pier 41 Portal. Off The Embarcadero opposite Powell Street. Former freight car barge terminal, which served the North Bay and Sausalito.

Fisherman's Wharf. This is a neighborhood district that is bounded by Grant Avenue, The Embarcadero, Van Ness Avenue and Bay Street. Many famous seafood restaurants are nestled here, and so is the fishing fleet. The Wharf didn't become a tourist mecca until the 1950s. Other attractions at the Wharf are **Ghirardelli Square**, the **Cannery**, **Hyde Street Pier** and the **San Francisco Maritime Museum**, **Aquatic Park** and **Pier 45**, which is home to the Liberty ship *Jeremiah O'Brien* and the World War II submarine *USS Panpanito*.

The Cannery. Leavenworth, Beach and Jefferson Street. A small shopping complex which opened in 1966. Formerly a Del Monte fruit canning plant.

Ghirardelli Square. Beach, Larkin, North Point and Polk Streets. The former chocolate manufacturing plant, one of the first small-scale shopping developments in the U. S. Opened 1964.

San Francisco Maritime Museum. End of Hyde Street, at the east end of **Aquatic Park**. Contains the ferryboat *Eureka*, the square-rigger *Balclutha*, and other noteworthy ships.

Outbound trip to 17th and Castro. Includes Beach Street and Market from 5th Street westward

Longshoremen's Hall. Beach and Mason Streets. A round building with a copper roof set in triangular sections.

Golden Gate Theater. Taylor and Golden Gate (opposite 6th Street).

New Federal Building. 7th and Mission Streets.

U. S. Court Of Appeals Building. 7th and Mission Streets. Beaux-Arts style.

United Nations Plaza. A broad pedestrian walkway starting west of 7th Street and leading to **Civic Center** Plaza **and** City **Hall**. The Beaux-Arts **Old Federal Building** lines the north side of the promenade between Leavenworth and Hyde Streets.

Orpheum Theater. Market and Hyde Street (opposite 8th Street).

Main Library. Grove between Hyde and Larkin Street Opened in 1997; although modern, it matches other buildings in Civic Center Plaza.

Hotel Whitcomb. Market and 8th Streets. A 1906 Earthquake survivor.

Merchandise Mart. Market, 9th and 10th Streets.

Fox Plaza. Market, Hayes and Polk Street. Replaced the ornate Fox Theater in 1963.

Civic Center Plaza. This urban park is fronted on the east (Larkin Street) by the **Main Library** and the **Asian Art Museum**, which used to house the Main Library; the north (McAllister Street) by the **State Building**; the west (Polk Street) by the Bakewell and Brown-designed **City Hall**; and the south (Grove Street) by the **Bill Graham Civic Auditorium**. All but the Main Library are built in the Beaux-Arts style; the library building matches the style of the others. On the west side of Van Ness are **Davies Symphony Hall**, Van Ness and Grove; the War Memorial **Opera House**, Van Ness and Grove, the **Veterans Building**, Van Ness and McAllister (where the United Nations was born), and the **California Public Utilities Commission Build-ing**, Van Ness and McAllister. Davies Symphony Hall and the CPUC building mirror each other in modern architectural style; the others are Beaux-Arts structures.

SFMTA Headquarters. 1 South Van Ness at Market Street.

San Francisco Lesbian, Gay, Bisexual and Transgender Community Center. Market and

Octavia Blvd. Located in the Victorian-era **Fallon Building** and a modern building next to it.

U. S. Mint. An Art-Deco building sitting atop Mint Hill at Buchanan and Hermann Streets; also fronts Mint Yard, formerly Duboce Avenue.

Mission Dolores. Dolores at 16th Street. Founded in 1776 as Mission San Francisco de Asis, the oldest building in San Francisco.

Swedish-American Hall, Market near Steiner. Multi-gabled building.

Castro District. The premier gay/lesbian neighborhood in the United States. Castro Street is a vibrant shopping district. In addition to being served by the F-Line and Muni Metro, also served by buses 24, 33, 35 and 37.

Castro Theater. Castro south of Market and 17th Streets. 1923 Timothy Pflueger-designed movie theater; Shows mostly revival films.

Other Neighborhoods and Attractions Accessible by Public Transit

Pacific Heights, north central San Francisco. Buses 22, 12, 24 and 3.

Marina District, north central San Francisco. Buses 30, 22 and 28.

Palace Of Fine Arts/Exploratorium, Lyon and Beach Streets. The last remaining structure from the 1915 Panama-Pacific International Exposition. The **Exploratorium** is a world-renowned children's museum.

Cow Hollow/Union Street, north central San Francisco, south of the Marina District. Buses 47, 49, 45 and 22.

Western Addition, central San Francisco. Buses 38/38L, 2, 3, 22, 31, 5.

Presidio of San Francisco, west of Cow Hollow and Marina Districts and north of the Richmond District. Bus 43.

Golden Gate Bridge. San Francisco icon from 1937. Bus 28 and Golden Gate Transit.

Richmond District, northwestern San Francisco. Buses 1, 5, 31, 38/38L, 44, 28, 29, 18.

Golden Gate Park, central western San Francisco. Stretches from Stanyan Street on the east to Ocean Beach on the west and bordered by Fulton Street (north side) and Lincoln Way (south side). Home to the **De Young Museum** and **California Academy of Sciences**. Buses 5, 33, 44, 28, 29, and 18, and N-Judah streetcar.

Lincoln Park, northwestern San Francisco. Buses 1, 2 and 18. Houses the **California Palace of the Legion of Honor** fine arts museum.

Land's End and the **Cliff House**, extreme northwestern corner of San Francisco, fronting the Pacific Ocean. Bus 38L and a short walk.

Inner Sunset District, south of Golden Gate Park. N-Judah streetcar; buses 6, 43, 44, 28, 29.

UCSF Medical Center, east of Inner Sunset District. On Parnassus Avenue. N-Judah streetcar and buses 6 and 43.

Outer Sunset District, southwestern San Francisco. N-Judah and L-Taraval streetcars, buses 28, 29, 18.

San Francisco Zoo, southwestern San Francisco, off Sloat Blvd. L-Taraval streetcar, buses 18 and 23.

West Portal, southwestern San Francisco, west of Twin Peaks. K, L and M streetcars, buses 17 and 48.

Stonestown/San Francisco State University, southwestern San Francisco. M-Ocean View streetcar, buses 28, 29, 17 and 18. Stonestown Galleria is a shopping mall, one of the first in the United States.

Ocean Avenue/Ingleside District, southern San Francisco, between Junipero Serra Blvd. and San Jose Avenue. K-Ingleside streetcar.

City College of San Francisco, Phelan and Ocean. K-Ingleside streetcar, buses 43, 49 and 29.

Outer Mission/Excelsior District, southern San Francisco. Buses 14, 49, 29, 43, 44 and 54.

Visitation Valley, southeastern San Francisco. T-Third Street streetcar.

Bayview District, southeastern San Francisco. T-Third Street streetcar, buses 23, 24, 44, 54 and 29.

Dogpatch District/Central Waterfront, eastern San Francisco. T-Third Street streetcar, buses 22 and 48.

Union Iron Works Historic District, eastern San Francisco, off 3rd and 19th Streets. Old shipyard, where some Muni streetcars were built. T-Third Street streetcar, bus 22.

Potrero Hill, eastern San Francisco. Buses 22 and 48.

Mission Bay and **UCSF Mission Bay Campus**, eastern San Francisco. This is a fast-developing area of the city. T-Third Street streetcar.

SoMa District, south of Market Street and fronted by San Francisco Bay on the east and southeast, Mission Creek on the south, and 11th Street on the west. N-Judah and T-Third Street streetcars and numerous north/south bus lines.

AT&T Park, home of the *San Francisco Giants*. 24 Willie Mays Plaza (King and 3rd Streets. N-Judah and T-Third Street streetcars.

Mission District, central San Francisco, boarded by 16th Street on the north, Potrero Avenue on the east, Cesar Chavez Street on the south, and Guerrero Street on the west. Centered along Mission Street. Large Latino district. Buses 14/14L, 49, 22, 27, 48 and 67.

Bernal Heights District, eastern central San Francisco. Hilly district east and south of the Mission District. Buses 14/14L, 49, 67, 24.

Excelsior District, Outer Mission. Market Street Railway's first bus line, 52-Excelsior, served this hilly neighborhood on the same route from its inception in the early 1930s, and into the Muni era, until 1979.

Chinatown, north of downtown. Stretches north/south along Kearny, Grant and Stockton Streets, but the side streets are just as interesting. Buses 8X, 1, 12 and 30/45.

North Beach, northeastern San Francisco. Along Columbus Avenue. Buses 8X, 30, 45 and the Powell/Mason cable car.

Russian Hill, northeastern San Francisco. Powell/Hyde cable car and buses 45 and 19.

Nob Hill, north of Union Square. All cable cars and buses 1 and 27. The **Fairmont Hotel**, **Mark Hopkins Hotel**, **Grace Cathedral** and **Masonic Auditorium** are atop Nob Hill.

Cable Car Carbarn and Museum. Washington and Mason Streets. Built 1887; rebuilt 1907 and 1984. Home for San Francisco's premier icons.

Haight-Ashbury District, central San Francisco. Of hippie fame. Stretches along Haight Street from Fillmore to Stanyan and the east edge of Golden Gate Park. Buses 6, 22, 24, 43 and 33. N-Judah streetcar skirts the south edge through **Cole Valley**.

Dolores Park, bounded by Church, 18th, Dolores and 20th Streets. J-Church streetcar and 33 bus.

Noe Valley District, central San Francisco. J-Church streetcar and buses 24 and 48.

Twin Peaks, elevation approximately 900 feet. Served by bus 37 connecting with the F-Line and Muni Metro at Church and Castro.

Some Restaurants listed in Chapters 10 and 11. (Note: This is a listing only. Although the author has dined at some of these locations, he makes no recommendations whatsoever.)

Tadich Grill, California between Front and Battery. Seafood, specializing in fresh fish. Oldest restaurant in San Francisco, established 1849.

One Market Plaza Food Court, Steuart opposite Don Chee Way. Many food places, including *Lena's* and *360° Burritos*. Closed weekends.

Rincon Annex Food Court, Mission between Steuart and Spear. In the old Rincon Annex Post Office building. A variety of restaurants.

Ferry Building Farmer's Marketplace, Ferry Building. A variety of restaurants.

Boulevard, Stuart and Mission (in the Audiffred Building. Upscale restaurant serving regional American cuisine with a French touch.

Waterfront Restaurant, Pier 7. Upscale restaurant serving American and seafood dishes.

Pier 23 Restaurant, Pier 23. A "waterfront dive" serving mostly American food. Also a jazz joint.

Fog City Diner, Embarcadero and Battery. Mostly American food.

Teatro ZinZanni, opposite Embarcadero and Sansome. European food, dinner only. Includes a theater-style revue. Advertises as "Love, Chaos and Dinner."

Houston's, Embarcadero between Chestnut and Bay Streets. American-style.

Pier 39. Many restaurants with varied cuisine.

Fisherman's Wharf, Jefferson between Powell and Hyde Streets. Many seafood restaurants, but also including **Boudin Bakery** and **Rainforest Café**.

Castagnola's, Jefferson and Jones. Seafood.

Scoma's, Pier 47 (off Jefferson and Jones). Seafood restaurant, specializing in fresh fish.

Zuni Café, Market between Franklin and Gough. Regional French and Italian cuisine.

Azteca, Church and Market. Mexican food.

Chow, Church and Market. American fare.

Café Flore, Market and Noe. American brunch and dinner.

Orphan Andy's, 17th Street opposite the F-Line terminal. American. Open 24 hours; breakfast at all times.

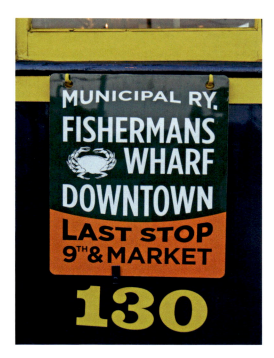

Dash sign on Muni B-Type 130.
All Muni, Market Street Railway and United Railroads cars used these metal signs to identify destinations along their routes until the introduction of PCCs in the 1940s and 1950s.
Peter Ehrlich

Logo of Melbourne 496.
Peter Ehrlich